W9-DDN-601

The UFO Controversy in America

The UF⊚ Controversy
in America

David Michael Jacobs

INDIANA UNIVERSITY PRESS

Bloomington & London

Photo of alleged UFO taken in McMinnville, Oregon, in 1950. The Condon report stated that this photo appears to be neither a hoax nor a conventional flying object.
(UNITED PRESS INTERNATIONAL PHOTO)

SECOND PRINTING 1975

Copyright © 1975 by Indiana University Press
All rights reserved

Published in Canada by Fitzhenry & Whiteside Limited, Don Mills, Ontario

Manufactured in the United States of America

Library of Congress Cataloging in Publication Data

Jacobs, David Michael, 1942–
The UFO controversy in America.

Bibliography
Includes index.
1. Flying saucers.   I. Title.
TL789.J26 1975   001.9′42   74-11886
ISBN 0-253-19006-1

To My Mother and Father

Contents

Foreword

Scientific controversy has a rich history. And in modern times no controversy in science has had the global extent, the awareness by the public, the display of scientific argument and prejudice, the involvement of the media, and the scientific dilution of, and gross distraction from, the main issues by religious fanatics, visionaries, and charlatans, as has the phenomenon of the Unidentified Flying Object (UFO).

The UFO controversy has a relatively long history, but until now this has been only partially and not coherently documented from about the turn of this century to the present. There is only sporadic documentation in earlier centuries. Indeed, in earlier times there could hardly be said to have been a controversy, although the phenomenon apparently was present.

The need of a sober non-partisan compilation and documentation of the controversy itself arises precisely because the UFO phenomenon has elicited as strong an emotional and partisan response as any scientific controversy in history. Certainly it has involved far more people, and on a global basis, than the classic scientific controversies on, say, meteorites, continental drift, mechanical nature of heat, relativity, and even biological evolution and natural selection. The latter, however, is perhaps the only controversy in which basic emotional responses, buttressed by deep-seated religious and personal prejudice, played so major a role.

Indeed, there is an interesting anti-parallelism between controversy surrounding the theory of biological evolution and that surrounding the UFO phenomenon. In the gradual rise of the concept of biological evolution, there was first the slow acceptance at the top echelons of biological science before these concepts filtered down to the popular levels. It was at these lower levels, however, where the greatest emotional and surcharged prejudicial responses were generated. Human dignity, it seemed to the man on the street, was at stake, as was religious orthodoxy, and the new concepts were stubbornly resisted and openly combated by the "grass roots" very much more than by the scientific establishment. One has to recall the famous Tennessee "monkey trial" in which the Darwinian concepts were ably but unavailingly defended by Clarence Darrow and vehemently opposed by William Jennings Bryan to gauge the extent of rampant emotionalism surrounding the whole subject.

With the UFO phenomenon there is a parallel, but one with the opposite sign. Here the phenomenon arose and was reported at the grass roots levels (as in the case of meteorites, as a matter of fact) and it was, in contrast, the highest scientific echelons that generated the emotional storm against allowing unprejudiced examination of the claimed observations of thousands upon thousands of persons judged sane by conventional standards.

One may expect unbridled emotional responses in scientific matter from the untutored public; one is aghast to find it among one's scientific colleagues. One should expect that they, above all, would be conversant with the history of science, which has furnished so many, many examples of violent opposition to new ideas and concepts, opposition which was forced to give way to acceptance in the face of overwhelming evidence. Above all, the ideals of science call for calm and unprejudiced examination of the evidence, duly and properly presented.

And therein lies the rub! The UFO evidence has not been properly presented at the Court of Science. The parallel of meteorites comes at once to mind. For centuries there had been stories of stones having fallen from the sky. Peasants reported finding such stones as later they plowed their fields. Why should the French Academy of Science take seriously the untutored peasants' incredible stories of stones having fallen from the skies? Clearly impossible! And by the same token, why should science take seriously incredible stories about strange craft in the sky? Stones don't fall from the sky, and strange craft, exhibiting behaviors totally unknown and not encompassed in modern science, can't exist.

One glaring difference: many of the observers of the UFO phenomenon have by no means been "untutored peasants." Professors, scientists, air-traffic controllers, engineers, pilots, persons holding elective office as well as truck drivers, farmers, and school children have reported much the same things. And as in the case of meteorites, the reports have come from all around the world.

But the data on the UFO phenomenon have had to run an insidious gauntlet that the meteorites were spared. Discoveries of meteorite falls did not become the fabric of cultists, pseudo-religious aberrants; meteorites were not regarded as sent by other-world intelligence bent on helping and reforming the benighted people of the earth. Nobody concocted a story about riding a meteorite to Venus and there meeting glorious "perfected humans" who imparted "platitudes in stained glass attitudes."

But let it be clearly understood: such UFO associated stories have been relatively few and certainly were not generated by pilots, policemen, air-traffic controllers, and persons holding public office and other highly responsible positions. These were quite clearly generated by persons for whom the concept of "flying saucers" satisfied some psychological fantasies and peculiar inner needs. Unfortunately, though few in number, such persons were generally uninhibitedly vocal and insensitive to ridicule; they were given ample press and often generated a cultist following. Meteorites were not so encumbered. Nor was final acceptance of meteorites and of other concepts obstructed by stories generated by misidentification and misperceptions. The untutored in what can be seen in the sky, and those unaware of the vagaries of perceptions, are legion. Stimulated by accounts of truly strange sights in the sky or near the ground, and anxious to partake in the excitement, this legion innocently but devastatingly heaped large piles of UFO stories onto the market. Although these were soon revealed for what they were—"unidentified" only to themselves and certainly not to others who could easily identify the source of the misidentifications—this all served to muddle the primary issues.

It was in this atmosphere of confusion and misinformation that the Condon Committee, the Air Force sponsored group at the University of Colorado headed by the late Dr. Edward Condon, was conceived. It labored long to produce a scientific mouse, and a deformed mouse at that, one with two dissimilar heads: one, the summary of the investigation by Dr. Condon, which summarily dismisses the entire subject as unworthy of scientific attention, and the other, a series of attempts, often agonizing—and unsuccessful in four times out of five—to devise a natural explanation for the UFO report selected for study. Clearly, the right hand head did not know what the left hand head was doing.

It was nonetheless quickly accepted, and with an audible sigh of relief in scientific circles, that Dr. Condon had succeeded in giving the subject a half-million dollar burial, with unctuous gestures befitting an interment ceremony. But it turns out that the corpse had not even attended the funeral. As amply detailed in the last chapter of this book, the UFO phenomenon presented itself to full view in the Fall of 1973, especially in the United States and in France, despite the overwhelming opinion that the subject had been put to rest by science itself. Once again, it was merely history repeating. How many times before had overcaution and established science seemingly buried a disturbing concept!

It is interesting to contemplate, had the Condon Committee had the benefit of Dr. Jacobs's comprehensive study of the UFO controversy, how different the final report might have been.

But we have Dr. Jacobs's work now at hand. It is not my aim here to summarize it—the reader should have the pleasure of having the entire story unfold as he reads—but it is, I believe, both my privilege and duty to say a word about the UFO phenomenon itself, the subject of the controversy. Since it is impossible to treat the controversy without introducing to some extent the subject itself, as Dr. Jacobs has of necessity done, I will limit myself to an overview, based primarily on my long acquaintance with the subject. My involvement with UFOs began in 1948 when I became astronomical consultant on "flying saucers" to the Air

Force. In the ensuing years I observed at firsthand both the phenomenon of continued UFO reports and the manner in which it was being treated (mistreated would be the better word) by science, the public, and by the Air Force.

Just exactly, then, what was and is the UFO phenomenon about which so many words have been spent?

First off, a quarter of a century has clearly shown, to all who are willing to look, that after the dross is removed—i.e., accounts from the untutored, the pranksters, and the relatively few but vocal lunatic fringe—there remains a profoundly impressive body of data which can truly be said to constitute a new empirical set of observations. The only possible way to gainsay this is to accuse a veritable host of persons—from all walks of life, from all parts of the world, and adjudged sane and responsible from their personal records—of being crazy or of lying. These are persons whose testimony in a court of law would be unquestioned.

Now it is quite true that these remaining accounts are unbelievable by ordinary standards. That is precisely why they constitute new empirical evidence, in the same way that meteorites once did—or radioactivity, atomic fission, anomalous motion of the perihelion of Mercury, which the new Theory of Relativity finally explained. They do represent something new. And that is precisely why they are important. They may signal a whole domain of nature (for intelligence is part of nature) as yet unexplained.

Specifically what is new? The reported sporadic and unpredictable appearance of "craft" by day, and lights (frequently brilliant) and "craft" by night, whose non-random behavior (and thus presumably guided or programmed by intelligence) is totally unexplainable by our present scientific technology.

What sort of behavior? The reported ability to execute trajectories, often but not always silently, that no known man-made craft could generate or follow; the ability to hover, and then to accelerate to high speeds in periods of the order of seconds (and generally without a sonic boom); on occasion to change shape, and to produce durable physical effects on both animate and inanimate matter; to be, on occasion, unmistakably detected on radar, yet to be peculiarly localized and preferential in their manifestation (that is, their appearance at times and places when and where they would be least likely to be detected, and their avoidance of level flight which would of necessity open them to observation by people along the way). The pattern in the "close encounter" cases is almost universal: a rapid descent to a landing or near landing, a stay of the order of only minutes, and the ascent, at usually a high angle, and disappearance either through distance or by some other means (it is often reported that at a height of a few hundred feet the bright luminosity vanishes). The choice of locale is statistically significant. The close encounter cases simply do not occur on the White House lawn or between halves at the Rose Bowl game, but in desolate spots, generally some distance from habitation and where detection would be least expected. In a small percent of the close encounter cases, robot-like or human-like "creatures" are reported.

A growing number of my colleagues and I have been driven, albeit reluctantly, into the bold step of accepting the more-than-amply reported UFO phenomenon as something that really *is* new, something not yet encompassed by our present science. There will indeed be a twenty-first century science, and a thirtieth century science, to which the UFO phenomenon may be as natural as television, atomic energy, and DNA are to twentieth century science, as these were quite foreign to eighteenth and nineteenth century science.

In any event, the UFO phenomenon presents us with a fantastic challenge. Off-the-shelf explanations just won't do. We've tried these for more than a quarter of a century, and they just don't wash. Acceptance of the UFO as a new empirical phenomenon worthy of very serious study is growing not only among scientists, engineers, and technically aware persons, but by educators and the socially aware and the politically astute. There is a growing recognition that here is indeed something new.

And anything new almost surely creates controversy. The controversy about UFOs has been, however, no ordinary one. It has brought into play a veritable host of human concerns: science and scientific prejudice, human emotions, bureaucratic authority, the press and other media, charlatans, religious fanatics—the list could be extended.

Dr. Jacobs's most admirable work has put the UFO controversy into scholarly perspective. It is indispensable reading for any who seek an informed view of the tortuous history of the UFO phenomenon. And now that the controversy has been ably and fairly presented by Dr. Jacobs, where does that leave the actual subject matter—the UFO phenomenon itself? Where can we logically go from here? Can the controversy be resolved? And more precisely, can it be resolved by science, or are we in a realm beyond the legitimate concerns of science?

One can certainly hold—and I for one do—that nothing that intrigues the mind of man is automatically ineligible for scientific approach. As logic is the basis of all scientific endeavor, even the most bizarre subjects can be approached in a logical manner. The methodology may differ from one subject area to another, but not the logical substrate. In determining causal relationships, logic demands that we isolate variables and hold as many as possible constant—all but one ideally—while the effects of running one variable through its total feasible range are noted. This has "paid off" in the classical physical sciences. If the variables are too numerous, as they frequently are in the behavioral sciences, statistical methods prove fruitful.

Unfortunately, little has been done in this direction, the Condon Committee notwithstanding. Any school child learns that in science one tests hypotheses. What he generally does not learn is that the hypothesis to be tested must logically follow from, and be suggested by, the data. As Dr. Jacobs indicates, many of the members of the Condon Committee did not apply this stricture. Without once asking what the overall, observed nature of the UFO phenomenon was—which could easily have been learned from a serious survey of a statistically significant number of well documented and truly puzzling cases—they set out to test the hypothesis that UFOs were visitors from outer space! And the relatively few cases they examined were studied individually, as though that one case—and only that one—existed. No attempt was made to find patterns, relations between the thousands of cases from all over the world (which were available in copious literature), and then to consider various testable hypotheses. This would be like asking, in times past, whether the Northern Lights represented interstellar communications, and concluding that since the data did not support this hypothesis, the Northern Lights were hallucinations, hoaxes, or sheer imagination.

This is clearly not the place to criticize the Condon Report. It is proper, however, to enter a plea for the proper scientific study of the UFO phenomenon and to profit from our mistakes.

One must first determine, if the controversy is ever to be resolved, whether a legitimate body of data really exists—that is, whether UFO reports, at least in part, represent truly new empirical observations. I am convinced, from my long acquaintance with the subject, that they most certainly do. But the majority of scientists still tend to reject this, often on emotional grounds, and in all cases because they forget another cardinal rule: A scientific opinion demands of the opiner that he be "acquainted with the literature."

When the nature of the UFO controversy is understood—and this book is dedicated to that end—and when the interdisciplinary nature of the phenomenon is grasped (no one knows to what discipline the subject belongs simply because not enough yet is known of the subject), a meaningful start can be made on a truly scientific study of the subject, which can then be approached as scientific subjects should be approached—without prejudice or emotional bias.

CENTER FOR UFO STUDIES
EVANSTON, ILLINOIS

J. ALLEN HYNEK
CHAIRMAN, DEPT. ASTRONOMY
NORTHWESTERN UNIVERSITY

Acknowledgments

I have incurred many debts in the past years as part of this project. I thank William L. O'Neill for originally encouraging me to go forward with this study. I owe my greatest academic debt to Paul K. Conkin, who patiently oversaw the manuscript, diligently corrected its errors, and good-naturedly kept my thoughts on an even keel throughout the writing. His rigorous thinking and sound advice were invaluable in helping me gain a perspective on the UFO controversy.

While I was conducting the research, James and Coral Lorenzen and Richard Greenwell at the Aerial Phenomena Research Organization (Tucson, Arizona) and Stuart Nixon of the National Investigations Committee on Aerial Phenomena (Kensington, Maryland) gave encouragement and immeasurable help by allowing me complete use of their organizations' files. I am particularly grateful to Richard Greenwell for his cogent criticisms of the manuscript, and to Betsy McDonald for giving me access to her late husband's files. J. Allen Hynek also allowed me to research his files, and my discussions with him at Northwestern University filled many gaps in my knowledge of his and the Air Force's roles in the UFO controversy. Judy Endicott and the staff at the Albert F. Simpson Historical Archives at Maxwell Air Force Base in Montgomery, Alabama, were especially helpful to me in my research there.

I thank Roger Keeran for listening to countless rehashings of my theories and helping me over many rough spots in my writing and ideas. Lynn and Charles W. Hieatt deserve gratitude for the friendship and support they gave during the trying days of writing.

The debt I owe to Irene D. Jacobs for listening to my ideas, reading and editing my writing, and giving moral support over the past three years is so large that mere acknowledgment becomes absurd in the face of it.

The UFO Controversy in America

Cartoon from the *Chicago Times-Herald*, April 12, 1897. (COURTESY OF THE CHICAGO HISTORICAL SOCIETY)

Engraving from *Chicago Times-Herald*, April 12, 1897. (COURTESY OF THE CHICAGO HISTORICAL SOCIETY)

James E. McDonald. (COURTESY OF BETSY MCDONALD)

The 1952 Samford news conference. From left are Capt. Roy James, ATIC radar specialist; Maj. Gen. Roger Ramey, director of Operations; Capt. Edward Ruppelt, head of Project Blue Book; Maj. Gen. John A. Samford, director of Intelligence; Col. Donald L. Bower, chief of Technical Intelligence Division, ATIC; and Mr. B. L. Griffing, ATIC civilian electronics specialist. (UNITED PRESS INTERNATIONAL PHOTO)

Major Hector Quintanilla in 1967 at the Project Blue Book office. (PRIVATE FILES)

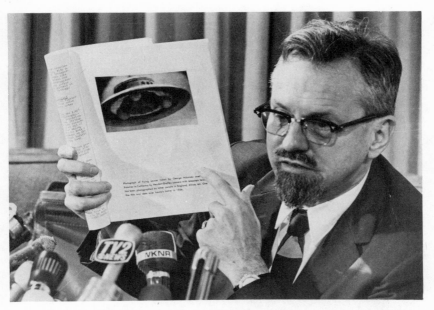

J. Allen Hynek at the "swamp gas" news conference in Detroit, March 1966. Here he is commenting on the resemblance between a photo of an alleged UFO, taken by contactee George Adamski, and a chicken brooder. (UNITED PRESS INTERNATIONAL PHOTO).

Donald E. Keyhoe, circa 1962.

Major Robert Friend, third from left, and members of the FTD UFO Panel, 1959. (COURTESY OF ROBERT FRIEND)

James and Coral Lorenzen of the Aerial Phenomena Research Organization in their new headquarters in Alamagordo, New Mexico, 1955. (COURTESY OF APRO)

Some Words of Explanation

[Unidentified flying objects (UFOs) have been a source of continuing controversy.] Steeped in ridicule and existing on the fringes of scholarly pursuit, the subject of unidentified flying objects has a history of its own. [This involves the Air Force's efforts for over twenty years to cope with the UFO phenomenon, the growth of national organizations dedicated to investigating it, and the scientific community's fear or reluctance to study the subject because of the ridicule attached to it.] It also involves press coverage of the subject, motion pictures and television shows about it, and the small group of people who have made a living capitalizing on the fantasy aspects of UFOs. The debate over unidentified flying objects in America has been surrounded by emotion, ignorance, misinformation, and, above all, loose thinking. I do not attempt to solve the problem of the origin of the phenomenon. Rather, I try to explain some of the reasons why so many people expended such large amounts of time and energy on it. My focus is on describing and, in part, analyzing societal and individual responses to the appearance of a mysterious phenomenon.

There are semantic difficulties inherent in a discussion of unidentified flying objects. No words exist to describe a person who studies the UFO phenomenon, one who believes UFOs do or do not represent an anomalous phenomenon, one who believes UFOs are products of extraterrestrial intelligence, or one who reputably claims to have an experience with a UFO. The lack of precise language prompts people to use the terms *flying saucer* and *unidentified flying object* synonymously. They are different. The term *flying saucer* conveys the idea of objects intelligently controlled and extraterrestrial in origin. [The term *unidentified flying object* denotes just that, an unidentified flying object regardless of speculations about its origin. I have tried to use the two terms in the way that the participants used them. There also is a difference between a UFO sighting and a UFO report. The first is an event that happens to a person, and the second is the description that the person gives of the event. Moreover, there are two types of UFO reports: those that investigators can explain given sufficient information, and those that investigators and analysts cannot explain even with sufficient information. Unhappily, these two types of reports do not have different labels, and the context in this study will have to make the meaning clear. Semantic rigor was not a characteristic of the debate over UFOs.

Finally, a word about the time span of this study. The UFO sighting waves dictated my chronology. The first major sightings took place in 1896 and 1897. I had to leap to 1947 (with a short interlude around World War II) because there were no known large-scale sighting waves in America between 1897 and 1947. The sighting waves prompted public reaction. Therefore, the history of the debate coincides with the times when people reported unidentified flying objects in American skies.

1

THE MYSTERY AIRSHIP:
PRELIMINARIES TO THE CONTROVERSY

[Thousands of people in the United States in 1896 and 1897 said they saw airships in the skies over Alabama, Arkansas, California, Colorado, Illinois, Indiana, Iowa, Kansas, Kentucky, Michigan, Minnesota, Missouri, Nebraska, Oklahoma, South Dakota, Tennessee, Texas, West Virginia, and Wisconsin. The sightings started in California in November 1896 and continued until May 1897, with a break from January to the middle of March.

The airships appeared most often as dirigible-type machines, cylindrical or cigar shaped and driven by a motor attached to an air screw or propeller.[1] When witnesses said they saw an airship, they implicitly differentiated between it and a glider or a heavier-than-air "flying machine." Also, most people distinguished between an airship and a balloon, which was definitely round and had a basket attached to it. They expressed a popular belief that the solution to aerial navigation would be through an airship rather than heavier-than-air flying machines, which had not yet assumed the importance in the popular imagination that they would after the Wright brothers' experiments in 1903. Consequently, many of the early designs for the "machine that would conquer the air" looked like dirigibles with a passenger car on the bottom.

Descriptions of the objects varied greatly, either because the witnesses were inaccurate or because they viewed different airships. In Omaha, Nebraska, an airship sighting interrupted a Knights of Ak-Sar-Ben initiation ceremony. According to the excited witnesses, the object was "at least eighteen inches in diameter, the reflection from which passed along what appeared to be a steel body, the length of which could only be estimated at from twelve to thirty feet." In Chicago, on April 10, 1897, the *Chicago Tribune* reported that people observed a slender object, seventy feet long with approximately twenty-foot wide structures resembling wings or sails just above the body. In Mount Carroll, Illinois, witnesses described an airship eight to ten feet long and two or three feet high. "A dim outline of it could be seen, which appeared to be shaped like an egg," in Wausau, Wisconsin. An airship over Dallas, Texas, was "in a luminous, hazy cloud" and had "sails or wings outstretched on both sides of its cigar-shaped body"; "on both ends," the report said, "there were large rotating fans projecting from the sails at an angle of about 45 degrees, the one in front being elevated, while the one at the rear was depressed, somewhat resembling the body of a bird." Witnesses estimated its length to be about two hundred feet. In Fort Worth, Texas, an airship looked like a sixty-foot long "passenger coach," pointed at the ends and with batlike wings.[2]

Witnesses repeatedly reported lights on the object, usually the first indication of an approaching airship. Colored or bright white lights plus an intense red or white searchlight were the most common features of the airship descriptions. In Fort Atkinson, Wisconsin, "the white light . . . ahead and a red light at the rear made the affair look like a machine about fifty feet long and flying about 500 feet above the earth." The Benton Harbor, Michigan, airship had blue, red, and green lights. Occasionally the searchlight on the airship was so brilliant that, for example, when it appeared in Everest, Kansas, at 9:05 P.M., the "full power of the wonderful lamps were turned on, and the city was flooded with light." Often the unusual color of the white searchlight made it seem phosphorescent. Sometimes the lights came from the side of the ship and moved independently of it. As thousands of gaping spectators watched in Milwaukee, "the machine, or whatever it was," hovered directly over the city hall and the lights on it moved backward and forward, "as if signalling to the earth." In Guthrie, Oklahoma, "its outlines were indistinct, but a light was thrown out from the front and at times there were flashes of light from the sides." Frank Dickson, editor of the *Edna* (Texas) *Progress*, saw two airships "400 feet apart communicating with each other by means of red and green lights."[3]

The airships' movements ranged from erratic to smooth. In Guthrie, Oklahoma, the object "sank almost to the ground just north of the city, and then rose straight into the air at great speed and disappeared in the darkness of the night." Often the airships "bounced" or "undulated" due, people speculated, to the flapping of "wings." For late nineteenth-century Americans, an airship's ability to maneuver against the wind proved that it was under control. A dispatch from Nashville, Illinois, pointed out that "the fact that the object traveled from the northwest while the wind was from the southwest goes to prove it was not a balloon."[4]

Like all other aspects of the airships, reported speeds varied greatly, from as slow as 5 miles per hour to as fast as 200 miles per hour. Occasionally witnesses made more accurate measurements of an airship's speed. A railroad engineer from Burlington, Iowa, estimated an airship's speed at 150 miles per hour by comparing it to his train's speed. But most people could not make such estimates and simply reported that an airship traveled slowly or "at a terrific rate of speed."[5]

Sometimes people heard noises emanating from a sighted object. In Burlington, Iowa, witnesses heard a "hissing sound," in Decatur, Michigan, a "sharp, crackling sound," and in Cameron, Texas, a "humming" noise. In general, though, either the objects made no sounds or no one heard them.[6]

All the reports indicate that more than one object was being sighted, both because of simultaneous or almost simultaneous sightings and because of the differences in perceived details. Nevertheless, people found it difficult to accept the idea of many airships. The *Chicago Times-Herald* reported, for example, that "the 'air ship' has been seen again—that is, in this vicinity. To be sure, it was also seen in Kankakee, Mount Carroll and other places at the same time, but the people in these cities must have been mistaken—or else there is a whole flock of air ships cavorting about through the heavens. The real 'air ship' [is] the one that was seen here." Another reporter, trying to explain how witnesses could report an airship in two different places in a short period of time, theorized that it was "speedy" and "covers vast areas of ground." Once in a while either an airship would return to the area or another airship would appear there: a sensation ensued in Middleville, Michigan, when citizens sighted an airship flying north at 9:00 P.M. and another one flying east at 10:30 P.M.[7]

Often witnesses reported hearing sounds as an airship passed over them at low altitude. Citizens in Sacramento heard voices coming from an airship; others claimed to have heard music, and one man said he heard someone on board say "go up higher, or collide with the church steeples, etc." In Farmerville, Texas, and Galesburg, Michigan, witnesses heard voices but could not understand them. "Sweet strains of music could be heard" in Fontanelle, Iowa, as well as "the workings of its machinery." Observers in Belton, Texas, heard the "passengers' " voices but could not understand them "on account of the velocity" of the craft.[8]

From time to time people said that items, usually letters, dropped from the airships. The *Milwaukee Sentinel* reported that several letters, fastened to iron rods that were rusted from the rain, purportedly dropped from an airship as it passed overhead: "The suspicion that the letters were 'planted' was not apparently well founded, for no hardware dealers in this vicinity have sold any such rods as the letters were wired to." The letter supposedly stated that the airship *Pegasus*, traveling from Tennessee to South Dakota, used steam for propulsion and could carry as much as a thousand pounds; the airship, the note maintained, would "revolutionize all present methods of locomotion." The letter did not disclose the inventor's identity but asked the "finder" to keep the note until a member of the Masonic fraternity called for it. Citizens in Newport, Kentucky, also found a letter describing an airship's traveling speed (forty miles per hour) and other details;

"Captain Pegasus" had signed the note. In Dupont and Lorain, Ohio, people supposedly found similar notes.[9]

Occasionally witnesses reported seeing occupants on board or near an airship on the ground. In Lovelady, Texas, one witness saw an object resembling a moving man in the airship's lower part. Several people in Girard, Illinois, who arrived at a landing spot after they had seen an airship rise and "disappear," found footprints which did not lead anywhere. "It was evident that they were made by someone who had jumped out of the ship to repair some of the machinery on the outside." In Belle Plaine, Iowa, on April 15, 1897, airship witnesses reported seeing "two queer looking persons on board, who made desperate efforts to conceal themselves"; the witnesses said the occupants "had the longest whiskers they ever saw in their lives." Some people in Belton, Texas, "distinctly" saw ten passengers on board an object. Witnesses in Sacramento reported seeing a cigar-shaped machine "operated by four men who sat aside the cigar and moved as though they were working their passage on a bicycle." In Cleburne, Texas, a man who claimed that "he had not touched a drop of anything except water during the evening" saw an airship speed by "just above the tops of the houses" with a passenger in it. "The passenger gave him the go-ahead sign that brakemen give on the railroad." Once in a while witnesses saw animals as well. The city marshal of Farmerville, Texas, said that when the object passed over him at about two hundred feet he could "see two men in the ship and something resembling a large Newfoundland dog." He also reported hearing the occupants talk, although he could not understand the language, which sounded like Spanish.[10]

Clearly the strangest occurrence in these 1896-97 sightings was the reported contacts between witnesses and airship occupants. These frequent reports substantially influenced the thought of the period about what the airships were and who was responsible for them. Sometimes the contact reports were so sketchy that it is difficult to ascertain exactly what happened, if anything did indeed happen. For example, a report from Downs Township, Illinois, simply said that "while [the witness] was at work in a field, an airship alighted near him and . . . six people disembarked therefrom, remained a few minutes and conversed with him, and then jumped aboard, ascended and sailed away." The *Harrisburg* (Arkansas) *Modern News* reported that ex-senator Harris (of that state) encountered an airship and occupant who said he had a special "Hotchkiss" gun on board and was thinking of going to Cuba to "kill Spaniards"; he offered Senator Harris a ride which the senator refused. One of the earliest claims of a detailed contact occurred in California in 1896. The witness told the *San Francisco Call* that, while searching in the woods for a deer, he had come across six men working on an almost completed airship who swore him to secrecy; but now that he was sure this was the airship people had seen, the witness said, he would give a detailed description of the encounter.[11]

In 1897 witnesses reported a whole series of contacts with people making repairs on their airships. Several "presumably truthful" citizens of Chattanooga, Tennessee, said they "came upon the vessel resting on a spur of a mountain near this city. Two men were at work on it and explained that they had been compelled to return to earth because the machinery was out of order. One of the men said his name was 'Prof. Charles Davidson.' He is alleged to have said that the vessel left Sacramento a month ago and had been sailing all over the country." [12]

John M. Barclay in Rockland, Texas, saw something that "made his eyes bulge out." Hearing a whining noise on his farm and the dogs "barking furiously," he grabbed his rifle and went outside to investigate; he immediately noticed an airship circling his farm and then saw it land in a pasture next to his house. When he was about 150 feet from the ship, "an ordinary mortal" met him and told him to lay his gun aside because no harm was intended; the occupants wanted lubricating oil, chisels, and a bluestone, for which they paid him. When Barclay tried to inspect the airship, one occupant prevented him from going near it but told him that someday they would return and take him for a ride. The airship, Barclay said, took off "like a shot out of a gun." [13]

In Stephenville, Texas, some of the most prominent men in the community—including a judge, a state senator, and a district attorney—saw an airship which the occupants were repairing. One witness spoke to two of the airship passengers, who gave their names as S. E. Tilman and A. E. Dolbear; they refused to allow the witness to come near the airship but explained that New York "capitalists" were financing them and that air navigation shortly would be an established fact. Then they boarded the ship and, "bidding adieu to the astonished crowd assembled," sailed away.[14]

Some people who claimed to see occupants with the airships reported coming across them in secluded places. Judge Love and his friend, Mr. Beatty, were fishing near Waxachie, Texas, when Beatty (while going upstream for a better fishing spot) discovered a "queer looking machine" in the woods and a group of "five peculiarly dressed men" near it. One of the men, who spoke "fairly good English," explained this was one of the famous airships and invited the witnesses to examine it. The man told them the airship came from "regions in the north pole" since, "contrary to popular belief, there is a large body of land beyond the polar seas." He explained that his people descended from the ten lost tribes of Israel and had been living in this inhabitable land for centuries; the people spoke English because Sir Hugh Willoughby's 1553 North Pole Expedition party (which supposedly was lost) and United States raiding parties had been stranded there and taught them the language. They were forced to build airships, the leader said, because they did not have timber for locomotives or sea ships. Now twenty airships were sailing around the United States and Europe, he explained, and all would meet on June 18 and 19 at the Tennessee Centennial Exposition where anyone could inspect them. Judge Love said good-bye to the occupants, and "We then shook hands with the crew and they stepped into their ship, rose in the air and started toward Waco. The description of the ship I have given you is a very meager one, but you can all go to the Nashville Exposition June 18 and 19 and see for yourselves." [15]

Similarly, when C. G. Williams walked across a field in Greenville, Texas, a light suddenly "frightened [him] almost out of [his] senses." An airship had landed near him and three men came out of it, two of whom started to work on the "rigging" of the ship.

As Williams began to write down what was happening, the third man interceded: "See here, young man, don't give this thing away. We are experimenting with this vessel. . . . We expect to revolutionize travel and transportation." The visitor explained that he had been experimenting with flight in a little town in New York State. He and the other two men had intended originally to take a short trip, but the flight went so well that they decided to keep going and soon found themselves over Indiana; they were returning home in a few days to make some improvements on the ship. They used electricity to get the airship off the ground and wind power (to turn the large wheel in front of the airship) once in the air, the visitor said. He predicted that in a short while people would hear from him and there would be a "full description of the modern wonder, the airship." The visitor said that if Williams would mail some letters for him, without copying the addresses, in return the visitors would come back and take him on a ride to South America.[16]

Perhaps the most baffling of all contact stories concerned a man named Wilson. The first incident occurred in Beaumont, Texas, on April 19, 1897. J. B. Ligon (local agent for the Magnolia Brewery) and his son Charles noticed lights in the Johnson pasture a few hundred yards away and went to investigate. They came upon four men standing beside a large, dark object; one man asked Ligon for two buckets of water. Ligon consented and then questioned one of the men, who said his name was Wilson. The man explained that he and his companions were traveling in a flying machine; they had taken a trip "out on the gulf" and were returning to a "quiet Iowa town" where the airship and four others like it had been made. Wilson explained that electricity powered the propellers and wings.[17]

The next day, April 20, Sheriff H. W. Baylor of Uvalde, Texas, went to investigate a strange light and voices in back of his house and encountered an airship and three men. One of the men gave his name as Wilson from Goshen, New York. Wilson inquired about C. C. Akers, former sheriff of Zavalia County, whom Wilson said he had met in Fort Worth in 1877 and wanted to see again. The surprised Sheriff Baylor replied that Captain

Akers was now at Eagle Pass in the customs service and that he often visited him. Wilson, somewhat disappointed, "asked to be remembered to the captain on the occasion of his next visit." The men from the airship wanted water and requested their visit be kept secret from the townspeople. Then they boarded the airship, and "its great wings and fans were set in motion and it sped away northward in the direction of San Angelo." The county clerk also saw it as it left the area. One week later (on April 27) the *Galveston Daily News* printed a letter from C. C. Akers, who said he had indeed known a man in Fort Worth named Wilson, who was from New York, educated, and about twenty-four years old. Akers said Wilson "was of a mechanical turn of mind and was then working on aerial navigation and something that would astonish the world"; Wilson, Akers theorized, seemed to have enough money to work on his inventions, and "having succeeded in constructing a practical airship, would probably hunt me up to show me that he was not so wild in his claims as I then supposed." Akers concluded by saying: "I have known Sheriff Baylor many years and know that any statement he may make can be relied on as exactly correct." The next reported incident with a man named Wilson occurred in Kountze, Texas, on April 23. An April 25 article in the *Houston Post* said that two "responsible men" observed an airship which had descended for repairs; the occupants on board gave their names as Wilson and Jackson.[18]

The *Houston Post* published an account of an incident that purportedly occurred in Josserand, Texas, on April 22, and that was similar to the Wilson incidents, although the name was not mentioned specifically. A whirring sound awakened Frank Nichols, a prominent farmer, who looked out his window to find "brilliant lights streaming from a ponderous vessel of strange proportions" in his cornfield. "With all the bravery of Priam at the siege of Troy," Nichols went outside to investigate. Before he could get to the object, two men accosted him and asked for some water from his well: "Thinking he might be entertaining heavenly visitants instead of earthly mortals permission was readily granted." The men invited Nichols to visit the ship, where he talked freely with the crew of six or eight individuals. Although "in his short interview he could gain no knowledge of its [the airship's] working," crew members told him that the ship's motive power was "highly condensed electricity." This airship was one of five that they had built in a small town in Iowa with the backing of an immense stock company. The *Houston Post* article concluded by saying: "Mr. Nichols lives at Josserand, Trinity County, Texas, and will convince any credulous [*sic*] one by showing the place where the ship rested." [19]

The last reported sighting that might involve a man named Wilson—because of its similarities with the other Wilson stories—occurred in Deadwood, Texas. In its April 30 edition, the *Houston Post* published a letter describing the event. At about 8:30 P.M., H. C. Lagrone heard his horses, which were "old gentle stock, . . . snorting, running and bucking around like a drove of bronchos on a regular stampede." Going out to see what was happening, he saw a bright white light circling around the fields nearby and illuminating the entire area; eventually the light descended and landed in a field. Lagrone thought this might be the much publicized airship and went to the landing spot. He found a crew of five men, three of whom entertained him while two others went for water with rubber bags. The men informed him that this ship was one of five that had been flying around the country recently and was the same one that had landed in Beaumont a few days before; these ships were "put up" in an interior town in Illinois. But the men were reluctant to say anything about the inner workings of the ship because "they had not yet secured anything by patent." They did say they expected to set up a factory in St. Louis and "at once enter into active competition with the railroads for passenger traffic." The crew, Lagrone noted, "was careful not to forget earthly things even though traveling in the heavens. They were well supplied with edibles of all sorts—likewise drinkables; had a good supply of beer and champagne, also had a full supply of musical instruments." Lagrone also reported a curious sidelight to this sighting: the airship passed close to a religious camp meeting and some of the participants who saw the craft "went into paroxysms of alarm" while others thought it was a messenger from God.[20]

Perhaps the most famous occupant incident during the 1896–97 wave of sightings took place in Leroy, Kansas, on or about April 19, 1897. Alexander Hamilton, his son Wall, and his tenant Gid awoke to cattle noises. Going outside they discovered —to Hamilton's "utter amazement"—"an airship slowly descending over my cow lot about forty rods from the house." The cigar-shaped object was three hundred feet long with a carriage made of "panels of glass or other transparent substance alternating with a narrow strip of some other material"; a large searchlight and smaller red and green lights were attached to it. As it descended to thirty feet above ground and the witnesses came to within fifty yards of it, Hamilton could see "six of the strangest beings I ever saw" inside. The occupants were "jabbering" but Hamilton could not understand anything. Then the witnesses noticed that a heifer was attached to a red "cable" emanating from the airship and also was caught in a fence. Unable to free the heifer, the witnesses cut the fence and "stood in amazement to see ship, cow and all rise slowly and sail off." The next day a neighbor recovered the calf's hide, legs, and head a few miles away.[21]

Hamilton was deeply affected and complained that when he tried to sleep he "would see the cursed thing with its big lights and hideous people." Distressed by the incident, Hamilton later said, "I don't know whether they are devils or angels or what but we all saw them and my whole family saw the ship and I don't want any more to do with them." The newspaper that carried Hamilton's account also printed an affidavit from eleven prominent community members, such as the postmaster, sheriff, justice of the peace, banker; it said they had known Hamilton "from 15 to 30 years" and "believe his statement to be true and correct." Eight days later a similar affidavit appeared in the *Burlington* (Kansas) *Daily News.*[22]

All these varied reports of occupants agreed on one detail: each described them as ordinary human beings and not as creatures from another world. These descriptions played a major role in molding contemporary thought about the airship. The public seemed convinced that if an airship existed, a secret inventor, perhaps named Wilson, must have made it. This is how the public thought an airship would probably be developed.

The above reports, from seemingly reliable witnesses, contrast sharply with several apparent hoaxes perpetrated during the period, generally to demonstrate that the entire airship wave was a lot of nonsense. Excited witnesses usually exposed these hoaxes immediately.

First recorded was the April 5, 1897, hoax in Omaha, Nebraska. According to the *St. Louis Post-Dispatch*, two men sent up a balloon with a basket of burning shavings attached to it, and the wind carried the balloon over the center of the city—hence the solution to the airship mystery. Five days later the *Des Moines Leader* reported a hoax in Burlington, Iowa: the hoaxers sent a tissue paper balloon up over the city and, as the *Leader* said, people called the local newspaper office swearing they had seen the airship complete with red and green lights; one reputable citizen swore he heard voices. This convinced the newspaper that "the Nebraska-Iowa-Illinois airship is a pure fake." A more elaborate hoax took place in Waterloo, Iowa, where several men secretly constructed a thirty-six-foot canvas and wood airship, complete with "compressors and generators." They guarded it, allowing no one "to inspect the machinery, and any attempt to cross the rope fence . . . was met with an order to stay out." The airship "operators" told the five thousand visitors about how they had come from San Francisco and how they had landed. When the "crew" said that "one man had fallen overboard just before landing," some of the distraught citizens organized a party to search the river for him; then they "discovered that the entire affair was a joke." Hoaxes also occurred in Chicago, in Fond du Lac and Portage, Wisconsin, in Muncie, Indiana, and in Des Moines, Iowa. Of course, none of the hoaxes—being hoaxes—flew.[23]

Enterprising reporters perpetrated many journalistic hoaxes. These generally are easy to identify because of their tongue-in-cheek tone, with an accent on the sensational. Yet because so many of the legitimate stories were fantastic, some of the journalistic hoaxes appear equally convincing. The *Dallas Morn-*

ing News printed a story that may have been a hoax. It supposedly took place in Aurora, Texas, on April 17, 1897. "Early risers of Aurora," the writer said, "were astonished" at seeing an airship "traveling due north, and much nearer the earth than ever before." It seemed that the "machinery was out of order" because it was traveling slowly and descending. "It sailed directly over the public square," the article said, and then "collided with the tower of Judge Proctor's windmill and went to pieces with a terrific explosion, scattering debris over several acres of ground, wrecking the windmill and water tank and destroying the judge's flower garden." Although the body of the one occupant was "badly disfigured, enough . . . has been picked up to show that he was not an inhabitant of this world"; in fact, a United States signal service officer, an astronomy expert, said "he was a native of the planet Mars." Moreover, some papers the occupant had "are written in some unknown hieroglyphics, and can not be deciphered." Since the ship was wrecked, the writer explained, it was not possible "to form any conclusion as to its construction or motive power. It was built of an unknown metal, resembling somewhat a mixture of aluminum and silver, and it must have weighed several tons." The last sentence in the article was: "The pilot's funeral will take place at noon tomorrow." [24]

This report contains many elements found in other sightings of the period: a ship flying over a town, evidence pointing to Mars as the home of the occupant, the opinion of an "expert," unknown metal. And although the collision itself seems somewhat strange, especially the reference to the flower garden, some of the sincere sightings were just as strange. Nevertheless, a 1966 follow-up investigation seemed to substantiate the hoax theory. There was a Judge Proctor living in the Aurora area, but "that is the only part of the story that anyone recognized. Two life-long residents of the Aurora area—Miss Mag Morris and Mrs. Lou Inman (88 and 93 respectively)—scoffed at the story." [25] In 1973 UFO researchers resurrected this story and claimed to have circumstantial evidence that the event took place. However, they failed to establish its authenticity. In contrast to this story, other literary hoaxes were much less subtle, the author purposely giving himself away by saying—in the last line—that he was writing from an insane asylum (or something to that effect).

Concurrent with these hoaxes, numerous people around the country claimed to be the airship's secret inventor. The first identified himself during the Sacramento–San Francisco 1896 sightings. The *Sacramento Daily Record-Union* reported that Mr. Collins, a prominent attorney, claimed that the airship's inventor was one of his clients whom he could not name because of a pledge of secrecy. The client was a wealthy man who, after studying flying machines for fifteen years, came to California from Maine to get away from the prying eyes of other inventors, and had spent at least $100,000 on his invention, for which he had applied for a patent. He kept his identity secret because he feared that someone might steal his patent if people knew his machine worked. According to the newspaper, the attorney claimed to have seen the machine on the ground and in flight. The next day the *Sacramento Daily Record-Union* printed a retraction of Attorney Collins's statement, explaining that the *San Francisco Bulletin* had tracked down Collins's client, the alleged inventor of the airship, who was only a wealthy dentist. The article reported that Collins denied making any statement about knowing the airship's inventor but did admit that a man had come to him with a patent for an airship and wanted the attorney to represent him in this matter. Collins's client seems to have had nothing to do with an airship other than making arrangements for patent plans.[26]

Five months later, on April 12, 1897, the *Chicago Tribune* reported that "A. C. Clinton" had written to the directors of the Trans-Mississippi Exposition (to be held in Omaha, Nebraska) claiming to be the inventor of the airship. Clinton said he would prove it in Omaha if the exposition directors would give him 870,000 square feet of space. "I truly believe I have the greatest invention and discovery ever made," he proclaimed. A few days later Clinton A. Case wrote a similar letter to the Omaha newspaper. It soon became obvious that A. C. Clinton and Clinton A. Case were the same person. Case, a violin maker in Omaha, claimed to have discovered the secret of aerial navigation and declared he was the man who had been sailing about the sky recently. Aerial pioneer Henry Maxim saw Case's plan and said it represented nothing new in the field. Case had tried to get capital for his invention before 1896 but no one would invest. There is no evidence that Clinton A. Case ever built an airship and he was not granted the land he requested at the Trans-Mississippi Exposition.[27]

On April 19, 1897, the *Louisville Courier-Journal* reported that Harry Tibbs claimed to be the inventor of the mysterious airship, which needed only a bit more work before it was ready for flight. Tibbs supposedly was a studious man interested in engineering and had been conducting research on an airship for some time. A while after this report, a friend of Tibbs purportedly received a letter from him saying that the airship was a success: he had made a voyage in it from Cincinnati to Erie, Pennsylvania, and "it works like a charm." Tibbs's description of the ship was similar to those many witnesses had made. Tibbs explained that he was keeping his invention a secret because he was afraid someone would copy his idea and beat him to Washington.[28]

Sometimes an enterprising reporter, in an effort to solve the airship mystery, would "find" the inventor. An article in the *Detroit Free Press* called John O. Pries of Omaha the secret inventor, although Pries vigorously denied the story. The reporter's proof was that witnesses had seen an airship hover over Pries's house on two different occasions and that Pries had made small models and drawings of airships as a hobby.[29]

In addition to the mystery inventor claims, some people declared that they had taken photographs of an airship. Walter McCann took a widely publicized photograph in Rogers Park (Chicago) while three other men witnessed the event and numerous people said they saw an airship in the vicinity. The *Chicago Times-Herald* printed a pen and ink etching of the photograph and an etcher's "expert" analysis. The etcher, who apparently knew something about photographic analysis, conducted chemical tests to see if anyone had tampered with the print. His results showed the photograph to be a good print, "genuine in every particular," and "a mighty fine piece of photographic work at that." But on that same day the *Chicago Tribune* announced that the supposed photograph of an airship was a fake. An "expert photographer" examined the photograph and said it had a "perspective impossibility" because "no camera could have caught so much within the scope of its lenses." Moreover, the *Chicago Tribune* noted that a man appeared in the picture who seemed to have his arms outstretched and a camera in them, as if he was taking the picture of the airship. "This suggests," the *Chicago Tribune* said, "the thought that perhaps this wonderful Kodak takes pictures of itself and its manipulator as well as of air ships." Yet the picture published in the *Chicago Times-Herald* did not show a camera in the man's hands.[30]

There were other reports of photographs, but no one verified their authenticity. The *Cincinnati Commercial-Tribune*, hostile to the idea of an airship, took a fake picture of one to demonstrate that people could be misled and to suggest that everybody who thought he saw the object was fooled.[31]

The debate over the authenticity of the Rogers Park photograph demonstrates the intense public interest in airship sightings, especially among people who had already seen an airship and those who wanted to see one. Indeed, excitement was so great that reporter after reporter saw fit to describe it. A reporter for the *Detroit Free Press* said "the section of Iowa where the ship has been seen is fairly crazy with excitement. People throng the streets of all the towns and villages in hopes of catching a glimpse of it, and the telegraph wires are hot with messages about it." In Dallas, St. Louis, and Chicago the airship was "the sole topic of conversation," as it was in many other cities and towns where it supposedly had been; in fact, some people stayed up all night hoping to get a glimpse of the aerial wonder. After an airship had passed over Kansas City, Missouri, "hundreds of people [were] still on the streets watching intently for a return of the airship." "Expectation ran high" among people in Milwaukee who gathered in the streets when they heard an airship was coming toward their city; any flash of light, such as from trolley poles of street cars, drew exclamations of wonder from the knots of citizens clustered in the streets. A *St. Louis Post-Dispatch* reporter interviewed people arriving by train in Milwaukee from the north and northwest areas of the state and found that "the airship was the one topic of conversation in the region through which they passed." In Chicago the traditional greeting of hello was replaced with "Have you seen the airship?" [32]

For people who saw an airship at close range or who had encounters with one, their excitement was mixed with fear and terror. A man in Richmond, Texas, who saw an airship ran terrified into his house. An airship's appearance in Springfield, Tennessee, caused the witnesses to be "nonplussed," and some people in the area were "overcome with abject terror. Many of them shouted and prayed as if they thought the millennium was at hand." In Paris, Texas, one man fell down on his knees upon seeing an airship and prayed for his and his family's safety; he said the airship was actually "the return of Noah's ark with wing-like attachments on its way toward the Mississippi bottoms, its mission being to save [his people] from the perils of the overflow in that section." In Hillsboro, Texas, a lawyer was driving his horse and buggy when he saw a brilliant flash of white light directly over his buggy; the light "frightened [him] to death." His horse also was frightened and "snorted, reared, and plunged madly, trembling meantime like a leaf." [33]

Colonel Peoples of Cameron, Texas, was out in the field with his forty convict-workers, a newspaper article reported, when a "very low" aerial "monster" suddenly appeared over the field. The object seemed to be in trouble; there was "great commotion" on board the ship and "many apparent signals were given with strange-colored banners or flags. Strange streamers or streaks of peculiar, dazzling white lights seemed to shoot up to the sky from aboard this strange craft." Eventually the object took off and the convicts thought that "evil days had drawn nigh" and their "day of deliverance had come." The article said this strange story "was given in good faith to the [*Dallas Morning*] *News* reporter and is vouched for by all the men on Col. Peoples' plantation." [34]

Airship witnesses were so certain of the reality of their experience that many were vociferous in opposing the prevailing scientific skepticism about the phenomenon. An article in the *Chicago Times-Herald* said people who had seen the airship "were ready to debate the matter without fear of being ridiculed, and their opinions were coolly arrived at." In reaction to the theory that the supposed airship was a star, R. W. Allen, a pharmacist, said he was "willing to take the consequences of expressing the opinion" that the star theory was wrong. He claimed that he and six other men had observed the object's movements carefully and "no star ever acted in the manner displayed by the lights we saw." The object undulated with the regularity of a "pulse beat"; it had red, green, and white lights on it and flew rapidly toward the northwest. An airship witness in Milwaukee charged that "anyone who claims that the thing I saw floating over the city hall is a star simply don't know what he is talking about." [35]

On the other hand, other witnesses feared public ridicule so much that reporters began to stress the witnesses' reliability and truthfulness: in Belle Plaine, Iowa, a "reputable physician" saw the spectacle; in Fort Atkinson, Wisconsin, "reputable citizens" watched the object; in Mount Carroll, Illinois, "persons whose honesty and truthfulness are beyond dispute" observed an airship; in Denton, Texas, two "credible witnesses" saw the object and one witness was a woman "whose reputation for truthfulness can not be assailed." A man who reported sighting an airship over Evanston, Illinois, said he "was afraid of being laughed at and declined to give his name." A *Chicago Tribune* article about this sighting said "many reliable people" claimed to have seen the mysterious airship. Witnesses who saw an airship in Omaha were careful to give their full names to the newspapers to emphasize their reliability. In Brenham, Texas, the newspaper took an offensive stance when it published Mr. John R. Pennington's report. The article said people could tell airship stories all day and "the public would scarcely pause to hear them, much less to give the story more than a passing thought, but Mr. John Pennington is a man of unquestionable integrity and not in the habit of talking to hear himself talk." [36]

It was indeed necessary for the public and especially witnesses to be concerned about their reputations in light of what many scientists and other professional people said about the sightings. In 1896 the famed aviation pioneer Octave Chanute, who was working on an airship of his own, said he did not have the patience to read the full account of the California airship because of its "absurdities." He was certain about the eventual mastery of air travel but did not expect "one fortunate achievement" to solve the complex problem. He was confident that the airship reports would not fool the public. Unknown to Chanute, Attorney Max L. Hosmar, secretary of the Chicago Aeronautical Association, seemed to have the complete explanation for an airship sighted in Chicago: he announced that Chanute invented it and had gone to California to oversee a test flight from San Francisco to Chicago. The Aeronautical Association planned to give Chanute and his crew a reception when they arrived, but the airship came sooner than expected because "conditions" must have been "extremely favorable." The next day Hosmar had second thoughts about his initial solution because it seemed impossible for Chanute to arrive so soon, "scarcely three weeks since the journey was begun." Hosmar revised his statement, saying Chanute's airship was someplace between San Francisco and the Rocky Mountains.[37] Chanute's airship did not arrive in Chicago; in fact, it never left the ground in San Francisco.

Scientific opinion about the cause of the mysterious objects in the sky was divided. Professor Riggs, an astronomer at Creighton College, thought the first airship seen in Omaha was the planet Venus; it was impossible that an undetected "fellow in the back woods" could invent an airship when air researchers had been trying unsuccessfully for years. Professor G. W. Hough of the Dearborn Observatory (in Evanston, Illinois) watched an airship-like object with a telescope and declared it was the star Alpha Orionis, which people could see with the naked eye usually around 8:00 P.M. The star, at its brightest, "resembles a ball of fire," and the atmosphere made the star's rays change from white to red to green. The next day the *Chicago Tribune* criticized Professor Hough's theory: it "is open to the suspicion of professional jealousy on the part of a man who does not like other people to see things in his realm that he does not see." Hough immediately issued another statement explaining that the star Alpha Orionis has been "roaming through its regular course in the firmament 10,000,000 years, and why it should have been settled upon in the last three weeks and pointed out as the headlight of a mysterious aerial vessel is hard to explain." [38]

Astronomer Arthur C. Lunn of Lawrence University, who claimed to have observed the phenomenon personally, explained that it was not an airship but the star Betelgeuse in the constellation Orion; he told how atmospheric conditions contributed to the illusion that the object changed colors and bobbed up and down. Professor G. C. Comstock of the University of Wisconsin's Washburn Observatory generally agreed; the brightest stars in the sky were Jupiter, Venus, and Sirius, he said, any of which could be mistaken for an airship. [39]

Professor Henry S. Pritchett of Washington University (in St. Louis) took a more cautious approach. At first he placed little stock in the airship stories, he said; but due to corroborative evidence, he now was inclined to treat the matter seriously and believed "something unusual has been seen in the heavens." He joined the *Chicago Tribune* in criticizing Hough's star theory: Venus was the bright star, not Alpha Orionis, and witnesses had seen the object on cloudy nights. However, Pritchett could not identify the object. He first thought it was a balloon but changed his mind because the object did not have the characteristics of a balloon. He did think it was possible that a secret inventor had developed an airship and he said that scientists at Washington University were going to try to solve the problem. [40]

Professor M. S. Koenig, identified only as an electrician from New York, stated that he knew a former workman in one of Edison's laboratories who had discovered a way to overcome the laws of gravity. At last report this person was living in San Francisco and working on an airship. "Of course this sounds remarkable," Koenig said, "but if there is an airship prowling above the clouds, I firmly believe it is engineered in some such manner." Apparently someone used Koenig's statement to fashion a hoax. Citizens of Astoria, Illinois, discovered some letters supposedly dropped from an airship. One letter was addressed to "Edison" and was signed "C. L. Harris, electrician airship No. 3." Edison took this opportunity to comment publicly on the airship sightings. He declared the letter a "pure fake" and said he had never heard of C. L. Harris. Scientists would probably construct airships in the near future, Edison thought, but it was absurd to imagine that someone could do so secretly at that time. He suggested that the whole affair was a hoax and the objects were colorful gas-inflated balloons.[41]

Most newspapers agreed with Edison that the airship was a hoax and printed editorials to this effect. The *Sacramento Daily Record-Union* attributed the sightings to balloons. Anyone who thought the airships were real was mistaken: "No one went flying through the air on Tuesday night on a machine with a powerful electric light." The editorial did admit, however, that people had seen a light. On the next day the paper carried another editorial that articulated the most common thought about airship witnesses—they were drunk—and placed the airship in the hoax tradition of the sea serpent: "The sea serpent never appeared off the Atlantic coast when there was any dearth of whiskey"; the same was true of the airship, which "cannot be verified properly without a liberal use of stimulants." Similarly, the *Birmingham* (Alabama) *News* thought "if the airship business continues, the Prohibitionist party will be driven into calling an extra session to formulate plans for an emergency campaign." An editorial in the *Chicago Tribune* equated the airship sightings with the sightings of a sea serpent every year in Lake Michigan. The *Kansas City* (Missouri) *Star* declared simply that the airship was Venus and people who thought otherwise had "more imagination than astronomy." The paper charged that San Francisco newspapers had initiated the airship hoax and placed the airship in a long tradition of elaborate hoaxes, including the Kansas meteor and the Prince of Wales's trip to America to see the Fitzsimmons-Corbett fight.[42]

Taking an ironic stance, the *Chicago Tribune* said the "vessel is purely a celestial body which has taken on a few terrestrial attributes in order to accommodate itself to the limitations of human imagination." Some people, the editorial pointed out, even agreed with the "preposterous supposition" that the light was the planet Venus. This could not be true because "a man who knew the facts" said that "Venus does not dodge around, fly swiftly across the horizon, swoop rapidly toward, then soar away until lost in the southern awry [sic]." Ironically, many newspapers used this last statement to support the belief that the airship was not Venus.[43]

Agreeing with the hoax theory, the *Des Moines Leader* said airship stories were one of the "most successful fakes in an era of such successes" and a plot that telegraph operators had devised. Operators had kept the airship hoax alive by constantly reporting it in their vicinities, but "when the rest of the public began to take a hand, the airships got too numerous; the reports would conflict, and it was evident that either there was a whole family of the ships or else somebody was manufacturing storues [sic]." The editorial concluded that similar overworked imaginations had deceived the rest of the country. Madison's *Wisconsin State Journal* attributed the airship to drunks, apparitions, optical illusions, wishful thinking, overzealous newspapermen, and stars. It stated flatly that "there is no airship." To prove the airship a hoax, the *Cincinnati Commercial-Tribune* had a photographer take a fake photograph of an airship to show how such evidence could be the product of trickery. The *Baltimore News* said dryly: "Last summer it was free silver, now it is airships; what next, nobody knows." [44]

In contrast to the above editorials, the *Memphis Commercial Appeal* simply stated that "the airship seems to be an accomplished fact." The *Dallas Morning News*, reluctant to admit that someone had invented an airship, remarked that "nobody need be at all astonished if the airship of fancy should in due course of experiment and invention become an airship in fact." In an article entitled "The Airship Serial," the *Galveston Daily News* expressed confidence in the future of aerial navigation and in technology's ability to overcome eventually the problems of the air. In a more practical approach, the *St. Louis Post-Dispatch* believed the airship would influence frontier taxation and smuggling: "Customs houses would be useless, and the army of officers that now collects customs on imports would have to seek other employment." Also, "Mr. Dingley and his tariff protection would be 'knocked out.' " [45]

As soon as airship stories appeared, imaginative ways of

dealing with them emerged as well in the press. Would-be poets spun verses to describe the phenomenon, like the one that appeared in the *Sacramento Daily Record-Union*:

> I see'd it! I see'd it!
>   Away up in the air,
> And the gooses and the duckses
>   Stopped in their flight to stare
> At the aerphone, or balloon-phone,
>   A sailin' round up there.
> I see'd it! I see'd it!
>   'Twas a funny-lookin sight,
> A sailin' round the stars
>   With its incandescent light—
> Sashaying first with Jupiter,
>   Then dancin' round the moon,
> An' bowing to Andromedear—
>   Was the electrified balloon.
> I see'd it! I see'd it!
>   And a friend of mine will swear
> That he too see'd the new masheen
>   A flyin' round up there.
> He's way up in astronomy,
>   An' never tells a lie,
> An' knows the name of all them things
>   A shinin' in the sky.

Several other newspapers printed similar poems, some of them combining political satire with the airship mystery. One such effort in the *St. Louis Post-Dispatch* concluded:

> That agent of Prosperity
>   That travels in Advance.
> I says it "was", for now, alas!
>   'Tis fallen in the dust;
> The bag above it filled with gas,
>   By some mischance did bust;
> And Hanna and McKinley dig
>   Each other on the sly,

And grin while thinking of the big
Explosion in the sky.

With its poem, the *Dallas Morning News* printed a cartoon that
pictured an airship, labeled "The Advance-Agent of Prosperity,"
floating over crowds of farmers; the title of the cartoon was "The
Secret of the Airship Disclosed." [46]

There were other cartoons on the subject as well. They
ranged from serious attempts to illustrate an airship, to political
commentaries, to humorous statements. A cartoon in the *Chicago
Times-Herald* depicted various Chicago nominees running riot in
a car suspended beneath two balloons filled with the hot air of
campaign oratory. The *St. Louis Post-Dispatch* carried two cartoons, one of a drunk person standing near a light pole seeing two
cigar-shaped airships in the sky—one marked "Domestic" and the
other "Havana"—and the second showing people looking at the
object through various types of appliances, including a whiskey
bottle, a wine bottle, and a glass. [47]

Although many newspapers and scientists ascribed the
airship to hoaxes, hallucinations, alcohol, and the like, some
people thought it existed and tried to account for its presence and
seemingly inexplicable behavior. The most common theory was
that a secret inventor had developed an airship. Another theory
held that extraterrestrial visitation was possible—the most popular
source being Mars. Schiaparelli's remarkable discovery in 1877 of
"canals" on the Martian surface, the appearance of "seasons" on
the planet, and science fiction literature of the day all created a
general interest in the possibility of life on Mars. Jules Verne and
H. G. Wells had helped popularize the idea that airships came
from Mars. Wells's 1897 story "The Crystal Egg" told about a
Martian television-monitoring device that people had found on
earth. Moreover, a commonly held belief was that the Martian
landscape was habitable, its air breathable, its costumes conventional, and the inhabitants human-like. [48]

The idea of an inhabitable Mars appeared in press and
witness accounts too. The *St. Louis Post-Dispatch* said something
was in the sky well worth scientific attention: "these may be

visitors from Mars, fearful, at the last, of invading the planet they have been seeking." The *Post-Dispatch* suggested sending the Martians "a message of peace and goodwill as well as a hospitable invitation to alight." After people in Girard, Illinois, saw a machine on the ground, approached it, and watched it rise and fly off, they found footprints in the area; they concluded that "something has happened above the clouds that man has not yet accounted for." People in Texas thought the airship was an exploring party from another planet, and the *Washington Times* conjectured it was a reconnoitering party from Mars. The *Memphis Commercial Appeal,* also speculating about extraterrestrial visitation, decided that even if "the inhabitants of Mars or some nearer planet have succeeded in overcoming the force of gravitation, it is impossible that human life could be sustained while making the voyage to the earth. It must be the work of man, and of someone who inhabits this earth." [49] Although these extraterrestrial speculations were limited because of the more seemingly plausible secret inventor theory, they nevertheless form a link between the 1896–97 airship mystery and the modern UFO controversy.

Another popular idea was that the airship was an elaborate advertising scheme. A reporter in Omaha hypothesized that the airship might be an advertisement for cigarettes, and other people in that city thought, if not for cigarettes, it was a gimmick for another product. Citizens of Madison, Wisconsin, were convinced that the circus in nearby Baraboo was using the airship as a clever advertising scheme, especially since people in cities on the circus route reported seeing an airship. One company did, in fact, capitalize on the airship's publicity: Beck's Stove and Range Company published a humorous drawing of an airship and confessed that the whole affair was a publicity stunt. In a semiserious statement, the company described how it had made the airship and gave a short history of the ship's flights. In conclusion, the advertisement cautioned: "Don't you believe that any air-ship is genuine unless it bears our Trademark." [50]

A related theory, which an Omaha newspaper developed, was that the airship was the second part of a confidence scheme.

Several years before, a man in Omaha had charged gullible people twenty-five cents to sit in a stadium and see an airship fly. Of course the flight never materialized, but now the hoaxers, the newspaper theorized, had obtained a real airship and had come back to give people their money's worth. The airship crew was afraid to land because the bilked people "have always been convinced that it was a confidence scheme, and notwithstanding McKinley's election, confidence has not yet been restored to these people." [51]

Other theories approached similar levels of absurdity. A man in Hempstead, Texas, thought the airship was actually fireflies or "lightning bugs" which could give off very bright lights and seemed to have characteristics in common with the airship: "On dark nights they fly high and are very rapid in their movements, throwing flashlights every few seconds, often at longer intervals." A Washington State man, in a letter to the *Sacramento Daily Record-Union*, said the solution to the airship mystery was a pelican; he had captured one, tied a Japanese lantern around one of its legs, and turned it loose—hence, the airship sightings. A theory put forth in Atlanta, Texas, suggested the airship "is the property of a gang of cracksmen [burglars], who by the aid of the searchlight and X-rays, under the management of scientific experts, sail over the towns and look through the walls of the houses and bank vaults and locate the booty; that they return on a later date and secure it, and then disappear by the aid of their airship." [52]

Despite all the observations of the airship phenomenon and both serious and humorous speculation about its nature and origin, the question of what it was remains. Not all of the hundreds of consistent and detailed sightings can be dismissed as hoaxes, illusions, or hallucinations. The most logical and reasonable explanation, in the context of American society in 1896–97, was the secret inventor theory—that perhaps a powered, controlled flight of an airship actually occurred before present records indicate. Is it possible that not one but many airships, intelligently powered and controlled, flew through American skies during this period?

European inventors were far ahead of their American

counterparts in developing an airship. Henri Giffard of France built the first navigable (but not practical) one in 1852; it traveled seventeen miles at a speed of five and one-half miles per hour. But it was underpowered and Giffard could not circle or return to the place from which he had started. Frenchmen Albert and Tissandier applied an electric motor to an airship in 1883 and 1884 and enjoyed a slight amount of success in navigating it; yet this machine, too, was underpowered and could not maintain itself against the wind current. In 1884 Charles Renard and A. C. Krebs made a more successful flight in France. Their nonrigid dirigible with an electric motor could travel about thirteen miles per hour and return to the point from which it left. The experiment proved that an airship could be practical. However, the power source was still inadequate and the airship could travel only a short distance and carry very little weight.[53]

David Schwartz built the first completely rigid dirigible in Germany in 1897. Although the trial flight failed, the machine was an important development in that it used a gasoline-powered engine. Two other Germans, Wolfert and Baumgarten, built the first dirigible with an internal-combustion engine but the ship exploded before its trial flight. Development of the modern dirigible began in France in 1898 with Alberto Santos-Dumont's first airship. Its nonrigid body with two internal-combustion engines was controllable. In 1901 Santos-Dumont thrilled France by traveling seven miles in thirty minutes, spectacularly rounding the Eiffel Tower to return to his starting point.[54]

American airship builders during the 1880s and 1890s experimented as well, but few ever completed a machine. In 1884 Arthur DeBausset, a Chicago physician, designed an electrically powered vacuum tube that was supposed to carry people over great distances at high speeds. He organized a stock company and began soliciting money, but he failed to obtain the funds and could not build his airship.[55] Six years later Edward J. Pennington of Racine, Wisconsin, organized the Aeronautical Company and built a twenty-four-foot model of a projected airship. Pennington's model remarkably resembled the "mystery airship" sighted in 1896 and 1897: it had a cigar-shaped gas bag with wings attached on the sides, a large railroad-like car hanging from the bottom of the bag, and storage batteries to light the car. But Pennington, like DeBausset, could not raise the necessary funds to actually build the ship. His exaggerated claim that the ship could travel at two hundred miles per hour prompted press ridicule, especially from the *Chicago Tribune*, which dampened his fund-raising efforts.[56]

In the 1890s American air pioneers Chanute, Lilienthal, Langley, and Pilcher were conducting heavier-than-air experiments. However, these contrivances had no similarities with witnesses' descriptions of the airship and, as far as historians know, no motor-powered airships flew in America in 1896 or 1897. (A bicycle-powered airship did fly for short distances at the Tennessee Centennial Exposition in May 1897.[57]) In 1900 A. Leo Stevens built the first motor-driven navigable airship flown in the United States. After this, others experimented with limited success, and in 1904 Thomas Baldwin's four years of experimenting resulted in the flight of the first practical dirigible in this country—the *California Arrow* in Oakland, California.[58]

In the late 1890s many people in the United States obtained patents for proposed airships. Most people believed someone would soon invent a flying machine, and many wanted to capitalize on the fame and fortune that certainly would come to the first person to launch an American into the skies. As soon as someone had a glimmer of an airship design, he immediately applied for a patent. These would-be inventors constantly worried over possible theft or plagiarism of their airship designs, for even a patent could not insure that someone might not steal or copy part of a design. As a consequence, most people kept their patents secret. Given this atmosphere and numerous European and American experiments with flight, it is not surprising that secret inventor stories so captured the public imagination and seemed such a logical explanation for the mystery airship. To some Americans the possibility did exist that "Wilson" of Texas airship fame *was* the inventor and pilot of the mystery airship. And, in fact, independent inventors *did* invent a heavier-than-air flying machine.

Nonetheless, all evidence indicates that scientific knowledge about powered flight in 1896 and 1897 could not have led to the invention of airships with the characteristics witnesses described.[59] And even if an independent inventor had been able to design and fly a successful airship, the problem of secrecy would have been almost insurmountable. An inventor would have found it nearly impossible to spend time and money designing an experimental craft and test flying it without someone discovering his activities. Moreover, in light of the number of different airships reported in many states during 1896 and 1897, a mysterious inventor would have had enormous difficulties concealing himself.

The airship phenomenon of 1896–97 constitutes the first major wave of documented unidentified flying object sightings in America (although not the first sightings per se). Occurring at a time when technology could not duplicate the characteristics witnesses described, the sightings created a national controversy. Although most people expected an airship in the near future, the immediate reaction of those who had not seen the object was hostile; they simply would not believe it was there. Neither the numerous newspaper accounts stressing the reliability and honesty of the witnesses, the descriptions of object characteristics completely unlike any natural phenomena, nor the knowledge that nothing else was in the sky could convince most people to believe an airship existed. In contrast, for the people who had sighted an object, no amount of persuasion or reason could dissuade them from believing they had seen an actual airship.

To explain the enigma, the public then, as did the public later, looked first for rational explanations—those that would make sense in terms of the scientific and the experiential knowledge of the time. When these were not completely satisfactory, the public turned to more irrational theories. An airship seemed so far out of the realm of current technological knowledge that a gap resulted in people's idea of what should be and what was. Since airships, given the technology of the times, could not have existed, then witnesses who claimed to have seen one obviously had not seen one. Most arguments against the airship idea came from individuals who assumed that the witnesses did not see what they claimed to see. This attitude is the crucial link between the 1896–97 phenomenon and the modern unidentified flying object phenomenon beginning in 1947. It also was central to the debate over whether unidentified flying objects constituted a unique phenomenon. Lying low for the first half of the twentieth century, while air technology mushroomed, the phenomenon of strange objects in the sky and the furor over it appeared again in 1947 and became a private and public battlefield.

2

THE MODERN ERA BEGINS:
ATTEMPTS TO REDUCE THE MYSTERY

The modern debate over the existence and origin of unidentified flying objects centered on the Air Force's investigation of
the phenomenon. Beginning in 1947, the Air Force started to
collect and evaluate reports. When it had acquired what it
considered to be adequate information, it determined that UFOs
represented nothing unusual in the atmosphere. The methodology
the Air Force used in arriving at this conclusion became a focal
point of the controversy. But even before 1947, when the modern
controversy began, the United States twice had been involved
with large-scale sightings of unidentified flying objects, first in
World War II and then in postwar Sweden.

The first sightings occurred when Allied bomber pilots
reported that strange balls of light and disc-shaped objects
followed them as they flew over Germany and Japan. The
American pilots dubbed these UFOs foo-fighters, after a pun on
the French word for fire (feu) appeared in the popular comic strip
Smokey Stover: "Where there's foo, there's fire." The foo-fighters
danced off the bombers' wingtips or paced the planes in front and
back. Naval personnel at sea also saw the objects maneuvering in
the sky. At first the Allies thought the objects were static
electricity charges; then rumor had it that they were either
German or Japanese secret weapons designed to foul the ignition
systems of the bombers. Later many servicemen decided that the

absence of overt foo-fighter hostility meant the objects must be psychological warfare weapons sent aloft to confuse and unnerve American pilots. Ironically, after the war the American public learned that the Germans and Japanese had encountered the same strange phenomenon and had explained it as Allied secret weapons. The United States Eighth Army made a cursory investigation of the foo-fighters and concluded that they were the product of "mass hallucination." [1] No one was overly concerned with them at the time because they did not appear to be hostile. Their explanation or source, however, remains a mystery.

The second wave of sightings occurred in Western Europe and Scandinavia, where from 1946 to 1948 many people reported seeing strange, cigar-shaped objects. Witnesses in Sweden and Finland sighted the objects close to the Soviet border, making American intelligence agents curious. They feared that these ghost rockets, as they were called, might be secret weapons the Russians developed with the help of German scientists and captured designs from the Peenemünde, Germany, secret proving ground. Army intelligence dispatched General James A. Doolittle to investigate the reports in cooperation with the Swedish government. The investigators explained 80 percent of the objects as misidentification of natural phenomena but made no conclusion about the other 20 percent. The Swedish government tried to use the ghost rocket sightings as a rationale to buy new and sophisticated radar equipment from the United States. It hoped that the new radar would be able to track and recover one of the rockets. But the United States Army, having determined that there was only a small possibility the ghost rockets were secret weapons, refused to sell the radar to Sweden.[2]

While Sweden was experiencing its wave of UFO sightings, the modern era of sightings in the United States began. On June 24, 1947, Boise businessman Kenneth Arnold, an experienced mountain and licensed air rescue pilot, was flying his private plane from Chehalis to Yakima, Washington, when he decided to look for a downed plane missing for some days. While searching, Arnold saw nine disc-shaped objects flying in loose formation and making an undulating motion, like, he said, "a saucer skipping over water." Arnold timed the speed of the objects as they passed between two points and calculated them to be traveling over 1,700 miles per hour—an unprecedented speed for 1947. He told his story to the ground crew in Yakima. When he flew on to Pendleton, Washington, his story had preceded him and skeptical newsmen awaited him. But because Arnold was such a reputable citizen (pilot, businessman, deputy sheriff), skepticism changed to wonder and the journalists reported the incident as a serious news item.[3]

The Arnold sighting was vital for modern UFO history in the United States. As a result of his description of the objects, the newspaper headline writers coined the term *flying saucer*,[4] which rapidly spread around the world as the most popular phrase to describe UFOs. The phrase allowed people to place seemingly inexplicable observations in a new category. Witnesses scanning the sky could now report that they saw something identifiable: a flying saucer. Moreover, the term subtly connoted an artificially constructed piece of hardware; a saucer is not a natural object. Consequently, when a witness said at that time that he saw a flying saucer, he implied by the use of the term itself that he had seen something strange and even otherworldly. The term also set a tone of ridicule for the phenomenon. The idea of saucers flying on their own volition was absurd. The term allowed people to laugh at the very notion of an unusual object in the sky without having to confront the circumstances behind the event. Saucers do not fly. It was ludicrous for a witness, using the only phrase available to him, to say that he saw one. Therefore, he obviously did not see one. The term itself made the actual event seem invalid.

Perhaps the greatest importance of the Arnold story is that it encouraged people all over the country to come forth with their own reports about strange objects in the sky. Many of these sightings occurred *before* Arnold's. In this sense the Arnold sighting acted as a dam-breaker and a torrent of reports poured out. Newspapers printed hundreds of these accounts. Independent UFO investigator Ted Bloecher studied the 1947 wave of sightings and found that, with 850 reports, it was one of the largest sighting years on record. Some reports went back to January, but the peak did not come until July, one month after the Arnold story broke.[5]

The press went through stages in its attitude toward the 1947 sightings. At first it reported the stories fairly and impartially. But as some of the stories became more fantastic and as newsmen vainly searched for proof, they added ridicule to their reports—a ridicule stimulated by the fact that no one had found a flying saucer or could offer concrete evidence that such things even existed. Many previously skeptical newsmen began to feel that nothing unusual or anomalous had existed in the sky in the first place. By the end of July newspaper reporters automatically placed any witness who claimed to see something strange in the sky in the crackpot category. Kenneth Arnold became victim to this belated ridicule and stated: "If I saw a ten-story building flying through the air I would never say a word about it." An Air Force investigator privately noted in mid-July that Arnold was "practically a moron in the eyes of the majority of the population of the United States." [6]

News reporters had some evidence on which to base their skepticism. Along with the authentic 1947 sightings came numerous hoaxes that, as in the 1896–97 period, added to the confusion. The most important hoax of the time took place at Maury Island near Tacoma, Washington. This hoax would not have been so sensational were it not for a tragedy that occurred in the course of its investigation. Harold Dahl and Fred Crisman claimed to have encountered a flying saucer at close range while boating off Maury Island. They said the flying saucer had dropped fragments of slaglike metal on them during the incident and they had picked up some of this material. Kenneth Arnold, who had been keenly following UFO reports since his sighting, heard about the two men and phoned army intelligence officers in California to tell them about the sighting. The army immediately dispatched two officers to interview Crisman and Dahl. But the interview never took place because the two army men were killed in a plane crash en route to Washington. Later under Air Force interrogation Crisman and Dahl confessed they had created the entire episode in hopes of selling the story to a magazine.[7]

Numerous minor hoaxes occurred as well. Vernon Baird, a

pilot, reported seeing a bunch of "yo-yo's" while flying over Montana. A Los Angeles newspaper printed the story on July 6, 1947, and other newspapers around the country quickly picked it up. Baird later said it was all a joke he had cooked up while shooting the breeze with the boys around the hangar. Other people thought it would be good fun to make saucer-shaped objects and leave them in people's yards so that they could discover a crashed saucer. One midwestern newspaper offered $3,000 to anyone who could prove that flying saucers existed, and this prompted many individuals to perpetrate hoaxes to collect the reward. As in 1896–97, some people tried to capitalize on the saucer craze. A publicity agent sent his clients pie plates inscribed with their names. Another press agent advertised a radio show featuring the "Flying Saucer Blues." [8]

Some people, of course, viewed the situation seriously. The Washington Air National Guard equipped all its pilots with cameras in hopes of getting a picture of a flying saucer. When the pilots were unsuccessful, this added to the suspicion that nothing unusual had been in the sky to begin with. But lack of photographic evidence was not the only thing making people suspicious. A constant stream of explanations for the reports helped as well. This urge to explain, as it may be called, became an integral part of the UFO controversy. Although this behavior was evident to a lesser degree in the 1896–97 sighting wave, it came to full fruition in the twentieth-century sighting waves. Prompted perhaps by the tremendous increase in scientific knowledge of the world and the universe, scientists seemed to put limits on the expansion and direction of that knowledge. Instead of attempting to discover if any of the reported UFO observations represented anomalous phenomena, scientists, academics, and other professional people simply categorically denied that the observations were of anomalous phenomena, and many denied that the witnesses had seen anything at all. Because these explanations came from "experts," people accepted them more readily. The urge to explain became a severely limiting factor in the study of unidentified flying objects.

The *San Francisco Chronicle* published a group of explanations for the Arnold sighting. One United Air Lines pilot thought Arnold had seen the reflection of his instrument panel off his cockpit window. A meteorologist suggested Arnold had seen strange objects because he had become slightly snowblind. A University of Oregon astronomer said Arnold was the victim of persistent vision, the result of staring at the sun for long periods of time.[9]

Some scientists began to notice the UFO interest and to issue explanations for it. At a meeting of the American Association for the Advancement of Science in Chicago on December 26, 1947, Dr. C. C. Wylie, an astronomer at the University of Iowa, suggested that the UFOs were an example of national mass hysteria. He blamed the sightings on "the present failure of scientific men to explain promptly and accurately flaming objects seen over several states, flying saucers and other celestial phenomena which arouse national interest." This failure, he explained, caused the public to lose confidence in the "intellectual ability of scholars." Gordon A. Atwater, an astronomer at the Hayden Planetarium, told the *New York Times* that the first sighting reports were authentic but that most subsequent reports were the result of a "mild case of meteorological jitters" combined with "mass hypnosis." Dr. Jan Schilt, Rutherford Professor of Astronomy at Columbia, explained that a speeding plane had churned up the atmosphere, thereby causing distorted light rays that were responsible for the sightings. Dr. Newborn Smith of the United States Bureau of Standards laughed the whole thing off as another Loch Ness monster story.[10]

The *New York Times* also interviewed Soviet Foreign Minister Gromyko and air pioneer Orville Wright. In a lighthearted manner Gromyko suggested that the UFOs were discs from Soviet discus throwers practicing for the Olympic Games. Orville Wright believed that no scientific basis for the objects existed and darkly hinted at a more sinister explanation: "It is more propaganda for war to stir up the people and to excite them to believe a foreign power has designs on this nation." In the same article, the *Times* quoted Leo Crespi, Princeton psychologist, as saying the real problem was whether a flying saucer was an illusion with objective reference or whether it was "delusionary in nature." [11]

Not all the explanations were serious. The *New York Times* began a long antipathy to the subject of UFOs by printing a tongue-in-cheek editorial suggesting that the objects were "atoms escaping from an overwrought bomb," Air Force antiradar devices, visitors from another planet, or afterimages of light on the human eye. Yet another suggestion was that the objects, all being silver, were coins that "high-riding government officials" scattered to reduce the country's overhead. The *New York Times* consistently took this humorous stance during the first five years of the controversy. *Life* magazine followed suit, printing a suggestion from Harvard anthropologist Ernest A. Hooton that saucers were "misplaced halos searching for all the people who were killed over the Fourth of July." The *Life* article compared the UFO sightings to those of the Loch Ness monster.[12] As had happened in 1896–97, many magazine writers with flashes of humorous "insight" insisted on equating flying saucers with the Loch Ness monster or sea serpents.

These early attempts to explain the phenomenon contain nearly all the assumptions the public and the Air Force made throughout the controversy. Almost everyone assumed the objects were real but easily explained—that witnesses had simply mis-identified conventional phenomena. An August 1947 Gallup Poll projected that 90 percent of the adult population had heard of flying saucers and that most people thought the objects were illusions, hoaxes, secret weapons, or other explainable phenomena. According to the poll, very few people thought the objects came from space.[13] This poll raised a crucial question: Were people able to distinguish between atmospheric and man-made phenomena?

The agency best able to make this differentiation at the time was the Air Force. It took on the task, sending all reports to the Technical Intelligence Division of the Air Materiel Command, at Wright Field in Dayton, Ohio. This division quietly received reports throughout 1947. Because national defense was its primary responsibility, it initially was interested in whether the objects might be secret weapons. Intelligence personnel thought it was possible that either the Soviets had developed a fantastic secret weapon, the same one the Germans supposedly were working on at the Peenemünde proving ground, or that another branch of the United States military had developed a secret weapon unknown to the Air Materiel Command. The investigators at first did not connect flying saucers with the foo-fighters, ghost rockets, or the 1896–97 airships.

Although privately interested in the phenomenon, the Air Force's public position was that the saucers were probably misidentifications. On July 4, 1947, an Army-Air Force spokesman said the military had not developed a new secret weapon that might be responsible for the sightings and a preliminary study of UFOs had "not produced enough fact to warrant further investigation." He dismissed the Arnold sightings as not realistic enough to deserve more study. In the same announcement, however, the Air Materiel Command said it was, in fact, investigating the matter further (particularly sightings in Texas and the Pacific Northwest) to determine whether the objects were meteorological phenomena. It thought perhaps they were solar reflections on low-hanging clouds, or "large hailstones which might have flattened out and glided a bit." [14]

Because sources for the early years of the Air Force's UFO investigation are scarce, one necessarily has to rely on Edward Ruppelt's *The Report on Unidentified Flying Objects* for much of the information. As head of the Air Force UFO investigation group from 1951 to 1953, Ruppelt had access to files now no longer available. In his book he explained that the Air Materiel Command (AMC) in 1947 had no formal structure within which to investigate sighting reports and that the staff hesitated to do so on its own—without specific orders. To the people at AMC, no orders meant the Air Force was not officially interested in the subject. Nonetheless, the staff did collect reports in a haphazard manner, filing newspaper accounts and reports made to other military bases. Finally, AMC received classified orders to investigate all reports it collected.[15] Because the order was classified, and the objects might be Soviet weapons, the Air Force insisted that the investigation be secret and tightened security.

Ruppelt said that the Air Force "top brass" wanted to solve the problem quickly. This created a certain amount of pressure and the staff began making frantic attempts to find answers. According to Ruppelt, two main schools of thought resulted. Some Air Force investigators thought the objects were terrestrial —either Russian secret weapons, atmospheric phenomena, or a secret navy circular plane called the XF-5-U-1 or the Flying Flapjack. The navy had scrapped the circular plane project in 1942, but the Air Force investigators did not eliminate the possibility that perhaps it had started the project again without the Air Force's knowledge. Other Air Force intelligence personnel thought the objects might be extraterrestrial—spaceships or space animals. Eventually both groups merged to investigate what seemed to be most likely and immediate: the Soviet secret weapon theory.[16]

In the meantime public speculation and interest were growing. Many people thought the atomic bomb might in some way have caused the sightings. This prompted David Lilienthal, chairman of the Atomic Energy Commission, to state publicly that the UFOs were not a result of the testing program.[17]

At the end of 1947, after having officially received 156 reports, the Air Force decided that the problem required a more complete investigation than the one in progress at AMC. On September 23, 1947, Lieutenant General Nathan F. Twining, commander of the Air Materiel Command, wrote to the commanding general of the Army-Air Forces saying that "the phenomenon reported is something real and not visionary or fictitious"; the objects appeared to be disc shaped, as large as aircraft, and controlled "either manually, automatically, or remotely." Twining said it most likely was possible to build an aircraft with similar flight characteristics, but "any developments in this country along the lines indicated would be extremely expensive, time-consuming and at the considerable expense of current projects." Twining thought the military must still consider the possibilities that the objects were of domestic origin, that one might crash and provide positive physical evidence of its existence, and that they might be of foreign origin and "possibly nuclear." But because the military could only speculate about the objects, Twining recommended that "Headquarters, Army-Air Forces issue a directive assigning a priority, security classification and Code Name for a detailed study of this matter." In the meantime, AMC would continue to collect the data as they came in.[18]

Major General L. C. Craigie accepted this recommendation and issued an order, on December 30, 1947, to establish an Air Force project to study the phenomenon of unidentified flying objects. The project, code name Sign, would be at Wright Field (now Wright-Patterson Air Force Base) under the auspices of the Technical Intelligence Division of AMC and would carry a 2A restricted classification (1A was the highest). Its function was to "collect, collate, evaluate and distribute to interested government agencies and contractors all information concerning sightings and phenomena in the atmosphere which can be construed to be of concern to the national security." The main purpose was to determine whether UFOs were a threat to the national security. Project Sign, known publicly as Project Saucer, began work on January 22, 1948.[19]

Two weeks before Project Sign's establishment, a famous sighting occurred that occupied much of the project staff's time and attention for the next year. On January 7, 1948, witnesses in the Louisville, Kentucky, area saw a cone-shaped, silvery object, tipped with red, about 250 to 300 feet in diameter, moving in a southerly direction. They reported the sighting to the state police, who called Godman Air Force Base to ask if anyone there had seen it. The flight controllers went outside and quickly saw the object as it floated overhead. After deciding it was not a plane or weather balloon, the flight controllers radioed four Air National Guard F-51 planes, which were coming into base, to take a look. One plane was low on fuel and landed, but the other three, with Captain Thomas Mantell in the lead, went up to observe. As Mantell climbed to reach the object, it sped away from him and climbed higher; he had no oxygen equipment in his plane and could not follow. But being obviously excited about the object and reporting it was metallic and "tremendous in size," he decided to climb to 20,000 feet to try to overtake it. As he did this he lost consciousness, his plane went into a dive and crashed, and Mantell died.[20]

The Mantell incident resulted in more sensational press coverage. The fact that a person had dramatically died in an encounter with an alleged flying saucer increased public concern about the phenomenon. Now a dramatic new prospect entered thought about UFOs: they might be not only extraterrestrial but potentially hostile as well. And as if this were not enough to increase public curiosity, the people at Project Sign explained that Mantell had died while trying to reach the planet Venus, which he had apparently mistaken for a flying saucer. The press and the public were incredulous. This official explanation began an enduring theme in the UFO controversy: that the Air Force conspired to keep important information from the public. (Three years later, the navy disclosed that a secret, high altitude, photographic reconnaissance Skyhook balloon was in the area and Mantell probably died trying to reach it.[21] Ultimately the Air Force concluded that Mantell had died chasing the Skyhook, but it could never definitely establish the presence of that balloon.)

After the Mantell incident the people at AMC began to work earnestly on the problem. They assumed that conscientious observers had sighted real objects and that UFOs were not products of misidentification. According to Ruppelt, Project Sign staff thoroughly investigated every possibility that the objects could be Soviet secret weapons of German design. AMC even contacted those German designers in America to see if it were possible for the Soviets to have used the designs to develop flying saucers. In every case the answer was negative.[22] Furthermore, AMC reasoned that the outside metal would not hold up under the tremendous heat at the reported speeds, and if the objects were actually Russian secret weapons, the Soviets would be foolish to fly them over hostile territory where they might crash and the Americans could recover them.

The Project Sign staff was left with some unsettling implications. If the objects were real but not Soviet or American, and if their flight characteristics did not match the state of technology at the time, then perhaps they were not ordinary; perhaps they came from another planet. One group at Project Sign began to explore this possibility seriously. Ruppelt found a memorandum in the project files stating that thinking of the objects in human terms was unproductive; thinking of them in nonhuman terms might help explain their maneuvering characteristics.[23] Nevertheless, another group at Sign was not convinced and maintained that the objects were not extraordinary but rather manifestations of psychological quirks, or man-made, or natural atmospheric phenomena mislabeled. But at this time the group favoring the extraordinary hypothesis won the day and the Sign investigators focused on the possibility of extraterrestrial origin.

By the time Project Sign began its investigation in 1948, press ridicule of UFO witnesses was intense, and newspapers, losing much of their initial enthusiasm for the subject, printed fewer articles about sightings. This enabled Sign personnel to work with maximum privacy and minimum disturbance from February to the beginning of August. But on July 24, 1948, another famous and controversial sighting catapulted the UFO controversy into the headlines again. Captains Clarence S. Chiles and John B. Whitted, flying an Eastern Air Lines DC-3, saw a large light, traveling at a tremendous speed, fly toward them. As the light-object approached, the startled pilots noticed it was cigar shaped, had two rows of windows around it with light coming from them, and had a red orange flame coming out of one end. Chiles and Whitted became alarmed as the object streaked past the DC-3 at about seven hundred miles per hour, made a sharp angular turn, climbed into a cloud bank, and then seemed simply to vanish. The one passenger awake at the time said he saw a bright flash of light go by his window but could not provide any details. A pilot flying another plane in the vicinity reported seeing a bright object in the sky at about the same time. Later, people on the ground also reported witnessing a similar object at about the same time as the DC-3-object encounter.[24]

For the first time two obviously competent witnesses and a

passenger had seen a UFO at close range. The sighting, classified unknown, had a great impact at Sign. The people at AMC now felt it was time to present their findings. They wrote an unofficial "Estimate of the Situation," classified top secret. The Estimate traced the history of UFO sightings, including the ghost rockets and American sightings before 1947; it concluded that the evidence indicated the UFOs were of extraterrestrial origin. The Project Sign staff sent their report through channels, all the way to Chief of Staff General Hoyt S. Vandenberg. The general decided the report lacked proof and sent it back to Sign where it died quietly. A few months later the Air Force declassified and burned the report.[25]

According to Ruppelt, the failure of the "Estimate of the Situation" to receive official blessing resulted in a policy change at Project Sign. The people who had suggested that the objects were extraordinary and perhaps extraterrestrial suddenly lost influence and the people who believed the objects were ordinary gained prestige. A subtle change in climate ensued and the proponents of the extraterrestrial hypothesis found themselves championing an unpopular theory. The prevailing opinion at AMC was that UFOs could be explained in conventional terms.[26]

On the whole, Sign's UFO investigations were fairly good. Its main problem was that the staff was too inexperienced to discriminate between which sightings to investigate thoroughly. Because of unfamiliarity with the phenomenon, the staff spent inordinate amounts of time on sightings that were obviously aircraft, meteors, or hoaxes. The staff also spent much time looking into the private lives of witnesses to see if they were reliable. Sign checked routinely with FBI field offices and criminal and subversive files of police departments, and the staff interviewed the witnesses' fellow employees, friends, and acquaintances. The Sign staff, however, did a creditable job considering that these early sightings usually contained too little information on which to base any kind of judgment and that the Air Force had no standardized method of reporting sightings.

In February 1949, Project Sign issued a report reflecting the philosophies of the group that thought the objects were extraordinary and of the group that thought they were ordinary. The report concluded that the staff had not found enough evidence to either prove or disprove an objective existence to flying saucers. On the one hand, positive proof of the existence of UFOs could come only from hard data, i.e., the remains of a downed saucer. On the other hand, "proof of non-existence is equally impossible to obtain unless a reasonable and convincing explanation is determined for each incident," and the staff acknowledged it had not been able to do this for 20 percent of the sightings.[27]

Furthermore, the staff said it did not have enough evidence to conclude that the objects did *not* represent a security threat to the United States, even though it had no evidence to suggest the objects were Russian weapons. Since the staff arrived at "simple and understandable" causes for some of the objects, "there is the possibility that enough incidents can be solved to eliminate or greatly reduce the mystery associated with these occurrences." However, the Project Sign staff believed that evaluating UFO reports was a necessary activity for military intelligence agencies: the sightings were "inevitable," and during war "rapid and convincing solutions of such occurrences are necessary to maintain morale of military and civilian personnel." For this reason alone the staff thought the Air Force should train competent people to handle the problem. The report recommended that the Air Force expend only a minimum effort to collect and evaluate the data on flying saucers: "When and if a sufficient number of incidents are solved to indicate that these sightings do not represent a threat to the security of the nation, the assignment of special project status to the activity could be terminated." The Air Force should handle subsequent investigations of the phenomenon routinely, "like any other intelligence work." The report also recommended improving procedures for obtaining accurate measurements by using photography and radar and by relying more on simultaneous ground and air sightings.[28]

The Project Sign report included an interesting appendix by James E. Lipp, of the Rand Corporation, on the feasibility of the objects being extraterrestrial. Lipp's reasoning was as follows: because earth is the only evolutionary life-producing planet in our solar system (he had eliminated all others in his study), the objects do not come from another planet in our solar system; assuming that probably one planet in each solar system has an environment conducive to producing evolutionary, intelligent life, and assuming that earth is "average in advancement and development," then a fifty-fifty chance exists that such forms of life are advanced enough to engage in space travel; therefore, the objects are more likely to come from planets in other solar systems; but, Lipp explained, even if life on other planets had developed space travel, the distance between earth and those planets and the time necessary to reach earth probably would prohibit other life from coming here. Besides, Lipp argued, if the extraterrestrials were here they would have contacted us by now. Lipp concluded that it was possible extraterrestrials were visiting earth but that it was highly improbable. In addition, "the actions attributed to the 'flying objects' reported during 1947 and 1948 seem inconsistent with space travel"—as he had formulated it.[29]

Project Sign's recommendations set the tone for the controversy over unidentified flying objects for the next twenty years. In 1949 the cold war was becoming heated and it was natural for Sign to recommend continued military intelligence control over the investigation of sighting reports. Sign never envisioned a nonmilitary, systematic study of the phenomenon. The staff believed that even if the alleged objects were nonhostile, and therefore not properly within the jurisdiction of the military, the military should still be involved with the subject because of the potential morale problem during wartime. As a further result of this reasoning, and apart from the growing ridicule attached to the subject, the military's control of the UFO investigation may have inhibited the scientific community from conducting its own study of UFOs; all "good" data were in Project Sign's classified files. Therefore, military inquiry may have prevented nonmilitary, systematic inquiry—even in the unlikely case that scientists would have found an interest in the phenomenon.

After the Project Sign staff issued its report, the project took on a new look based on the ascendancy of the group that believed UFOs did not represent any type of extraordinary object.

According to Ruppelt, Air Force officials abruptly terminated the plan to expand Project Sign's investigation by placing UFO teams at every Air Force base. New staff people replaced many of the old personnel who had leaned toward the extraterrestrial hypothesis. In the future, Sign personnel would assume that all UFO reports were misidentifications, hoaxes, or hallucinations. J. Allen Hynek, later scientific consultant for the Air Force's UFO project, said that after the Sign report came out the atmosphere at the UFO office was markedly chillier than before.[30]

The new look meant a new name as well. On December 16, 1948, the Air Force director of research and development ordered Project Sign's name changed to Project Grudge, which, under the United States Joint Services Code Word Index, referred to "Detailed Study of Flying Discs." Its purpose was the continued collection and evaluation of UFO data. Grudge retained the 2A security classification and its UFO files were closed to the public. The Project Grudge staff tried to implement Project Sign's recommendations, both by explaining every UFO report received and by assuring the public that the Air Force was investigating the UFO phenomenon thoroughly and had found no extraordinary objects in the atmosphere. Instead of seeking the origin of a possibly unique phenomenon, as Sign had done, Grudge usually denied the objective reality of that phenomenon. In this way Grudge shifted the focus of its investigation from the phenomenon to the people who reported it. Grudge also made a concerted effort to alleviate possible public anxiety over UFOs by embarking on a public relations campaign designed to convince the public that UFOs constituted nothing unusual or extraordinary.[31]

As part of this new public relations focus, the Air Force made its first major public statement on UFOs by giving its "whole-hearted co-operation" to writer Sidney Shallett's two-part article about UFOs for the *Saturday Evening Post*. The article appeared on April 30 and May 7, 1949. Shallett believed most UFO sightings were balloons, atmospheric phenomena, and ordinary objects. He dismissed pilots' reports as being "strange tricks" that "the sun, stars, and senses can play upon you in the wild blue." Shallett conceded that a few UFO sightings remained unidentified, but most of these were probably the products of "vertigo and self-hypnosis brought about by staring too long at a fixed light." Shallett discussed hoaxes in detail and gave many examples of easily identifiable sightings, some of which army and Air Force generals had made. He quoted Air Force General Carl Spaatz: "If the American people are capable of getting so excited over something which doesn't exist . . . God help us if anyone ever plasters us with a real atomic bomb." Shallett also suggested a psychological explanation. Americans, living in a "jittery age," induced in part by an "atomic psychosis" and the possibilities of space travel and planned earth-orbiting satellites, easily saw Martians and saucers.[32]

The first installment of Shallett's article concluded: "if there is a scrap of bona fide evidence to support the notion that our inventive geniuses or any potential enemy, on this or any other planet, is spewing saucers over America, the Air Force has been unable to locate it." The second part ended with a quotation from Dr. Irving Langmuir, a Nobel Prize winner in chemistry, a consultant for Project Sign, and, as Shallett admitted, the most outspoken foe of the existence of flying saucers in the United States. Langmuir's final advice to the Air Force on the UFO issue was "Forget it!"[33]

According to Ruppelt, the Air Force had hoped the article would stem the tide of reports flowing into AMC. But apparently the article failed; a few days after the second part appeared, UFO sightings hit an all-time high. The Air Force, thinking the article caused the sightings, tried to counter this reaction by issuing a lengthy press release saying that UFOs were nothing but products of mass hysteria and the misidentification of natural phenomena. Ruppelt explained the public reaction to the article in two ways. He said, first, that several people at Project Grudge thought the sightings continued because Shallett had admitted that a few UFOs remained unidentified. According to some of the Grudge staff, this made Shallett prosaucer. Second, Ruppelt said, the article was too biased; instead of alleviating the public's doubts, it planted a seed of doubt in the public mind about the Air Force's investigating method. Some people started studying the subject on their own because they could not reconcile Air Force concern six months back with the subsequent lack of concern.[34]

Throughout 1949 the Air Force worked on gathering evidence to prove that UFOs as a unique phenomenon did not exist. For this the Air Force had the help of the project's new scientific consultant, J. Allen Hynek, a professor of astronomy at nearby Ohio State University and head of the McMillan Observatory. Hynek had read about the UFO sightings in the newspapers. He thought the whole business was a joke and that no scientist could possibly take it seriously. But when the Air Force asked him to become its scientific consultant on the subject, he accepted the contract because, as he later said, he enjoyed a sporting challenge. Hynek's job was to sift astronomical phenomena from the UFO reports, as part of the Air Force's efforts to explore every conceivable possibility that witnesses who thought they saw something extraordinary were mistaken. These findings were, of course, classified. Six months after Project Grudge began this official investigation, it was ready to issue its final report in August 1949. (The Air Force released a summary of the report to the press on December 27, 1949.)

Project Grudge reported on 244 cases it had investigated. As the Project Sign staff had recommended, Grudge made an effort to explain every sighting even though many of the explanations seemed forced or highly speculative. The case of a T-6 training plane pilot illustrates these tactics. The pilot noticed a light near him as he was beginning to land and tried to get closer to see what it was, but the light seemed to take "evasive action." The pilot blinked his navigation lights but got no answer. He flew even closer to the light but it went up and over his plane. He tried to get closer again, and again the light turned. He attempted to get between the light and the moon, but the light turned so tightly that he could not do it. This scene went on for ten minutes. Finally the pilot made a pass at the light and turned on his landing lights. He could see that it was a "dark gray and oval-shaped" object, which finally made a "tight turn and headed for the coast." Four Air Force witnesses who had been watching from the ground completely corroborated the pilot's story. The Air Weather Service, which specializes in weather balloons, investigated and said the object was "definitely not a balloon." Hynek also investigated and said that there was no astronomical explanation. The object was neither another airplane nor an hallucination. Project Grudge, though, explained that the object was a weather balloon but did not reveal how it had arrived at this conclusion.[35]

Grudge's final report also included the results of Hynek's investigation of the Mantell case. His conclusions were ambiguous, but Hynek speculated that Mantell had chased Venus. Yet because Venus is only a pinpoint in the daylight sky, even at its brightest, Hynek further speculated that if Mantell did not chase Venus he probably chased a balloon or maybe two balloons. Later in a press conference an Air Force major said Mantell had definitely chased Venus. (Hynek changed his interpretation in 1952, saying the UFO was not Venus.) At the time, Hynek and the Air Force had no knowledge of the navy's secret Skyhook balloon.[36]

Even though the Grudge staff (working primarily with Hynek) did everything it could to explain all the sightings, 23 percent remained unidentified. For these, Grudge looked to psychology. The final report stated: "There are sufficient psychological explanations for the reports of unidentified flying objects to provide plausible explanations for reports not otherwise explainable." The Rand Corporation, which had a contract with the Air Force to study reports of sizes and shapes of UFOs, found nothing in the reports "which would seriously controvert simple rational explanations of the various phenomena in terms of balloons, conventional aircraft, planets, meteors, bits of paper, optical illusions, practical jokers, psychopathological reporters and the like." Project Grudge concluded that "there is no evidence that objects reported upon are the result of an advanced scientific foreign development; and therefore, they constitute no direct threat to the national security." It also concluded that "all evidence and analysis indicated that UFOs were the result of the misinterpretation of various conventional objects," or "a mild form of mass hysteria and war nerves," or hoaxes that publicity seekers and "psychopathological persons" perpetrated. Grudge recommended, therefore, that the investigation and study of UFO reports should be down-graded and AMC should collect only those reports "in which realistic technical applications are clearly indicated." A note attached said that "further study along present lines would only confirm the findings presented herein." [37]

Project Grudge, still unsure of public reaction, brought up a phase of the phenomenon that was to occupy much of the Air Force's time and attention: the reported sightings could be dangerous. "There are indications that the planned release of sufficient unusual aerial objects coupled with the release of related psychological propaganda would cause a form of mild hysteria," the report said. "Employment of these methods by or against an enemy would yield similar results." Therefore, "governmental agencies interested in psychological warfare should be informed of the results of this study." Moreover, Grudge recommended that its conclusions be made public in an official press release to dispel "public apprehension." [38]

The importance of public relations in the UFO controversy is evident in the staff's recommendation that the project be reduced in scope. The Grudge staff thought that the very existence of an organized Air Force investigatory body might encourage people to believe that something strange was flying in the skies. With this in mind, the Air Force issued a press release on December 27, 1949, announcing the termination of Project Grudge. The Air Force decided that now was the time to disengage itself from the public side of the controversy. It transferred Project Grudge personnel elsewhere and stored all its records. While this was going on, however, the Air Force intelligence director, in a directive to the Project Grudge staff, announced that the project had not really disbanded and that the order to do so was premature. The director explained that the Air Force would continue to collect UFO reports but would handle them through normal intelligence channels rather than by a special project.[39]

In fact, the Air Force immediately launched a classified study of a strange phenomenon—green fireballs—that competent and reliable observers had reported between 1947 and 1949. These objects closely resembled meteors except for their bright green color, flat trajectories, slow speeds, and sighting location (only northern New Mexico at the time). The Air Force's Cambridge Research Laboratory coordinated the study, called Project Twinkle, which was part of Project Grudge. The Air Force decided it would set up observation posts in areas of high fireball activity. The men in these posts would be armed with cameras, telescopes, theodolites, and any other equipment that would help them in their observations. The Air Force set up the first posts at Vaughn, New Mexico, where citizens had frequently reported seeing green fireballs. When the posts went into operation, however, green fireball sightings stopped completely. The men scanned the skies for six months with no luck. Meanwhile a rash of UFO sightings occurred at Hollomon Air Force Base 150 miles to the south. So the Air Force packed up and moved its observation posts to Hollomon. But virtually the same thing happened. Although some pilots and civilians made a few UFO reports around the area, the observation posts could report nothing tangible after six months of watching. Some scientists in the Air Force thought it might be significant that the sightings had stopped as soon as the Air Force started observing, but the Air Force concluded that sinking more funds into the program was a waste and dropped the project.[40]

From the beginning of 1950 until the middle of 1951 Project Grudge remained in a state of suspended animation. Once again, as with the Project Sign report, Grudge's recommendations discouraged independent civilian investigation. Grudge, in spite of its conclusion that UFOs were not hostile, continued its collection and classification policy and hence the near military monopoly over sighting reports. Even though the Air Force was no longer officially interested in the problem, Grudge refused to declassify its data or recommend that a nonmilitary group study the problem further. Even in late 1951 Grudge refused to declassify the Project Twinkle report because it feared that undue public speculation would stir up interest in UFOs.

Project Grudge personnel had anticipated a large amount of publicity about the Grudge final report. But press reaction was subdued and mainly limited to noticing that the Air Force had issued the report. Why the expected publicity did not materialize is a matter of conjecture. Ruppelt's speculation was that the report, being so ambiguous and such an obvious attempt to explain every sighting, served to hinder news reporters from believing it or writing about it as the final explanation for the sightings. Whatever the reason, the Project Grudge final report received slight publicity, whereas articles about the UFO phenomenon steadily increased in number. Although most people, according to a 1950 Gallup Poll, believed UFOs represented secret weapons, hoaxes, misidentifications, and the like, a growing number thought UFOs might be "something from another planet." [41] This interest, continued widespread reports of sightings, and the possibility that money could be made in the UFO business all helped to increase the number of newspaper and magazine articles.

True Magazine, in late 1949, commissioned Donald E. Keyhoe, a retired Marine Corps major, to write an independently researched article on flying saucers. Born in 1897, Keyhoe was an energetic and peppery man who had been a pilot and an aviation writer. As chief of information for the Department of Commerce in 1927, he had accompanied Charles Lindbergh on his triumphant United States tour after his trans-Atlantic flight. Then in 1928 Keyhoe wrote a well-received book about the tour called *Flying With Lindbergh*. In 1940 Keyhoe wrote *M-Day*, which described what the United States government planned to do economically and industrially in the event of war. He had also written many magazine articles about aviation in the 1930s and the 1940s. In 1949 he turned his attention to solving the flying saucer mystery. Keyhoe still had many friends in the upper echelons of the military and went to them for information. He received none, perhaps because Grudge wanted to play down the entire UFO affair and put a stop to reports. In fact, he alleged that every military person he contacted gave him the "silent treatment." [42] Keyhoe sensed a big story. He interpreted the silence to mean official tight security which, in turn, meant that the Air Force was hiding something important. To Keyhoe only one thing could be this important: the flying saucers came from outer space.

Keyhoe's article, entitled "The Flying Saucers Are Real," appeared in the January 1950 issue of *True*. He concluded: "living, intelligent observers from another planet" had been scrutinizing earth for 175 years; the intensity of the visits had increased during the past two years; there were three basic types of spaceships; and the manner in which the extraterrestrials observed earth was similar to American plans for space exploration expected to come into being within the next fifty years. Keyhoe reviewed various sightings, including the Mantell and Chiles and Whitted cases, and discussed the opinions of several "unnamed authorities" on the origin of the saucers. He refrained from attacking the Air Force because he did not know the reasons for the "cover-up." But he speculated that the Air Force was covering-up to prevent a panic (as in the Orson Welles's 1938 *War of the Worlds* broadcast) and to prepare the public for the startling disclosure that the saucers were from another planet. Keyhoe used his imagination liberally in the article. When he could not see a clear reason for Air Force policy or actions, he surmised the reason and stated it as fact. Scholarship and reliable information were not strong points of the article. It was, nevertheless, a sensation and Keyhoe became the leading private UFO "authority" in the country. This issue of *True* was the most widely sold and read in the magazine's history. Indeed, it was one of the most widely read and discussed articles in publishing history. In the face of this massive publicity, Air Force efforts to assure the public that the article did not reflect the facts accurately were futile.[43]

True followed Keyhoe's article with another sensational flying-saucers-are-real story in March. Navy Commander R. B. McLaughlin, a member of a team of scientists at the White Sands (New Mexico) secret guided missile development grounds, explained "How Scientists Tracked the Flying Saucers." The navy cleared McLaughlin's article even though he contradicted Project Grudge's findings. He discussed how, in the process of launching and tracking a Skyhook balloon, scientists (whose specialties he did not name) caught sight of a strange silvery object near the balloon. One scientist had a theodolite (a surveyor's instrument for measuring horizontal and vertical angles), another a stop-watch, and the third a clipboard. They began to record as much information as they could as soon as they saw the object. Before it sped away from view, they were able to ascertain that it was 40 feet long, 100 feet wide, and traveling at an altitude of approximately 56 miles and a speed of 25,200 miles per hour. McLaughlin was convinced that the object "was a flying saucer, and further, that these discs are spaceships from another planet." [44] The Keyhoe and McLaughlin articles were the first in a national magazine to present a case for extraterrestrial explanations for UFOs and to contradict official Air Force findings. The articles set the stage for a battle that was to rage for the next twenty years.

Still one more element was to enter that battle arena—Frank Scully's book *Behind the Flying Saucers*, published in 1950. Scully was a former *Variety* columnist who had previously written *Fun in Bed*, *More Fun in Bed*, and *Junior Fun in Bed* for bedridden people. With this background, Scully presented his book on UFOs as a serious work. In it he related the content of a lecture he had heard at the University of Denver. The lecturer was Silas Newton, described as being a millionaire Texas oil man. In the lecture Newton recounted the experiences of his friend and scientist, "Dr. Gee." The doctor had told Newton that the Air Force captured three landed saucers and found sixteen, four-foot-tall, dead occupants in them. The Air Force took the occupants for examination to "scientists," one of whom was Dr. Gee. Scully described the occupants and the material composition of the craft. He explained that the water the spacemen drank was "twice as heavy" as earthly water, that the men had no cavities in their teeth, and that the spaceship's metal was much harder than anything known on earth. Neither Newton nor Dr. Gee knew why the Air Force kept this a secret, but Newton theorized that it was to avoid panic.[45]

In the remainder of the book, Scully discussed some of the famous sightings, Einstein's special theory of relativity, and newspaper articles on UFOs. The Dr. Gee story, of course, was a hoax. However, Newton *had* given the lecture at the University of Denver and it seemed that Scully actually believed the story. The police arrested Newton and Mr. GeBauer (the mysterious Dr. Gee) two years later on a charge of fraud. They had bought a worthless piece of war surplus equipment for $4.50 and were trying to sell it as a surefire device for detecting potential oil wells. The price? A mere $800,000.[46]

In spite of the book's content, it still had a large impact and became a best seller. It was the first American book on UFOs, and *Time, Saturday Review, Science Digest,* and many other magazines carried reviews of it.[47] But perhaps it was most important as a forerunner of the special breed of saucer disciples—the contactees—who were to emerge a few years later. Scully's book also added to the already great public confusion. The Air Force had discounted all extraterrestrial theories and had tried to find natural explanations. Keyhoe had contended that UFOs came from outer space and that the Air Force knew about them. Then Scully had said that the Air Force not only knew about them but had actually captured some. The public immediately linked Scully to Keyhoe. This basic confusion between legitimate UFO theory (that the objects might be extraterrestrial) and the Scully brand of hoax was to plague UFO investigators from this time on.

Keyhoe, meantime, was busily expanding his article for a book with the same title, *The Flying Saucers Are Real* (1950). In addition to the information in the article, the book contained some new ideas on the reasons for Air Force secrecy. Keyhoe's book, like his article, was based on conjecture, personal opinions from unnamed scientists, some factual information, and a large amount of loose thinking. Because the Project Grudge files were secret, Keyhoe had no way of knowing what was really happening and was forced to rely on people's opinions, official press releases, and the little information he could get out of his friends in the military. For example, Keyhoe used the following conversation as a legitimate method of gaining information:

> "Charley, there's a rumor that airline pilots have been ordered not to talk," I told Planck. "You know anything about it?"
> "You mean ordered by the Air Force or the companies?"
> "The Air Force *and* the C.A.A."
> "If the C.A.A.'s in on it, it's a top level deal," said Charley.[48]

Keyhoe's "facts" seemed similar to Scully's "facts," and many critics failed to see any difference at all.

Because Keyhoe tried to get information but could not, he became more concerned with the secrecy aspect than with explanations for UFOs. Keyhoe concluded that the Air Force was "badly worried" when witnesses first reported UFOs in 1947. The Air Force knew "the truth" about Mantell's death, he said, and had established its investigatory agencies to conceal the truth about UFOs from the public. The Air Force changed this policy in the spring of 1949 and "decided to let facts gradually leak out, to prepare the American public." This, explained Keyhoe, was why the Project Sign report included a section on the feasibility of extraterrestrial visitations and why the Air Force had accepted his *True* article as part of its "public education program." But the Air Force misinterpreted the unexpected public reaction to the article as evidence of hysteria and began to deny the existence of saucers.[49] Keyhoe's Air Force secrecy angle later provided him with the basis for three more books and the impetus for establishing a large national UFO organization.

By 1950 other people also were speculating about the origin of the flying saucers, and the parade of explanations continued. David Lawrence's *U.S. News and World Report* featured an article that purported to solve the flying saucer mystery once and for all. The article said flying saucers were real and "top Air Force officials know where the saucers originate and are not concerned about them." The reason for this lack of concern was that the saucers were actually navy secret weapons, the old Flying Flapjack XF-5-U-1 that Project Sign had investigated and found abandoned in 1942. This article appeared at the same time that commentator Henry J. Taylor made a similar statement on a national radio broadcast. Although the Air Force denied the story, the old secret weapon theory revived for a short time. *Newsweek* printed this story under the heading "Delusions." Despite these explanations for UFOs, by May 1950 reports hit an all-time peak and came into AMC at the rate of about seventeen a month.[50]

The Air Force still tried to downplay the entire UFO

phenomenon. Newsmen even asked President Truman about UFOs, and he seriously denied ever having seen one. White House Press Secretary Charles G. Ross, in April 1950, said the Air Force's final report on the subject "was so conclusive" that the project closed down. When the *New York Times* asked Secretary of Defense Louis Johnson about the flying saucers, the question, as the reporter put it, "brought grins from the man who ought to know." Later a Department of Defense press officer said the Air Force had no intention of reopening Project Saucer.[51]

In January 1951 the Air Force for the second time cooperated with someone writing an article on UFOs. Columnist Bob Considine, in *Cosmopolitan* magazine, made the most vicious attack to date on "believers." Project Grudge personnel allowed Considine to see certain classified documents in the Pentagon and at AMC and to interview Air Force officers. In "The Disgraceful Flying Saucer Hoax," Considine characterized people who saw flying saucers as "true believers," "gagsters," "screwballs," members of the "lunatic fringe," and victims of "dementia," "cold war jitters," "mass hypnotism," "hallucinations," and "mirages." The whole UFO issue was "purely idiotic," and saucers "wholly nonexistent." Considine interviewed Air Force Director of Intelligence Colonel Harold E. Watson, who said that the entire sad affair was simply "nonsense." Not only that, added Considine, but it cost "the taxpayers a tremendous amount of money—for nothing." [52] (One of the private citizens mentioned in the article sued Considine for libel. In 1954 a judge ruled in favor of Considine. Although the judge admitted that the article was libelous, he believed that the part directly related to the plaintiff could not be construed as such.[53])

One month after the Considine article, *Time* magazine announced that all UFOs were actually Skyhook balloons, a theory widely accepted for a time. But Dr. Anthony Marachi, an Air Force chemist, argued that the Skyhook theory led people to a false sense of security because, in actuality, a foreign power launched the saucers. Marachi recommended that the United States identify the foreign power before Americans experienced another Pearl Harbor.[54]

By the summer of 1951 Project Grudge had so drastically reduced its staff that only one person, a lieutenant, served as investigator. The large number of sightings in 1950 gave way to a substantial decrease in 1951. In April, May, and June of 1951, only seventeen sightings were reported to AMC.[55] It appeared that the Air Force, after eighteen months of effort, had finally succeeded in its campaign to eliminate UFO reports and reduce the mystery surrounding the phenomenon.

THE 1952 WAVE:
EFFORTS TO MEET THE CRISIS

In 1952, after a dormant period of nearly two years, the Air Force again found itself plagued with the unidentified flying object mystery. The Air Technical Intelligence Center (ATIC), formerly the Intelligence Division of the Air Materiel Command, received the most sighting reports ever recorded—1501 for the year. Many were concurrent radar and visual reports from Air Force pilots and radar personnel. In an attempt to meet the challenge, ATIC authorized the reorganization of Project Grudge, and eventually the Air Force gave it a more prestigious position in the official hierarchy. Under the leadership of Captain Edward J. Ruppelt, the project staff designed and instituted plans to systematically study the UFO phenomenon. It sought the assistance of engineers, physicists, and astronomers, among others, implemented new and more efficient reporting procedures, contracted for a computer-based study of reported UFO characteristics, made plans to study UFO maneuver patterns, and developed special radar and photographic detection methods. This upsurge in activity resulted in renewed press and public interest in the phenomenon and a concomitant change in Air Force press policy. The year 1952 marked the high point of the Air Force's UFO investigation and the beginning of styles of thought that dominated the Air Force's attitude toward UFOs until 1969.

A dramatic sighting on September 10, 1951, stimulated the

Air Force to revitalize and bolster the dormant project. A T-33
pilot and his passenger, an Air Force major, saw what appeared to
be an unidentified flying object over the Fort Monmouth, New
Jersey, area. The witnesses described an object thirty to fifty feet
in diameter, round, silver, nonreflecting, and flat, which hovered
below the plane. The pilot dived in an attempt to intercept it but
failed. The object hovered for a short time, flew south, made a
120-degree turn, and continued on its way out to sea. At this same
time a radar operator at the Army Signal Corps radar center (Fort
Monmouth) was demonstrating radar equipment to a group of
visiting Air Force officers. He picked up a fast moving object
above the center and tracked it at speeds from 400 to 700 miles
per hour; but the object was so erratic and fast that the operator
lost it. The next day Fort Monmouth radar once again picked up
unidentified flying objects with the same maneuver patterns. This
time, however, the objects disappeared and returned several times
and moved so fast that the radar operators could not track them
automatically.

According to Ruppelt, the sightings caused a sensation at
Fort Monmouth. An Air Force major and a group of officers had
witnessed either the objects or their radar returns. The astonished
radar operators wrote to ATIC, Ruppelt said, requesting an
investigation. The director of Air Force intelligence, Major
General C. B. Cabell, saw a copy of the letter and requested more
information about the Air Force's UFO program. He dispatched
Lieutenant Jerry Cummings (head of Project Grudge) and his
superior, Lieutenant Colonel N. R. Rosengarten (chief of the
aircraft and missiles branch of ATIC) to Fort Monmouth to
investigate.

Cummings and Rosengarten completed the investigation,
tentatively classifying the objects as balloons and anomalous
propagation (freak radar returns caused by unusual atmospheric
conditions), and then they briefed General Cabell and his staff on
the general status of the UFO project. Cummings related the
history of the Air Force program, its shortcomings, and its current
status; he explained that reputable persons reported UFO sightings to Project Grudge at a steady rate. Apparently convinced of

the legitimacy of the problem, and with no publicity or fanfare, General Cabell ordered ATIC to launch a new UFO project.[2] Since the Air Force had just released Cummings from active duty, Rosengarten appointed Captain Edward J. Ruppelt, a decorated World War II bombardier, to head the project.

Ruppelt, who had a reputation as a good organizer, had just been reactivated from the reserves because of the Korean conflict and was assigned to ATIC as an intelligence officer. He had a layman's interest in the subject and had familiarized himself with Grudge before his appointment. In late September 1951 he set to work. First he read all the old Grudge and Sign records. Then he filed and cross-indexed every Sign and Grudge UFO report according to an object's color, size, location, and time of sighting. The cross-indexing helped his staff to determine general characteristics of the reports and to compile statistical data. Although the Air Force gave Ruppelt some clerical aid, the process was slow.[3]

Being familiar with the factionalism that had permeated previous UFO projects, Ruppelt resolved to avoid such conflicts if possible. He made clear that open speculation or argument about the origins of unidentified flying objects or the legitimacy of the reports was taboo and even ousted several staff members who advocated one theory or another. Ruppelt was determined to reserve judgment until his staff processed all available information. As part of his reorganization, Ruppelt arranged for his staff to write a classified report each month on current specific investigations and on the overall status of the project.[4] He appointed Dr. J. Allen Hynek, already an Air Force consultant in astronomy, as chief scientific consultant to Project Grudge and placed him on Air Force contract. Sensing the need for increased scientific help on UFOs, Ruppelt actively sought the cooperation of other interested scientists in return for briefings on the UFO situation.

One of Ruppelt's first problems was obtaining fresh UFO reports, because the Air Force had no routine way of quickly gathering them. Even reports from Air Force servicemen came in haphazardly and sometimes after a delay of up to two months. Consequently, the investigators found it difficult to obtain information that was fresh in the minds of witnesses. In addition to delays, the Project Grudge staff also encountered a serious ridicule problem. In an informal survey of Air Force pilots, Grudge found them reluctant to report UFO sightings because of possible ridicule from the press and from their fellow pilots and officers. One pilot summed up the attitude well: "If a space ship flew wing-tip to wing-tip formation with me, I would not report it." The Project Grudge staff worried that if an unconventional vehicle with extraordinary performance and characteristics appeared, "its detection would be hampered by the reluctance to report sightings." [5]

To overcome delay and ridicule, Ruppelt sought a compulsory method of reporting UFOs quickly and routinely. First, to speed up the reporting process, he requested a revision of the existing Air Force directive. Then he and his staff intensively briefed Air Force officers to acquaint them with the UFO situation and to show that the Air Force now treated UFO reports seriously. Ruppelt also recognized the need for a standardized questionnaire for UFO reports, hoping it would alleviate the imprecision and random quality that had characterized previous reports; the Air Force agreed to contract with Ohio State University to develop such a form. In addition, finding that newspapers carried many sighting reports not sent to ATIC, Ruppelt subscribed to a clipping service.[6]

One of Ruppelt's most ambitious projects in late 1951 was to obtain a statistical study of reported UFO characteristics. Although he did not expect such an analysis to reveal the origin of the UFO phenomenon, he did believe it would yield valuable data. Accordingly, the Air Force contracted the study to the Battelle Memorial Institute, a private research organization. Ruppelt's final project in 1951 was based on a suggestion from General Cabell. He thought electronic means of UFO detection might be valuable and suggested that radar used in conjunction with photographic equipment could help detect UFOs. Project Grudge immediately sought to implement this idea.[7]

Although Project Grudge made progress and seemed to enjoy Air Force favor, it lacked sufficient funds to do its work well. The Air Force gave Ruppelt a few people to help with investigations and some clerical staff for the office, but thorough investigation of more than a few monthly reports was still impossible. Even when a staff member, usually Ruppelt, conducted a field investigation, lack of money frequently prevented him from following up all leads. Investigators often had to pay for their own transportation to and from an investigation site when military transportation was unavailable. Similarly, the Air Force would not give Ruppelt funds for a related materials library; to help out, Hynek volunteered to buy the books with money from his own Air Force contract. The monetary difficulties indicated Grudge's continuing low priority in spite of its buildup.[8]

Six months after Ruppelt began his reorganization of Grudge, the Air Force decided that the project deserved more support. Ruppelt's aggressive briefing policy, his basic organizing procedures, and an increase in the number of sightings during the first three months of 1952 prompted the Air Force to promote Grudge from a project within a group to a separate organization. The Air Force changed the code name to Project Blue Book and gave it the formal title of the Aerial Phenomena Group.[9] Normally a change of this nature would mean a change in leadership as well; an officer with the rank of colonel or higher usually headed a group. Ruppelt, however, had been so effective that the Blue Book division chief, Colonel Donald Bower, decided to retain him as project director.

Ruppelt also received new help: ATIC's electronics group, analysis group, radar section, and investigating group now worked directly under Project Blue Book; and because of the contractual arrangements for the statistical study and the questionnaire, the scientists at Battelle Memorial Institute and Ohio State University could also help Ruppelt directly. Around this time, Joseph Kaplan, a University of California at Los Angeles physicist and a member of the Air Force Scientific Advisory Board, visited the new project at Wright-Patterson Air Force Base in Dayton, Ohio. He had come up with a good idea. Realizing that accurate measurements of any UFO were essential but difficult to obtain, Kaplan suggested an analysis of the color spectrum of an object by use of a special diffraction grid placed over the lens of a camera. When an unidentified flying object came into view, the camera photograph would put the spectrum on film and the staff could compare the object's spectrum with those of known objects (such as meteors and stars) to determine whether the object was unknown. ATIC and Blue Book were enthusiastic about this plan, and for the remainder of 1952 Kaplan and Air Force scientists tested possible diffraction grids and cameras for suitability under all conditions.[10]

With Kaplan's plan in the development stage, Ruppelt decided to act on General Cabell's radarscope suggestion. He contacted the Air Defense Command, which had about thirty radarscope cameras around the country, and specially briefed its top officers as well as the Joint Air Force Defense Board; they agreed to work out plans for Blue Book to use the cameras. Ruppelt also briefed the scientists at the Cambridge Research Laboratory (the Beacon Hill Group) who were Air Force technical advisers. They suggested that special sound equipment, left unattended in areas of high UFO activity, might be a useful and inexpensive detecting device. Also, the Pentagon, wanting to be informed of Blue Book's activities, assigned Major Dewey Fournet as Pentagon liaison man. Fournet was a party to all major developments, investigations, projects, and theories that came out of Blue Book during 1952, and he acted as the Pentagon's chief source of information from the project.[11]

As well as giving Ruppelt and Project Blue Book more authority, the Air Force implemented Ruppelt's proposed change in UFO reporting methods. On April 5 it issued Air Force Letter 200-5 (published on April 29) directing the intelligence officer on every Air Force base in the world to telegram preliminary sighting reports to ATIC and all major Air Force commands immediately and then to write a more detailed report and mail it to ATIC. A copy of these reports also went to the Air Force director of intelligence in Washington. Furthermore, the new directive allowed the Blue Book staff to communicate directly with any Air Force base or unit without going through the normal chain of command.[12] This new reporting method resulted in ATIC receiving reports quickly and gave Blue Book more control than it ever had before: the intelligence officers had to report all sightings, and Blue Book staff members could decide, on the basis of preliminary information, which reports to investigate immediately.

Two days before issuing Air Force Letter 200-5, the Air Force publicly announced that it was still studying UFOs and would continue as long as some sighting reports remained unexplained. It also alerted all Air Force field commands to report UFOs. The press release warned, however, that the public should not interpret this action as meaning the Air Force had come to any conclusion about the subject.[13] ATIC and the Pentagon also decided to cooperate with the press, replacing their "no comment" with the policy of explaining as much as possible to the public.

Even before Project Grudge became Project Blue Book, the press had shown a renewed interest because of the number of sightings reported. The press's first test of the official cooperation policy came in the early part of March 1952. Robert Ginna, a writer for *Life* magazine, visited ATIC to gather material for a feature article on UFOs, which he was writing with H. B. Darrach. They had already been to the Pentagon, where they received as much help as they needed. The Blue Book officers were especially cooperative, declassifying sighting reports at Ginna's request. Blue Book wanted to arrange for copies of all the UFO reports *Life* received from its reporters around the world to be sent to the project.[14]

Life published the Ginna and Darrach article in its April 7 issue. "Have We Visitors From Space?" was one of the most influential articles ever printed on UFOs, rivaling even the original Keyhoe *True* article. Ginna and Darrach explained that the Air Force used radar, jet interceptors, and photographic equipment in its study, and that it had no reason to believe flying saucers were hostile or a foreign power's weapons. Blue Book, they said, actively solicited sighting reports from scientists, pilots, weather observers, and private citizens. The authors noted that discs, cylinders, and similar objects of geometrical form, luminous quality, and solid nature had been and might then be present in the earth's atmosphere. "These objects," the authors stated, "cannot be explained by present science as natural phenomena—but solely as artificial devices created and operated by a high intelligence." No power on earth, they argued, could technologically duplicate the performance of the objects.[15]

The article aired in some detail ten reports never before published, some of which ATIC declassified for the authors. Ginna and Darrach concluded that psychological aberrations, secret weapons, Russian weapons, Skyhook balloons, or atomic test results did not explain adequately these ten sightings. To support their conclusions, they went to Dr. Walther Reidel, former chief designer and research director of rockets and missiles at Peenemünde, Germany, who now worked for an aircraft company in California. Reidel said that earth material would burn up from the friction that the reported objects' maneuvers created and that human pilots could not withstand the centrifugal force. He interpreted the lack of jets or jet trails to mean that the UFOs used an unknown power source. "I am completely convinced," he said, "that they have an out-of-world basis." [16]

Ginna and Darrach also included remarks from Dr. Maurice A. Boit, a prominent aerodynamicist and mathematical physicist. Boit believed the circular design, while being impractical for earth's atmosphere, had significant advantages for space flight. "The least improbable explanation is that these things are artificial and controlled. . . . My opinion for some time has been that they have an extraterrestrial origin." Ginna and Darrach concluded by posing several questions: Where do they come from? Why are they here? What are their intentions? Are they benign? "Before these awesome questions, science—and mankind—can yet only halt in wonder. Answers may come in a generation—or tomorrow. Somewhere in the dark skies there may be those who know." [17]

For the first time a national magazine of *Life*'s stature had come close to advocating the extraterrestrial hypothesis, and reaction to the article was widespread. From April 3 to April 6 over 350 newspapers across the country mentioned the article. ATIC received 110 letters concerning the article, most of them about UFOs sighted over the past two years and theories on the objects' origin, propulsion, and the like. *Life* itself received over

700 letters. When the press questioned the validity of the *Life* article, the Air Force did not, as in the past, issue a blanket denial. Instead, it stated that "the article is factual, but *Life*'s conclusions are their own." [18]

The *New York Times*, maintaining its consistently hostile attitude toward the extraterrestrial hypothesis, printed a rebuttal to the *Life* article. *New York Times* science writer Walter Kaempffert complained that Ginna and Darrach were "uncritical." He attacked the validity of some of the reports by citing inconsistencies and argued that most of the sighted objects were balloons, since they dated from the time of the old Skyhook balloon project. Using information from the Grudge report, Kaempffert said the Air Force had accounted for 99 percent of all sightings and lacked sufficient information on the other 1 percent. For Kaempffert, UFOs had as much reality as the Loch Ness monster. In a similar vein, a *New York Times* editorial suggested that the Grudge report should have put an end to all this nonsense once and for all. But "the idea was too fantastic to die. After all, the sea serpent was with us for decades and it took several years before the Loch Ness monster was buried." [19]

Blue Book braced itself for a flood of reports as a result of the *Life* article, assuming that its sensational nature would prompt people to see things in the sky. The day after the magazine appeared, ATIC received nine reports; the next day the reports dropped off.[20] Yet the number of monthly reports did increase considerably, from the normal ten to twenty reports in previous months to ninety-nine in April and then to seventy-nine in May,[21] although Ruppelt could not attribute the increase to the *Life* article.

One consequence of this increase and of the *Life* article was a surge of press inquiries to Blue Book, so much so that Ruppelt and his staff felt the inquiries interfered with their regular duties. To help out, the Air Force appointed a civilian, Albert M. Chop, to handle all press relations through the Air Force Office of Public Information in the Pentagon. Chop received his information from Ruppelt directly and from the Pentagon liaison officer, Major Dewey Fournet. A second result of rising activity in Blue Book was that Thomas K. Finletter, secretary of the Air Force, personally requested a briefing on UFOs. Afterward Finletter issued a press statement saying that although there was no concrete evidence to prove or disprove the existence of the so-called flying saucers, a number of sightings remained that Air Force investigators could not explain. As long as this was true, Finletter stated, the Air Force would continue to study UFO reports.[22]

By June 1952 Project Blue Book was a dynamic, ongoing organization. Ruppelt's briefing policy had made the UFO problem visible to many Air Force and military groups. The diffraction grid plan, the radarscope plan, the new reporting directive, the Battelle Institute study, the Ohio State questionnaire project, and the monthly status reports all enhanced the prestige of Blue Book and indicated that the Air Force was working intensely and seriously on the UFO mystery.

In June ATIC officially received 149 reports—more than in any previous month in history. The reports came from nearly every section of the country. The Blue Book staff had all it could do to simply screen, classify, and file them; Ruppelt had to discontinue the monthly status reports so that his staff could deal with all the sightings, and the Air Force tried to meet the growing number of reports by increasing Ruppelt's staff to four officers, two airmen, and two secretaries. But the staff still was able to investigate only a fraction of the cases and, in deciding whether a case warranted field investigation, had to rely more and more on the judgment of the base officer who sent in the reports.[23]

Air Force intelligence officers in the Pentagon became concerned about the increase in reports and summoned Ruppelt to Washington to give a special briefing to Director of Intelligence General Samford, members of his staff, intelligence officers from the navy, and people Ruppelt claimed he could not name (possibly CIA members). At the briefing some intelligence officers told Ruppelt that they were seriously considering the possibility that the UFOs were extraterrestrial. They directed him to obtain more positive information of scientific value.[24] Ruppelt hoped that the diffraction camera plan would fill this need and continued work on it with a new sense of urgency.

With the upsurge in sighting reports, Harvard astronomer Donald H. Menzel outlined the solution to the UFO mystery in *Look* and *Time*. The key to the UFO problem, he said, was in mirages, reflections, ice crystals floating in clouds, refraction, and temperature inversion (the condition whereby a layer of cold air is sandwiched between layers of warm air); in fact, Menzel argued, temperature inversion could account for nearly all nighttime visual and radar sightings. To prove his point, Menzel conducted an experiment. He half filled a glass cylinder with benzene and floated a layer of acetone on the top; the benzene acted as a layer of cold air and the acetone as a layer of warm air; the fluids simulated temperature inversion. He then shot a beam of light through the cylinder, and the light curved down as the layers of solution bent it; he agitated the cylinder and the light seemed to move. Thus he accounted for the source of a saucer and its movements. The temperature inversion theory was most appropriate, he said, for desert sightings where "saucer reports are more frequent" and to explain radar returns of UFOs. Menzel concluded: "I believe that these saucers will eventually vanish—most appropriately, into thin air, the region that gave birth to them." He felt sad because saucers were a "frightening diversion in a jittery world." Menzel thought he was bravely acting as the realistic, scientific debunker, and described himself as the man "who shot Santa Claus." [25]

In July *Look* followed its Menzel article with one by J. Robert Moskin who, like Darrach and Ginna, had been to ATIC and had received full cooperation from the Blue Book staff.[26] Moskin quoted Air Force Chief of Staff General Hoyt Vandenberg as saying the Air Force would continue to study the phenomenon as long as unexplained sightings existed; Vandenberg warned that "with the present world unrest, we cannot afford to be complacent." Moskin described Blue Book's radar and diffraction grid plans, the sound equipment idea, and alluded to the Battelle study. Although personnel at key atomic installations around the country had sighted UFOs, he noted, there was no evidence that the saucers were spying on or threatening the atomic programs. "But," he hinted darkly, "this fear still lies deeply in some responsible minds."[27]

Moskin made an important point in his article. He described how intelligence men had attempted to correlate sightings with societal events, such as war tensions, atomic tests, and publicity about flying saucers. "They offer no pattern," he concluded, "no explanation that satisfies the experts. And long ago the Air Force gave up the easy idea that all the excitement is just the result of mass hysteria." Moskin stated that the Air Force felt sure the solution to the problem was either misinterpretation of conventional objects, optical phenomena (as Menzel described), man-made objects, or extraterrestrial objects. Even though Ruppelt said there was no direct indication that the objects were a threat to national security, Moskin concluded, "that doesn't mean they are not a potential threat." [28]

In July ATIC received 536 reports, more than three times the number received in June. They came in steadily from all over the country and peaked on July 28, when ATIC received nearly fifty reports on that one day. The situation assumed near panic proportions. The Blue Book staff thought the country was in the midst of a full-scale flying saucer scare, mainly as a result of the *Time, Life,* and *Look* articles. However, the staff could find no evidence to substantiate this idea; in fact, it found that, except for the increase a few days after the *Life* article, the number of reported sightings was about the same immediately before the articles appeared as immediately afterward, on a daily basis. To help meet the challenge of the mass of reports, ATIC received the cooperation of the Air Weather Service to try quickly to learn if a sighted object was a weather balloon or a temperature inversion. Project Blue Book stopped issuing monthly reports and the entire staff worked on screening and filing the reports, some staff members working a sixteen-hour day. The Pentagon liaison officer, Major Dewey Fournet, began working full-time to keep the Pentagon informed about all the reports.[29]

During these hectic summer months a series of sensational and important sightings occurred over Washington, D.C. On July 10 the crew of a National Airlines plane saw a strange, bright light just south of Washington in Quantico, Virginia. On July 13 another air crew spotted an unusual object about sixty miles south of the capital; the object came directly up to the plane from below, hovered for a few minutes, and then flew straight up at a tremendous speed. On July 14 a Pan American Airlines crew reported seeing eight UFOs near Newport News, Virginia. The next day observers on the ground reported a UFO in the same area.[30]

On July 19 and 20, between 11:40 P.M. and 3:00 A.M., a group of unidentified flying objects appeared on two radarscopes at the Air Route Traffic Control Center at Washington National Airport.[31] The objects moved slowly at first, about 100 to 130 miles per hour, and then shot away at "fantastic speeds." During this same time, several airliner crews reported seeing mysterious lights moving erratically up, down, and sideways; the objects slowed down, speeded up, and hovered. The visual sightings corresponded with the radar returns.

Early that morning Chief Radar Controller Harry Barnes recommended an intercept. At 3:00 A.M. the Air Defense Command scrambled two F-94 jet fighters. The squadron charged with protecting the capital from attack by air was usually stationed at Bolling Air Force Base just across the Potomac, about two miles from the Capitol building. Earlier that day, however, the Air Force had secretly moved the squadron a hundred miles away to New Castle County Airport in Wilmington, Delaware, because of runway repairs at Bolling. It took the jets about half an hour to get from New Castle to the Washington National Airport area. When the jets finally arrived, the Air Route Traffic Control Center vectored them to the targets' positions, but the objects disappeared as the jets neared, and the pilots were unable to make visual contact.[32] At the same time, people on the ground reported seeing strange lights making erratic maneuvers. (There are indications that other airline pilots saw the objects but were reluctant to file reports for fear of ridicule.) Some of the objects had appeared over the restricted air corridors above the White House and the Capitol.

During the night radarscopes continued to track targets in the Washington, D.C., area. At one time all three radar installations at Washington National Airport, and also those at Andrews Air Force Base in Maryland, picked up the same targets three miles north of the city. Early in the morning the Air Route Traffic Control Center at Washington National Airport called Andrews Air Force Base to report it had a target that appeared to be directly over the Andrews' radio tower. The radio operators rushed out and saw "a huge fiery-orange sphere" hovering directly above them. The press swamped Al Chop, the Pentagon public information officer, with inquiries; he said he could not comment until the Air Force had studied the situation. The Air Force refused to admit that it had scrambled a jet interceptor.[33]

Events calmed down until the following weekend. On July 26, at 10:30 P.M., Air Route Traffic Control Center radar once again picked up unidentified flying objects. Tracking began immediately. A half hour later the Air Force command post in Highlands, New Jersey, scrambled jets still at New Castle Airport to intercept the objects. As on the previous weekend, the objects disappeared from the radar screens when the fighters arrived; the pilots saw nothing and returned to the base. As soon as the targets disappeared from the radar screens, people in Newport News, Virginia, began to report unidentified flying objects—bright lights rotating and emitting alternating colors. A few minutes later Langley Air Force Base in Virginia saw a strange light and ordered another jet scramble. It vectored the jet to the object. The pilot spotted the light but, as before, it disappeared "like somebody turning off a light bulb" when he attempted to approach it. The jet did manage to obtain a radar lock-on to the invisible target for a few minutes.[34]

When the jet returned to Langley Field, the targets reappeared over Washington. Once again officers at the traffic control center at Washington National Airport ordered jets to investigate. This time, however, the returns stayed on the radarscopes even after the jets entered the area. A game of tag ensued. Each time the jets were able to get close enough to the targets for close-range observation, the objects sped away. At one point in the chase a pilot noticed the lights were surrounding his plane and nervously asked the ground controllers what to do. Before they could answer, the lights moved away from the plane and left the area. After twenty minutes of fruitless chasing, the jets ran low on fuel and returned to base. The pilots had seen only lights in the sky. Al Chop and Dewey Fournet watched the radarscopes during the entire chase sequence. During this same time the radar operators noticed weather targets, the results of a mild one-degree temperature inversion surrounding the Washington area. The operators claimed that they could easily tell the difference between the actual targets and the returns from this weak temperature inversion.[35]

These Washington sightings were the most sensational to occur since the Mantell incident in 1948. They made headlines around the country, even replacing front-page news of the Democratic National Convention in many newspapers. At 10:00 A.M. on the morning after the sightings, presidential aide Brigadier General Landry, at the request of President Truman, called intelligence authorities in Dayton, Ohio, to find out what was happening in the skies over Washington. Ruppelt took the call and personally briefed Landry on the phenomenon. Later Ruppelt learned that Truman had been listening in on the conversation.[36] The next day an unidentified Pentagon spokesman (probably Chop) told the *Washington Post* that the Air Force was "fairly well convinced" the objects were not a menace to the country. While the Air Force could not discount the extraterrestrial hypothesis, it leaned toward the theory that the objects represented a new kind of physical phenomenon about which it knew very little. "One thing I would like to do," the spokesman said, "is dispel the belief of some that we are holding something back. We are not." [37]

The Pentagon and Blue Book were swamped with press and congressional inquiries about the UFO situation. So many calls came into the Pentagon alone that its telephone circuits were completely tied up with UFO inquiries for the next few days. The

Air Force was keenly aware of the dangers involved in jamming communications in the military's nerve center. As Al Chop said later, the Air Force "had to do something to keep the people quiet." [38] It decided to hold a press conference to allay fears and rumors. On July 29, 1952, the Air Force held the longest and largest press conference since World War II. The spokesmen at the conference were Major General John A. Samford (director of Air Force intelligence), Major General Roger A. Ramey (chief of the Air Defense Command), Colonel Donald L. Bowers (ATIC's chief of the Technical Analysis Division), Ruppelt, several civilian electronics experts, and radar expert Captain Roy L. James, who knew about the Washington sightings only from newspaper reports.

Samford headed the conference. He said the Air Force was reasonably well convinced that the radarscope sightings on the past two weekends were the result of temperature inversions (one of Menzel's solutions); the radar equipment had picked up ground lights reflecting off a layer of cold air between two layers of warm air. Captain James supported this by providing technical details on temperature inversions. Samford then explained that the Air Force was planning to call in outside scientists to examine the Washington sightings more closely (there is no evidence it ever did this). He said the diffraction grid scheme, still in the planning stage, had top priority and would help in gaining accurate scientific measurements of the objects. The Air Force could not account for the fact, Samford admitted, that some of the airline pilots had actually seen the objects. No astronomer had ever seen a flying saucer, he claimed, but the Air Force had received a certain number of reports of unknown objects from "credible observers of relatively incredible things"; these unknowns constituted about 20 percent of the total reports. Finally Samford explained that none of the UFOs seemed to be a threat to the national security. Although all the participants at the conference seemed to agree, Ruppelt later said that Dewey Fournet and a navy radar expert, who were both in the radar room during the July 26 sightings, were not invited to attend the conference because they did not subscribe to the temperature inversion theory.[39]

The news conference had a soothing effect on the nation's press. Most reporters and editors fully accepted the Air Force's version of the events on July 19 and 26. The sightings also prompted another round of the urge to explain. The *New York Times* volunteered the information that the Air Force press statements in the Samford news conference were the result of its analysis of "the thousands of plausible reports of apparitions that have poured in during the last six years." Radar detected the objects over Washington, the *New York Times* explained, because it could not distinguish between birds, ribbons of tinsel, cellophane, and rain. The newspaper suggested that the Air Force should continue studying UFOs only because it could gain knowledge about meteorological conditions. Bill Lawrence, writing in the *New York Times*, asserted that the explanation for the UFOs should be sought in the realm of mass psychology rather than in scientific legitimacy. Taking a similar stance, the *Christian Science Monitor* chalked up the sightings to inadequately understood natural phenomena and "the vagaries of the human mind." The American people had problems enough, the paper said, without worrying about either "heterogeneous oddities which so far display no menace or outbreaks of fancy without credible foundation." Herbert B. Nichols, a special correspondent for the *Monitor*, explained that the public remained interested in flying saucers because it loved a mystery and "why spoil it?"[40]

The *Baltimore Sun* compared flying saucers with the Loch Ness monster and the British "silly season." The reason Americans saw more flying saucers was that America was a larger country and had a longer silly season. The *Milwaukee Journal* explained that it took very little imagination to see a flying saucer, and if imagination were not enough, "a little alcoholic stimulation will help." Writer Elliot Lawrence, in an article in *Coronet* magazine, interviewed a man who had once witnessed a secret demonstration of a saucerlike craft; the inventor had blueprints for a spaceship that could "skip through the air like a flat stone."

The witness did not know where the inventor was at present but thought he had gone to the Soviet Union before the war and was still there. Therefore, the saucers were probably Russian secret weapons.[41]

Some of the press was not so enthusiastic about the conference. The *Washington Post*, which had been in on the inner workings of the Washington sightings, decided upon a wait-and-see attitude. It criticized Menzel's theories: radar had "detected twelve different objects" and the radar sightings were the most impressive to date. "The best advice at this point," the *Washington Post* said, "would be to keep your mind open and your fingers crossed." The *Denver Rocky Mountain News* found the Air Force's inability to identify the origin of UFOs "incredible" and "terrifying." The *News* suggested that the Air Force tell the public if these were military secret weapons; if the Air Force was unable to identify the objects, then "it should not boast about its scientific and military advances until it comes up with the right answer." [42]

C. B. Allen, columnist for the *New York Tribune*, expressed a minority viewpoint: the Samford news conference "had gone far toward its obvious purpose of debunking the whole snow-balling phenomenon of 'Flying Saucers.' " Drew Pearson believed the news conference was important because the Air Force had admitted for the first time that personnel had recorded radar and observational data at the same time, and he implied that the objects could be from another planet. *Life* magazine also noted that the Air Force had admitted concurrent radar, ground, and observational sightings. A *Life* reporter had asked the Air Force about the jet interceptors that it had originally denied dispatching; after a confrontation, the Air Force admitted to the jet action but made no other comment. The *Life* reporter posited that perhaps the Air Force had "known more about the blips than it admitted." [43]

The Washington sightings also prompted a full expression of the urge to explain among scientists. Physician Edgar Mauer, writing in *Science*, believed it was time to examine the problem of the existence of saucers in physiological spheres "other than the psyche," since scientists had not been able to come up with a plausible explanation. Mauer's analysis: "flying disks are motes in the eyes of a dyspeptic microcosm or perhaps some abnormal cortical discharges in the migrainous." Professor C. C. Wylie, head of the astronomy department at the University of Iowa, said "the object" over Washington was the planet Jupiter. Unless the Air Force gave the complete answer to the sightings in clear astronomical terms, Wylie argued, "belief in visitors from outer space will be strengthened in those who cannot distinguish between speculation and scientific reasoning." The distinguished Dr. Gerard Kuiper, head of the Yerkes Observatory in Williams Bay, Wisconsin, said the objects were weather balloons.[44]

Dr. Jessie Sprowls, professor of abnormal psychology at the University of Maryland, told the country in a radio interview that the reports were the product of hallucination. His advice was "Just sort of forget about it." Dr. Horace Byers, chairman of the meteorology department at the University of Chicago, attributed the sightings to "junk" in the skies, such as balloons, meteors, reflections, clouds, and the like. "I know of no reputable scientist who places any credence in reports that so-called flying saucers come from a mysterious or unexplained source," he said. Dr. Otto Struve, University of California astronomer, explained that the evidence for the reality of flying saucers "appears to be completely negative to an astronomer." Dr. I. M. Levitt, director of the Fels Planetarium in Philadelphia, agreed with the inversion theory and said the sightings were due to mirages and temperature inversions. Dr. Donald Menzel asserted again that the sightings would disappear "when the present hot spell is over." Even Einstein had an opinion about the flying saucers. When a Los Angeles evangelist asked him to comment, Einstein replied: "These people have seen *something*. What it is I do not know and I am not curious to know." [45]

While the major wave of sightings was in progress, in the summer of 1952, Dr. J. Allen Hynek discreetly polled for the Air Force forty-four astronomers around the country on their views about UFOs. He found that 5 percent claimed to have seen a UFO. This, Hynek explained, was understandable because they spent more time watching the skies than most people; however, astronomers also could discriminate between what was unusual and what was not. In probing their attitudes toward the subject, Hynek found that 16 percent were completely indifferent, 27 percent mildly indifferent, 40 percent mildly interested, and 17 percent very interested. Most of them believed that UFO reports could be explained as misidentifications of conventional objects. But when Hynek took the time to explain the exact nature of the phenomenon and to describe some of the more puzzling cases, "their interest was almost immediately aroused, indicating that their general lethargy is due to lack of information." Hynek also found an "overwhelming fear of publicity." A newspaper headline to the effect of "Astronomer Sees A Flying Saucer" would be "enough to brand the astronomer as questionable among his colleagues." Hynek concluded that most astronomers were not actually hostile to the subject but did not want to become involved because of publicity and the tenuous and unreliable nature of the data.[46]

The Washington sightings marked the high-water point of the 1952 wave. ATIC received 326 reports in August, down 210 from the July total. The Blue Book staff concentrated on filing and screening. The monthly status reports remained suspended but work on the questionnaire, the statistics project, and the diffraction grid continued.

The UFO sightings had had an ominous effect on the military. Not only was the Pentagon swamped with UFO inquiries and Blue Book immersed in a huge backlog of reports, but air bases and installations around the country were feeling the effects as well. On August 1, 1952, the *New York Times* reported that the Air Force had been getting so many flying saucer inquiries that "regular intelligence work had been affected." An Air Force spokesman (probably Fournet) reported that one full-time man was already working on the press inquiries and still other people in other departments had to answer some of the questions. The *Christian Science Monitor* said that Captain F. R. Shafer, commanding officer of the Air Force Filter Center in South Bend, Indiana, was receiving so many UFO reports that he was forced to spend a few hours every day studying them. The same was true, the report said, for Captain Everett A. Turner of the Chicago Filter Center; his weekends had been hectic, devoted to screening and sending in his reports to Washington and ATIC. General Ramey appeared on the nationally televised CBS show "Man of the Week" a few days after the Washington news conference to answer questions about UFO reports. Essentially saying the same things that Samford had said at the conference, Ramey also noted that the Air Force was trying to come up with "fast answers" in order to avert hysteria.[47]

Perhaps Air Force Chief of Staff General Hoyt Vandenberg best summed up the rising feelings of many Air Force officials in an interview with the *Seattle Post-Intelligencer*. After reiterating that UFOs were neither extraterrestrial, products of foreign technology, nor secret weapons, he bluntly stated that he did not like the "continued, long-range occurrence of what might be called mass hysteria about flying saucers." He went on to say that "The Air Force has had teams of experts investigating all reports for several years, since the end of World War II, and they have never found anything to substantiate the existence of such things as flying saucers." [48]

Donald Menzel reflected this growing Air Force attitude as well. *Look* quoted him on September 9 as saying once again that the UFOs in Washington, D.C., were mirages. Menzel had examined the case and decided that the reason both the pilots and radar saw the same objects was that both were "operating under the same meteorological conditions." Furthermore, Menzel reasoned, it was highly unlikely that the objects were extraterrestrial: if they have spaceships, then they probably have radio, and if they have radio, they would have contacted us. "If inter-planetary travelers came here they wouldn't hang around like ghosts; they'd get off their ships and have a look at us. Wouldn't you on Venus?" Menzel remarked that the flying saucer scare could be dangerous "in the sense that if an enemy were to attack us tomorrow, it might take 24 hours for the people in the target area to make up their minds whether it really was a terrestrial enemy or somebody from Venus." [49]

Although the 1952 wave of sightings generated growing

anxiety, it also created more genuine interest. The increasing number of articles about UFOs seemed to have contributed to the interest; Ruppelt found that in a six-month period 148 newspapers carried 16,000 items about UFOs. Many previously skeptical people now wanted to know more about the phenomenon. As a result, some professional people initiated projects to study the flying saucer reports. In Wisconsin a group of electronics engineers and technicians from a reserve unit of the Army Signal Corps set up Project Vortex, the purpose of which was to receive information about UFOs and to conduct research. The *Wichita (Kansas) Beacon* organized thirty part-time reporters to be on "camera alert" for UFOs. Ohio Northern University initiated an independent UFO investigation that scientists at the university would conduct. In spite of the increased public interest in the phenomenon during the summer months, the university stated, "little has been done to adequately screen information and to aid in presenting a scientific appraisal of this phenomenon to the general public." Moreover, there was a need for a private organization to collect the data objectively and distribute the results of a careful study to the public. Ohio Northern hoped that its proposed study would "lead to a more logical appraisal of phenomena observed in all walks of life." With this announcement Ohio Northern began soliciting reports and worked on the data for the next year.[50]

During 1952 two private research groups came into being. The first was Civilian Saucer Investigation of Los Angeles, founded by Ed Sullivan, a technical writer for North American Aviation Corporation. The organization included scientists from the Los Angeles area with Dr. Walther Reidel its most prominent member. The second was the Aerial Phenomena Research Organization (APRO), formed by Coral Lorenzen, a private UFO researcher in Sturgeon Bay, Wisconsin. Basically a collecting organization, APRO attempted to work independently of the Air Force and come to its own conclusion based on what evidence the group could amass. The organization published a bimonthly newsletter, *The A.P.R.O. Bulletin*.[51] With small membership, these two organizations were the first major independent groups established for the specific purpose of looking into the UFO mystery.

Professional organizations now began to take an interest in the subject. In October 1952 the American Optical Society sponsored a symposium on UFOs and invited Drs. Hynek, Menzel, and Liddel (of the Bendix Aviation Corporation and a member of the Atomic Energy Commission) to give papers before the society. In his paper, Menzel reiterated his familiar theories of mirage, reflection, refraction, temperature inversion, and the like. For Menzel these theories could explain *all* sighting reports that the Air Force now listed as unknown.[52]

Urner Liddel took a similar stance in his paper, "Phantasmagoria or Unusual Observations in the Atmosphere." Frankly stating that he prepared the paper because "the nation was in the throes of a flying saucer scare," he thought it worthwhile "to take any action which might alleviate the hysteria." Liddel's analysis was that "hucksters of science" caused much of the flying saucer scare. These people were mainly newspaper reporters who fed on the scare because it provided a "lucrative business." Liddel then attempted to explain some sightings, concluding that all reports basically stemmed from reflections, mirages, and psychological inadequacies. Furthermore, he argued, conditioned fear of atomic weapons and the secrecy surrounding them as well as the UFO sightings around atomic installations had contributed to the current "mass hysteria." "Thus, just as ghosts are seldom seen outside [away from] cemeteries or haunted houses, so flying saucers are seen at points of greatest fear psychosis." Liddel concluded that he knew of "NO" evidence leading to the extraterrestrial hypothesis and that all unexplained reports were due to insufficient scientific data.[53]

Hynek took a different approach. He directly attacked Menzel's and Liddel's theories and for the first time departed publicly from his hostility to the idea that UFOs were not ordinary objects. The events of 1952 had affected him. Instead of believing, as did many Air Force people, that all UFO reports were the result of hysterical public reactions to illusions, Hynek slowly began to rethink this position in light of the quality and puzzling aspects of the reports. In his paper he gave several examples of particularly puzzling unexplained cases. He reasoned that if the reports were not of natural phenomena, then an obligation existed to "demonstrate *explicitly* how . . . specific reports can be explained in terms of balloons, mirages, or conventional aircraft." [54]

Hynek became the first scientist in the country to note the destructive effect of ridicule, and he emphasized that ridicule of witnesses and the phenomenon itself acted against scientific interest in the subject: "nothing constructive is accomplished for the public at large—and for science in the long run—by mere ridicule and the implication that sightings are the products of 'birdbrains' and 'intellectual flyweights.' . . . Ridicule is not part of the scientific method and people should not be taught that it is." Taking a more practical stance, he concluded that the UFO problem was one of "science-public-relations" in that the "chance has consistently been missed to demonstrate on a national basis how scientists can go about analyzing a problem." After the symposium Hynek filed a report with Project Blue Book saying that the Liddel and Menzel papers were worthless; the two men had not studied the evidence or the literature and were not qualified to speak on the subject. Hynek felt his trip to the society was unproductive.[55]

Some people in the Air Force were beginning to think Hynek was right, that perhaps UFO reports did represent something unknown or even extraterrestrial. The Air Force's investigation of the Fort Monmouth incident—the September 1951 sightings which were a major influence in the decision to reorganize Project Grudge—concluded that one of the four major radar and visual reports, the one from the T-33 pilot, remained unexplained.[56] Moreover, the official explanation for the Washington sightings, in spite of Samford's temperature inversion statements, listed them as unknown. Project Blue Book consulted with scientists working on the Battelle statistical plan about Menzel's theories and they agreed that "none of the theories so far proposed would account for more than a very small percentage of the reports, if any." [57]

Pentagon liaison officer Fournet wanted to look into the situation more closely. After meeting with Ruppelt and two

Pentagon officers (Colonels W. A. Adams and Weldon Smith), Fournet and the other three men decided to study the maneuvers and reported motions of the objects to determine whether they were under intelligent control. This idea had been around for some time, and the mass of data collected in the summer now made such a study feasible. If the study showed that the objects moved in a definite pattern (rather than randomly), then the Air Force would have to consider the extraterrestrial hypothesis a serious alternative. Ruppelt and the Pentagon officers assigned the problem to Fournet, who began work on it immediately.[58]

By the end of 1952 the sighting wave subsided. The frantic days of the past summer gave way to the routine of receiving an average of fifty reports each month for the last three months of the year. The Air Force had taken in a record number of 1,501 reports for the year—nearly twice the total number of reports received during the previous five years. And yet despite this number, Ruppelt estimated that the Air Force received reports of only about 10 percent of the total sightings in the country.[59]

With the number of reports declining, Project Blue Book resumed its prewave activities. It started issuing its status reports again. It sent the Ohio State University questionnaire (completed in October) to everyone who filed a report; this greatly improved the quality of received reports. The Battelle Institute's statistical study also was progressing. The scientists decided to stop collecting data at the end of 1952, because they assumed that additional reports would yield similar data, and they hoped to complete their study some time in 1953. The diffraction camera plan was in the final stages of development. ATIC and Dr. Kaplan had hit upon the idea of using special two-lens Videon cameras, which could take stereoscopic pictures; ATIC planned to put a diffraction grid over one lens and leave the other free to take a normal picture of a suspected UFO. The cameras were accurate, inexpensive, and fairly simple to operate. ATIC began to negotiate in December with Air Defense Command headquarters to place the cameras in air bases around the country and also to mount the grids on the lenses of F-86 gun cameras to take pictures from the air.[60]

The groups cooperating with Blue Book also made progress.

The Air Defense Command had nearly completed its radarscope plan and directed personnel to place all radarscope cameras on a twenty-four-hour alert. In addition, ADC made the Ground Observers Corps (a group of civilians who watched the skies for enemy planes that might have broken through the radar network) available to Blue Book and told the members to report any UFOs to ADC, which would then forward the reports to ATIC.[61] The navy directed all naval units to report UFOs directly to Air Force headquarters, ATIC, or the Air Defense Command. The Air Weather Service began to give full cooperation to Blue Book, supplying the project with data about weather conditions, balloons, inversions, and the like.

The year had been exceptionally hectic, and the Air Force breathed a collective sigh of relief at the end of 1952. The great mass of UFO reports had created a climate in which Fournet, Hynek, and others had begun to consider seriously the extraterrestrial hypothesis as one of many explanations for the sightings. But for others in intelligence circles the 1952 sightings had the opposite effect. They firmly believed the reports signified only psychological manifestations of a society caught in the grips of a potentially dangerous scare. By 1953 a growing number of people in the Air Force and the Central Intelligence Agency began to think that—for reasons of national security—the number of UFO reports had better be reduced drastically, if not eliminated altogether.

4

THE ROBERTSON PANEL AND ITS EFFECTS ON AIR FORCE UFO POLICY

Official policy on UFOs switched dramatically in 1953. After building its investigatory capacity in 1952, Project Blue Book by the end of 1953 could no longer adequately investigate or analyze UFO reports and functioned mainly as a public relations and collecting office. This change was due primarily to the recommendations of a group of scientists who formed the Robertson panel. The convening of this CIA-sponsored panel was a pivotal event in UFO history. Although much of the information concerning the impetus for the panel remains in CIA and Pentagon files and is therefore unavailable, sufficient information is accessible to reconstruct most of the events leading to the Air Force's policy reversal.

The CIA became interested in the UFO phenomenon during the 1952 wave of sightings.[1] The CIA and some high-ranking Air Force officers, including Generals Vandenberg and Samford, thought the mass of UFO reports might constitute a threat to the national security. It was possible for the Soviet Union, or any other "enemy," to use UFOs as a decoy in preparation for an attack on the United States. It was possible that a deliberately confused American public might think attacking enemy bombers were UFOs. At the least, a foreign power could exploit the flying saucer craze to make the public doubt official Air Force statements about UFOs and thereby undermine public confidence in the military. Moreover, the volume of sighting reports in 1952 had clogged normal military intelligence channels and this certainly would pose a danger during an enemy attack.[2]

With the information from the Battelle Memorial Institute's statistical study, it would be possible to assess the dangers UFOs might represent. But a snag developed in the plans. The Battelle Memorial Institute was not ready to present its findings. At a preliminary meeting in early December 1952, Battelle representatives strongly recommended that the proposed CIA meeting be postponed until Battelle could make the results of its study available to ATIC. Battelle's problem was that the data it was working with were unreliable, and it could not document what it felt should be supported by facts from the analysis. Sometimes critical information was missing from a report, and even in a well-documented report an element of doubt always existed about the data because of its anecdotal nature. This made positive identification of the reported objects difficult.

Since the need for precise data was important for identification, Battelle suggested that the Air force set up controlled experiments in areas of high UFO activity. These areas could be stocked with skywatch equipment (radar, cameras, measuring equipment, etc.). All conventional objects crossing the area would be known in advance. Therefore, any unidentified flying objects could be recognized at once by a simple process of elimination. Once Battelle had data from these controlled experiments, it would apply the information to past unidentified sightings and would lay the flying saucer controversy to rest once and for all. Furthermore, the Air Force would benefit from this experiment because it would then know just how much attention to pay to a massive wave of sightings like the one just passed. The Air Force could make positive statements reassuring the public that the military had everything under control.

But against Battelle's objections and mindful of the potential threat to national security, the CIA decided to go forward. It convened a distinguished panel of nonmilitary scientists to analyze the Blue Book data. Five outstanding scientists in the physical sciences, two associate panel members, and various Air

Force and CIA representatives met from Wednesday, January 14, to Saturday, January 17, 1953, in Washington, D.C.[3]

Dr. H. P. Robertson, formerly at Princeton and the California Institute of Technology and an expert in mathematics, cosmology, and relativity, chaired the panel. At that time he was director of the Weapons System Evaluation Group in the Office of the Secretary of Defense and a CIA classified employee. Panel member Samuel A. Goudsmit, an associate of Einstein, discovered electron spin in 1925 in Holland, helped found a school of theoretical physics, and headed a mission at the end of World War II to investigate the Germans' progress in developing the atomic bomb. In 1953 he was on the physics staff of the Brookhaven National Laboratories. Luis Alvarez, a high-energy physicist, contributed to a microwave radar system and the atomic bomb and received the Nobel Prize for physics in 1968. Thornton Page, former professor of astronomy at the University of Chicago, was a physicist at the Naval Ordnance Laboratory during World War II and in 1953 was deputy director of the Johns Hopkins' Operations Research Office. Lloyd Berkner, the final panel member, had accompanied Admiral Byrd on the 1928–30 Antarctic expedition, had been a physicist with the Carnegie Institution's Department of Terrestrial Magnetism, had headed the radar section of the Navy Bureau of Aeronautics, and had served as executive secretary of the Department of Defense's Research and Development Board in World War II. Later he became special assistant to the secretary of state and at the time of the panel was one of the directors of the Brookhaven National Laboratories.[4]

Two associate panel members were J. Allen Hynek and Frederic C. Durant. Hynek was only invited to selected meetings. Durant, an army ordnance test station director, past president of the American Rocket Society, and president of the International Astronautical Federation, wrote the summary of the proceedings. Also present were Ruppelt, Dewey Fournet, ATIC chief General W. M. Garland, Navy Photo Interpretation Laboratory representatives Lieutenant R. S. Neasham and Harry Woo, and CIA personnel: Dr. H. Marshall Chadwell, Ralph L. Clark, and Philip G. Strong.[5]

The panel convened on Wednesday without Lloyd Berkner, who did not arrive until Friday afternoon. It began by reviewing the CIA's interest in UFOs. Dr. Robertson requested that panel members investigate the reports according to their specialties. For example, astronomer Thornton Page should focus on nocturnal lights and green fireballs and physicist Alvarez on radar cases. Then the panel watched two color films, both taken in daylight and showing maneuvering light sources in the sky. Nicholas Mariana had taken one movie in Great Falls, Montana, and navy Commander Delbert C. Newhouse the other in Tremonton, Utah. The Mariana film showed two objects flying behind a building and a water tower. The Newhouse film, which the Air Force had kept classified, showed twelve objects flying in loose formation through the sky. The Project Blue Book staff believed the films were among the best evidence it had to give credence to the extraterrestrial intelligence hypothesis.[6]

Ruppelt briefed the panel on Blue Book's methods of tracking down UFO reports. Hynek described the Battelle Memorial Institute study, which was still in progress. The panel discussed a few case histories and saw a special movie of sea gulls in flight that tried to duplicate the Newhouse film. It then heard a report on Project Twinkle, the Air Force's attempt to decipher the green fireball mystery. General Garland spoke, explaining that more intelligence efforts coupled with better briefings should be used to sort and collect UFO reports. He recommended declassifying reports completely on a continuing basis and increasing ATIC's UFO analysis section. Later, Hynek outlined a skywatch program which might be an inexpensive adjunct to current astronomical programs. Trained astronomers could photograph a UFO while doing other work through a program of this kind. Hynek suggested ten different observatories where Blue Book could implement this plan.[7]

On Friday morning Dewey Fournet read a paper on reported UFO movements, concluding that the extraterrestrial hypothesis might be the key to the mystery. Although impressed that Fournet had been with the UFO project for fifteen months and was an aeronautical engineer, the panel members could not accept his interpretation of what they perceived as "raw, unevaluated reports." During the three days of examining Blue Book data, the panel reviewed eight cases in detail, fifteen in general, and saw two movies. It discussed tentative conclusions and recommendations on Friday afternoon and commissioned Robertson to draft the final report. The members spent the next day correcting and altering the draft. The panel had spent a total of twelve hours studying the UFO phenomenon. The panel adjourned Saturday afternoon, January 17, ending the most influential government-sponsored, nonmilitary UFO investigation of the 1950s.[8]

Probably because of time limitations and the small number of reports the panel members examined, they disregarded apparent anomalistic evidence in certain UFO reports. For example, the Navy Photograph Interpretation Laboratory spent 1,000 hours analyzing the Newhouse film and concluded that the objects in the film were neither birds, balloons, aircraft, nor reflections; rather, they were "self-luminous." The laboratory based its analysis on the assumption that Newhouse's distance estimates were accurate. Rejecting this analysis, the panel members reasoned that Newhouse probably was mistaken in his distance estimates. As S. A. Goudsmit said, "by assuming that the distance was less, the results could be explained as due to a formation of ducks or other birds, reflecting the strong desert sunlight but being just too far and too luminous to see their shape. This assumption yielded reasonable speeds and accelerations." The panel concurred in the bird explanation. The panel used similar reasoning to interpret the Mariana film. Mariana saw two jet planes about to land at a nearby air base just before his sighting. He testified, however, that he knew the difference between the planes and the objects. But because the jets and the two objects had appeared near the same place at about the same time, the panel decided Mariana was mistaken and had taken a film of the jets.[9]

After reviewing the data, the panel found no evidence that UFOs represented a *direct* threat to the national security. The Air Force's concern over UFOs "was probably caused by public pressure," due to the number of articles and books on the subject.

Nevertheless, the panel warned that "having a military source foster public concern in 'nocturnal meandering lights' " was "possibly dangerous." The implication was that military interest in the objects might encourage people to believe the objects were a *potential* threat to national security. The panel also concluded that the reports represented little, if any, valuable scientific data; the material was "quite irrelevant to hostile objects that might some day appear." Assuming that visitors would probably come from our solar system, Thornton Page noted that astronomical knowledge of the solar system made the existence of extraterrestrial intelligent beings extremely unlikely. Page also incorrectly assumed that UFO reports occurred only in the United States, and the idea that extraterrestrial objects would visit only one country seemed "preposterous." [10]

Even though the panel did not believe UFOs were a direct threat to the national security, it did find a potentially dangerous threat in the reports. The panel commented that "the continued emphasis on the reporting of these phenomena does, in these parlous times, result in a threat to the orderly functioning of the protective organs of the body politic." The reports clogged military intelligence channels, might precipitate mass hysteria, and might make defense personnel misidentify or ignore "actual enemy artifacts." In language reminiscent of Project Grudge's recommendations, the panel found that the reports could make the public vulnerable to "possible enemy psychological warfare" by cultivating a "morbid national psychology in which skillful hostile propaganda could induce hysterical behavior and harmful distrust of duly constituted authority." [11] At last the military had found the threat to national security—the UFO *reports,* not the UFOs. The solution of the UFO problem now assumed another dimension. The real enemy had finally been identified. The battle was joined.

Based on its conclusions, the panel made four recommendations. The first concerned Blue Book's diffraction camera, radarscope, and skywatch plans. It suggested using the diffraction cameras not to collect UFO data but to allay public anxiety, especially because the plan was the result of public pressure.

Similarly, it recommended implementation of the radarscope plan because it could help explain natural interference in the radar screens. But it rejected Dr. Hynek's expanded skywatch plan. "A program of this type," the panel argued, "might have the adverse effect of overemphasizing 'flying saucer' stories in the public mind." In a second proposal, the panel suggested that the two major private UFO research organizations, the Aerial Phenomena Research Organization and the Civilian Saucer Intelligence, "be watched because of their potentially great influence on mass thinking if widespread sightings should occur. The apparent irresponsibility and the possible use of such groups for subversive purposes should be kept in mind." Third, the members recommended that national security agencies take steps immediately to strip the UFO phenomenon of its special status and eliminate the aura of mystery it had acquired. This could be done by initiating a public education campaign so that people could recognize and react promptly to true indications of hostile intent.[12]

Finally, in its fourth proposal, the Robertson panel outlined a detailed program of public education with two purposes: "training and 'debunking.'" Training would help people identify known objects so that there would be "a marked reduction in reports caused by misidentification and resultant confusion." Debunking would reduce public interest in UFOs and therefore decrease or eliminate UFO reports. The education program, by using the mass media, would concentrate on "actual case histories which had been puzzling at first but later explained. As with conjuring tricks, there is much less stimulation if the 'secret' is known." Such a program would reduce "the current gullibility of the public and consequently their susceptibility to clever hostile propaganda." The panel suggested that the government hire psychologists familiar with mass psychology as consultants; it named a few, including Hadley Cantril who had written a book on the 1938 *War of the Worlds* broadcast. The panel also recommended that the Air Force use an army training film company, Walt Disney Productions, and personalities such as Arthur Godfrey in this massive educational drive. In a key discussion before making recommendations, the panel members decided that a limited expansion of Blue Book's investigatory capacity was needed to increase the percentage of explained reports; this also was necessary to reinforce the proposed educational program.[13]

A few panel members may have prejudged the UFO issue. At the meetings, Page refused to take the subject seriously and Robertson had to chastize him for joking about the UFO reports. Writing in 1965 to a person interested in UFOs, S. A. Goudsmit said he had not changed his mind about the UFO phenomenon since the panel meetings; he still believed the subject was "a complete waste of time and should be investigated by psychiatrists rather than physicists." Furthermore, the extraterrestrial theory was "almost as dangerous to the general welfare of our unstable society as drug addiction and some other mental disorders." Hynek was aware of these attitudes, and although the panel members did not ask him to sign the final report, he later stated he would not have signed it even if they had asked. He argued that the panel made a judgment about UFOs in less than four days whereas he had spent more than four years studying the problem and was unable to arrive at any conclusions.[14] When asked why he did not speak out against the panel, Hynek replied that he was only "small potatoes" then; not only would the Air Force have ignored him, but he would have jeopardized his standings with the Air Force and with the astronomical community.[15]

The Robertson panel conclusions were roughly similar to those of the 1949 Projects Sign and Grudge reports. Sign also wanted the Air Force to "eliminate or greatly reduce the mystery" associated with UFOs. Grudge found that enemies could use UFOs to create a "mild form of hysteria" in the public and recommended publicity to dispel "public apprehension." [16] Both Sign and Grudge found that UFOs represented no direct threat to national security. Also, the Robertson report, like the Sign and Grudge reports, set the tone of future Air Force UFO policy. The panel did not recommend declassification of the sighting reports and did not exercise its apparent opportunity to move the study from the military to the academic community. Rather, because of the UFO reports' threat, the panel implied that the Air Force should *tighten* security, continuing the situation whereby nonmilitary personnel could not obtain the technical and anecdotal information the Air Force had amassed over the last four years, and also increasing public suspicions derived from secrecy. The panel believed the dissemination of information would lead to increased public awareness of UFOs and this would eventually mean an increase in reports. It assumed that keeping quiet would make UFOs disappear.

The Robertson report also had critically important public relations ramifications. It enabled the Air Force to state for the next fifteen years that an impartial scientific body had examined the data thoroughly and found no evidence of anything unusual in the atmosphere. More importantly, the panel gave the Air Force's UFO program the necessary military raison d'être it needed to continue: it had to mount a major effort against UFO reports because they were a threat to the national security. The Air Force could now sidestep the substantive issues of the nature and origin of the objects and concentrate on the public relations problems involved in eliminating UFO reports. Blue Book was therefore relieved of its main investigating burden. Yet since the Air Force's overall mission was to monitor everything in the skies, Blue Book would still investigate and analyze UFO reports, but on a greatly reduced scale.

The panel submitted its formal conclusions and recommendations to the CIA and, as far as can be ascertained, to the Pentagon and higher echelons of the Air Force. Robertson showed the final report to General Cabell (former director of intelligence), who expressed satisfaction with it. The CIA did not give a copy of the report to Ruppelt or his staff in 1953, although it did release a summary to Blue Book a few years later. But shortly after the panel adjourned, the CIA summoned Ruppelt and Garland to its headquarters to tell them about the recommendations. As Ruppelt repported it, the officials explained that the Robertson panel had recommended expanding Blue Book's staff, using instruments for more accurate measurements, and terminating all secrecy in the project by declassifying sighting reports.[17] If Ruppelt understood and reported correctly, it remains a mystery why the CIA gave out this false information. The panel members had recommended continued use of some plans in their discussions but had not made this the focus of their formal recommendations.

Armed with these CIA "recommendations" and orders from his superiors to follow them, Ruppelt began implementation. He tried to have the Newhouse film declassified and shown to a press conference. This was to be a major event because in 1952 the press had heard rumors of the film and Fournet had fought hard with the Air Force Office of Information to release it. But just before the showing was to take place, Air Force officials stopped it and the press conference. According to Ruppelt, the military believed the sea gull theory was weak. Moreover, the new publicity policy was to keep silent.[18]

Other events happened at Project Blue Book that Ruppelt could not account for. Toward the end of 1952 the Air Force began to work out a nationwide plan to set up cameras in connection with radar units (this plan was different from the plan to take photographs of radarscopes). The cameras would photograph any UFO that radar picked up and would provide accurate measurements of the objects. The Air Force hoped this plan would either take the place of the diffraction grid camera plan or supplement it. Suddenly, and seemingly without reason, the Air Force abandoned it, saying the diffraction cameras would suffice. Even the radarscope plan, which the panel had suggested, was not producing valuable information. Thus, the diffraction camera scheme, which was ready for implementation, assumed even more importance. The Air Force placed about a hundred Videon cameras equipped with diffraction grids in air bases around the country and tested them. After a few weeks of testing, however, it found that because of chemical decomposition the grids were slowly disintegrating and losing their light-separating ability. It decided to try to repair or substitute the grids but never did, finally abandoning the entire idea. After one full year of work, the Air Force allowed the diffraction camera plan to die, although the Videon cameras without grids remained in operation at the bases.[19]

In the face of growing Pentagon opposition to mounting a

full-scale UFO investigation, Ruppelt conceived an idea to supplement his diminishing Blue Book staff. During wartime the 4602d Air Intelligence Service Squadron, a unit within the Air Defense Command, gathered intelligence from captured enemy pilots. But during peacetime the unit only simulated this activity and had no other duties. In a February 1953 briefing to high-ranking ADC officers, Ruppelt suggested that the 4602d take over Project Blue Book's field investigation. The men of the 4602d would get on-the-spot investigation experience and also expand Blue Book's field work. General Garland liked the idea and, with General Burgess, worked out the transfer plan, which became operative in December 1953. It was the last major expansion of Blue Book's activities.[20]

Ruppelt temporarily left Blue Book in February 1953 for a several-month assignment in Denver. Since his replacement never came, this left a staff lieutenant in charge. When Ruppelt returned he found that the Air Force had reassigned several members of his staff and had sent no replacements. Eventually the Blue Book staff dwindled to Ruppelt and two assistants. This was not in keeping with the panel's recommendation, as Ruppelt understood it, to expand Blue Book. According to Ruppelt, his superior officers gave him orders to build up Blue Book; yet every time he tried to add personnel or expand in any way, the Air Force refused to concur. Ruppelt left Blue Book permanently in August 1953. As a reserve he had been reactivated for the Korean War; now that it had ended he accepted a position in private industry. No replacement came for him and he turned over his command to Airman First Class Max Futch.[21] The fact that an airman commanded the project demonstrates the priority the Air Force placed on it.

Dewey Fournet left the Pentagon in the same year. These two departures meant that the last effective military support for the continued study of UFOs based on the premise that they could be extraterrestrial vehicles had vanished. Hynek still supported such study, but he was a civilian and could only submit suggestions. Moreover, although he believed the Air Force should study the subject systematically, he feared ridicule from the academic community if he came out strongly for a continued systematic investigation. Hynek simply kept quiet and continued in his role as consultant.[22]

During the first half of 1953, even as the Air Force decided to downplay publicity about UFOs, popular UFO speculation boomed. Donald Keyhoe headed the field when an excerpt of his book *Flying Saucers From Outer Space* appeared in an October issue of *Look* magazine. Keyhoe began the book in the summer of 1952, acting on Blue Book's new liberal attitude toward the press. Having heard General Samford say at the July 1952 press conference that the Air Force had no reason to classify sighting reports, Keyhoe asked Al Chop, Pentagon UFO information officer, for numerous classified reports. The Office of Information routinely denied Keyhoe's request. But Chop, who was leaning toward the extraterrestrial hypothesis, asked Dewey Fournet to help. Fournet, who also tended toward the extraterrestrial theory, went to Ruppelt and had all the sightings that Keyhoe requested declassified and turned over to him. With these sightings, Keyhoe had enough information for his new book.[23]

The Air Force feared that the excerpt of Keyhoe's book in *Look* would result in another rash of sighting reports. To combat this, it pressured *Look* into including an Air Force disclaimer in the article. The disclaimer stated that the information contained in the article was unofficial and that the Air Force had found nothing unusual about the objects. In addition, *Look* allowed the Air Force to insert parenthetical remarks disputing certain points throughout the article.[24]

As well as trying to neutralize the expected impact of the *Look* article, Air Force officials charged that Keyhoe had obtained his sighting reports fraudulently and that the Air Force had no record of releasing them. Keyhoe went directly to Al Chop to counter this claim. (Chop had resigned his press information post in March 1953.) He willingly signed an affidavit stating that he had released the sighting reports, which were from official Air Force files, to Keyhoe. Eventually the Air Force admitted this was the case. The entire affair deepened Keyhoe's conviction that a massive cover-up was taking place within the Air Force to keep vital information from the public. He believed high-ranking Air Force officials knew UFOs represented extraterrestrial intelligence, and because they had not informed the public of this, Keyhoe felt certain it meant only one thing: a conspiracy of silence. Keyhoe's book, *Flying Saucers From Outer Space*, came out in October 1953 and was one of the most widely read books of the decade, selling over half a million copies.[25] Through its sales, Keyhoe kept his position in the forefront of private UFO investigators.

Although Keyhoe believed more than ever in an Air Force cover-up, he admitted in his book that he might have been wrong about the Air Force trying to cover up information in the early days of the controversy. But, he said, "they knew a lot more than they were telling now." He contended that the Air Force kept facts from the American public to prevent possible panic and hysteria. Keyhoe had heard the argument that an enemy possibly could use the flying saucer scare to its advantage. But he turned the argument on its head. By 1954, Keyhoe wrote, the Russians would have, according to the Joint Chiefs of Staff, the ability to stage a massive atomic attack. Keyhoe reasoned that the Russians, just before the attack, could claim the saucers were actually secret weapons. "By starting false rumors of Russian saucer attacks, they might cause stampedes from cities, block defense highways, and paralyze communications just before an A-bomb raid." Therefore, a "grave danger" existed if the Air Force refused to correctly identify the saucers as extraterrestrial vehicles.[26]

Keyhoe had learned many of the basic facts. He had obtained the sighting reports from Blue Book files; he had heard rumors of the Robertson panel meetings and recommendations, although he could not verify them; he accurately identified the people within the Air Force sympathetic to his reasoning by establishing a direct line to the Air Force through Fournet and Chop. The problem was his interpretation of these facts. He had no way of knowing all the Air Force and CIA reasons for their actions. But because he lacked access to all the information, his interpretation—that the Air Force blocked full release of information about UFOs to avoid public panic and hysteria—seemed to be the only answer to the Air Force's puzzling behavior. For Keyhoe all outward indications of the Air Force's actions led to the conspiracy thesis. Because Keyhoe's facts were basically correct, the Air Force could not invalidate or refute his interpretation unless it disclosed fully the rationale for its activities. Therefore, the Air Force's main counterattack in 1953 was to issue press releases denying Keyhoe's claims and to ward off additional publicity. This only reinforced Keyhoe's contentions and the effect was circular: the more the Air Force denied Keyhoe's conspiracy charge, the more it seemed to be covering up.

At about the same time that Keyhoe released his book, Donald Menzel published his long-awaited book on the subject as well. Menzel was the first American scientist to write a book on UFOs, and Harvard University Press published it. He had not changed his mind about the phenomenon. As in previous articles, he explained again in *Flying Saucers* that the objects were mainly uncommon atmospheric occurrences: temperature inversions, reflections, lenticular clouds, sun dogs, mock suns, ice crystals floating in the clouds, optical illusions, and, especially, mirages. The very idea that UFOs represented extraterrestrial intelligence was ludicrous. People who accepted this idea were lunatics, cultists, religious fanatics, or, at best, frightened and confused.[27]

Menzel, thinking that a direct attack on specific sighting reports was the best way to explode the "saucer myth," attempted to solve each major sighting that had achieved notoriety. The foo-fighters of World War II were the sun's reflections shining off imperfections of a bomber wing tip; Captain Mantell had chased a mock sun; the "windows" and structures that Chiles and Whitted had described were products of overexcited imaginations, although Menzel could not explain what it was they saw. To show how self-seekers had taken advantage of the gullible public, Menzel dwelled on the famous hoaxes of a few years before. He erroneously claimed there were more hoaxes than legitimate reports in the beginning of the phenomenon, and he spent an entire chapter describing Frank Scully's 1950 semihoax, *Behind the Flying Saucers*, and the events surrounding it.[28]

Menzel also dealt with the 1896–97 airships and thereby

moved these sightings into the UFO debate. Menzel believed the airships were either twinkling stars that appeared to move because of atmospheric refraction, cigar-shaped lenticular clouds, or mirages. The entire airship affair was a product of mass illusion; people wanted to see an airship and therefore did. To back up his argument, Menzel quoted Edison's statement that airship sightings were ridiculous. This, Menzel said, effectively burst the airship bubble and the sightings stopped after newspapers around the country published Edison's statement. If a person sighted an airship after the publication of Edison's remarks, Menzel reasoned, the sighter obviously had not read the article.[29]

To reinforce his arguments Menzel once again stressed the potential dangers of UFOs in psychological warfare. Americans were suffering from a case of "international jitters," Menzel said, and had been conditioned to report anything unusual because they were anxious about an atomic war. Also, science fiction writers had conditioned the American public to believe in other intelligent life in the universe; therefore, the public interpreted anything unusual in the sky as being evidence for this. Menzel saw no difference between the 1952–53 flying saucer scare and the hysterical reaction to the Orson Welles 1938 invasion from Mars broadcast. Menzel, as did the Robertson panel, believed the sightings represented a possible danger to the national security. "The public is afraid of saucers—and we need only a match to set off a nation-wide panic that could far exceed that of the Invasion from Mars. In fact, if a foreign power were to pull off a surprise attack on the United States, millions of Americans would conclude that the flying saucers from Mars or Venus were finally landing!"[30]

Menzel's book was successful. Published at the same time as the Keyhoe book, many libraries had to decide which book to purchase. They more often bought Menzel's book because he was an established scientist. Sometimes libraries bought both and put the Menzel book in the science section and the Keyhoe book in the science fiction section. One librarian was so hostile to Keyhoe's book that he decided "no amount of rationalizing about 'future historical importance,' 'balanced collections,' and 'public demand,' can justify their expenditure of tax dollars for books such as Keyhoe's—books whose purpose seems to us to satisfy a jaded taste for the bizarre and the sensational."[31] In addition, Keyhoe's popularity and looseness in thinking helped legitimize Menzel's views. Menzel wrote his book in an acceptable scientific manner. This, coupled with the subject's inherent illegitimacy, enabled Menzel's views to achieve substantial influence in the scientific community.

While the Keyhoe-Menzel debate raged, the Air Force, mindful of the previous year's hectic summer, moved to regularize and simplify its UFO investigating and reporting methods. First it issued Air Force Regulation 200-2 in August 1953, which superseded Air Force Letter 200-5. The regulation required an air base UFO officer to make a preliminary report of a sighting, and it spelled out exactly all the questions he was to ask of the UFO witnesses. The air base officer decided what priority to assign a report according to his determination of the report's intelligence value. The following year the Air Force amended AFR 200-2, stipulating that only the 4602d would make investigations. If a unit was not in the vicinity of a sighting, an air base officer was required to make a preliminary report and send it to the 4602d unit nearest him, which would determine if a field investigation was warranted. AFR 200-2 also took a firm public relations stance: it prohibited the release of *any* information about a sighting to the public except when the sighting was positively identified. In addition, while Air Force Letter 200-5 had stated that sightings should not be classified higher than restricted, the new regulation (200-2) said all sightings should be classified restricted at the very least. Finally, the regulation directed ATIC to continue analyzing UFO data as they came in from the 4602d units.[32]

The new regulation gave the Air Force strong control over the sighting reports it received, and it hoped this control would mean increased identification of the objects. The prohibition against giving out sighting information reflected the Air Force's attempts to institute the Robertson panel's desire to end public speculation about UFOs with the concomitant threat of increased reports. For the first time the Air Force had institutionalized secrecy at the air base level. To further ward off publicity leaks, the Joint Chiefs of Staff followed up 200-2 with Joint-Army-Navy-Air Force-Publication (JANAP) 146 in December 1953. Under the subheading of "Canadian-United States Communications Instructions for Reporting Vital Intelligence Sightings," the Joint Chiefs of Staff made releasing any information to the public about a UFO report a crime under the Espionage Act, punishable by a one-to-ten-year prison term or a $10,000 fine. JANAP 146 applied to anyone who knew it existed, including commercial airline pilots.[33] This action effectively stopped the flow of information to the public. Only if Blue Book could positively identify a sighting as a hoax or misidentification would the Air Force release information to the public. The policy was in effect until December 1969, when the Air Force terminated its involvement with UFOs.

The Blue Book status reports subtly reflected the Air Force's new attitude toward sightings. Instead of issuing monthly reports as before, Blue Book issued only four more status reports, all during 1953 and the first two in January and February. The reports displayed a certain defensiveness and concern for public relations. For instance, Blue Book mentioned in all four reports that the decline in sighting reports was due to a decline in newspaper publicity. There was a "direct relation" between newspaper publicity and UFO reports: one "highly publicized sighting would again trigger off another 'saucer' scare with resulting pressure on the Air Force and ATIC." Because of possible public hysteria, Project Blue Book was preparing a fact sheet for the public information officer in Washington to release. "Thus the Air Force cannot be accused of withholding information." ATIC's concern with public relations was further demonstrated in its new policy of channeling *all* its releases and information through the Secretary of the Air Force's Office of Public Information.[34]

Blue Book's last major ongoing project in 1953 was the Battelle Memorial Institute's statistical study of UFO characteristics. The institute had finally completed the study. It concluded that the objects did not appear to represent anything unknown or outside the capabilities of human technology, even though earlier in the year the institute acknowledged that the data were highly unreliable. Instead of immediately issuing the report to the press, evidence suggests that the Air Force decided to delay the study's release until the most opportune time.[35]

Thus the Air Force's involvement with the UFO controversy changed character rather completely during 1953. A year earlier, Blue Book, under Captain Ruppelt, had tried to set up procedures whereby it could systematically study the UFO phenomenon, at least within the bounds set by its limited funds and resources. But by the end of 1953 the opportunity for such an investigation was gone. Project Blue Book had only three staff members, its investigating capabilities had gone to another command, and most of its projects had died for lack of funds. Ruppelt, Fournet, and Chop were no longer involved and General Garland never again raised his voice in defense of a UFO investigation. The CIA-sponsored Robertson panel changed Blue Book's role from seeking the causes of sightings to keeping the sighting reports at a minimum or, preferably, stopping them completely. Although Project Blue Book continued its work, it would never again be able to conduct a program of thorough investigations. From 1953 to 1969 Project Blue Book's main thrust was public relations.

In the private sector, Ohio Northern University's study of UFOs also ended fruitlessly in 1953. Although the researchers had found that about 20 percent of the reports seemed to be of genuinely unusual phenomena, they could not make an adequate scientific study because they had received only 54 reports from the public out of the 200 they estimated they needed for scientific analysis.[36]

The CIA recommendations became critical for future Air Force action. It would claim for years afterward that it had conducted an adequate scientific investigation, complete with instruments (radarscope camera and Videon diffraction grid) to measure UFO characteristics. Moreover, the Air Force would use the Robertson panel as proof that it had sought the most able scientific evaluation. Meanwhile, the Air Force had unexpected help in its public relations efforts. A growing number of flying saucer "believers," who subscribed to the views of a new group of people called contactees, emerged in 1953 to confuse the controversy even more. But that is another story.

5

CONTACTEES, CLUBS, AND CONFUSION

As public interest in unidentified flying objects grew, the UFO phenomenon entered popular culture. Because of its nature, the phenomenon easily lent itself to science fiction, fantasy, sensationalism, and hoax. In the early and middle 1950s two groups in American society exploited the sensational aspects of the phenomenon. As would be expected, the Hollywood movie industry entered the scene early, capitalizing on the growing audience for stories associated with UFOs. But the group that captured public attention most was the contactees—people who claimed personal contact, communication, and interaction with beings from another planet. Rising to popularity at the same time as the Air Force was trying to reduce the number of UFO reports, the contactees increased publicity on the subject and counteracted many of these Air Force efforts. Similarly, the contactees hindered the attempts of people concerned about the UFO phenomenon to convince the public and the Air Force to treat the phenomenon seriously. Ironically, the contactees also aided the Air Force by making seemingly ridiculous claims and inviting widespread ridicule of all UFO witnesses. The contactees did not participate directly in the debate over the origin of UFOs, but they embodied many of its elements and became, above all, a divisive force in the controversy.

Since the 1950s there have been many instances when reputable individuals claimed to have close encounters with UFOs. Occasionally, people with no discernible reason to lie, who were respected members of a community—teachers, ministers, policemen—claimed to have seen occupants or beings in or near a UFO. Puzzled and frightened, these witnesses usually reported their experiences to the police or Air Force because they wanted a reasonable explanation for such a fantastic experience. They often asked for anonymity and were not interested in gaining publicity or money. Their UFO experience seemed to be an aberration from the normal flow of their daily lives. Nothing in their backgrounds suggested that they hallucinated or perpetrated a hoax (although a serious investigator could not ignore these possibilities). Sometimes these witnesses presented evidence of their experience in the form of corroborating witnesses, flattened and scorched grass, broken tree limbs, and deep depressions in the ground. Often they claimed that these encounters produced strange side effects, such as electrical failures, automobile engine failure, and radio interference.[1]

This group was completely different from the psychologically aberrant individuals who, apparently because of mental problems, had delusions of communicating with extraterrestrial beings. These people often claimed to receive signals from outer space or to have mystical encounters with spacemen. Their experiences did not constitute deviations from their daily lives, and their stories usually were incoherent, inconsistent, or part of a pattern of psychical or occult experiences. Like the first group, these people generally did not seek publicity or fabricate hoaxes intentionally.[2]

The contactees represented an entirely different type of UFO witness. They exhibited behavior consistent with the assertion that they fabricated hoaxes. They did not report their "experiences" to a reputable investigatory agency. Instead, they publicized them by writing books and articles, presenting lectures, and appearing on radio and television shows. Indeed, the contactees had no fear of ridicule and eagerly sought publicity. They often organized special flying saucer clubs based on their experiences and used the clubs to help publicize their stories. Also, their "experiences" often differed markedly from all other UFO observers, in that some contactees claimed to have taken a ride in a flying saucer and described the ride and the planets they visited in great detail.

Moreover, most contactees reported that space people had charged them with a mission, which, they said, was why they had to seek publicity.

The five major contactees who rose to national stardom in the 1950s were George Adamski, Truman Bethurum, Daniel Fry, Orfeo Angelucci, and Howard Menger. Each attracted a large following. The five men also knew each other and reinforced each other's claims.

George Adamski was the most famous contactee of the 1950s. He worked as a handyman in a four-stool cafe near Mount Palomar, California. Previous to his encounters with the space-men, he had billed himself as "professor" and had written a tract about a body of thought he devised and called the "Royal Order of Tibet." [3] Failing to gain recognition as a mystic, he turned to science fiction to capitalize on his interest in astronomy and photography. His main endeavor in this genre was a novel he wrote in 1946 about an imaginary trip to the stars.[4]

When UFO sightings began, Adamski conceived of a way to take advantage of the current interest. The product of this idea was *Flying Saucers Have Landed*, which he coauthored with British writer Desmond Leslie in 1953. In the book Adamski related his contactee experiences. They began in 1946 when he "actually saw with [his] own naked eyes a gigantic space craft." The next year Adamski saw 184 saucers one night passing over him one after the other "as if in review." Unfortunately he took no pictures of this extraordinary procession. From then on, he said, he observed the saucers regularly.[5]

Adamski's first "contact" came on November 20, 1952, when he and four friends saw a spaceship land about one mile off the road in Desert Center, California. He told his friends to wait at the car and rushed to the landing spot, taking pictures all the way (he had two cameras with him). When he neared the craft, a man with long blond hair confronted him. The man was from Venus. Adamski and the Venusian conversed telepathically and by sign language; the Venusian told Adamski that he had come to Earth to stop atomic testing because the radiation from fallout was damaging the other planets in the solar system. The Venusian did not want his picture taken because then he would no longer be able to roam incognito among the earthlings. The Venusian expressed an interest in a roll of Adamski's film and asked to borrow it, promising to return it soon. Adamski consented and the Venusian then allowed him to take pictures of the spacecraft as it took off and left the area. Adamski took over seven rolls of film that day; but, as luck would have it, he forgot to focus one camera and the other was not working properly. The result was one blurry photograph. After the Venusian took off in his spacecraft, Adamski looked in the desert sand and discovered the Venusian's footprints, which had strange hieroglyphics in the middle of the soles. Adamski just happened to have some plaster of paris with him and made casts of the footprints. He and several friends attempted in vain to decipher the hieroglyphics.[6]

Adamski's major work, *Inside the Space Ships*, appeared in 1955. He told how he met incognito space people in Los Angeles bars and cafes. At various times they invited him aboard Martian, Venusian, Saturnian, and Jupiterian spaceships. On board these ships Adamski met beautiful Martian and Venusian spacewomen and the elder philosopher of the space people—the Master. While the women served refreshments, Adamski and the Master engaged in long and deep conversations about the state of the universe and Earth's position in it. The Master described other planets' social and political systems and made it clear that Earth was primitive. The space people were benevolent beings who had come to save mankind from eventual atomic destruction and, as the Master explained, to stop the Earth's atomic radiation from harming the other planets. The space people had a dual mission: to save the earthlings from themselves and to save the universe from the earthlings. They told Adamski that they had selected individuals to carry their message to the people. Jesus had been one of these messengers; Adamski was another. He had to carry their message to the Earth people and bear the ridicule of those who would not believe him.[7]

Truman Bethurum followed Adamski's lead in 1954 with *Aboard a Flying Saucer*. Bethurum was then a mechanic laying asphalt in the California desert. One night eight to ten little men awakened him as he slept near his rig, and he noticed a flying saucer near them on the ground. The little men took the curious Bethurum aboard the scow, as they called it, and introduced him to the captain, a gorgeous woman named Aura Rhanes. She was similar to Earth women except for her extraordinary beauty. Aura explained that she and her crew came from a planet called Clarion, which was in the same solar system as Earth. Astronomers could not see Clarion because its orbit always placed it directly behind the sun. The Clarionites had been coming to Earth for many years and were able to walk around unnoticed. They were "very religious, understanding, kind, friendly and . . . trusting." They had come to Earth, Aura explained, to reaffirm the values of marriage, family, and fidelity, because a "dreadful Paganism" was at work and the Clarionites did not want to see Earth people destroy themselves. Aura feared atomic war and wanted to prevent Earth from blowing itself up, an event that would cause "considerable confusion" in space. In the course of their lengthy discussions, Aura explained to Bethurum in detail the idyllic quality of life on Clarion, a life that Earth people could enjoy if they thought and behaved correctly.[8]

Before the Clarionites departed for home, Bethurum met with them eleven times. Sometimes he saw them in cafes, but there they ignored him because they did not want to reveal their identities. When they finally left and Bethurum told his story, no one believed him except George Adamski, who encouraged him to publicize his experiences. Bethurum thought Adamski was a great man and an authority on space travel.[9]

In the same year (1954) "Dr." Daniel Fry's *White Sands Incident* came out. One night, when Fry was working in an unspecified capacity at the White Sands Proving Ground in New Mexico, he saw a flying saucer land near him. He walked up to it and heard a voice say: "Better not touch the hull, pal, it's still hot!" This frightened him but the voice was reassuring: "Take it easy, pal, you're among friends." [10] The voice, which later identified itself as "A-lan," invited Fry into the saucer and explained the details of the saucer's power. Fry remembered the conversation and carefully recorded the technical data:

When certain elements such as platinum are properly prepared and treated with a saturation exposure to a beam of very high energy photons, the binding energy particle will be generated outside the nucleus. Since these particles tend to repel each other as well as all matter they, like the electron, tend to migrate to the surface of the metal where they manifest as a repellent force.[11]

Alan, as Fry called the voice, whisked him to New York City and back in about thirty minutes. During the flight Alan told Fry to write a book about this experience to prevent the world from falling into the "terrible abyss" that nuclear weapons brought about. The spacemen, Alan explained, were forced to contact Fry because they would upset the "ego balance" of the Earth's civilization if they showed themselves. Alan said the key to peace and happiness for Earth was *"understanding"*: if all the nations on Earth would just understand each other, then there would be no more war.[12]

Orfeo Angelucci, a mechanic at an aircraft corporation, continued the contactee tradition in 1955 with his mystically oriented *Secret of the Saucers*. Angelucci's experiences began when he saw a flying saucer land in a Los Angeles field; he inspected the craft and heard a voice, which identified itself as a "space brother," explain that he was visiting Earth to record the "spiritual evolution of man." He was concerned that Earth's "material advancement" was endangering life's evolution. A few weeks later Angelucci saw another flying saucer in the same location and entered it on impulse. Inside a voice revealed the secrets of the saucer's power. He took a ride in the saucer and was so impressed that, during the flight, he underwent a mystical-religious experience that demonstrated his kinship with the space people. After the flight he met a spaceman named Neptune who instructed him about the universe and life in space.[13]

Angelucci then began to meet the spacemen in mundane places. For instance, one contact took place in a Greyhound bus terminal. Unable to keep these experiences a secret, he gave weekly talks, published a newspaper, and attended flying saucer conventions, where he met Adamski, Bethurum, and other contactees whom he admired greatly. One day he realized he had had amnesia for a week and eventually discovered that he had been spiritually transported to another planet. There he met the beautiful Lyra and her friend Orion, who explained that Angelucci had been a spaceman also named Neptune in another life. They exposed Angelucci to all the wonders of their beautiful planet and told him that Earth had better change its course—by mankind working together benevolently—or a calamity would ensue in 1986. Angelucci returned to Earth knowing that in his first life he was a spaceman with his spiritual heritage in the heavens. In a later contact, Angelucci met Jesus, who told him the space people were on Earth to help mankind and were traveling incognito everywhere. "This is the beginning of the New Age," Jesus said. At his last meeting with Lyra, Angelucci drank from the crystal goblet and finally understood that, even though he must return to the mundane world, he, Lyra, Orion, and the other Neptune were joined together forever in love.[14]

Howard Menger, a self-employed sign painter, was the fifth of the major contactees. He told about his experiences in *From Outer Space To You* (1959). Menger had his first contact as a child. He was playing in the woods when he chanced upon a beautiful woman who told him that the space people were watching over him. He did not have another contact until he was an adult but sensed during all those years that the space people were helping him. He felt they had helped save his life in World War II when he was in hand-to-hand combat with the Japanese. When the space people finally contacted Menger again, they revealed that they came from Mars and Venus. They took him to the moon and gave him a guided tour of the wonderful buildings and sights there. Menger explained that the moon's atmosphere was similar to the Earth's and that he could breathe the air easily. Eventually Menger learned that he was a reincarnated Jupiterian put on Earth to perform good deeds for the benefit of mankind. At one of his lectures about his experiences, he met a beautiful woman, Marla, whom he immediately recognized as being a spacewoman, even though she did not know this herself. Menger divorced his wife and married Marla; they made a "natural couple," destined for each other because of their common heritage. During his lecture tour, Menger met contactee George Van Tassel, who accompanied him on the tour. Later Menger met George Adamski and said he was a "great soul." [15]

The Adamski, Bethurum, Fry, Angelucci, and Menger stories all contained similar concepts. They defined the contactee literature genre and illustrated the contactees' anthropomorphic style of thinking. These concepts possibly reflected the contactees' anxieties about post–World War II American society and, more specifically, the prospect of atomic war, the role of religion in a technological society, the yearning for peace and harmony in the cold-war political climate, and the possibility of extraterrestrial visitation. An analysis of these themes is at least essential for understanding why the contactees became so popular.

According to the contactees, space people came from utopian planets free from war, poverty, unhappiness, or want. Everyone on Clarion was employed and poverty was unknown. No Earth-like problems existed, although some extraterrestrials did mention enemies. Moreover, the space people, if not immortal, lived thousands of years and usually could be reincarnated in another life. The planet Angelucci visited had "eternal youth, eternal spring and eternal day." The contactees portrayed the space people as rational, technologically advanced, perfected "humans" who understood the disastrous implications of Earth's technology. Angelucci's space people told him that "man's material knowledge has far outstripped the growth of brotherly love and spiritual understanding in his heart." [16]

Operating within a common fear of the 1950s—the inevitability of atomic war—the contactees invested the space people with missions that promised society a release from cold-war tensions. The space people came to help Earth people avoid war, stop atomic testing, and help mankind work together for a benevolent society. But they were not completely altruistic and were working for their own interests as well as those of Earth. They wanted to stop atomic testing because the leaking radiation affected their planets; they wanted to stop an atomic war because it would upset the solar system's delicate balance. The contactees avoided potentially troublesome political issues in the 1950s by having the nonideological space people expound these beliefs and by taking an anticommunist stance in their literature.

In keeping with the aliens' humanity and benevolence, they came from planets where civilization was based on a god-figure, such as the "Infinite Father" or "Infinite Creator." The space people lived within a religious ethos that supported their moral reason for coming to Earth. They placed Jesus in a secondary position and did not worship him because he died on Earth for Earth people. The contactees said that either the space people or God had sent Jesus to Earth to fulfill a mission. Jesus, the Master told Adamski, "was sent to be reincarnated on your world to help your people, as had others before him." His death taught the space people to carry on their mission "in a way less perilous to those concerned than actual birth on your planet." For Angelucci's aliens, Jesus was an "infinite entity of the sun" and "not of earth's evolution." [17] In this sense, the contactees transformed Jesus into a spaceman and allied God, Jesus, and the space people into a unified system. Moreover, because both Jesus and the contactees were space messengers, the contactees compared themselves to Jesus and thereby strengthened the impact of the religious implications of their experiences. Although the contactees never claimed to be on a religious par with Jesus, the parallel was still clear.

Apart from religious and ideological implications, the contactees dealt with a host of more mundane problems. In explaining why aliens did not land publicly, they juxtaposed the space people's benevolence with the Earth people's hostility and psychological frailty. It was these Earth qualities that prevented the aliens from landing publicly. As Adamski said: humans would have a "tremendous amount of fear" of the space people and probably would "tear [them] to pieces." Daniel Fry's Alan explained that most Earth people would consider the space people "potential tyrants" and would try to destroy them. Menger's space friends feared that a landing would result in hysteria and panic and, Menger reasoned, "there would be endless investigations and controversy, and the work and message the space people have come to deliver would be snowed under by red tape." But contacting selected Earth people was not a problem for the space people. Regardless of where the aliens were from, be it Mars, Venus, Jupiter, or Clarion, they looked like human beings, except that the women were fantastically beautiful. Thus, the space people were able to mingle incognito with humans.[18]

If the space people looked just like Earth people, why did they not carry out their own mission instead of having a human do it? The contactees did not answer this question. They sidestepped it with self-conscious explanations of why the space people chose them in particular. They chose Adamski because, in photographing saucers for many years, his thoughts "inevitably" reached them and demonstrated his "sincerity." They chose Bethurum simply because he "happened to be close" when the scow landed. They selected Fry because he had one of those rare brains that could receive as well as send telepathic signals. Also, the "buffetings of fate" gave Fry an "unusual depth and breadth of perception and understanding" which made him an ideal contact. The aliens contacted Angelucci because he was simple, humble, publicly unknown, and possessed a "higher vibrational pattern" than other men. Aliens singled out Menger because he was one of them, a "rebirth" from another planet. Presumably these characteristics made it easier for the contactee to carry out his prescribed mission.[19]

Along with these personal qualities, all the contactees had the experience of entering and/or flying in a saucer. This experience seemed to undergo an evolution in the contactee literature. Adamski, who wrote first, observed the saucer close up but could not enter it. Bethurum, the second contactee of 1953, entered the saucer but it did not leave the ground. The next year Fry claimed that he went from New Mexico to New York City. In Adamski's second book (1955), he claimed to have flown to the moon; he did not actually land but saw all its wonders—inhabitants, cities, plants—through a special viewing apparatus. He saw Venus the same way. Angelucci went further. In addition to riding in a saucer, he was mystically transported to the planet Lucifer, previously a piece of a larger planet that had existed in another time zone and had been destroyed in an ancient war before the aliens were benevolent. In Menger's 1959 account, his flying saucer landed on the moon, where the inhabitants gave him a sightseeing tour. Menger was the only one of the five major contactees who claimed to have landed on a celestial body after a flight in a flying saucer.

Similarly, each claimed to have had the earliest contact, Menger's pre–World War II claim topping the list. The escalation of contactee claims appeared to be a function of trying to outdo one another in their efforts to be *the* most important contactee. Yet most contactees seemed reluctant to become too sensational. They preferred not to overextend themselves scientifically. Menger, who constantly escalated his claims over the years, eventually found himself in completely indefensible scientific positions, and subsequent astronomical discoveries forced him to recant on many of his positions.

The heart of contactee literature was in the mission the space people gave the contactee. This mission provided the central rationale for the contactee's publicity-oriented behavior. Adamski had to impart the Master's knowledge to Earth people so that they could avert the disaster of an atomic war. Bethurum's task was to make sure the Earth people understood Aura Rhanes's message: unless Earth changed its ways, "the water in your deserts will mostly be tears." Fry obeyed Alan's order to spread the word about universal *"understanding"* to prevent the Earth's nations from engaging in an atomic holocaust. Alan passionately directed Fry to "tell the story through your newspapers, your radio and television stations. If necessary, shout it from the house-tops, but let the people know." The space people warned Angelucci of a terrible war of extreme devastation and charged him with a Christ-like mission: "For the present you are our emissary, Orfeo, and you must act! Even though the people of Earth laugh derisively and mock you as a lunatic, tell them about us!" Later he emphasized, "As you love your brothers of Earth, Orfeo, fight to your dying breath to help them toward a world of love, light and unity." Menger's friends did not specifically forecast a catastrophe but did tell him that wars, torture, and destruction would result from people's "misunderstanding"; Menger had to inform others of his experiences in the hope of promoting better understanding.[20]

The contactees had to make the Earth people believe them but had difficulty obtaining reasonable evidence to support their claimed experiences. Because Adamski's space people did not want him to take their pictures, he had to rely on the Venusian's footprints and a few blurry photographs. The Air Force analyzed Adamski's photos and decided they were probably hoaxes. Bethurum's evidence was a note written in French that Aura Rhanes had supposedly translated into English and Chinese. Angelucci and Fry offered no evidence, preferring to have their stories stand on their own merits. Menger was the only major contactee to offer tangible evidence. One day he chanced upon a cabin in the woods with a Saturnian inside who was playing the piano; the Saturnian told Menger that he too could play this enchanting music, even though he did not know how to play the piano. Menger arrived home to find that he could play the music he had heard, and he immediately made a commercial record album. On another occasion, one of Menger's space friends gave him a "space potato," which supposedly had five times the protein of an Earth potato. Menger also built a small "free energy motor" from the space people's telepathic instructions; it did nothing in particular, but Menger considered it good evidence of alien visitation.[21]

Not having any reasonable evidence of their own, the contactees often used the Air Force's role in the controversy to prove that flying saucers existed. Adamski and Bethurum said the Air Force's secrecy in investigating UFOs constituted proof that flying saucers existed. Angelucci implied that the Air Force was a party to the space people's plans: the Air Force was handling the issue of extraterrestrial visitation "precisely as those visitors have anticipated and desired them to do." If the Air Force were to release all it knew about flying saucers, "It would be the beginning of national panic that no amount of sane reasoning could quell." All this, of course, proved the existence of flying saucers.[22]

A composite contactee formula was as follows. People from a

utopian planet accidentally or by design contacted an unsuspecting human. The extraterrestrials gave the contactee a ride in their spacecraft, explained the workings of the craft, told about their own planet's civilization, and predicted dire events to take place on Earth that also would affect the other planets. They endowed the contactee with a mission that, if successful, would avert the calamity, allowing Earth to exist in peace and harmony. The contactee, having little or no proof, embarked on a publicity campaign to get his message to the people.

Adamski, Bethurum, Fry, Angelucci, and Menger were the most prolific and publicized contactees but not the only ones. Minor figures existed as well, all of whom used the above formula and all of whom had their local followings. Buck Nelson flew to Mars, Venus, and the moon; as proof, he offered to sell packets of hair from a 385-pound Venusian St. Bernard dog. The space people took George Van Tassel on a flying saucer ride and explained the "true history" of the beginnings of life on Earth. George Hunt Williamson, one of the alleged witnesses to Adamski's first contact, claimed he could communicate with men from Mars by using a ham radio set and Ouija board. It seemed that the Martians had heard other earthlings communicate by radio and had "managed to dope out the language." Lauro Mundo claimed to communicate telepathically with the space people. Dana Howard went to Venus, married a Venusian, and raised a family—all while she was napping on her living room couch.[23]

Some contactees not only publicized their experiences but used them to appeal directly for money. George Van Tassel said the space people had dictated designs for a rejuvenation machine that would guarantee everlasting youth; all he needed was $42,000 to develop the plans. Otis T. Carr claimed to have plans for a genuine flying saucer and succeeded in raising many thousands of dollars to build it. Although most contactees seemed to be in the flying saucer business primarily for money, at least one, Gabriel Green, saw the political potential as well. His California-based organization, The Amalgamated Flying Saucer Clubs of America, published *Thy Kingdom Come*, a semireligious magazine. Using the organization and magazine as a political base, Green ran for the presidency of the United States in 1960 on a space and peace platform but dropped out of the race before the election. Then he ran for the Senate in 1962, garnering over 171,000 votes.[24]

The contactees' chief problem was gaining publicity for their messages and themselves. They did this by writing books, pamphlets, and tracts, presenting lectures, and attending flying saucer conventions where they could sell their literature and deliver their lectures. George Van Tassel's annual Giant Rock Convention in Yucca Valley, California, became the largest and most highly publicized of such events. In 1954, its first year, the convention attracted over five thousand people. Here the contactees gathered to lecture about their experiences. Spectators could buy books, pamphlets, photographs, records, and other souvenirs from the contactees' booths on the grounds.

The conventioneers generally assumed that the space people looked favorably upon the meeting and a participant was sure to spot a flying saucer near the area. If this did not happen, Van Tassel would sometimes send up a balloon with flares attached to it to create some excitement and controversy. At times the space people would make their presence known in mysterious ways. Gray Barker, a popular contactee-oriented author and publisher, once found some blood near his book stall. He and others immediately were convinced that it was "space blood" from an extraterrestrial. Because the blood did not clot as they had expected, this, Barker claimed, substantiated his theory that space people walked among them. The faithful rallied to Barker's side and attacked the skeptics who wanted an analysis of the blood before they would judge its origin. The skeptics won the debate later when the analysis proved the blood's menstrual origin.[25]

Numerous flying saucer clubs held their own conventions and invited a contactee to lecture. Green's club sponsored some tremendously successful conventions in Los Angeles in the late 1950s; thousands of people attended and one convention agenda included over forty-five speakers for a two-day event. These conventions became part of the contactees' lecture circuit. If business was slow, contactees sometimes would sponsor their own conventions, as Howard Menger did on his front lawn where excitement ran high when people spotted several blue lights rising from the back of Menger's barn. Buck Nelson, who claimed to have eaten dinner with the rulers of nearly all the planets in the solar system, held a convention at his home in Missouri and was left with over nine thousand hot dogs when only three hundred people attended.[26]

The contactees were media events, and radio and television shows helped them gain publicity. The sensationalism of the contactees' claims always provided good entertainment. In New York, Long John Nebel furnished the most consistent outlet for contactee stories on his late-night radio talk show; Menger's fame was chiefly due to his appearances on the Long John show. Steve Allen's nationally televised "Tonight" show featured many contactees, as did the NBC "Betty White Show" on which Truman Bethurum appeared several times. In addition to the national shows, many locally broadcast shows helped feed the growing public feeling that the contactee and the contactee-oriented groups made up the essence of the UFO phenomenon. The public found it difficult to distinguish between contactee experiences and those of reputable witnesses. For example, a television producer would invite Keyhoe to appear on a show with a contactee, not understanding the difference between these two people. Keyhoe usually refused these invitations because he did not want to be associated in any way with the contactees.[27]

The growth of flying saucer clubs in the mid-fifties clearly indicated the contactees' success in gaining publicity and their subsequent domination of the UFO scene. These clubs were of two types: contactee clubs and contactee-oriented clubs. Many contactees organized their followers into local and national clubs designed to propagate their message. Daniel Fry, using Alan's message about the importance of understanding in world politics, formed *"understanding"* units. With fifteen in California alone and more around the country, Fry had a ready market for his publication *Understanding*. George Van Tassel established the College of Universal Wisdom, the entrance requirement being a subscription to Van Tassel's journal, *Proceedings*. George Adamski formed the Adamski Foundation, and Truman Bethurum the Sanctuary of Thought.[28]

The majority of flying saucer clubs were contactee-oriented. They were not centered around an individual contactee, but the members believed contactee stories or, at least, kept an open mind. Most of these people did not discriminate between Keyhoe's brand of serious UFO investigation and contactee claims. In 1954 the anticontactee *Saucers* magazine illustrated this confusion when it polled its readers about whom they considered to be the best authors on UFOs. Keyhoe came in first, followed by Adamski, Scully (*Behind the Flying Saucers*), and Fry. Similarly, the Space Observers League of Spokane, Washington, fully supported Keyhoe and his theories and unhesitatingly accepted Daniel Fry's claims. Over 150 contactee-oriented clubs existed in the mid-1950s. Invariably, they held conventions and sponsored contactee lecturers. Also, the contactee clubs blended into occult areas, such as astrology and mysticism, and were able to assimilate many of the previously existing occult and psychic clubs which originally were not a part of the flying saucer world. For example, an editorial in *The Spacecrafter*, the newsletter of the Phoenix, Arizona, Spacecraft Research Association, said the club's objective was to "acquaint ourselves with as many facts as possible concerning UFO's, Metaphysics, Mysticism, and other related subjects." [29]

Some contactee-oriented clubs subscribed to one of the more outlandish flying saucer theories. It held that if a person learned too much about flying saucers, or if he discovered the "secret" of their origin, then he might expect a visit from the mysterious and frightening Men In Black (MIB). The MIBs were aliens from an unknown planet who would silence any unfortunate individual by threats, harassment, or worse. The MIB theory was remarkably resilient and provided a constant source of anxiety for some individuals who delved deeply into the saucer mystery.[30]

The contactees and their publicity posed a serious threat to legitimate UFO investigation and research groups. These groups thought the contactees were confusing the public about whose activities were legitimate and whose were not. In addition, non-contactee-oriented UFO investigation groups were not nearly as popular as the flying saucer clubs and did not have as much support. The investigation and research groups tried to solve the UFO problem and refused to accept contactee claims, even though the members read about them in periodicals. As the contactees gained popularity, the investigation groups took on the difficult task of exposing them but were not often successful, for the contactee controversy created factions within their ranks. *Orbit*, a publication of one research group and one of the best periodicals in the early 1950s, folded partially because its readers shifted to contactee-oriented journals. Similarly, the Grand Rapids Flying Saucer Club, which published *UFORUM*, died when members became split over contactee claims. Most noncontactee groups published articles determinedly hostile to contactee claims. James Moseley's *Nexus* and *Saucer News*, Max Miller's *Saucers*, Lex Mebane's *Civilian Saucer Investigation Newsletter, The UFO Newsletter*, and other periodicals featured extensive exposés of Menger, Adamski, Van Tassel, and others.[31]

To Keyhoe and Coral Lorenzen (the latter of the Aerial Phenomena Research Organization), the contactees were dangerous enemies. From 1953 to the early 1960s, Keyhoe and Lorenzen spent much time trying to correct the damage to the legitimacy of UFO research. Keyhoe complained to Lorenzen in 1954 that he spent a lot of time "cleaning up" after the contactees or "getting the record straight" about their claims. Lorenzen wanted to expose Adamski by proving his photographs were fakes but, as Keyhoe pointed out, "Knowing it and proving it are, unfortunately, not the same thing." [32]

Eventually some of the exposés began to have an effect on the contactees' claims. Adamski's "witnesses" recanted many of their statements and considerably weakened his case, although he maintained his claims until his death in 1965. When evidence mounted in 1959 that Howard Menger's experiences were fallacious, he tried to salvage his veracity by claiming his story was "allegorical" and his book "fact/fiction." A New York lawyer, Jules B. St. Germain, developed a scheme to prove George Van

Tassel's experiences a hoax. He mailed Van Tassel some fake flying saucer and occupant photographs that he had taken in his home; Van Tassel insisted immediately that the photographs were "conclusive proof" and used them to bolster his own contactee claims. When Van Tassel appeared on the Long John Nebel show, St. Germain also appeared unannounced and asked Van Tassel about the photographs. Van Tassel insisted on their authenticity and St. Germain took the opportunity to expose the hoax, thereby putting Van Tassel in an embarrassing and indefensible position. Daniel Fry, stung by charges that he had fabricated his story, offered to take a lie detector test. He failed it. He later claimed that the test was rigged against him. Eventually many minor figures dropped out of the flying saucer world and some were imprisoned for fraud. Space ride claimant Rheinholdt Schmidt and saucer builder Otis T. Carr received prison sentences when convicted of bilking people out of thousands of dollars to develop a flying saucer or to mine for "free energy crystals." [33]

In spite of the exposés, Angelucci, Adamski, Fry, and Bethurum steadfastly refused to recant no matter what evidence their critics used against them. The contactee clubs thrived during the 1950s, even though their numbers decreased by the late 1950s and early 1960s and the minor figures faded. The contactees' influence on the public and press hampered serious UFO researchers' efforts to legitimize the subject. The UFO phenomenon had always encountered ridicule, such that many reputable individuals were afraid to report sightings and scientists refused to view the subject seriously. Indeed, ridicule was probably the most decisive factor that prevented professional people and the public from treating the subject seriously. The contactees' emergence and their popularity and publicity succeeded in entrenching even deeper the ridicule factor in the public imagination. From the mid-1950s to 1972, people with little knowledge of the phenomenon constantly confused the "lunatic fringe" with serious UFO investigators and researchers. Civilian Saucer Intelligence of New York in its newsletter bemoaned the fact that contactees received so much publicity in the news media. This massive publicity, the article stated, "conspires to help the audacious 'contactee' on his path to fame and fortune—and in the process, to help wreck the reputation of flying saucers, which are more and more indissolubly linked, in the public mind, with the fantasies of these well-publicized tale-spinners." [34]

The contactees scared off many people who were genuinely interested in the subject. Even Ruppelt purportedly felt the effects of the contactees. He revised his 1956 book in 1959 and totally reversed his open-minded position; he stated positively that UFOs as a unique phenomenon did not exist and attempted to erase his identification with the phenomenon. Although no one can know for sure his reasons for this reversal (he died of a heart attack in 1960), his wife stated years later that the constant agitation of the contactees and their followers, along with lack of proof for the extraterrestrial hypothesis, contributed to Ruppelt's reversal. The Air Force was pleased with the reversal, and Project Blue Book chief Robert Friend fed Ruppelt information through the Office of Information to help him write the new chapters. [35]

Serious UFO researchers dismissed the people who believed the contactee stories (contactee followers) as psychologically disturbed innocents with a will to believe or, simply, "the lunatic fringe." The situation was more complex than this. It involved a logical belief system that evolved in contactee follower thinking and acted as a buffer to outside attacks on them. As such, it is necessary to separate the contactees from their followers.

Contactee followers believed, as did legitimate UFO investigators and researchers, that flying saucers (UFOs) existed. The difference between the two groups was the reasoning that followed the belief. Most serious UFO investigators either refused to speculate on the origin of the objects or believed the extraterrestrial hypothesis best explained the evidence. They were split over whether to accept reputable witness claims of occupant sightings as part of the evidence, and many were hostile to any claims of communication. When a contactee claimed direct social intercourse with an alien and had no reasonable evidence to back up even the fact that he had sighted a UFO, most serious UFO investigators denied the claim as a fabrication.

The contactee followers, on the other hand, were not so

concerned with the evidence. Believing the saucers existed and, from available reports, were products of an extraterrestrial intelligence with a highly advanced technology, the contactee followers accepted contactee claims based on the contactees' sincerity. They did not ask for evidence. Moreover, already assuming that the aliens could routinely explore space, the contactee followers logically accepted the notion that the aliens must have overcome the problems of advanced technology (pollution, waste, and destructive weapons). And if their technological capabilities had not destroyed them through war, it was probably because they desired to preserve life and were able to do so. Hence, the aliens had a moral sense. Therefore, when a contactee sincerely said he met a moral, benevolent, technologically-advanced space person from a utopian world who wanted to help save Earth, the contactee followers' logic dictated that the contactee was telling the truth. The key here is the sincerity of the contactees; all the major ones seemed to have had more than the required amount. Serious investigators were always struck by the contactees' sincerity and how people seemed to *want* to believe them.

The contactee followers, then, based their belief on their own logical system. They did not ask What are they? or Are they here? but *Why* are they here? They went past the accepted thought of serious UFO investigators and directly dealt with the implications of extraterrestrial intervention in human affairs. John Godwin, in *Occult America*, equated the contactee followers with the New Guinea Cargo Cultists. This was perhaps unfair. The contactees did not regard the space people as deities. They were always careful to say that the space people had advanced to their high level only with God's help. The aliens' religion was compatible with Christianity. Believers did not have to respect and admire atheists. The contactees characterized themselves as messengers and did not insist that they were deities (although they came close to this position by equating their mission with Jesus' mission).[36]

Robert Ellwood, a religion scholar, suggested that the role of messenger placed the contactee in the shaman tradition. This argument has merit. The shaman is a man in special communication with the spirit world, fighting evil spirits for the good of the community. He acquires his role either through heredity or a sudden, unexpected vision, trance, or seizure. If the contactees did have a shaman role, then the contactee groups could be sects. Most groups possessed a body of writings or teachings and a dogma to guide the members' thought and behavior.[37]

Other scholars have not been so generous in their appraisal of the contactee followers. Because of the religious and sensational aspects of contactee thought, some academicians have characterized the contactee followers as insane or as lunatics. H. Taylor Buckner, a Berkeley sociologist, observed that the typical contactee club members were poorly educated, elderly, widowed or single women with physical and mental infirmities, older infirm men, and younger "schizophrenics." Although such people most probably belonged to these clubs, they were not the only members. People of all ages, classes, and, to a lesser degree, educational backgrounds, belonged. For instance, Leon Festinger's small, Minnesota-based, contactee-oriented group, discussed in *When Prophecy Fails*, consisted mainly of young and educated people. Basically, though, contactee followers were gullible people who, through lack of adequate factual information about the UFO phenomenon, formulated a belief system that easily incorporated the contactees' claims as fact.[38]

Like the contactees, the Hollywood motion picture industry moved in early to capitalize on public interest in UFOs. The first films with flying saucer themes predated contactee literature by two years, perhaps because the industry was quicker to realize the market potential of the flying saucer theme. The subject of flying saucers was ideally suited for the movies. Using spectacular special effects, a film maker could exploit the sensational implications of the extraterrestrial hypothesis. Both the movies and the contactees dwelled on the fantasy aspects of UFOs, but whereas the contactees pictured the extraterrestrials as basically beneficent but with a potential for hostility, Hollywood portrayed the space people as both beneficent and hostile, with an emphasis on the latter. For most motion pictures about flying saucers, the destructive potential of hostile beings from an advanced extraterrestrial civilization was a standard theme.[39]

The first and perhaps best film with a flying saucer motif was Robert Wise's *The Day the Earth Stood Still*.[40] Released in 1951, it contained most elements of later contactee literature. A handsome benevolent being from a utopian planet landed his saucer near the White House and brought the message that atomic testing was harming other planets. The alien was semi-immortal; his life span, which only God could end, could be hundreds of years long. The Earth people reacted with hostility and attempted to detroy him, but he escaped, mingled with the populace, and succeeded in delivering his message to Earth's major scientists. The film brought together the themes of the alien as beneficent, the Earth people as hostile, the dangers of the atomic bomb, the alien's ability to walk on Earth incognito, and immortality. But the film left out the messenger—the contactee. Because the themes in the film were so much like later contactee literature, it is possible that some contactees may have drawn upon the film as a source for their ideas.

The 1951 Howard Hawks film *The Thing* was the first to present the extraterrestrials-as-hostile theme. In it an alien crashed in a flying saucer and brought havoc to a group of scientists who tried to capture him. The movie portrayed the alien as intelligent but bent on purposeless, irrational destruction. The alien strongly resembled Frankenstein's monster. In the end, Earth people destroyed the alien and the movie avoided the problem of the alien's origin and his purpose on Earth. Some of the other characters in the movie reflected popular thought about the Air Force's UFO investigation in 1951 by poking fun at the Project Grudge report, which stated that all UFO sightings were mistakes. After Earth people confirmed the existence of the downed flying saucer, they read portions of the Grudge report aloud amidst general hilarity and ridicule.

The *Red Planet Mars* (1952) did not picture a flying saucer but did portray Martians who could communicate with Earth through radio signals, à la George Hunt Williamson. In *It Came*

From Outer Space (1953) extraterrestrials accidentally crashed on Earth and tried to repair their craft when hostile Earth people confronted them. The extraterrestrials managed to escape before they were hurt. Only one Earth person in the town tried to keep the townspeople from destroying the aliens. Although not a contactee, this man-hero interceded on the aliens' behalf to give them time to repair their craft. *The War of the Worlds* (1953) featured hostile extraterrestrials who attempted to destroy Earth but met defeat at the hands of bacteria in Earth's atmosphere. The idea that a small group of extraterrestrials wanted to colonize Earth was the central theme in *This Island Earth* (1955). A benevolent alien with a moral sense believed that the colonization plan was wrong and saved Earth by killing his fellow aliens and then committing suicide. *Invasion of the Saucer Men* (1957) parodied other saucer films. It featured a feebly humorous account of extraterrestrials who overtook people by injecting alcohol into their veins and making them drunk. The aliens melted when lights were shined on them.

Even Keyhoe's book, *Flying Saucers From Outer Space*, underwent the Hollywood treatment and became a standard science fiction film, *Earth Versus the Flying Saucers* (1956). It did accurately portray UFO shapes and maneuvers based on actual witness reports. But the aliens in it were hostile and addicted to blowing up Earth rockets as they were sent aloft. The aliens wanted to subjugate Earth and went on a destructive rampage against the earthlings and their cities. The hero-scientist invented a special antimagnetic weapon with which he finally destroyed the aliens. The film's producers persuaded Keyhoe to sell them the rights to his book by telling him that they were making a documentary on UFOs. When the feature came out, Keyhoe was angry; he refused to make personal appearances for the film and tried unsuccessfully to have his name removed from the credits.[41]

The rise of the contactees and of flying saucer movies came at the same time as the Air Force's new policy on reducing UFO reports. The Air Force's increased secrecy coupled with contactee publicity fed the UFO controversy. The public was confused. On the one hand, it heard about the alleged Air Force cover-up and, on the other hand, it read about UFO sightings in the press and either heard about or read Keyhoe's books. In the resulting confusion it tended to equate Keyhoe with the contactees, which hindered Keyhoe's determined fight to bring respectability to a systematic study of the UFO phenomenon.

Moreover, the contactees, their followers, and Hollywood movies in the mid-1950s hardened the aura of illegitimacy surrounding the UFO phenomenon. While the contactees and the movie industry gave the UFO phenomenon publicity the Air Force wanted to avoid, they also—by focusing on the sensational and fantastic—lent credence to the Air Force position that reports of unique aerial objects of possible extraterrestrial origin were groundless. At the least, the movies and contactees created a misleading impression about the nature of the phenomenon. Correcting this impression occupied much of Keyhoe's and other serious investigators' energies during the 1950s. Keyhoe's attempts to disassociate legitimate UFO investigators from contactees and their fellowers complicated his continuing fight with the Air Force. The skirmishes continued in the 1950s, with both sides using new resources and reinforcements to try to win the battle.

6

1954 TO 1958:
CONTINUED SKIRMISHES
AND THE RISE OF NICAP

After the contactee and civilian UFO organizations entered the UFO controversy, they engaged in a series of skirmishes with the Air Force over its UFO program. During this period from 1954 to 1958, the civilian UFO groups found a leader in the National Investigations Committee on Aerial Phenomena (NICAP). The Air Force reorganized its investigative and public relations systems, and both parties formulated their positions on the issues of Air Force secrecy, congressional investigations, and publicity about UFOs.

The skirmishes centered around the Air Force's position as keeper of the knowledge. It was the only official agency that continually collected, investigated, and analyzed sighting reports. The Air Force had the most comprehensive data available tucked away in its classified files. The civilian UFO organizations, following Keyhoe's lead, criticized it for what they thought was a conspiracy of silence to prevent panic among the people. They demanded that the Air Force make the files public. But the Air Force refused, because of the Robertson panel's report and because the files did contain some classified intelligence information. By continually reacting to Air Force pronouncements, regulations, and policies, the civilian groups made the Air Force the prime mover in the controversy and thereby relinquished some of their own autonomy. Yet the Air Force stimulated this reaction by denying the potential significance of the UFO phenomenon and by suspecting the civilian groups' intentions.

Air Force secrecy policies made UFO proponents somewhat paranoid. Civilian UFO investigators James Moseley and Leon Davidson thought UFOs were actually American secret weapons. Moseley said the Air Force used them to "absorb excess radioactivity" in the atmosphere. Davidson, while originally thinking they were secret weapons, later developed the theory that UFOs were nothing but a CIA "front"; the CIA, Davidson explained, had maneuvered or created all UFO club activity, contactees, books, and so on to confound the Soviets about our technological capabilities.[1] The clearest example of extrapolating sinister ideas from noninformation was Keyhoe's theory that the top levels of government perpetrated the flying saucer "conspiracy": "Actually, the Air Force is not the only agency involved; the CIA, National Security Council, FBI, Civil Defense, all are tied in at top levels. The White House, of course, will have the final word as to what people are to be told, and when." Keyhoe also believed the Air Force conspired against him personally. He wrote Coral Lorenzen, head of the Aerial Phenomena Research Organization, in August and September of 1954, that it might try to "muzzle" him by recalling him to active Marine Corps duty and putting him under military restrictions. He thought the Air Force might try to silence Coral Lorenzen as well and devised a written signal for her to use in case this happened.[2]

In this atmosphere of suspicion and near paranoia, the Air Force moved to counter the criticism by reorganizing its UFO program to minimize public interest and to implement the Robertson panel recommendations. In March 1954 it appointed as head of Project Blue Book Captain Charles Hardin. And because Hardin's two-man staff could not investigate the large number of UFO reports coming into ATIC, the task fell on the 4602d Air Intelligence Service Squadron (AISS), a division of the Air Defense Command. Actually Ruppelt began this transfer during his last months as head of Blue Book, but his purpose was to supplement and expand Blue Book's investigative capabilities, not abolish them.[3] The transfer meant that Blue Book would analyze and evaluate the data, only making special field investigations when ATIC felt they were important enough.

The first activity in the reorganization was to teach the 4602d personnel, who were trained only to identify planes, how to investigate and evaluate UFO reports. Hardin, Hynek, and members of the 4602d devised a "UFOB Guide" for this purpose. The manual described the characteristics of balloons, aircraft, meteors, and so on, and also explained some of the problems field investigators were likely to encounter. It became the standard guide for all Air Force field investigations.[4]

In late 1954 the 4602d started its program of making preliminary investigations and screening out reports too fragmentary for evaluation or easily explainable by known activities or phenomena. The 4602d then sent the rest of the reports to ATIC for analysis and evaluation, and ATIC informed the 4602d if a follow-up investigation was warranted. Almost immediately, however, the 4602d found itself doing ATIC's job of analyzing the data in an effort to find solutions to the sighting reports. The Air Force did not consider this a violation of AFR 200-2. Instead, it saw that the field investigators could save ATIC much trouble by their on-the-spot identifications and moved to regularize this aspect of the 4602d's function by declaring that the squadron should conduct follow-up investigations when the evidence suggested that a positive identification could be made.[5]

At first the 4602d classified a large number of reports as unknown. This was unacceptable. In February 1955 an ATIC officer told the commander of AISS that investigators should strive to solve as many cases as possible to reduce unknowns to a minimum. To help with this task, because the very nature of UFO reports militated against positive identifications, the Air Force devised a new classification system. Whereas previously investigators placed reports in either the identified, insufficient data, unreliable, or unknown categories, the Air Force now broadened the identified category to include probable and possible. These vague subcategories allowed the investigators to identify a report based on their estimate of the probability or possibility that the sighting was a known phenomenon. If investigators could not definitely identify a sighting, they could solve the problem, and the case, by placing it in one of these two broadly defined categories. In press releases and final Blue Book evaluation statistics, the probable and possible subcategories disappeared and Blue Book listed the sightings simply as identified.[6]

In March 1955 the Air Force issued a revision of the "UFOB Guide" to the 4602d. In it the Air Force differentiated between unsolved and solved cases. Unsolved cases had contradictory and conflicting data. All others the investigators could solve, the guide explained, in a truly "scientific" manner by looking at the direction in which the preponderance of data leaned and then placing the report into one of the categories of *identification* as outlined in the guide. The "UFOB Guide" called upon investigators to use "common sense" which, presumably, would rule out the possibility that the witness had observed anything truly extraordinary.[7]

The new methods of investigating and identifying UFO reports worked marvelously. The percentage of unknowns fell from 60 percent in August 1954 to 5.9 percent in 1955 and then to 0.4 percent in 1956. Of the 335 reports the 4602d investigated in the last half of 1956, it forwarded only two to ATIC as unsolved. By the end of 1957 the 4602d had virtually taken over ATIC's job of analyzing UFO reports.[8]

The modus operandi of the 4602d was that the UFO problem was a public relations problem and no one could ever have seen anything truly extraordinary in the sky. The Air Force assumed that UFO sightings resulted from the "Buck Rogers trauma"—a mixture of technological advance, cold-war fears, and the influence of science fiction. The only justification for investigating UFO reports, therefore, was that enemy guided missiles might resemble UFOs and the Air Force had to investigate these reports for national defense reasons.[9] The 4602d envisioned its job as that of allaying public hysteria by systematically squelching rumors that UFOs represented an invasion from outer space. But the 4602d realized it would have only partial success in stopping reports, since "emotionally unstable" people still reported UFOs, and in great numbers. Indeed, the number of reports coming in disturbed the 4602d, and it looked to public relations for part of the answer: perhaps the very knowledge that the 4602d investigated UFO reports created public hysteria which, in turn, created more UFO reports. Whatever the reason, though, the 4602d was never able to affect the number of reports sent to it.

The 4602d's methodology allowed the Air Force to broaden its public relations campaign. With strategically placed personnel making immediate identifications, the Air Force claimed that its investigating capabilities were more "scientific"; the more accurate information coming into ATIC was reducing substantially the number of unknowns. Using the data gathered through the new procedures, the Air Force stepped up its campaign to emphasize that its UFO program was not secret and that UFOs were not unusual. The Air Force explained that the 20 percent to 30 percent unknown rate for the previous 1947 to 1952 period resulted from inadequate data and poor reporting and cited the current less than 10 percent unknown rate as evidence for this explanation.[10]

But no matter what statistics the Air Force gave, it could not convince UFO proponents to accept at face value statements about its objectivity and openness. The Air Force refused to declassify its sighting reports and thus found itself in a dilemma: the same policies it defended handicapped its public relations efforts. By refuting the secrecy charges while at the same time refusing to declassify the sighting reports, the Air Force incurred even greater criticism and appeared to be covering up as the critics charged. Furthermore, in its zeal to dispel the notion that it had at one time considered the extraterrestrial hypothesis seriously, the Air Force denied that certain essential documents existed and that pivotal events had taken place. Spokesmen denied the existence of General Twining's 1947 letter, which stated that the objects were "real" and which was the impetus for the UFO program. They denied that the 1948 "Estimate of the Situation" had ever existed. They denied that Dewey Fournet had conducted a UFO maneuvers study in 1952. And they denied that the Robertson panel ever had met. Privately the Air Force contended that declassification of its UFO files could lead to another saucer scare; publicly it claimed that its classification policies were necessary to protect witnesses' names and the capabilities of classified electronic equipment that might have been involved in investigating a sighting.[11]

Mass media coverage in 1954 about UFOs boosted the Air Force's public relations campaign. Once again the urge to explain came to the fore. Charlotte Knight, in *Collier's*, explained that Air Force high altitude balloons accounted for virtually all UFO sightings. Siegfried Mandel, confused about the contactees, lumped Adamski and Keyhoe together when he reviewed several books on UFOs for the *Saturday Review*. Mandel said that these two writers exploited the anxieties of the times "to create infantile illusions, fears, and hopes ranging from facile solutions to world conflicts to the saucers-will-get-you bugaboo." He hoped readers "with a normal degree of objectivity" realized UFOs were "auto-suggestive myths." When extraterrestrial visitors arrived, Mandel stated positively, they would approach "reliable" people and "present unmistakable credentials of their galactic origin." He recommended Menzel's book as a "potent antidote" to the other writers. Wartime head of the German V-2 rocket development, Dr. Walter Dornberger, told a *Newsweek* reporter that UFOs were only violent eddies of air that spun so fast their atoms became unstable and emitted light; this accounted for 98 to 99 percent of all sightings and the rest were natural phenomena. "No one is going to convince me of visitors from space," Dornberger said, "until they bring in one of those little guys and sit him on my desk." [12]

Menzel reiterated his feelings at the International Astronomical Union in Dublin, Ireland; when some of the astronomers began to discuss UFOs, Menzel exclaimed that "such fantastic nonsense has no part in business dealt with on such a high scientific level as at these meetings." Even President Eisenhower seemed to help the Air Force's public relations endeavors. He stated at a news conference that a trusted Air Force official had told him the notion that UFOs came "from any outside planet or any other place" was "completely inaccurate." A *New York Times* reporter interviewed an Air Force spokesman after Eisenhower's comment and said that "If the Air Force were not tactful it might scoff at the whole business publicly." Later, after asking Air Force headquarters about UFOs, the same reporter explained that "talk about flying saucers is one of those delusions that from time to time sweep the popular mind, especially in times of stress." [13]

Meanwhile, the Air Force made more direct debunking efforts to prevent a saucer scare. An article in the March 1954 issue of *American Aviation* said that the Pentagon "definitely attributes" the latest wave of UFO sightings to Keyhoe's *Flying Saucers From Outer Space*, which, the article explained, gained notoriety by affecting an official air with the help of an Air Force "underling" (Al Chop) who was no longer with the service. [14]

Keyhoe continued his counterattack against the Air Force in his third book, *The Flying Saucer Conspiracy*, published in 1955. In it he again put forth his conspiracy-of-silence theory, but this time he had new facts to back it up: the issuance of Air Force Regulation 200-2, part of which prohibited the release of UFO reports to the public, and of Joint-Army-Navy-Air Force-Publication (JANAP) 146, which made public disclosure of a UFO sighting described in the JANAP form a criminal offense; the Air Force's insistence on including disclaimers in Keyhoe's *Look* article; and the efforts to discredit him. He concluded once again that high-ranking Air Force officials knew more than they were telling and that a small group of Pentagon conspirators were directing the Air Force policy to the country's detriment. This "Silence Group" within the Pentagon, Keyhoe said, used censorship to prevent hysteria. He realized that such action might be due to a high motive but warned that censorship endangered democratic institutions and that the "Air Force's insistence that it has no answer only heightens the possibility of hysteria." To bolster this theory, he listed over a hundred puzzling UFO cases and weak or ridiculous Air Force explanations for them. [15]

Believing that his new book would boost his cause, Keyhoe did not know that the Air Force still had an important card to play, a card it had been holding since 1953. It was Project Blue Book *Special Report Number 14*, the updated results of the Battelle Memorial Institute's statistical study of UFOs which Ruppelt had initiated in 1952. Although it is unclear why the Air Force decided to release *Special Report Number 14* at the same time that *The Flying Saucer Conspiracy* came out, Keyhoe's assertion that the Air Force did it to counteract his book seems consistent with the Air Force's policy of opposing any publicity that might lead to another saucer scare.[16]

Special Report Number 14 was puzzling. The purpose of the study was to determine, through statistical techniques, whether anything flying in the air "represented technological developments not known to this country." A secondary purpose was to develop a model of a flying saucer and to find common patterns and trends in the movements of the reported objects. But the researchers could neither devise any "verified" model of flying saucers (apparently assuming UFOs should come in one shape) nor find any physical evidence for them. Similarly, the researchers could find no patterns or trends in sightings, although, the report said, "the inaccuracies inherent in this type of data, in addition to the incompleteness of a large proportion of the reports, may have obscured any patterns or trends that otherwise would have been evident." [17]

The researchers did find that the more complete the data and the better the report, the more likely it was that the report would *remain* unknown. Nevertheless—even after saying they could not identify the unknowns—the researchers found that "the probability that any of the UNKNOWNS considered in this study are 'flying saucers' is concluded to be extremely small, since the most complete and reliable reports from the present data, when isolated and studied, conclusively failed to reveal even a rough model, and since the data as a whole failed to reveal any marked patterns or trends." Yet the researchers concluded that as a result of incomplete data and inadequate scientific measurements, "it cannot be absolutely proven that 'flying saucers' do not exist." But they also concluded that "on the basis of this evaluation of the information, it is considered to be highly improbable that any of the reports of unidentified aerial objects examined in this study represent observations of technological developments outside the range of present-day scientific knowledge." [18]

When Secretary of the Air Force Donald Quarles released *Special Report 14* on October 25, 1955, he made several statements to the press about the entire UFO issue. He said that no one had reason to believe flying saucers had flown over the United States and that the 3 percent unknowns during 1954 would be identifiable if more information were available (the latter being contrary to what the Battelle Institute found). Also, he explained that the Air Force had recently tested a new, circular, vertical-take-off jet and had contracted with a Canadian firm, the A. V. Roe Company, to buy a circular flying craft. These two planes, Quarles stated, would probably cause UFO sightings in the future. Keyhoe's reaction to this last statement was that it was calculated to deceive the public.[19]

The Air Force hoped the timely release of *Special Report 14* would quiet the UFO controversy once and for all, especially because the report was a scientific study that found no evidence for UFOs being interplanetary objects. But instead of laying the controversy to rest, *Special Report 14* created a new battlefront. Keyhoe and other civilian UFO proponents charged that the Battelle Institute had not analyzed the best cases for its study and had avoided using many important cases that the Air Force listed as unidentified in its files. Keyhoe asserted that the "cream of the crop" reports on which the Battelle Institute based its model of a flying saucer were in reality weak cases, and that the Institute deliberately used them to convey the impression that all witnesses saw different phenomena. Keyhoe criticized the Institute for being biased in favor of explaining the reports and for studying only a few foreign sightings and none before 1947, which intimated that the phenomenon began in 1947. Finally, Keyhoe faulted the Institute for using the statistics on unknowns to imply that only 9 percent of all sightings and 3 percent of the recent sightings were unknown; in fact, Keyhoe said, 20 to 30 percent of all sightings were unknown and the 3 percent was for the first three months of 1955 only.[20]

Ruppelt criticized *Special Report 14* as well. In a widely quoted letter (February 1956) to UFO researcher Max Miller, Ruppelt said the most astounding thing about the report was that it said all but a few UFOs were explainable. This shocked him because he had initiated the project and knew that the study's purpose was not to solve the overall UFO problem, as the Air Force made it out to be, but to find unknown technological developments. Moreover, Ruppelt said, "after spending a considerable amount of money, statistical methods were no good for a study like this. They didn't prove a thing. The results were such that by interpreting them in different ways you could prove anything you wanted to. This is not a good study." Ruppelt could not understand why the Air Force had held on to the report for two years and released a 1953 study in 1955 as the "latest hot dope." [21]

Special Report 14 also created another mystery and endless speculation about its significance. Project Blue Book had previously issued twelve status reports, the last one in September 1953. Civilians interested in the UFO controversy wanted to know what happened to report number 13, and what secret and perhaps sensational information it contained. UFO researchers spent much time over the years trying to find the phantom report, but to no avail. The Air Force claimed in 1973 that material intended for report number 13 was subsequently included in Special Report 14, but this did not stop the speculation. [22]

At first Special Report Number 14 seemed to have the desired effect. New York Times science editor Jonathan N. Leonard added to the paper's ongoing hostility toward proponents of the theory that UFOs had an extraterrestrial origin by using Special Report 14 as a basis for a scathing review of Keyhoe's The Flying Saucer Conspiracy, popular writer Harold T. Wilkens' Flying Saucers Uncensored, and Ruppelt's The Report on Unidentified Flying Objects. Leonard characterized all UFO proponents as cultists and said one subcult included those who believe in "heretical conspiracy in the depths of the Pentagon." Keyhoe, the chief cultist, wanted to become a martyr to the cause. Ruppelt's book was the "longest and dullest" of the three and, while more sensible, still well within the cultist range. But, explained Leonard, while these books were in preparation, "the Air Force released the results of a massive, intelligent, painstaking and detailed analysis of all flying saucer reports," employing "excellent scientists" with "elaborate apparatus." Leonard favorably outlined *Special Report 14*'s conclusions and called it a "cruel blockbuster" for Ruppelt and other "cultists." Captain Hardin, commenting happily on the review, reported that "It would appear from this review that the downgrading and subsequent release of Special Report 14 is serving well the purpose for which it was intended." [23]

In spite of Hardin's optimism, though, the criticism of *Special Report 14* was so intense that the Air Force and Blue Book became more sensitive than ever, and the controversy did not subside. Instead, the Air Force became embroiled in a protracted fight about making the report available to the public. Perhaps uneasy about the criticisms and inadequacies, the Air Force had printed only a hundred copies for in-house distribution, particularly for every major public information officer in the country. But pressure from UFO researchers persuaded California Representative John E. Moss of the House Subcommittee on Government Information to force the Air Force to print and distribute more copies.[24]

Despite its controversial nature, by 1956 *Special Report 14* had become the cornerstone of the Air Force's position on UFOs. This position, that the Air Force had "scientifically" studied UFOs and found no evidence for their existence as a unique phenomenon, was not limited to public pronouncements and press releases; it prevailed within the Air Force staff as well. Although Keyhoe charged that the Air Force stifled interest in UFOs, no information exists to indicate that any member of Project Blue Book or ATIC ever thought UFOs constituted anything other than an explainable phenomenon.

Captain George T. Gregory, who became head of Blue Book when Captain Hardin transferred in April 1956, best illustrated this attitude when he briefed members of the Air Intelligence Training School. Gregory, a zealous UFO debunker, told the staff that the 1952 sightings definitely resulted from publicity about the subject and that the growing number of UFO clubs, books, and articles criticizing the Air Force were contributing to a new surge of reports. According to Gregory, in 1952 the Air Force managed to rise above the hysteria of the times to investigate UFO reports *"quietly, solemnly* and *seriously."* He freely used Hynek's name to demonstrate the caliber of scientists who worked on the problem and found nothing unique in the atmosphere. Gregory enumerated all the latest techniques the Air Force used to study the phenomenon, such as the Videon diffraction grid and the radarscope camera. But he neglected to explain that the Air Force had installed the Videon diffraction grids even though they had failed and that the radarscope plan had been unsatisfactory. At the end of the briefing, Gregory distributed copies of *Special Report 14*, explaining that it contained the results from "a large panel of distinguished scientists" who had intensively studied and analyzed the phenomenon. *Special Report 14* proved, said Gregory, that there was a *"total* lack of evidence" to demonstrate that the objects were hostile interplanetary spaceships, that they represented technological development not known in this country, or that they threatened the United States.[25]

By 1956 almost all former ATIC and Blue Book personnel had left the project. Gregory and the new officers may not have been aware of the UFO program's previous history. It is clear that from 1956 to 1969 no one within ATIC seriously questioned the Air Force's UFO investigative or analytical methods. Even Hynek, with his vague misgivings, willingly participated in the Air Force's plan to rid itself of the UFO problem. Hynek described the characteristic style of thinking in the Air Force around 1956 as: "It can't be, therefore it isn't." [26] Given this philosophy, Gregory and the other staff people had little or no concern with verifying the facts or validating their methods and findings; UFOs were nonsense, and any reputable scientific study would most certainly conclude the same thing.

Gregory's method of analyzing reports reflected his opinion that the phenomenon did not merit serious attention. During his tenure he made the most strenuous efforts of any Blue Book project leader to identify UFO reports regardless of the information they contained. Under Gregory, Blue Book staff routinely classified all reports from youths age ten to seventeen as figments of their imaginations and placed the reports in the unreliable

144 The UFO Controversy in America

category. The staff automatically put most sightings reported through the "Canadian-United States Communications Instructions for Reporting Vital Intelligence Sightings" channels in the insufficient data category without soliciting more information. Blue Book extended the probable category to include sightings that presented no data to indicate the object could *not* have been an aircraft, balloon, and so forth. If a witness in his efforts to describe a UFO used words like *jet-like, balloon-like,* or *meteor-like,* Blue Book staff identified the object as a jet, balloon, or meteor. The staff did this even when the witness used the words to describe what the object did *not* look like. It also routinely placed some of the most interesting low-level or close encounter reports in the insufficient data category. Occasionally investigators mistakenly sent obvious meteor reports to Blue Book, and the staff diligently put them in the solved category. If Hynek or an investigator listed a sighting as possible, Blue Book put it in the probable category; if originally called probable, the project labeled it definite.[27]

Blue Book also continued in its efforts to eliminate reports because the Air Force still felt anxious about the steady stream of UFO publicity emanating from private sources. Perhaps the most serious threat to the Air Force in 1956 was the release of Clarence Greene's semidocumentary motion picture, *UFOs.* Greene had received the technical assistance of Chop, Fournet, and Ruppelt on the film and also had obtained copies of the recently declassified Great Falls (Montana) and Tremonton (Utah) UFO films of supposed UFOs in flight. Greene's movie featured Los Angeles journalist Tom Powers in the starring role as Al Chop; other actors portrayed Ruppelt, Fournet, and General Garland. Greene included interviews with Nicholas Mariana and Delbert C. Newhouse (the two men who had taken the UFO films), a portion of the Samford news conference, and dramatic reenactments of the Mantell incident and the Washington, D.C., sightings.[28]

Such publicity posed a severe threat to Captain Gregory and the Air Force, which mobilized its resources to counteract the film. Gregory kept a file of all the movie's reviews, notifications, and advertisements, carefully underlining every statement that might cause problems for the Air Force or generate interest in UFOs. From Richard Dyer McCann's review in the *Christian Science Monitor*, Gregory singled out the statement, "It will almost certainly stir up a storm of public controversy," and added the marginal note, "This is something that neither PIO [Office of Public Information] or ATIC would like to undergo again!" Gregory summed up the Air Force's attitude toward the film by using the phrase from the review: "This film may stir up a storm of public controversy similar to that which USAF was subjected to in 1952 with regard to UFOs as a result of the unwarranted sensationalism generated by so-called 'UFO experts,' writers, and publishers." In addition to keeping files, ATIC asked Hynek and Air Force officers to review the film before its release, and asked photo experts to compare copies of the Mariana and Newhouse films with the excerpts shown in the movie. ATIC Chief Scientist A. Francis Arcier met with agency officials to discuss the preparation of a case file giving the official Air Force explanation for every sighting portrayed in the film. And, finally, ATIC devised a standard response to all inquiries about the movie in which it referred the person to *Special Report 14.*[29]

When the film was released in May 1956, the "storm of controversy" the Air Force so feared turned out to be little more than a light mist. *UFOs* was successful, but it did not cause flying saucer hysteria, criticism of the Air Force, or more UFO reports. Nonetheless, the Air Force still had reason to believe its UFO debunking campaign was inadequate, for the number of sighting reports began to rise again. In the peak sighting year, 1952, ATIC received 1,501 reports. In the following three years, 1953, 1954, 1955, it received 509, 487, and 545 reports, respectively. Then in 1956 it received 670 reports.[30] Public interest in the subject increased with the reports, and the discrepancies between the sightings, Air Force pronouncements, Keyhoe's theories, and the public perceptions of the problem came to a head in 1956 with the formation of the National Investigations Committee on Aerial Phenomena (NICAP).

A group of private citizens interested in UFOs and dissatisfied with Air Force policies met in October 1956 to organize the Flying Saucer Discussion Group. They proposed to investigate UFOs and the possibility of space flight. Club member and space propulsion researcher T. Townshend Brown, the club's first director, wanted scientists and other influential citizens to back the club. With the help of Keyhoe, Brown appointed to the board of governors a retired army brigadier general, two physicists, two ministers, and two businessmen, among others. The most prestigious man on the board was missile pioneer and former head of the navy's guided missile program, retired Rear Admiral Delmer S. Fahrney. Brown changed the club's name to the more professional sounding National Investigations Committee on Aerial Phenomena and had the organization incorporated on October 24, 1956. A major problem confronting the new organization was to keep the "crack pots" out and to become "respectable" enough to draw professional people. Keyhoe purposely stayed in the background, not wanting reporters to "jump on it [NICAP] and picture it as a Keyhoe-inspired deal." [31]

From the beginning Brown ran into trouble. He had estimated that $85,000 a year would cover salaries and expenses and set the membership fees at from $15.00 for regular members to $1,000 for founders. Expenses mounted but the expected funds did not materialize. By the end of 1956, when only two months old, the fledgling organization hovered on the brink of bankruptcy. Tensions between Keyhoe and Brown over Brown's financial policies peaked in January 1957 at a climactic membership meeting. Keyhoe attended and seemed content with watching and listening only. But when Brown decided to place his own name in nomination for chairman of the board of governors, a position he wanted in addition to being director, Keyhoe could not contain himself. He stood up and accused Brown of mismanaging the funds and steering the organization on too radical a course (he referred to Brown's dubious antigravity propulsion theories). A shouting match ensued and Keyhoe issued an ultimatum to the board and to Brown: either Brown resigned from NICAP or Keyhoe would personally advise Admiral Fahrney and other board members to resign. Faced with this ultimatum, the board capitulated; the next day it forced Brown to resign, elected Admiral Fahrney chairman, and appointed Keyhoe to replace Brown as the new director of NICAP.[32]

Keyhoe finally had an organizational tool for challenging the Air Force on a national scale. He had been formulating plans since 1954, when he told Coral Lorenzen that a "wide public demand" for Air Force declassification or congressional hearings on UFOs was needed to combat the top-level conspiracy. "If enough intelligent believers could get together and use all possible influence, through their congressmen, senators, and any other means at hand, it might force a quick policy change in Washington." [33] Keyhoe's strategy to solve the UFO problem to his satisfaction and uncover the conspiracy was either to force or to wait for a "big breakthrough," which could take several forms: a flying saucer could land on the White House lawn, thereby putting an immediate end to the UFO controversy; a series of spectacular sightings could occur, which would create enough public pressure to force the Air Force to reveal all its findings; or rational argument could swing the public to Keyhoe's position, giving him the leverage to compel the Air Force to disclose its "hidden" findings publicly. The latter method was, of course, the only way Keyhoe could control the breakthrough.

All UFO organizations drew a degree of ridicule, but NICAP tried to keep its share to a minimum. Keyhoe's position as director plus the people on the board of governors gave NICAP dignity, and it attracted many individuals who would usually not have joined a UFO organization. Within a few months after Keyhoe's appointment, the board of governors consisted of Fahrney, Vice-Admiral R. H. Hillenkoetter (the first director of the CIA), Dewey Fournet, J. B. Hartranft (president of the Aircraft Owners and Pilots Association), retired Rear Admiral H. B. Knowles, Army Reserve Colonel Robert B. Emerson, retired Marine Corps Lieutenant General P. A. delValle, Dr. Marcus Bach (professor of religion at Iowa State University), Dr. Charles A. Maney (professor of physics at Defiance College in Ohio), Reverend Leon LeVan, Reverend Albert Baller, columnist Earl Douglass, and radio-TV commentator Frank Edwards. These men gave NICAP the prestige and national outlook that no other UFO organization had. Furthermore, NICAP had a distinguished group of special advisers: Al Chop, Captain C. S. Chiles (of the 1948 Chiles and Whitted sighting fame), Captain R. B. McLaughlin (author of the *True Magazine* article on tracking a UFO), Warrant Officer Delbert C. Newhouse (who took the famous Tremonton, Utah, motion picture), and Wilbert B. Smith (former head of the Canadian government's UFO project).[34]

Fahrney inaugurated NICAP's public role with a press conference, which the Associated Press carried nationally. He stated that neither the Soviet Union nor the United States could duplicate the UFOs' observed speeds and accelerations and that the flying objects seemed to be intelligently controlled because of "the way they change position in formations and override each other." With over five hundred newspaper articles about the press conference, the new organization began with a burst of publicity.[35]

Meanwhile, Keyhoe's reorganizing plans advanced rapidly. He cut the membership fee to $7.50, arranged to publish a monthly bulletin, slashed the organization's overhead, and put it on a bare bones financial policy by, among other things, moving to offices with lower rent and dismissing salaried employees. Most important, he changed the organization's emphasis. Unlike Brown, Keyhoe wanted to use NICAP as a pressure group to force congressional hearings on the Air Force's UFO program; Congress could require the Air Force to release its UFO data to the public and also prompt a fair and impartial scientific investigation. More conservative than other UFO organizations, NICAP at first avoided any claim that UFOs were extraterrestrial. By assuming that Air Force records and sighting reports would prove the extraterrestrial origin of UFOs, NICAP in effect gave the Air Force this responsibility. Through this stance, NICAP placed the Air Force in the position of being the expert in the field and relinquished some of its ability to act independently of the Air Force. For nearly all of NICAP's existence, it was inextricably connected with Air Force policies and whims.[36]

Keyhoe's main vehicle for his lobbying efforts was the organization's publication, the *UFO Investigator*. The first issue created much public comment because it contained a previously undisclosed radar-visual sighting that Civil Aeronautics Administration control tower operators had made.[37] Each succeeding issue presented information designed to counteract Air Force claims of UFO "solutions." Before long the newsletter and Keyhoe's aggressive reorganization policies led to a considerable membership, numbering approximately 5,000 by 1958. But regardless of the large numbers of people joining and paying $7.50, NICAP existed in a constant state of financial crisis. Keyhoe had to finance the newsletter after the first few issues and, in large part, the entire organization with his personal funds. With careful nurturing, however, NICAP quickly assumed leadership over the scores of smaller UFO organizations spread around the country.

NICAP's only potential rival organization was the Aerial Phenomena Research Organization (APRO), which James and Coral Lorenzen had founded in 1952. But the Lorenzens were pleased to see NICAP's formation and did all they could to help the new organization. They did not agree completely with Keyhoe's conspiracy thesis but, at least in 1957, did not argue with it. APRO was, from its inception, a small organization, content to report UFO sightings and events. It had neither the resources nor the inclination to take on the Air Force or Congress; it had avoided severe monetary problems and preferred to remain within its financial limits.

The Air Force looked upon the establishment of NICAP with Keyhoe at its head as an ominous development. The influential people on the board of governors did nothing to ease the Air Force's anxiety. It was distressed especially over Keyhoe's efforts to obtain congressional hearings, fearing that the publicity from such hearings would touch off another saucer scare. Moreover, hearings would imply that the Air Force was not doing its job properly. In the face of increased criticism from UFO proponents and the newly formed NICAP, the Air Force expanded its rationale for keeping UFO data classified. In 1957 Major Robert Spence, deputy chief of the operations branch of the Public Information Service, told private researcher Max Miller that the Air Force could not give him its photographic files "without making them available to all." This was undesirable because the "man hours and cost would be exorbitant" and, more importantly, it would interfere with the Air Force's normal missions and operations. Similarly, General Joe Kelly assured Keyhoe in 1957 that the Air Force would not turn over its UFO files to NICAP because it would then have to do the same for the other organizations. The Air Force classified UFO reports, Kelly said, to "safeguard the National Security" because often a case involved a specific radar or classified weapons system.[38]

Concurrent with major public relations problems from NICAP, the Air Force went through another reorganization of its UFO project. In July of 1957 the Air Defense Command disbanded the 4602d and reassigned UFO investigating duties to the 1006th Air Intelligence Service Squadron (AISS). The Air Force took this opportunity to divide public relations responsibilities between the Office of Legislative Liaison for Congress and the Office of Public Information for the public, thereby allowing Air Force intelligence to be "completely divorced" from the public relations aspect of the controversy.[39]

The Air Force revised AFR 200-2 in February 1958 to formalize the new procedures. Also, the revised regulations recreated the system of air base commanders conducting initial investigations of all UFO sightings in their areas and continued ATIC's formal UFO responsibility for analysis and evaluation. If ATIC believed more extensive study was required, revised AFR 200-2 stated, it should submit a request to have 1006th personnel conduct the investigation. At the same time, the Air Force added the order to AFR 200-2 that "Air Force activities must reduce the percentage of unidentifieds to the minimum." The Air Force continued its firmly held belief that reducing the number of unidentifieds would cut down on the number of new sighting reports. It hoped people would begin to understand that a strange something in the sky was not necessarily a spaceship and, therefore, would not report such sightings to the Air Force. In revising the regulations, the Air Force tried to eliminate "any and all portions of [AFR 200-2] which might provoke suspicion or misinterpretation by the public." (Keyhoe, in *The Flying Saucer*

Conspiracy, had criticized the Air Force for its secrecy policies as outlined in AFR 200-2.) The new procedures also countered the contactees' publicity efforts; the Air Force gave the FBI names of individuals who were "illegally or deceptively bringing the subject to public attention." These changes, the Air Force hoped, "should do much toward the relief of [Air Force intelligence] in the UFO program." [40]

The change to the 1006th encountered problems immediately. Within a few months of the transfer, the Air Force reduced the funds for the 1006th, making curtailment of its investigating functions necessary. The Air Force limited the 1006th's duties to conducting investigations only upon request of the ATIC commander or the director of intelligence in Washington, D.C. The 1006th remained with the UFO program until its reassignment in July 1959, at which time the Air Force used the 1127th Field Activities Group stationed at Fort Belvoir, Virginia. This group made few investigations. [41]

The Air Force's organizational and regulation changes had no effect on the number of sighting reports coming into ATIC. Despite the campaign to downplay the subject, 1957 represented another peak year in UFO reports. Whereas ATIC recorded 670 sighting reports in 1956, it received over 1,000 in 1957. The average held steady at from 27 to 39 sightings per month for the first six months of 1957; then the reports increased in July and August to about 70 a month, decreased slightly to 60 in September, increased to over 100 in October, and finally climbed to over 500 for November and December together. [42] The country was experiencing another major wave of saucer sightings, approaching the scale of the 1952 "scare."

November, the month with the most reports, began with a spectacular group of sightings in Levelland, Texas. These cases were important not only for the public impact but for illustrating the Air Force's investigatory methods. The sightings began at 11:00 P.M. on the night of November 2 and ended at 2:00 A.M. on the morning of November 3. Two witnesses, driving just north of Levelland, saw a glowing, yellow and white, torpedo-shaped object flying toward them. As the object flew over the automobile, the car's motor and lights failed. The two witnesses left their car to view the object, and it came so close to them that they experienced "quite some heat," which forced them to "hit the ground." As the object left the area, the driver could start the car again and turn the lights on. The witnesses reported the incident to the police.[43]

One hour later, at midnight, a witness driving four miles east of Levelland came upon a brilliantly glowing, egg-shaped object resting in the middle of the road. As the witness approached the object, which he thought was about 200 feet long, the car's engine and lights failed. A few seconds later the object rose to a height of about 200 feet and disappeared. The amazed witness could then start his car and the lights worked properly. Five minutes later another person, driving eleven miles north of Levelland, reported to police that he had come upon a 200-foot-long glowing object sitting in the road; as he approached it, he said, his car engine failed and the lights went out; when the object rose and left the area, the engine and lights functioned normally again.[44]

At 12:05 A.M., a nineteen-year-old college freshman was driving nine miles east of Levelland when the engine and lights in his car failed suddenly; as he got out of his car to look under the hood, he saw an egg-shaped object sitting on the ground in front of him. The object, he said, was 75 to 100 feet long, glowed white with a greenish tint, and seemed made of aluminum. Frightened, he jumped back into his car and watched the object for about five minutes. Then the object "disappeared" and the witness could start his car. He did not tell anyone about the incident "for fear of public ridicule." (The next day, however, his parents convinced him to call the police.) Fifteen minutes after this last incident, another car stalled as it approached an object sitting on a dirt road nine miles north of Levelland. The object was glowing, but when it rose to an elevation of about 300 feet, it disappeared from sight. And once again the witness was then able to start the automobile.[45]

All of these reports came in to Patrolman A. J. Fowler of Levelland, who was on duty that night. He sent two deputies out to investigate; they reported seeing bright lights in the sky but had no engine problems. Several minutes after the deputies' report, a man driving just west of Levelland saw a huge orange ball of fire coming toward him; it settled on the highway about a quarter of a mile in front of him, covering the paved portion of the road. When the witness approached the object, his car engine and lights failed. As the object rose a few minutes later, the witness was able to start his car again. One-half hour later, a truck driver called Patrolman Fowler to report that, as he was driving northeast of Levelland, his truck engine and headlights failed when he came within 200 feet of a 200-foot-long, egg-shaped object on the ground. He said it glowed "like a neon sign." As he got out of the truck to investigate, the object shot straight up with a roar and flew away. His truck engine and headlights worked perfectly after the encounter.[46]

During this time other sheriff's deputies, aware of the UFO reports in the area, searched for objects. Sheriff Clem and Deputy McCulloch, while driving four or five miles outside the city, saw a streak of light with a reddish glow about 300 to 400 yards ahead of them on the highway; it lit up the entire area in front of them. Patrolmen Hargrove and Gavin were only a few miles behind the sheriff's car on the same road when they saw "a strange looking flash" which "appeared to be close to the ground" about a mile in front of them. Constable Lloyd Ballen reported the last sighting of the evening. He saw an object that, he said, traveled so fast it looked like a flash of light moving from east to west.[47]

In all, twelve people claimed to have seen an object and three more to have seen an unusual flash of light during a three-hour period. All of the witnesses reported a light rain or heavy mist in the area but *no storms or lightning.*[48]

The national news wire services picked up the sightings, which made headlines around the country. Public pressure on Blue Book to investigate these incidents was severe. An Air Force spokesman told a *New York Times* reporter that "a preliminary investigation had been ordered." When the reporter asked the significance of this, the spokesman replied, "We don't investigate all of them, after all." According to Hynek, the Blue Book investigation consisted of one man from the 1006th who arrived a few days after the sightings, took two automobile trips to question witnesses, and then told the sheriff that he had completed the investigation. The officer failed to interview nine of the fifteen witnesses and also erroneously stated that lightning had been in the area at the time of the sightings.[49]

Public pressure for an explanation was so intense that the assistant secretary of defense requested ATIC to immediately submit a preliminary analysis to the press. Although Captain Gregory called this request "a most difficult requirement in view of the limited data," officers at ATIC analyzed the information on hand and released a press statement a few days later. The ATIC officers said that contrary to the popular idea that many witnesses were involved in the sighting, only three people "could be located" who had seen the "big light." The object was visible for "only a few seconds, not sustained visibility as had been implied." Furthermore, the officers said, the key to the sightings lay in the presence of lightning and storm conditions in the area. The Air Force's final evaluation gave the cause of the Levelland sightings as "weather phenomenon of electrical nature, generally classified as 'Ball Lightning' or 'St. Elmo's Fire,' caused by stormy conditions in the area, including mist, rain, thunderstorms and lightning." The Air Force attributed the car engine and light failures to "wet electrical circuits." Privately Blue Book officers believed the Levelland sightings were "obviously another UFO example of 'mass suggestion.' "[50]

What concerned the Air Force most about the Levelland sightings was the amount of publicity they generated. Captain Gregory, operating within the accepted Air Force theorem that one sensationally publicized sighting would cause others, reported that the Levelland case had provoked a flood of other reports and "within three weeks this Division [ATIC] had received approximately 500 UFO reports as a result."[51]

To counteract the latest wave of reports, the Office of Public Information in the Pentagon released a fact sheet, which stated that "after ten years of investigation and analysis," with the help of a "selected scientific group," the Air Force was unable to discover any evidence for the existence of "Flying Saucers." Using Hynek's name and credentials, the fact sheet explained that "the

selected qualified scientists, engineers, and other personnel involved in these analyses are completely objective and open-
minded on the subject of flying saucers." These scientists "apply
scientific methods of examination to all cases in reaching their
conclusions." Moreover, "no report is considered unsuitable for
study and categorization and no lack of valid evidence of physical
matter in the case studies is assumed to be 'prima facie' evidence
that so-called 'flying saucers' or interplanetary vehicles do not
exist." To reinforce the fact sheet, an Air Force spokesman told
the *New York Times* a few days later that the Air Force gave all
reports the " 'most thorough' " analysis involving the services of
top-level scientists in many fields to be sure that the findings were
fair and impartial and " 'above all, informed.' " [52]

Donald Menzel, while attending a meeting in Stockholm,
once again supported the Air Force's conclusions and added some
of his own ideas about the wave of sightings. As many flying
saucers existed now, Menzel said, as did in 1947 and 1948 when
the scare first started; this was not surprising because they were all
due to mirages and other natural phenomena. And Menzel gave
another reason for UFO sightings, a reason that the Air Force
would use later in its official explanations of the 1957 wave of
sightings: "The current rash of flying saucers is tied in with the
sensitization of people to the Sputniks." Doubtless Soviet satellites
did create some UFO sighting reports; the larger wave of UFO
sightings in November of 1957 coincided with the launching of the
second Sputnik, but the sightings decreased to 136 in December
and to 61 in January of 1958. The 1958 rate, 627 for the year, was
a little less than the 1956 rate.[53]

The Air Force campaign to stop UFO publicity seemed to be
working. After the 1957 wave newspaper publicity about the
subject subsided considerably, and articles about UFOs became
rare because, as the Air Force reported, "the press is completely
satisfied with the periodic UFO 'fact sheets' made available to
them and the Air Force responses to specific UFO sightings." [54]
Public interest seemed to be waning by 1958 and the passions that
the UFO phenomenon aroused appeared much less intense,
although the UFO groups were still strong.

Keyhoe's appearance in February 1958 on the *Armstrong Circle Theater*'s television show, "UFOs: Enigma of the Skies," added new fuel to the controversy. Departing from the script he had hesitantly agreed to use, Keyhoe said on national television that the Air Force had three secret documents of which the public was unaware: the original letter from General Nathan Twining in 1947 establishing the Air Force's UFO project on the premise that UFOs were "real"; the 1948 "Estimate of the Situation" that favored the extraterrestrial hypothesis; and the Robertson panel report. But before he could complete even one sentence, the producers turned down the audio so that the home audience heard practically nothing. The producers explained that they had censored Keyhoe because they feared a libel suit against the network.[55]

In this case the Air Force seemed to take Keyhoe's side. It was unfortunate, it said, that the producers had cut off the audio, for "they enhanced rather than detracted from Major Keyhoe's position concerning his sensational and unsupported claims." Major Tacker, then Pentagon public information officer for UFOs, wrote that people tended to remember sensational accusations better than "the responsible statements of such qualified scientists who disclaimed such charges on the same program." The show prompted many letters to Keyhoe and to congressmen. But the Air Force received only six letters, and these, the Air Force said, were all from "cranks." This apparent lack of public criticism pleased the Air Force, and an ATIC officer wrote that "reaction from the CBS TV program has been beyond expectation." The show, he said, actually helped the Air Force because Keyhoe had "alienated himself with the press" by going beyond the script in his effort to criticize the Air Force.[56]

The skirmishes between civilian UFO proponents and the Air Force did not end. In fact, 1954 to 1958 was a transitional period, filled with minor debates, reorganizations, and policymaking. Of course, no period has a neat beginning and ending, and these minor battles continued into the 1960s. By about mid-1957, Keyhoe and NICAP were just beginning their full-scale battle with the Air Force. Although publicity about UFOs had greatly decreased, Keyhoe always had one great ally to rely on in his war with the Air Force—the UFO sightings. Continued sighting reports in addition to constant pressure from NICAP and other civilian groups created an even greater problem for the Air Force—the threat of congressional hearings on UFOs.

7

THE BATTLE FOR CONGRESSIONAL HEARINGS

Congressional hearings presented a serious threat to the Air Force. They might imply that the UFO phenomenon was vitally significant and that the government was very interested in it. This might lead to another "flying saucer scare," threatening to the national interest. Hearings might force the Air Force to declassify its files, contradicting Air Force claims that its files were open already. Hearings might prompt criticism of the Air Force's UFO investigation, criticism that would harm its public relations program. Therefore, preventing or limiting congressional hearings became a major objective for the Air Force from 1957 to 1964.

Handling the hearings problem and congressional inquiries about the UFO program fell to the Secretary of the Air Force Office of Legislative Liaison (SAFLL). It continually assured congressmen that the Air Force's UFO program was adequate to the task. Relying heavily on *Special Report Number 14* for its information, SAFLL told New Jersey Congressman Freling-huysen that there was a "total" lack of evidence to suggest that anything unusual was in the skies or that the objects were interplanetary vehicles. Writing to Representative Lee Metcalf (of Montana) in early 1957, Major General Joe Kelly of SAFLL defended the way in which the Air Force dealt with UFOs: its interceptors pursued UFOs "as a matter of security to this country and to determine technical aspects involved" and it kept the public informed and released summaries of evaluated UFO reports. "For those objects which are not explainable," Kelly said in support of the classification policies, "only the fact that the reports are being analyzed is considered releasable due to the many unknowns involved." [1]

Despite these assurances, some congressmen still considered holding public hearings on the subject. Under pressure from Keyhoe and NICAP, in January 1958 the Senate Subcommittee on Government Operations (Senator John McClellan, chairman) asked to meet with representatives from SAFLL to discuss the possibility of holding open hearings on the Air Force's UFO program. At the meeting William Weitzen, deputy of the Air Force research and development operations, said the Air Force saw no reason for hearings but would cooperate if the McClellan subcommittee thought them necessary. The participants discussed the UFO program, the beneficial aspects of the hearings, and the potentially harmful effects of hearings. Whereas hearings might show that the Air Force was doing its job, the participants said, the "uncontrolled publicity" that might result could be dangerous.[2]

The outcome of the discussion was that Richard Horner (assistant secretary of the Air Force for research and development) told subcommittee chief counsel Donald O'Donnell that hearings were "not in the best interest of the Air Force." O'Donnell, impressed with the Air Force's UFO program after hearing about its work, said he would advise the subcommittee to drop the issue. In an unsigned February memorandum, an Air Force officer said it seemed as if "there is no longer any basis for congressional, press, or public criticism of Air Force UFO activities." Because inquiries about UFOs drastically dropped after the launching of the second Sputnik and with better public understanding of American space efforts, he hoped that "public thinking will be more realistically conditioned, transcending from fantasy to fact." Several weeks later, on February 28, Major General Arno H. Luehman, director of information services, asked the McClellan subcommittee to certify that its "preliminary investigation" had "proved" the Air Force was conducting its

UFO investigation properly and was not withholding information from the public. The subcommittee refused to cooperate; the members did not want a previous press release to "shackle" them in case the situation changed.[3]

The Air Force prevented congressional hearings, but only for the moment. In June 1958, Ohio Representative John E. Henderson, after reading Ruppelt's book, sent a list of questions about UFOs to the Air Force. Still very sensitive about congressional opinion, Project Blue Book decided to respond with a special, comprehensive briefing for Henderson and other interested congressmen. According to an Air Force memorandum, congressmen complained that constituents constantly besieged them for information about UFOs and that, because the congressmen knew nothing about the subject, they experienced some "professional embarrassment." After the briefing the congressmen expressed confidence in the Air Force's UFO program and said they understood the problems in administering it. Rather than leaving responsibility to the Air Force, the congressmen agreed that they should advise their constituents on UFO matters and also that publicity would be "unwise . . . particularly in an open or closed formal Congressional hearing." The Air Force persuaded congressmen that private organizations and authors gave "undue impetus to the existence of 'flying saucers' " and stimulated "unfavorable public hysteria." To bolster its argument, the Air Force distributed to the congressmen classified portions of the Robertson panel report.[4]

Again the Air Force had only temporarily forestalled the threat of hearings. In August, John McCormack's House Subcommittee on Atmospheric Phenomena (part of the House Select Committee on Astronautics and Space Exploration) requested a briefing on UFOs. McCormack wanted a week-long hearing in "closed secret session, unrecorded, names of witnesses to be held in confidence," and decided to call as official witnesses Francis Arcier (the Air Force's chief scientific adviser), Captain Gregory, Majors Best and Byrne of Air Force intelligence, and Majors Brower and Tacker of the Office of Public Information. McCormack requested that Menzel, Keyhoe, and Ruppelt serve as outside witnesses. Air Force intelligence thought that if there must be hearings, the Air Force might benefit from them.[5]

McCormack opened the session by explaining it was not really a hearing; the subcommittee, according to an Air Force memorandum, merely sought "additional information on upper space that would be helpful to the appropriate executive agency." Gregory outlined major events in the history of the UFO program, from Project Grudge and its reorganization to *Special Report 14*. He correctly explained that Project Grudge concluded UFO reports were misidentifications of natural phenomena, war nerves, and the like, but he incorrectly stated that press publicity was the only reason for reorganizing Grudge and establishing Project Blue Book. Without mentioning any UFO sighting reports, Gregory said that the publicity about UFOs brought about the 1952 "hysteria." This publicity, according to Gregory, led people to question the Air Force's handling of the UFO menace. As a result, Gregory recounted, General Samford requested the CIA to review the Air Force's UFO program; it did so by forming the Robertson panel which, he incorrectly reported, had sixteen members (it had five).[6]

Gregory then outlined the panel's conclusions and recommendations and described the current Air Force UFO program. Without mentioning Project Blue Book's habit of lumping the probable and possible categories under the title of identified or the Air Force's policy of urging untrained air base officers to identify UFO reports at the base level, Gregory said Blue Book's improved investigating methods had reduced the unknowns from 30 percent to 10 percent. Without explaining that the diffraction camera plan never worked properly, Gregory declared that the plan, while "not wholly successful" because of "lack of operating personnel," produced no results to indicate the objects were not conventional. Gregory said *Special Report 14* found a "total lack of evidence" for extraterrestrial visitors but did not tell the subcommittee that the report called the evidence ambiguous. He used Hynek as an example of the caliber of scientists who had carefully examined the UFO phenomenon and found nothing unusual about it but did not say Hynek thought UFOs deserved increased systematic study.[7]

Gregory concluded by noting the rise of private UFO organizations, books, and clubs, and by chastising the organizations for continually trying to embarrass the Air Force. These self-appointed UFO groups, he said, constantly misinterpreted, exaggerated, or misquoted Air Force publications "all to the detriment of the Air Force." Gregory added that the Air Force "would be more impressed by all this were it not so profitable." Contrary to these private groups' claims, the Air Force neither did nor would suppress any evidence indicating that UFOs were a threat to the security of the United States. This briefing apparently relieved the subcommittee members, who "highly commended" Gregory and the other Air Force officers for their efforts. According to Air Force records, the members were "definitely pleased" with its approach to the problem and "apparently satisfied" with the results. The subcommittee was so satisfied, in fact, that one of its staff told Air Force representatives that it would call no more witnesses and "take no further interest in this matter."[8]

Once again the Air Force had defused an inquiry into the UFO program. But other congressmen, under continuous constituent pressure for public hearings, requested information from the Air Force on previous hearings, briefings, and the like. In response, SAFLL in 1959 devised a policy line for answering such inquiries. Not mentioning the Henderson, McClellan, or McCormack briefings, SAFLL said the Permanent Subcommittee on Investigations (part of the Senate Government Operations Committee) periodically requested information, which the Air Force furnished, and after preliminary investigation the subcommittee indicated that it did not intend to hold hearings. The Air Force, the policy statement continued, believed hearings "would merely give dignity to the subject out of all proportion to which it is entitled." Moreover, "the sensation seekers and the publishers of scientific fiction would profit most from such hearings, and in the long run we would not accomplish our objective of taking the aura of mystery out of UFO's." Not wishing to appear intransigent, the policy statement assured the reader that if "overriding considerations" should prompt a congressional committee to hold public hearings, "the Air Force stands ready to give its wholehearted cooperation" to such an endeavor. SAFLL also included in the policy paper some statements defending the Air Force's public information policies.[9]

Yet Air Force pronouncements explaining its classification policies often seemed contradictory. Richard Horner, assistant secretary of the Air Force for research and development, told Barry Goldwater in a January 1958 letter that allegations about the Air Force withholding information about UFOs were "entirely in error." But Horner also explained that many people who reported UFOs did not want details of the sightings made public and the Air Force respected their wishes. Writing to Senator Harry F. Byrd in January 1959, Major General W. P. Fisher (who replaced Joe Kelly as director of SAFLL) said the charge that the Air Force was withholding information "has no merit whatsoever." But, Fisher went on to explain, sometimes the Air Force did withhold information from the public to protect witnesses from "the idle curiosity of the sensation seekers" or to keep from "compromising our investigative processes." [10]

Congressional inquiries, threats of public hearings, and public pressure prompted two Air Force actions in late 1958: it issued another fact sheet in October and it undertook a staff study in December to evaluate its UFO program. The October fact sheet said "refinements" in Air Force investigatory processes had led to a decline in the number of unknown UFO reports. These refinements essentially meant integrating the probable and possible categories with the identified category, so that when the Air Force released its official statistics on UFO reports, it could claim that the unknowns, which were at 9 percent in 1953 and 1954 and at 3 percent in 1955, were only at 1.8 percent in the first six months of 1958. The fact sheet explained that Air Defense Command personnel conducted the investigations and then sent the data to ATIC for analyses and evaluation "by scientific means"; the UFO project often used the services of Dr. Hynek and other scientists to investigate individual cases or to conduct "detailed studies" of UFOs in general.[11]

As an example of the "scientific" aspect of Air Force procedures, the fact sheet mentioned, for the first time publicly, the 1953 Robertson panel. It explained that the Air Force convened the panel to conduct an "over-all examination of investigative procedures and findings on specific reports," and summarized the panel's conclusions and recommendations—without mentioning the educational program plans. Finally, the fact sheet explained that the Air Force classified reports "only in a few instances" to protect "elements in our Air Defense System" and did not comply with individual requests for information because "individuals who have assisted Air Force investigators" (the witnesses) might be embarrassed.[12]

Although the fact sheet's purpose was to relieve press and public pressure on the Air Force, it had limited effect on private UFO groups, and intelligence officers remained dissatisfied with the Air Force's ability to counter the inroads these groups had made in its credibility. Therefore, intelligence officers ordered a staff study to examine the public relations problems and to reevaluate its UFO program. The staff reported that civilian UFO groups frequently investigated a sighting from a biased viewpoint and then publicized it, pointing to inadequacies in the Air Force's handling of the case. Because the Air Force only investigated officially reported sightings, these groups could study and publicize sensational sightings never reported to the Air Force. These organizations knew the Air Force's deficiencies and used them to put it "in a defensive position." Moreover, the staff stated incorrectly, "Captain Ruppelt . . . is now affiliated with NICAP," which meant that Ruppelt and "political adventurist" Keyhoe "represent a formidable team from which plenty of trouble can be expected"; both were in the "business" for the money. Comparable situations existed in forty-nine other organizations, the staff explained, which "for various reasons" felt the need to do everything they could to discredit the Air Force. Often these groups reached witnesses before the Air Force did and primed them on what to say; the club members even remained in the room when the Air Force investigator asked his questions.[13]

The Air Force, the staff concluded, needed to increase its credibility. One problem was that the Air Force did not investigate all sightings and sometimes took a long time on those it did investigate. The time delay was crucial because it allowed UFO groups to complete their investigation quickly and put the Air Force on the spot. To complicate matters, the staff said, many Air Force investigators did not have the experience to handle complex situations; all they could do was ask questions as outlined in AFR 200-2. The staff recommended, first, that the Air Force assign eighteen to twenty men to temporary investigating duties and arm them with a UFO kit containing a standard operating procedure manual and other tools necessary for an adequate investigation; the men should be available at a moment's notice. Second, the Air Force should automatically investigate sightings reported to press people but not to it. Third, two members of the ATIC UFO group should be on alert each week for critical investigating duty. Implementing these recommendations, the staff felt, would help alleviate the problem of civilian UFO group criticism and also decrease the percentage of reports in the unknown and insufficient data categories (as of November 1958, 20 percent of all official reports were in these two categories).[14]

The ATIC commander tentatively approved the plan. But later Air Force headquarters dropped it, apparently deciding not to spend more money on a phenomenon that was no threat to the national security and that seemingly had no scientific value.[15]

In October 1958, one month before the staff undertook the above study, Major Robert J. Friend assumed Captain Gregory's duties as head of Project Blue Book. Friend was, according to Hynek, the only Blue Book chief who earned his respect. Having studied physics in graduate school, he had more extensive scientific training than other Blue Book chiefs, and he was a "total and practical realist" who understood Blue Book's limitations. No sycophant or bureaucrat, Friend was the fairest chief of Project Blue Book since Ruppelt. Although not an advocate of the extraterrestrial hypothesis, and to a certain extent a willing participant in the Great Keyhoe War, he nevertheless brought a new perspective to the project.[16]

When Friend took over the reins from Gregory, he immediately began to systematize the chaotic situation in Blue Book's office. He ordered an electric filer for reports, which Blue Book staff in the past had filed haphazardly or not at all. In his tenure he tried to institute a microfilming project to save the reports for posterity because he feared many had been pilfered. The Air Force decided the project was too expensive and never carried it out. Friend began cataloging the sightings according to color, size, geographic location, and the like, but the job was so enormous that the lack of additional help forced him to abandon the work. Friend also realized Hynek's value and supplied him daily with current UFO reports. More importantly, under Friend's direction and for the first time since the implementation of the Robertson panel recommendations in 1953, Blue Book began to reassess its role in studying the UFO phenomenon.[17]

The first indication of a new outlook for Blue Book came in February 1959 when Hynek called a meeting of key ATIC and Blue Book personnel to review public relations policies on UFOs, and also ostensibly because he was smarting from personal attacks. From 1957 to 1960 Hynek was codirector of the Smithsonian Institution's satellite tracking program and played a limited role in analyzing UFO reports. Hynek made clear at the beginning of the meeting that the Air Force "had done a good job of handling a very difficult program with the limited resources available" but that the Air Force could improve these resources and other facets of the program. Trying to smooth out some of the public relations and scientific problems, the participants suggested five changes.[18]

The first suggestion was to change the ambiguous appellation *unidentified flying objects,* although this was not the proper time to do so because such a change would supply "the UFO fanatics with ammunition for a new attack." But the participants did recommend changing the name of the statistical category *unknown* to *unidentified;* this, they thought, was less suggestive of mystery.

Second, the participants thought the Air Force should take advantage of favorable publicity: "Pictures and descriptions of the phenomena or objects determined as being probably responsible for a sighting should accompany a news release." [19]

Saying that the overall Air Force approach was not scientific enough, the participants' third recommendation was that the Air Force call in a panel of scientists once a month to discuss the UFO problem. Fourth, the participants thought Project Blue Book should review old, sensational, unknown cases—those that private UFO organizations were reopening "to the further embarrassment of the Air Force"—so that, given the "greater scientific knowledge" of the day, they "may be removed from the 'unknown' category and reclassified as a 'probable.' " Concerned about private UFO organization claims that people "held in high esteem by the public" sympathized with the organizations' views, the participants' fifth suggestion was for the Air Force Information Service to ask these individuals "for corroboration or denial and for further detail if in the affirmative." To relieve public pressure on Hynek, the participants decided to discontinue using his name in official press releases (which had begun to anger Hynek) and to have the Air Force Information Service answer inquiries addressed to him.[20]

Of the five suggestions, the Air Force implemented two: it changed the name of the unknown category to unidentified and, although it did not create an official scientific panel, it allowed Hynek to meet informally with some ATIC personnel each month. The purpose of the meetings was to review "troublesome cases," discern trends, and make suggestions for the future. The unofficial scientific advisory group, which Blue Book recruited, basically consisted of six men in addition to Hynek. They were astronomer L. V. Robinson, public relations specialist Theodore J. Hieatt, chaplain Captain R. Pritz, physicist V. J. Handmacher, psychologist Leroy D. Pigg, and Friend. The group met for the first time on May 5, 1959, and continued to convene about once a month until the end of 1960.[21]

The group recommended that the Air Force stop evaluating UFO reports on the basis of their potential hostility and, instead, step up its scientific evaluation of the phenomenon using the mass of available data rather than individual cases. The advisory group supplied a military reason for continued Air Force study of sighting reports: if Air Force personnel did not learn to discriminate between UFOs and space-probe equipment, in the future they might mistake UFOs for sophisticated enemy missiles. Air Force officials chose to ignore these recommendations, and by the end of 1960, the group, as Hynek said, "just petered out." Its effect was nil.[22]

The unofficial group of advisers had no impact primarily because ATIC, while the group met in 1959, conducted its own reassessment of the UFO project and arrived at different conclusions. Friend's outlook, continued private UFO group criticism, and increased expense for public relations all made the Blue Book staff think about getting rid of the UFO problem entirely. Friend realized that the Air Force's interest in UFOs only extended to determining whether they were threats to the national security or had intelligence value. He also realized that if the UFOs did not fall into one of these two categories, they were then a scientific problem and, as such, did not come within the purview of what the Air Force called the intelligence community. Because of Friend's attitude, ATIC ordered a second staff study to determine how to economize on the UFO program and how to devise a different policy toward it. This staff study became the most important of the UFO program to date.

The staff reported that the ATIC UFO program consisted of four essential tasks: investigating sightings for possible intelligence and/or scientific value; eliminating the "defensive attitude" of the program's public relations philosophy, such as "trying to prove that each object sighted is not a space ship"; informing the public that the UFO program, which evaluated each sighting, "is not essential to national security"; and using a public education program to "strip the shrouds of mystery" from the project because "many innocent people are duped by those who are using the UFO for personal gain." [23]

After twelve years of investigating and analyzing UFO reports—over 6,000 in total—ATIC had no evidence to suggest that UFOs were either space vehicles, a threat to national security, or of scientific value, the staff explained. The UFO program was a costly and "unproductive burden" on the Air Force, resulting only in "unfavorable publicity." The program, which strayed from its original intent, was 80 percent public relations efforts, primarily because members of more than fifty private UFO organizations "exploit unidentified flying objects for financial gain, religious or other more devious reasons at the expense of the Air Force." When dissatisfied with the Air Force's investigation, the staff said, these people convinced witnesses to complain to their congress-men, causing congressional hearings, unfavorable publicity, and more work for ATIC. Project Blue Book's staff, which included three full-time personnel, many part-time people, and the field investigators, "who must meet this problem on a day-to-day basis," could be more constructive on other programs.[24]

Given this situation, the staff considered four possible solutions. The "immediate elimination of the program" could certainly solve all problems but would destroy every advantage the Air Force had gained in the last twelve years, especially in public relations, and would undermine the average citizen's belief in the Air Force and give "UFOites" and "propagandists" more weapons. Complete disbandment was the eventual goal, the staff said, but "the public must first be conditioned in order that they be receptive of the idea." Thus, the Air Force should still receive and "give proper attention" to reports that might prove hostile or have scientific and intelligence value.[25]

A second solution was first to remove the program from the intelligence community, "where it is extremely dangerous to prestige," and then disband it completely. The Air Force could transfer the program to a more suitable branch of the service, such as the Office of Information Services; this would eliminate an intelligence program that was "open to public inspection" and lent itself to exaggerated importance. Then the Air Force would have to embark on a long-range educational program—using the press, radio, television, and motion pictures—to assure the public that it continued to monitor everything in the sky. One disadvantage was the likely "loss of prestige" in taking the program from intelligence and placing it in a public relations division. Another disadvantage would be the expense of a public education program, which would require new coordinative and liaison systems. But, the staff said, "the expense incurred in the public education program will more than pay for itself if this eventually leads to deactivation of the program." [26]

A third solution was to reassign the program from intelligence to an Air Force division with scientific and technical capability, such as the Air Research and Development Command (ARDC). This reassignment would provide the program with a fresh approach and greater scientific stature and would not result in loss of prestige. Such a transfer had a disadvantage in that the Air Force would have to establish new directives and lines of communication and train new personnel. The fourth and last alternative was to do nothing, to maintain the program in its special project status at ATIC. Yet the public tended to exaggerate the importance of a program connected with intelligence and such a wide-open program "has a tendency to reduce the prestige" of the entire intelligence community. The staff concluded that the best move was to transfer the UFO program to an Air Force division with scientific capability, which could implement an active public relations campaign with the goal of "the eventual elimination of the program as a special project." None of these possible solutions meant that the Air Force would stop receiving sighting reports, for it had to monitor all aerial objects. The Air Force wanted to eliminate the UFO *program,* not eliminate its watch over objects in the sky.[27]

After reaching the decision, ATIC attempted to interest the Air Research and Development Command in the program. Colonel Richard R. Shoop of ATIC explained to ARDC's commander, Lt. General Bernard Schriever, that the UFO program had potential scientific value in the areas of meteors, fireballs, space vehicles "(general)," missiles, radar, static electricity, meteorology, and upper-air physics. The UFO program's value to the Air Force, Shoop believed, lay not in intelligence but in exploring these areas for scientific purposes. ARDC was not convinced. Major General James Ferguson, ARDC vice commander, replied that more than half of the UFO program related to "nonscientific phenomena" and that the other portion, "while possibly associated with scientific processes, does not include qualitative data and is therefore of limited scientific value." Aerial phenomena observations, Ferguson said, would not "enhance" ARDC's research programs and, therefore, the proposed transfer was not "in the best interest of the Air Force." A letter from Hynek to ARDC strongly recommending the transfer failed to move Ferguson.[28]

ATIC next tried to transfer the UFO program to an Air Force public relations agency, such as the Secretary of the Air Force's Office of Information (SAFOI). In March 1960, ATIC deputy for science and components, Colonel Philip G. Evans, wrote to the ATIC commander, Major General Dougher, suggesting this transfer; A. Francis Arcier, ATIC chief scientist, concurred; he added that the prestige the UFO program might lose from a transfer to SAFOI was actually an advantage, because less prestige meant less importance. He recommended that Hynek remain the scientific adviser if ATIC transferred the program. ATIC made strenuous efforts to sell SAFOI on the idea of accepting the program, but SAFOI, like ARDC, wanted no part of it, for it also thought it would be inheriting a major public relations headache.[29]

While ATIC tried to transfer the program, two more books on UFOs came out and added yet more fuel to the Air Force–civilian UFO group fires. In *Flying Saucers: Top Secret*, Keyhoe outlined his activities from 1956 to 1960: the formation of NICAP, the *Armstrong Circle Theater* episode, and attempts to obtain hearings. Now more than ever, he said, he believed the Air Force was covering up to avoid panic, not only among the general populace but among its own pilots as well. According to Keyhoe, Air Force pilots heard rumors that UFOs had caused mysterious plane disappearances; if the Air Force admitted that UFOs existed, Keyhoe reasoned, the pilots would panic.[30]

Keyhoe, from his own perspective, was unable to arrive at a logical explanation for why the Air Force classified its files, denied the existence of extraterrestrial vehicles, and opposed congressional hearings. On the one hand, Air Force public policy statements about UFOs seemed to him contradictory, confusing, and sometimes erroneous. On the other hand, Keyhoe thought there was overwhelming evidence for the existence of extraterrestrial vehicles. Given this situation, Keyhoe reasoned that the only explanation to reconcile the two sides was his conspiracy-to-avoid-panic theory, with minor variations. Keyhoe tried to deal with an illogical situation in a logical manner.

In 1953 the Robertson panel gave the Air Force a reason for secrecy: UFO reports, by clogging intelligence channels, presented a threat to national security; therefore, the Air Force had to decrease the number of reports by downplaying the entire subject. But by 1960, the personnel change at Blue Book and, to some extent, at ATIC, the lessening of cold-war fears, the Air Force's confirmed belief that extraterrestrial vehicles did not exist, and the simple passage of time all obscured the original reasons for secrecy. In their place was the overriding public relations problem, questions about whether the Air Force was "doing its job," was lying to the people, or was competent to examine aerial phenomena.

Although the Air Force's goal was to eliminate the UFO program as a special project, it did not think it could take the apparent logical course of action—to open its files, announce the project unworthy of further involvement, and disband it. Instead, the public relations problem had assumed a life of its own. The Air Force, highly sensitive to bad publicity, looked at the conflict with civilian UFO groups as it would a war. Each attack was a battle; to declassify its files, stop its debunking campaign, or close down operations in the face of attacks was tantamount to surrender. The UFO enigma had only secondary importance, if that; the 1952 "hysteria" and the Robertson panel recommendations definitely had receded into the background. With the original reason for secrecy forgotten or neglected, secrecy to prevent bad press took prominence. It is doubtful that by 1960 anyone in the Air Force could remember the original reasons for the policies, and certainly not Keyhoe. Consequently, it was easy for him to conclude that the Air Force's action confirmed his theories.

Keyhoe would have had even more reason to believe high echelons of government conspired to keep information from the public had he known of the bizarre case the CIA had become involved in. The CIA had stayed away from the UFO controversy since it sponsored the 1953 Robertson panel. But in 1959 the Office of Naval Intelligence heard of a woman in Maine who claimed to be in contact with space people and brought it to the CIA's attention. Normally the government would have ignored this contactee-like case in which the woman used the common psychic device of automatic writing. But the Canadian government had also heard of this woman, and it sent Wilbert Smith, its UFO expert, to interview her. In her trance the woman purportedly correctly answered technical questions about space flight beyond her knowledge. After learning of this, the navy sent two officers to investigate. The woman persuaded one of the officers to go into a trance himself and try to contact the space people. He tried but failed.

When the two officers returned to Washington, they told CIA officials about their experience. The CIA arranged to have the officer who unsuccessfully tried to make contact try again at CIA headquarters. Six witnesses gathered in the CIA office to watch. The officer went into another trance and apparently made contact with space people. The other men in the room wanted proof. The officer in a trance said that if they looked out the window, they would see a flying saucer. Three men rushed to the window and were astonished to see a UFO. Two of these men were CIA employees and the third was with the Office of Naval Intelligence. At the exact same time, the radar center at Washington National Airport reported that its radar returns had been blocked out in the direction of the sighting. The CIA briefed Major Friend on these developments, and Friend sat in on a later trance session. He asked to be kept informed if anything else happened, but apparently nothing did. Friend thought Duke University's parapsychology laboratories should investigate the officer and the woman. But Project Blue Book never analyzed the sighting and what the men actually did see remains a mystery. The CIA did not treat the incident seriously yet took punitive actions against the men involved. It made sure they were transferred to other positions. As far as is known, the government never followed up on the sighting or the radar blackout.[31]

Although no one knew about this sighting, of course, the Air Force public relations policies in 1960 seemed to add support to Keyhoe's conspiracy theories, especially when Major Lawrence Tacker's *Flying Saucers and the U.S. Air Force* appeared. Tacker was an Air Force public information officer and the UFO project monitor for the press. He was angry that the Air Force "was being set upon by Major Keyhoe, NICAP and other UFO hobby groups who believe in space ships as an act of pure faith." He particularly objected to the "countless harangue[s] that the Air Force is withholding information." His book was supposed to set the record straight and end the debate.[32]

The short book was basically a compilation of press releases, fact sheets, and official pronouncements and, as such, was a good review of Air Force thought on UFOs in 1960. Tacker began with a short history of the UFO phenomenon, a history that illuminated the lack of basic knowledge within the Air Force of the phenomenon and the Air Force's involvement with it. Tacker maintained that one day in 1896 an airship sailed from Oakland to Chicago where it disappeared. Astronomers identified it as Alpha Orion, "but public opinion was that the object was an airship." Jumping to the 1947 and 1952 sightings, he claimed that lack of data was the only reason the Air Force did not draw "definite conclusions" and take the "aura of mystery" out of these sightings. The Air Force had taken the problem of UFOs seriously in 1952 and had "put a lot of effort into developing adequate and proper reporting, investigating, analysis, and evaluation procedures." This policy, he said, was still in effect, and "selected qualified scientists, engineers and other technical personnel" at ATIC kept Project Blue Book up to date so that the American public remained informed about UFOs.[33]

Tacker responded to four of the most common attacks on the Air Force, essentially the same four that Keyhoe made on the

Armstrong Circle Theater telecast in 1958. The first was that the Air Force had a document dated September 23, 1947, which proved that flying saucers existed. This referred to the Twining letter, which stated that the objects were "real" and authorized an Air Force investigation of UFOs, although Tacker did not identify it as such. His response to this charge was technically correct but deceptive: "There is no official Air Force report or document which states that . . . flying saucers are real." The Twining letter did not contain the term *flying saucers*. The second charge concerned the 1948 Estimate of the Situation document claiming that UFOs were interplanetary. Ruppelt, Fournet, and Hynek had verified its existence, but Tacker replied that ATIC never had an "official" document of this nature.[34]

In response to the third accusation—that a secret Air Force intelligence report on UFO maneuvers concluded that the objects were interplanetary (Dewey Fournet's late 1952 study)—Tacker stated bluntly that such a report was "non-existent." Finally, Tacker dealt with the charge that a secret panel of scientists in 1953 urged the Air Force to expand Project Blue Book and publicly release all UFO information (the Robertson panel recommendations as Ruppelt explained them). Tacker acknowledged the panel and accurately summarized its recommendations, but he omitted one: that national security agencies should institute a public education program immediately to strip the aura of mystery from UFOs.[35] He failed to give the reasons why the panel convened.

Tacker explained in the book that a team of selected scientists met each month (the unofficial UFO panel) to make sure the Air Force used "every means available" to pursue a "positive UFO investigation program," and that the Air Force conducted a "thorough information program . . . to keep the public informed." In spite of all Air Force efforts, Tacker said, "a small but articulate segment of people" mistakenly believed that the Air Force had not investigated the UFO problem scientifically and that it withheld information from the public. These people, according to Tacker, spoke out because the subject was so "novel and fascinating" that it supported over a hundred organizations, all of which expected the Air Force to release its data to provide "grist" for their publications. These organizations made "senseless and vicious" attacks on the Air Force, which "would be remiss in its duty to the American people if by its assistance it encouraged these clubs in their sensational claims and intentions." Tacker concluded by saying that the Air Force had a tremendous job in defending the country from enemies; if the Air Force diverted more money and personnel to investigate UFOs, it would seriously jeopardize the country's security, allow "sensation seekers" to "dictate our defense policies," and lay itself "open to the charge of gross impudence." [36]

That same year Tacker continued his defense of the Air Force with appearances on radio and television shows around the country. On the radio show "Washington Viewpoint" he outlined the "vast scientific resources" the Air Force used to analyze UFO sightings, resources such as the Air Research and Development Command, the Air Materiel Command, and scientific consultants from many different colleges and universities. Furthermore, Tacker said, the Air Force had "instantaneous communications world-wide," which enabled it to hear about a sighting anywhere in the world "in a matter of minutes." He compared this to a "small group of euphologists [sic] who have a typewriter and read a newspaper account of the thing, and—you see you really can't compare." [37]

Tacker's personal campaign had little effect. The civilian UFO groups continued their attacks, congressmen remained interested, and as a result the Air Force had to resist new threats of congressional hearings. In early July 1960, members of the Senate Committee on Preparedness, the House Armed Forces Committee, the House Science and Astronautics Committee, and the CIA requested Air Force briefings on the UFO program. The public increased pressure on congressmen, who were concerned particularly over charges that the Air Force investigation was inadequate. The Air Force gave a preliminary briefing to Stuart French of the Senate Preparedness Committee on July 13. French wanted to know about Air Force solutions to puzzling cases and requested résumés of several well-known sightings, including those in Washington, D.C., and in Levelland, Texas. He also felt that Project Blue Book should be capable of investigating cases that might have scientific significance.[38]

The French briefing was a warm-up for the major briefing on July 15, 1960. Present were Richard Smart from the House Armed Forces Committee, Spencer Bereford, Richard Hines, and Frank Hammit from the House Science and Astronautics Committee, and two men from the CIA (Richard Payne, technical adviser, and John Warner, assistant for legislative liaison to Allen Dulles). Air Force representatives included John McLaughlin (administrative assistant to the secretary of the Air Force), Major General Luehman (director of intelligence), Brigadier General E. B. LeBailley and Tacker (Office of Information), Brigadier General Kingsley and Colonel James C. McKee (Office of Legislative Liaison), Lt. Colonel Sullivan (intelligence), Major Boland (legislative liaison), Major Friend, and Hynek.

The congressmen were not as cooperative as others had been in the past. Bereford of the Science and Astronautics Committee said it had discussed UFOs and they appeared to have "scientific potential." Congressman Smart (of the House Armed Forces Committee) believed the Air Force withheld information from the public as well as from congressional committees. Although the Air Force assured him this was not the case, Smart remained skeptical. He was particularly unhappy that the Air Force investigated routine cases but was "limited" when a case required extensive scientific analysis. He indicated that his committee would be satisfied if it could say the Air Force had the "numbers and the capability" to investigate all cases that appeared to have intelligence, scientific, or public relations value. Also, he wanted the Air Force to keep his committee advised of all pertinent sightings and warned that future remarks to his constituents would be based on these conditions. Hynek had told Smart about ATIC's inadequate capability to investigate UFO cases with scientific potential, displaying his growing dissatisfaction with the Air Force; of course Hynek agreed with all of Smart's recommendations.[39]

For the Air Force, though, Hynek's growing restiveness was

unimportant, and the significant aspect of the briefing was that once again the Air Force had successfully prevented open hearings. As General Luehman said to the assistant chief of staff for intelligence, "All personnel attending the briefing were pleased with the results and the general consensus is that no public hearings will be held in the near future." [40]

Nevertheless, congressmen for the first time had expressed dissatisfaction with the UFO program and had suggested steps to remedy the situation. Hoping to put a quick end to congressional dissatisfaction, the Air Force immediately began to deal with Smart's recommendations. ATIC decided that to investigate cases with intelligence, scientific, and public relations potential, it would assign another man to Project Blue Book, which had a staff of only one commissioned and one noncommissioned officer. ATIC estimated it had to investigate from twelve to fifteen cases per year, at a probable cost of $200 per case, and needed an additional $3,000 to carry out the program; it also needed money to buy a Polaroid camera and a geiger counter for the investigators and $1,000 per year to raise Hynek's salary (he was receiving $3,000 per year as a consultant). ATIC officially requested the funds from the assistant chief of staff for intelligence (AFCIN).[41] While waiting for the extra money to come through, the Office of the Secretary of the Air Force authorized travel money in connection with the recommendations. But in September AFCIN informed ATIC that it would not allocate additional personnel or funds for Project Blue Book. ATIC would be able to institute Smart's recommendations in one way only: Blue Book could have "close telephone monitorship" with air base officers investigating a UFO sighting of "extreme importance." [42]

The Air Force did not relay this information to Smart, who inquired in November about the progress it had made toward implementing his recommendations. The Office of Legislative Liaison explained that the changes "had yet to be accomplished." In early 1961 Major Friend decided on a new course of action. Blue Book requested an increased budget for the fiscal year which allowed it to implement at least a compromise measure to satisfy Smart. Rather than use one officer full time, it decided to place four officers on an on-call basis; because UFO sightings were "cyclical and erratic," the four officers could handle the reports more expeditiously. This response seemed to satisfy Smart. Blue Book did use these officers from time to time during Friend's stay as head of the project but not afterward.[43]

Publicly the Air Force remained silent about its congressional briefings and investigatory problems. It continued to castigate its critics and assure the public that top-level scientists with command of all necessary facilities were conducting a rigorous scientific investigation of UFOs. The Air Force withheld nothing from the American public, it said, except in certain cases when the data required security classification. The July 1960 fact sheet criticized the many "self-appointed authorities on UFOs" who considered themselves "unofficial advisors to the United States Air Force Intelligence community." Because they did not have this authority under the law, the Air Force thought "it would be entirely inappropriate and even dangerous at times to exercise the Intelligence system in order to give them, or their organization, any notoriety or publicity." ATIC officials privately placed the blame for the July congressional briefings on Keyhoe, NICAP, and other civilian UFO organizations. Colonel Evans reflected this when he said that the 500,000-plus members claimed by the civilian groups belonged for "financial gain, religious reasons, pure emotional outlet, ignorance, or possibly to use the organization as a 'cold war' tool." NICAP and Keyhoe were of course the principal villains.[44]

Still, many congressmen continued to inquire about the UFO program. The Air Force replied, as it had done in previous years, with statements from the semiannual fact sheets. Once in a while it changed its official line. For example, writing to Senator Oren E. Long in April of 1960, Colonel Carl M. Nelson (legislative liaison) said the Air Force protected the identity of UFO witnesses "in order to encourage the public to report UFO's." Brigadier General Joseph Kingsley, deputy director of legislative liaison, wrote to John Carstarphen of the House Committee on Science and Astronautics in May 1960 and said that as Mr. Carstarphen could tell from the recent U-2 incident (the abortive mission over the USSR), the Air Force had a difficult job in defending against "known enemies" and their weapons systems and had committed all its resources to this end; one of the greatest problems in the UFO area was not to waste resources on false alarms or UFOs that did not constitute a threat to the country's security. Kingsley also told Carstarphen that the Air Force's refusal to lend its resources to private UFO groups was based on the 1953 Robertson panel, which found that UFOs constituted a threat to the "orderly function of the protective units of the body politic because an unwarranted mass of irrelevant information could clog vital channels of communication and continued false reports could hide indications of a genuine hostile attack." Similarly, Colonel Gordon B. Knight told Estes Kefauver in April 1960 that the Air Force did not honor individual requests for UFO information because it did not have the resources to do so and because most of the replies to the requests ended up in the files of private UFO organizations.[45]

These Air Force explanations did not convince everyone. House Speaker John McCormack, whom the Air Force briefed in 1958, doubted it had disclosed all it knew at that time. In fact, McCormack believed in 1960 that UFOs were "real" and not familiar objects or delusions. The reputation of many UFO witnesses impressed him and, with Keyhoe's urging, he began to think about holding another congressional investigation. In 1961 he directed Congressman Overton Brooks of the House Science and Astronautics Committee to look into the UFO problem. Brooks was sympathetic, and he appointed Minnesota Congressman Joseph Karth head of a three-man Subcommittee on Space Problems and Life Sciences and directed Karth to hold hearings on UFOs.[46]

Keyhoe had written letters to both Brooks and McCormack requesting these congressional hearings and proposing a plan in which both NICAP and the Air Force would present their evidence on the existence of extraterrestrial vehicles at an executive session of the subcommittee. There, Keyhoe said, NICAP would present proof of Air Force incompetency in dealing with UFO reports and proof of Air Force secrecy in making "contradictory, misleading and untrue statements" to congressmen and private citizens. Keyhoe wanted the Air Force representatives to answer all NICAP questions about specific cases and methods. In turn, said Keyhoe, NICAP would answer all Air Force questions. If, after hearing evidence on both sides, the executive session disproved NICAP's contentions, then Keyhoe would resign as director of NICAP, cease all publications, and dissolve the organization. If, on the other hand, the executive session decided that the Air Force was withholding information, then it should ask the Air Force to end its secrecy policies and NICAP would request that the government establish a new agency to "insure the speedy release of all UFO information, with the immediate purpose of reducing the grave secrecy-dangers [sic]." If the Air Force refused to participate in this plan, NICAP would urge public hearings. The full NICAP board of governors signed the proposal.[47]

In mid-1961 the Air Force heard about the proposed hearings for early 1962. To meet this new crisis the Office of Legislative Liaison began to direct its efforts toward heading off the hearings. But it could not prevent House Science and Astronautics Committee staff member Richard P. Hines from visiting ATIC to gather information for the hearings. When Hines, who had attended the July 1960 briefing, came to ATIC in August, Friend "thoroughly briefed" him on the Air Force method of conducting the UFO program, using "government-wide facilities . . . to provide data and/or assist with the analyses." ATIC officials, including Hynek, took Hines on a tour of the Aeronautical Systems Division facilities which, they said, gave support to the UFO program. Hines told Friend and Hynek that congressional interest in the program was due to pressures from "undisclosed sources" on John W. McCormack. The three men reasoned that Keyhoe was the culprit, especially since he had been behind previous congressional inquiries, had spoken on radio and television about the need for congressional hearings, and had urged NICAP members to write to congressmen. Hines left ATIC "favorably impressed" with the Air Force UFO program and enlightened about Keyhoe's intentions.[48]

A week later Hines wrote to Major Friend, addressing the letter "Dear Bob" and saying he had not talked to Karth yet but Chairman Overton Brooks had decided not to hold UFO hearings then or in the foreseeable future. "For this," Hines remarked, "I am sure both you and I breathe a deep sigh of relief." As a result of this decision, Hines explained, the " 'Plaintiffs' [meaning Keyhoe] have begun their clamor stimulated by notices in the press of our committee's interest in UFOs." [49]

The following week Congressman Karth wrote to Keyhoe viciously attacking him for trying to " 'be-little,' 'defame,' 'ridicule' " the Air Force. He accused Keyhoe of "malicious intent toward a great branch of the military." Previously, Karth said, he thought Keyhoe planned to "prove" the existence of spaceships but knew now that Keyhoe could not do it (Keyhoe never claimed he could prove this). Therefore, Karth concluded, he was not interested in holding hearings or "listening to headline-making accusations (prompted it seems by past gripes) in open debate between you and the Air Force." Karth became more agitated as the letter progressed. Answering Keyhoe's request for a face-to-face meeting before the executive session of the subcommittee, Karth said protocol called for the Air Force and NICAP to testify on different days, and Keyhoe obviously wanted the direct confrontation only to ask the Air Force embarrassing questions and indulge in "grandstand acts of a rabble rousing nature where accusations may be made THAT COULDN'T BE ANSWERED BY ANYONE—the Air Force or NICAP." Karth was quick to claim, however, that *I am not a captive of the Air Force,* I assure you." A few days later Major Friend quoted to Colonel Wynn what Karth had told a newspaper reporter: "[The reporter] was advised by that worthy gentleman that he would not be part of Major Keyhoe's cheap scheme to discredit the Air Force, and that there would be no hearing." [50]

Keyhoe weathered this attack and even managed to soften Karth's views. In answer to Karth's charges, Keyhoe replied that he wanted the confrontation with the Air Force to occur in closed session only and that NICAP did not have "evidence" that "UFOs were superior objects under intelligent control" and extraterrestrial. Moreover, the NICAP board of governors gave Karth "proof of NICAP's serious and patriotic purpose and its continued offer to cooperate with the Air Force." In place of its original plan, Keyhoe said, NICAP would offer its "massive UFO evidence" in accordance with congressional protocol. During the month of this exchange, Chairman Overton Brooks died. The new chairman, Congressman George P. Miller of California, expressed neither an interest in UFOs nor a desire for hearings. On September 19, 1961, Karth wrote to Keyhoe: "Now that we better understand each other, I would hope we could properly proceed with a new hearing early next year—providing that the new chairman authorizes hearings." Of course, the new chairman did not. Once more Keyhoe had watched the bait dangle in front of him only to see it withdrawn at what he thought was the critical moment.[51]

Events on the UFO home front in 1961 and 1962 did not go well for NICAP and Keyhoe. When the organization first started in 1958, Keyhoe maintained close and cordial contact with the Aerial Phenomena Research Organization (APRO) in Alamogordo, New Mexico (before it moved to Tucson, Arizona). Although never convinced of the grand conspiracy theme, Coral Lorenzen (director of APRO) supported NICAP by giving lip service to the idea. From 1959 to 1961, however, she grew steadily away from this position. She had worked for the Air Force in a civilian capacity at Holloman Air Force Base in New Mexico and had found no evidence for a conspiracy there, and she had the growing suspicion that the Air Force UFO program amounted to no more than public relations. Mrs. Lorenzen began to feel that NICAP's attacks on the Air Force were misguided. Moreover, APRO was more willing than NICAP to consider reports of UFO occupants. Although both groups strongly disavowed any connection with the infamous contactees, APRO would accept reports of occupant sightings if the evidence warranted it whereas NICAP steadfastly refused to accept such reports because they seemed too similar to the contactees' bogus claims. NICAP scrupulously avoided even the vaguest hint of hoax.[52]

The issues came to a head in 1961 and 1962 when both

organizations felt a financial squeeze. Lack of a major sighting wave had caused a decrease in press publicity about UFOs and public interest began to wane and membership to dwindle. Many people interested in UFOs belonged to both APRO and NICAP; the 1962 "recession" prompted some people to give up their dual membership. In an effort to retain APRO's membership, Coral Lorenzen wrote an editorial in the newsletter stating that NICAP was basically a lobby group and members should remain in APRO because it was more active in research than in uselessly attacking the Air Force. This editorial represented an open break in the simmering feud with NICAP, and the two organizations were never able to cooperate again.[53]

Other UFO club members had been sniping at Keyhoe as well. James Moseley of the Saucer and Unexplained Celestial Events Research Society (SAUCERS) thought the Air Force used Keyhoe to divert public attention from UFOs, and others believed Lorenzen was right and Keyhoe's energies would be best spent in matters other than lobbying. The ever present contactees were another problem that plagued Keyhoe constantly. He spent much time telling the press and NICAP members that he forbade contactees to join NICAP. But the contactees were a pesky lot. In 1958 George Adamski claimed on television and radio shows that he was a member of NICAP. Keyhoe found to his horror that his secretary, second in command at NICAP, secretly had issued Adamski and other contactees membership cards because she was convinced of their truthfulness. To Keyhoe this was treason in his own general staff and he accepted her resignation. On top of this, NICAP was in a continual state of financial crisis. Time and again Keyhoe sent out emergency pleas for donations to keep the organization solvent; the membership always contributed the necessary funds.[54]

Through the rival UFO proponent attacks, contactee troubles, and financial problems, Keyhoe steered a steady course aimed at Congress and the Air Force. Undoubtedly Keyhoe's most important activity in 1962 was to compile with Richard Hall (who had replaced Keyhoe's secretary) a document containing the best NICAP evidence to support the extraterrestrial intelligence theory. The document contained numerous detailed sighting reports from reputable individuals, scientists' statements, congressmen's statements, and the like. NICAP issued this compendium to all congressmen who expressed an interest in UFOs and in the Air Force's handling of the matter. Most often, however, NICAP pushed for congressional investigations simply by showing congressmen key UFO reports and examples of Air Force secrecy and by its letter writing campaign.[55]

The Air Force's public relations problems remained—even though the Office of Information, the Office of Legislative Liaison, and the Office of the Assistant Chief of Staff for Intelligence tried to avert congressional hearings, discredit NICAP and Keyhoe, and transfer the UFO project. And the sighting reports continued to come into ATIC at a steady rate of between 500 and 600 a year. ATIC received 474 reports in 1962, and this was far from the desired goal of no reports at all. Consequently, in 1962 ATIC made one final effort to transfer the UFO program.[56]

Edward R. Trapnell, assistant for public relations to the secretary of the Air Force, had become interested in the UFO program and requested a briefing from Lieutenant Colonel Friend (recently promoted from major). At the briefing, Friend and Hynek told Trapnell about the Robertson panel's recommendations and the Air Force's attempts to educate the public by stripping the UFO program of its "aura of mystery" and putting it in "its proper perspective." Trapnell "was amazed to learn" that UFO reports were, as Friend and Hynek had told him, three times higher in 1962 than the yearly totals in the 1947 to 1951 period, and he observed that "this could grow into a lifetime job unless headed off in some manner." [57]

Afterward, Trapnell met with Secretary of the Air Force Zuckert, Dr. Brockway McMillan (head of Air Force research and development), and Dr. Robert Calkins (president of the Brookings Institution); they suggested several transfer plans. The Air Force could transfer the UFO program to an agency such as the National Aeronautics and Space Administration, the National Science Foundation, or the Smithsonian Institution. Or the Air Force could contract it out to a private group, such as the

Brookings Institution, which would operate the program under the auspices of an Air Force scientific complex such as, for example, the Office of Aerospace Research. Or, third, the Air Force could contract the project to a private organization and not keep it under Air Force auspices. The organization could "make positive statements regarding the program and the Air Force's handling of it in the past and make recommendations regarding its future, i.e., disban[d] the program completely" or transfer it to NASA or the like.[58]

Lieutenant Colonel Friend took a dim view of the transfer, which past experience had taught him was all but impossible because no one wanted the public relations problem that went with it. Friend believed the only two alternatives left were either to disband the program or to contract it to a private organization under the Air Force's monitorship. Colonel Edward Wynn, who had taken over Colonel Evans's position as deputy for science and components, concurred with Friend but was even more pessimistic about any transfer possibility. Transferring it to NASA or the National Science Foundation "would only serve to convince a larger segment of the public that sightings are due to visits to earth by interplanetary space vehicles." Contracting the project out to another agency would be expensive, the public would think that the Air Force was secretly directing the private agency to make certain statements, and the Air Force still would have to investigate sightings even though the private group would analyze them. Thus, Colonel Wynn and the Foreign Technology Division (in 1961 ATIC became part of the Foreign Technology Division [FTD] of the Air Force Systems Command) thought the Air Force should embark on a public education program and eventually either disband the special project entirely while still investigating UFO reports at the air base level or, failing this, continue the UFO program in one of its scientific branches.[59]

Despite these arguments, the Air Force tried once again to get rid of the UFO program. But again its attempts to get NASA or the National Science Foundation to handle the program proved futile. In 1962 the Air Force finally gave up the entire idea. The program remained at FTD as a special project and without expanded resources.[60] The irony of the situation was that Keyhoe, through his persistent campaign against Air Force secrecy, unwittingly prevented the Air Force from approaching the problem more systematically. By keeping the UFO program and fighting public relations battles with Keyhoe, the Air Force found it had a burden that no other agency—private or public—wished to assume. In a sense, NICAP's fight to have the public recognize the seriousness of the UFO problem had, because of the Air Force's counter efforts, moved the UFO problem away from scientific scrutiny and closer toward Air Force control.

After all transfer plans dissolved, Lieutenant Colonel Friend retired as head of Project Blue Book in 1963 and Major Hector Quintanilla replaced him. Friend had realized that the UFO program did not belong in the intelligence community and had tried to transfer it to a more suitable branch of the service; when this failed, he had pushed for disbandment. Quintanilla, on the other hand, made no efforts whatsoever to improve Blue Book's capabilities or to transfer the project. He basically believed Blue Book was doing the best job it could and there was no reason to rock the boat by improving Blue Book's status. He looked on Blue Book as a collection and public relations agency, not as an investigatory or analysis operation. He maintained complete belief in the Air Force's ability to cope with the UFO problem and its public relations component, envisioning his role as that of caretaker.[61]

While Blue Book's outlook was changing, congressional interest declined and by mid-1963 reached a low point. According to available evidence, Georgia Congressman Carl Vinson made the last congressional inquiry into UFOs until 1966.[62]

In spite of a decrease in press and congressional interest and in the number of UFOs reported to ATIC, NICAP continued its constant pressure on Congress. In 1964 NICAP put together another compendium of facts surrounding the UFO enigma (basically a revised version of the previous compendium). Published privately as *The UFO Evidence*, the 200-page report contained the best evidence for extraterrestrial visitation NICAP could gather. It covered nearly every aspect of the UFO phenomenon, from details of over 700 sightings (at least 50 percent made by "trained or experienced observers") to congressional and scientific attitudes toward the subject. Complete with charts, graphs, photostatic documents, Air Force statements, and NICAP rebuttals, the book placed the UFO controversy in historical context based on NICAP's perceptions of events. NICAP mailed a copy to every member of Congress. Probably as a result of *The UFO Evidence* and incessant NICAP pressure on Congress, Blue Book began to package its reports more attractively. Instead of issuing semiannual fact sheets, it began in 1964 to print an annual booklet discussing in detail all the sightings and their statistical breakdowns, the Air Force's methodology, and the UFO program's history. It also included short articles and reprints on the improbabilities of extraterrestrial visitation.[63]

At this time Donald Menzel came out with his second book on UFOs, *The World of Flying Saucers: A Scientific Examination of a Major Myth of the Space Age.* Written with the help of science writer Lyle Boyd, the book basically rehashed Menzel's 1953 work. Although slightly more moderate in his remarks about "flying saucer enthusiasts," Menzel refused to criticize the Air Force investigation or to temper his statements about the absurdity of the extraterrestrial visitation theory. Branching out into the history of the UFO phenomenon, he attributed the saucer sightings in the late 1940s to the efforts of publisher Ray Palmer, who printed Kenneth Arnold's story ("I Did See the Flying Disks") in the first issue of *Fate* magazine. Menzel said the "panic" of 1952 was a result of Ginna and Darrach's *Life* magazine article, the *Look* article on "Hunt for the Flying Saucers," and the issuance of AFR 200-2. These, plus the summer heat wave, meteors, and the 1951 motion picture *The Day the Earth Stood Still*, all acted on people's imaginations and they started seeing flying saucers.[64]

Menzel went on to explain that the Robertson panel spent "five long days . . . analyzing every available act of evidence" relating to possible theories about UFOs and found no support for the extraterrestrial hypothesis. Menzel admitted that the Air Force should have declassified the panel's conclusions immediately because this would have ended the saucer scare at once. But, instead, "the UFO hysteria continued, and is still dying a slow and lingering death." The Air Force, of course, was enthusiastic about Menzel's book and called it "the most significant literary effort to date" on the UFO phenomenon.[65]

Hynek (now at Northwestern University), in the meantime, continued to change his attitude about UFOs and to call for increased scientific study. The 1964 Lonnie Zamora case in Socorro, New Mexico, further changed Hynek's mind.

While chasing a speeder at about 4:45 P.M., Socorro Deputy Marshal Lonnie Zamora heard a sound like a roar and saw flames off to his right in hilly desert terrain. He thought the dynamite shack there had exploded and abandoned the chase to investigate. He turned onto a dirt road leading to the dynamite shack. As he proceeded to the site, he saw a shiny, aluminum-like object, which he thought was an overturned car. He noticed two people in white coveralls standing next to the object. One of the people turned and looked straight at Zamora's car. The person seemed surprised and quickly jumped. Zamora began to hurry toward them thinking they needed help. He radioed to the sheriff's office that he was in the process of investigating an accident.[66]

Zamora approached to within a hundred feet of the object and got out of his car. He then heard a loud roar that changed in frequency from soft to loud to very loud. At the same time he spotted a strange blue and orange flame that appeared to be coming from the underside of the object. Zamora panicked. He turned and ran, bumping his leg against the car which made his glasses fall off. He glanced back a few times and noticed that the roaring object was egg shaped and had a red "insignia." He also noticed that the object had lifted off the ground to a height of about twenty to twenty-five feet. The continual roar frightened Zamora, and he ducked down and covered his head with his arms. At that point the roar stopped and a high-pitched whine emanated from the object; then complete silence. Zamora lifted his head and saw the object heading away from him against the wind. He jumped up, ran back to his car, and immediately radioed the sheriff's station and asked the radio dispatcher to look out the window and try to see the object. The radio officer failed to see it.[67]

Zamora then went to where the object had been and discovered burning brush in several places and depressed marks in the ground. Three minutes later a sheriff who had been listening to the radio conversation arrived on the scene. Zamora was shaken, sweating, and pale. The sheriff looked around the area and also found the burning brush and indentations. Later a gas station attendant reported that a customer had mentioned seeing an unusual oval-shaped object heading in the direction of Zamora's sighting just before it happened.[68]

This unusual case had important ramifications. The press heard about it and widely publicized it. Once again the public put pressure on the Air Force, congressmen, and the White House. Quintanilla dispatched Hynek to investigate the case personally. Hynek confirmed the burned areas and the depressions, and he sent soil samples to the Air Force for analysis. The analysis uncovered nothing unusual. Hynek interviewed Zamora at length. Zamora was by this time weary of interviews because he had already related his story countless times to police officers, the FBI, newsmen, and civilian UFO groups, including APRO and NICAP. Zamora impressed Hynek, who found the deputy marshal to be highly credible and reliable. Dr. Lincoln LaPaz, who had worked on old Project Twinkle, knew Zamora and testified to his honesty. Zamora was telling the truth, Hynek concluded. Hynek's report stated that this was one of the "major UFO sightings in the history of the Air Force's consideration of the subject." To the press he declared that the sighting was "one of the soundest, best substantiated reports." Privately Hynek cautioned Quintanilla that the UFO organizations would probably make a large commotion over this sighting.[69]

Quintanilla immediately began to work on the case with the assumption that Zamora had seen something. Quintanilla reasoned that the landing mechanisms of an experimental lunar landing module could have made the depressions in the ground. He discreetly contacted NASA, the Jet Propulsion Laboratory, and fifteen industrial firms to see if they were conducting any experiments with lunar landing modules in the area. In each case the answer was no. Quintanilla also established that no helicopters or aircraft were in the area at the time of the sighting and that the direction of the winds ruled out the possibility that the object was a balloon. Quintanilla had no alternative. He listed the case as unidentified. This is the only combination landing, trace, and occupant case listed as unidentified in Blue Book files.

The case had an impact on NICAP. Prior to this, NICAP had scrupulously avoided any occupant cases because they smacked of contacteeism. But because of Zamora's reliability and credibility, and because the Air Force listed this case as unidentified, NICAP began slowly to reevaluate its position. As a result, NICAP moved closer to APRO's stance regarding occupant cases and the sighting served to "liberalize" the organization.[70]

Perhaps the case affected Hynek the most: he now came to virtually the opposite position to that which he had held when he started as an Air Force consultant in 1948. He was ready to accept privately some sensational cases as being a legitimate part of the UFO controversy.

By the end of 1964 the UFO controversy had reached a type of stalemate. On the one side were Keyhoe, NICAP, and, to some extent, APRO. Keyhoe had some support in Congress and NICAP still had prestigious people on its board of governors. Also on this side were the sightings, an ever present source of embarrassment and concern for the Air Force, which had forced itself into the position of categorizing virtually every UFO witness as credulous, gullible, or easily deceived. NICAP's policies, popular pressure, and the sightings created congressional interest and the threat of hearings.

On the other side was the Air Force with its three-pronged counterattack: ATIC to evaluate the sighting reports, SAFOI to deal with public inquiries, and SAFLL to counter congressional hearings. The tool they used was elaborate briefings. While not containing complete fabrications, the briefings, except during Robert Friend's tenure, were certainly deceptive and designed to place the Air Force in the best possible light and its critics in the worst. Helping the Air Force in its public relations were the mass media and most scientists. The latter, believing Air Force press releases and without extensive research experience in the UFO phenomenon, derided the legitimacy of the subject and castigated the people who considered it important. Donald Menzel stood out in this group as the Air Force's leading scientist-ally, as the self-professed UFO debunker, and, as he characterized himself, "the man who shot Santa Claus."

In the middle of the warring factions stood Hynek. The amount of time he took to change his attitude, the better part of nine years, was a testament to his caution and his concern over other scientists' criticism of him for taking the subject of UFOs seriously. By 1964, though, it was questionable whether he was the Air Force's ally.

The opposing forces faced each other in a standoff. The Air Force public relations policies had to some extent decreased public concern over UFOs, but NICAP and APRO continued to bring the subject to public attention. Congress had not held hearings on the subject, as Keyhoe and NICAP wanted, but the Air Force had averted them only barely. Congress had pushed for expansion of the scientific aspect of the program, but the Air Force managed to avert this also. And within the Air Force itself, ATIC wanted to transfer the program but other divisions refused to take it. The two variables that NICAP and the Air Force could not predict were Hynek and the number of sighting reports. At the beginning of 1965, these two unknowns assumed paramount importance and opened another front in the continuing battle.

1965:

THE TURNING POINT
IN THE CONTROVERSY

For seventeen years, 1947 to 1964, the UFO controversy raged within the confines of special interest groups—the Air Force on one hand and the private UFO organizations on the other. The press, public, and Congress became involved sporadically, but for them the subject of UFOs and the controversy over the phenomenon had only fleeting interest, depending on the frequency of the reports. The Air Force and private group charges and countercharges remained unimportant for most people. The one group that might have given the subject dramatic interest and popular importance—the scientists—remained silent. But the period from 1965 to 1967 marked a turning point in the controversy. Those who had been on the periphery of the controversy became actively engaged in it. The press, public, Congress, and the scientific community all entered the debate over UFOs. As a result, the Air Force finally gave up its near monopoly of the UFO study and asked a university to examine the phenomenon.

The impetus for this turning point was the one unknown variable, and the crux of all the controversy—UFO sightings. Although ATIC recorded sighting reports at an average rate of 30 to 50 per month for the first six months of 1965, it received 135 reports in July and 262 in August. This began a wave that continued until the middle of 1967. The increase in reports prompted widespread press and public criticism of the Air Force

UFO program and an outpouring of popular articles and books on UFOs.

A long drought of press publicity on UFOs ended in 1965. Since 1957 the press had accepted the Air Force viewpoint and had refrained from criticizing it. Many newspapers even refused to carry sighting reports because editors decided the reports were only illusions, fabrications, or misidentifications of natural phenomena. Because no significant wave of sightings had occurred since 1957, newspaper editors thought the UFO fascination had ended. But in August 1965, following a series of spectacular UFO sightings in Texas, press interest revived.[1] The new attitude seemed to be a product of frustration over the Air Force's inability to explain UFOs. Since Air Force pronouncements had not affected the number of sighting reports, more newspaper editors and reporters became suspicious of the Air Force's role. Some newspapers even seemed to agree with NICAP's conspiracy theories.

The *Charleston* (South Carolina) *Evening Post* reported in 1965 that "something is going on 'up there' and we rather suspect the Air Force knows it." When the Air Force received a UFO report, the *Evening Post* stated, it "immediately begins to crank out of the wild blue yonder the same pre-recorded announcement it has been playing for 20 years: scratch, scratch, the Air Force has no evidence, scratch, scratch, the Air Force has no evidence. . . . If our courts shared the Air Force's professed suspicion of creditable witnesses our jails would be empty." The *Orlando* (Florida) *Sentinel* printed a compilation of newspaper editorials in early September 1965 and noted that many editorial writers had changed focus "from outright scepticism to at least tentative belief" in extraterrestrial visitation. If these editorial writers joined with congressmen interested in the UFO problem, the *Orlando Sentinel* predicted, then "perhaps something will happen," and the Air Force would be forced to open its classified UFO files. "Whether UFOs or not, the public deserves to know." [2]

The *Fort Worth Star Telegram* said "[the Air Force] can stop kidding us now about there being no such things as flying saucers. . . . It's going to take more than a statistical report on how many reported saucers turned out to be jets and weather balloons to convince us otherwise." The editor of the *Richmond* (Virginia) *News Leader* wrote that only imprudent people would deny the possibility that UFOs were real: "Attempts to dismiss the reported sightings . . . serve only to heighten the suspicion that there's something out there. The Air Force doesn't want us to know." For the *Alameda* (California) *Times-Star* the time was "long overdue" for governmental disclosure of all it knew about UFOs. "It would surprise no one today to learn that some UFOs are spacecraft from elsewhere in the solar system or beyond. In fact, it would even be more surprising to learn that they were not." [3]

The *Christian Science Monitor* remarked that recent sightings over Texas gave "the clearest evidence of all that something strange was actually in the sky." The *Monitor* called for a "thorough look at the saucer mystery." A week later *Monitor* natural science editor Robert C. Cowen said that although the Air Force has tried to brush off puzzling reports with handy explanations, "something is definitely going on that cannot yet be explained" and "the long standing saucer mystery begs for thorough scientific study." As if to soften a hastily taken stand, a few weeks later he wrote that additional data could clear up the puzzling reports and that he did not really believe in extraterrestrial visitation.[4]

By the end of 1965 ATIC had received 887 reports for the year. This large wave created great public interest in UFOs and the Air Force's investigation of them. As usual, the sighting wave also prompted a host of explanations. Astronomer Robert L. Brown of Southern Connecticut State College offered one of the most ingenious: saucer sightings were actually lunar dust; when the retrorockets on the Russian moon satellite (Lunik V) fired, a dust cloud rose up and the earth's gravitational field pulled it in; the dust could hover, become luminous, or move erratically; therefore, the saucer mystery could be "resolved in rather simple terms devoid of any reference to visitors from outer space." A spokesman for the Federal Aviation Agency gave reporters a more standard explanation when he said the sightings were due to the "long, hot summer," which "expedites the imagination." [5]

Some scientists expressed reservations about the Air Force's pat explanations for UFOs, and the *Wall Street Journal* printed some of these opinions. I. M. Levitt, director of the Fels Planetarium, who made national news in 1952 by calling the famous Washington, D.C., sightings mirages and temperature inversions, now urged the Air Force to admit that "there are natural phenomena taking place under our noses of which we know nothing. . . . The Air Force is trying to explain something that isn't susceptible to explanation." Robert Risser, director of the Oklahoma Science and Art Foundation Planetarium, criticized the Air Force explanation of the August sightings as stars. Those stars, Risser said, were not visible at that time of year and "the Air Force must have had its star-finder upside down during August." Dr. Frank Salisbury, a plant physiologist at Utah State University who was rapidly becoming a proponent of the extraterrestrial hypothesis as a result of studying UFO reports, said that people had to consider the tentative possibility that UFOs were "spaceships." [6]

Columnist John Fuller, in an article for the *Saturday Review*, greatly stimulated public interest in the subject. Fuller, a self-professed skeptic about UFOs, decided to investigate thoroughly "at least one specific case of UFO-chasing"; he contacted NICAP, which brought a case in Exeter, New Hampshire, to his attention. Upon investigation Fuller found two policemen and a nineteen-year-old college student who had observed at close range a large, metallic-like object that hovered silently over them. At one point the object swooped down and came so close to the amazed witnesses that they had to drop to the ground; the policemen went for their guns but did not draw. Fuller's article caught the attention of the G. P. Putnam publishing firm, which commissioned him to write a book on the Exeter sightings. He spent over a month in Exeter interviewing UFO witnesses and uncovered over seventy-five additional sightings. This experience convinced him that there was "overwhelming evidence" that UFOs were extraterrestrial. Before Putnam published Fuller's book, *Look* magazine printed excerpts from it and insured a wide readership.[7]

In the meantime, the subject of UFOs became a staple of

Fuller's *Saturday Review* column. By January 1966, a month before the *Look* article appeared, Fuller believed that "the truth" about UFOs would not remain hidden forever. "In fact," he said, "many are wondering if it isn't time for the government either to explain whatever it knows, or to order a research project to investigate the phenomenon and reveal the facts." When the Air Force interpreted what the two policemen and the college student saw as a mirage caused by a temperature inversion, Fuller began to consider seriously the idea of an Air Force cover-up about UFOs. These statements plus the *Look* article made Fuller a nationally known authority on UFOs. With the phenomenon so much in vogue, he added to UFO publicity by becoming a frequent visitor to television interview shows.[8]

Fuller was not the only UFO proponent to capitalize on media interest. During the last months of 1965 and the first months of 1966, Keyhoe and NICAP staff members appeared on the "Today" show, the "Tonight" show, NBC's panel show "Open Mind," "The Mike Douglas Show," and many radio shows, and accepted numerous speaking engagements. This visibility helped NICAP's continuing campaign to publicize the UFO phenomenon. From 1957 to 1966, Keyhoe, NICAP board members, and NICAP general members had appeared on over nine hundred television and radio shows and conducted over five hundred public discussions; Keyhoe himself was responsible for four hundred broadcasts and a hundred public talks.[9] The renewed interest in UFOs during 1965 to 1967 started a fad in television shows. Just as sighting reports in the early 1950s had stimulated motion pictures with flying saucer themes, the revived interest in the middle 1960s stimulated several television shows with either flying saucer or interplanetary travel themes. Among these were "Star Trek," which used a version of the 1948 Captain Mantell incident for one of its episodes, "Lost in Space," and "The Invaders," which continued the old motion picture extraterrestrial-as-hostile theme.

With the increased interest and publicity in 1965, the Air Force became worried. Hynek took advantage of this concern and wrote to Colonel Spaulding about the need for a scientific investigation of the UFO phenomenon. Hynek proposed that a panel of civilian scientists carefully review the UFO situation "to see whether a major problem really exists" and to make recommendations about the program's future status within the Air Force. The Air Force, now looking in earnest for a solution to its problem, took Hynek's suggestions under advisement and turned the UFO program's future over to the Public Information Office. On September 28, 1965, Director of Information General E. B. LeBailly wrote to the military director of the Air Force's scientific advisory board and said that the assistant deputy chief of staff for plans and operations (General Arthur C. Agan) had found Project Blue Book to be a worthwhile program deserving more support and that the Air Force should continue to investigate UFOs "to assure that such objects do not present a threat to our national security"; the project would remain at FTD.[10]

LeBailly also noted that reputable individuals, "whose integrity cannot be doubted," made many reports and that, in addition, reports sent to the Air Force represented only a small portion of the "spectacular reports which are publicized by many private UFO organizations." Using Hynek's suggestion, LeBailly requested "that a working scientific panel composed of both physical and social scientists be organized to review Project Blue Book—its resources, methods, and findings—and to advise the Air Force as to any improvements that should be made in the program to carry out the Air Force's assigned responsibility." [11]

The panel resulting from the LeBailly letter turned out to be the impetus for a new approach to the problem and for taking the investigation out of military hands. Called the Ad Hoc Committee to Review Project Blue Book, it featured Dr. Brian O'Brien as chairman and five other scientists as participants: Drs. Carl Sagan, Jesse Orlansky, Launor Carter, Willis A. Ware, and Richard Porter. All the scientists but Sagan were members of the Air Force's scientific advisory board. The committee met for one day in February 1966, at which time it reviewed the Robertson report of 1953 and heard a briefing from Quintanilla and the FTD staff.[12]

The committee members were satisfied that UFOs did not

threaten the national security, that the Air Force program was "well organized" albeit "quite limited," and that no UFO case represented technological or scientific advances outside of a terrestrial framework. Although the committee found that most unidentified reports lacked sufficient data, it also discovered some questionable identified reports that also lacked sufficient data and did not belong in the identified category. Assuming that it was always possible for a sighting to have scientific value, the committee recommended that the UFO program "be strengthened to provide opportunity for scientific investigation of selected sightings in more detail and depth than has been possible to date." To accomplish this, the committee suggested that the Air Force negotiate contracts "with a few selected universities to provide selected teams to investigate promptly and in depth certain selected sightings of UFOs"; a single university should coordinate the teams, which together should study a hundred sightings per year, devoting an average of ten man-days to each investigation and the resulting report. The committee recommended that each team have at least one psychologist, "preferably one interested in clinical psychology," a physical scientist, and an astronomer or astrophysicist, and that air base UFO officers should work with the teams. The committee hoped these new investigations would "provide a far better basis than we have today for a decision on a long term UFO program." [13]

In addition, the committee, being aware of the Air Force's public relations difficulties, recommended disseminating Project Blue Book reports among "prominent members of the Congress and other public persons" to give evidence that the Air Force took a scientific approach.[14]

The O'Brien committee represented both a break in and a continuation of Air Force UFO policy. It broke with policy in recommending that a university conduct a systematic, detailed study of UFO reports. It continued policy in recommending, in different language, that the Air Force resolve its UFO problem by getting rid of the program. Contracting out the investigation to a university was another means of transferring the program. The Air Force moved cautiously and it held back on implementing the recommendations. It waited to see if the new "flying saucer scare" would die down. It did not.

The sighting wave that began in July 1965 continued through 1967. In fact, more sightings came into Blue Book in 1966 and 1967 than in 1965, making this the first time sighting reports remained at very high levels for three consecutive years. Public interest grew enormously: a May 1966 Gallup Poll indicated that 96 percent of the people polled had heard or read about flying saucers; of these, 46 percent thought them to be "real," and 29 percent, "imaginary"; moreover, 5 percent of the people who had heard of flying saucers thought they had seen one personally—projected to the general population, this represented approximately nine million people.[15] Once again the flying saucer "hysteria" gripped the country, with one dramatic sighting after another filling newspaper and magazine articles. The Gallup Poll findings may have been due to one of the most widely publicized events in the history of the UFO controversy: the furor over the explanation of the Dexter and Hillsdale, Michigan, sightings in March 1966.

On March 20, 1966, eighty-seven women students and a civil defense director at Hillsdale College saw a football-shaped, glowing object hovering over a swampy area a few hundred yards from the women's dormitory. The witnesses claimed the object flew directly at the dormitory but then stopped suddenly and retreated back to the swamp. The object "dodged an airport beacon light," appeared to dim when automobiles approached the area, and then "brightened when the cars left". The witnesses watched the object for four hours. The next day five people—including two police officers—in Dexter saw a large, glowing object rise from a swampy area on a farm, hover for a few minutes at about 1,000 feet, and then leave the area. Over one hundred witnesses saw objects on these two nights in two Michigan cities sixty-three miles apart. The story of these somewhat routine sightings caught fire. Within a few days virtually every newspaper in the country and all national news shows carried the report. Reporters put intense pressure on the Air Force to investigate the incidents and arrive at a solution immediately.[16]

Quintanilla sent Hynek to the scene. When he arrived, he encountered a situation "so charged with emotion that it was impossible for [him] to do any really serious investigation." He had to fight his way through reporters to interview the witnesses, and the entire region "was gripped with near-hysteria." Police, he said, madly chased stars they thought to be flying saucers and people believed spaceships swarmed in the area. After his investigation, Hynek held a press conference to explain what happened. He claimed that the Air Force ordered him to hold the press conference; Quintanilla, on the other hand, claimed that Hynek informed him that he had the solution and therefore gave Hynek permission to hold the conference.[17]

Whatever the impetus, the press conference became a singularly important event in the history of the UFO controversy. It was the largest press conference in the Detroit Press Club's history. Hynek described it as a "circus," with a mélange of television cameramen, newspapermen, photographers, and others all "clamoring for a single, spectacular explanation of the sightings." Hynek explained that the faint lights people had observed could have been the result of decaying vegetation that spontaneously ignited and created a faint glow—this phenomenon is known as marsh gas. As soon as he handed out the written press statement, Hynek recalled, he "watched with horror as one reporter scanned the page, found the phrase 'swamp gas,' under-lined it, and rushed for a telephone." Journalism Professor Herbert Strentz, in his study of newspaper attitudes toward UFOs, pointed out that "press and public reactions to the 'swamp gas' theory were prompt, wide-ranging and generally hostile"; not one of the hundred witnesses involved in the sightings accepted the explanation.[18]

The swamp gas solution became an object of ridicule and humor throughout the nation. Cartoons lampooning the solution appeared in numerous newspapers and magazines, and press coverage of UFOs increased steadily during March and April 1966. *Life* magazine ran an eight-page feature on the Hillsdale sightings and UFOs, including full-page color photographs of various UFOs. Entitled "Well-witnessed Invasion by Something:

Australia to Michigan," *Life*'s story hit hard at the swamp gas explanation through interviewing witnesses and showing photographs of the area. An article in *The New Yorker* magazine stated acidly: "We read the official explanations with sheer delight, marveling at their stupendous inadequacy. Marsh gas, indeed! Marsh gas is more appropriate an image of that special tediousness one glimpses in even the best scientific minds." On the other hand, *Time* continued its ridicule of the idea that UFOs might be extraterrestrial and agreed with the swamp gas explanation; it called the current wave of sightings "primaveral deliriusion" and said the sightings exemplified an "American mythology." The *Wisconsin State Journal* (Madison) featured Hynek's explanation in red, front-page, banner headlines, and an editorial bluntly stated that the swamp gas theory "smells." [19]

The *New York Times* printed a witness's drawing of the Dexter UFO and compared it to a drawing of one of George Adamski's sightings; the *New York Times* lumped Adamski and the witnesses from Dexter in the same category. In the same issue, reporter Evert Clark wrote that Congress held back from investigating UFO sightings because it would "encourage the idea that there is more to the unidentified flying objects than mistaken sightings of natural and manmade objects"; an investigation "might frighten much of the public . . . by seeming to indicate concern in Congress." In another editorial, the *New York Times* continued to oppose the idea that the UFO phenomenon was unique: "people who are conditioned by television, comic strips and books to believe in flying saucers find it easy to see them in [man-made] phenomena," and the Michigan sightings typified people's "strange propensity for seeing what they want to see." But the *Christian Science Monitor* said the recent sightings and investigation in Michigan had "deepened the mystery" of UFOs, and "it is time for the scientific community to conduct a thorough and objective study of the 'unexplainable.' " Syndicated columnist Roscoe Drummond decided that the swamp gas explanation had signaled the time "for Congress to take charge" in an investigation and "a more thorough and objective search for the facts is in order." [20]

In early April 1966, probably in reaction to the Michigan sightings, CBS news began to investigate the UFO problem. The result was a nationally televised news show, "UFOs: Friend, Foe or Fantasy?," narrated by Walter Cronkite. In it, Donald Menzel reiterated his theory that UFOs were misidentifications of unusual atmospheric conditions. Secretary of the Air Force Harold Brown assured the viewers that the Air Force was not withholding information from the public. Ex-SAFOI officer Lawrence Tacker called attacks on the Air Force "senseless and vicious." Radar experts claimed that they had never picked up UFOs on their radarscopes. Several astronomers said that no one involved in tracking satellites or meteors had taken pictures of UFOs. Carl Sagan, a member of the O'Brien panel, talked of "flying saucer cultists." The theme of the show came across clearly: UFOs were misidentifications, delusions, hoaxes, and products of the will to believe and of societal stress.

To reinforce the "experts," CBS devoted long sections of the show to the contactees. The network sent a camera crew to the Giant Rock Convention, where the CBS staff interviewed George Van Tassel and other contactees. The show also included sections of a filmed interview with George Adamski, who had died a year before.

For "balance," CBS spoke with Keyhoe, who accused the Air Force of withholding information, with Hynek, who made a noncommittal statement, and with Charles Gibbs-Smith, an aviation historian, who strongly advocated the extraterrestrial hypothesis. Gibbs-Smith showed the CBS staff a film clip of what he said was a spaceship. The staff proved, beyond a doubt, that the film clip showed only a reflection of part of an airplane, thus successfully destroying Gibbs-Smith's credibility.

At the end of the hour-long show, Cronkite tried to sum up the various viewpoints. People should keep an open mind, he said, because "yesterday's fantasy is tomorrow's reality." Yet the viewers must remember, Cronkite intoned, that "while fantasy improves science fiction, science is more often served by fact." The show was televised in May, too late to have any effect on the fast-moving events of March and April.

The uproar over the latest wave of sightings in general and the Dexter-Hillsdale ones in particular was so great that Weston E. Vivian (Democratic congressman from Michigan) and Gerald R. Ford (then House Republican minority leader) responded to their constituents' concern and formally called for congressional hearings. In a letter to the House Armed Services Committee requesting the hearings, Ford enclosed several newspaper articles criticizing the Air Force investigation of the events in Michigan and the New Hampshire sightings. Referring to these and other public statements questioning the Air Force, Ford said "the American public deserves a better explanation than that thus far given by the Air Force"; to "establish credulity" about UFOs, he strongly recommended a committee investigation of the subject. Keyhoe, of course, quickly praised Ford's suggestion, telling the Associated Press that the Pentagon had a "top level policy of discounting all UFO reports" and that the Air Force for years had used ridicule to debunk sightings.[21]

The House Armed Services Committee acted on Ford's suggestion. On April 5, 1966—for the first time in the history of the controversy over unidentified flying objects—Congress held an open hearing on the subject. The committee, under the chairmanship of L. Mendel Rivers, invited only three people to testify: Secretary of the Air Force Harold D. Brown, Project Blue Book Chief Hector Quintanilla, and Hynek—all associated with the Air Force. The committee did not invite a NICAP representative, but a NICAP member submitted material for the record, hoping this would balance the Air Force testimony.[22]

Secretary Brown began the formal testimony by reading a statement outlining the Air Force views as made public in its press releases, fact sheets, and Blue Book reports; he included the LeBailly letter and the report of the Ad Hoc Committee to Review Project Blue Book (the O'Brien committee). Brown's main argument relied on the familiar refrain that no evidence existed to prove that UFOs threatened the national security or came from extraterrestrial origins.[23]

Hynek spoke next. Reacting to press criticism of his swamp gas explanation and rankling over charges that he was a puppet of the Air Force, Hynek said he would read a "daring" statement "which has certainly not been dictated by the Air Force." He made his now frequent point that UFOs deserved the scientific community's attention. He warned that complete adherence to the policy that all UFO reports had conventional explanations "may turn out to be a roadblock in the pursuit of research endeavors." The Air Force had claimed time and again that it could either identify an object or prove the sighting invalid if it investigated the case long enough; this, Hynek said, was an example of a "poverty of hypotheses" and investigators were apt to miss "matters of great scientific value" if the phenomenon did not fit the "accepted scientific outlook of the time." He called for a civilian panel of scientists to examine the UFO program critically and to determine if a major problem actually existed. Quintanilla made no formal statement.[24]

During the questioning following the formal testimony, Secretary Brown mentioned that he was considering the O'Brien committee's recommendation for a private study. The congressional committee seized on this and said several times how pleased it was to hear this. Hynek then pointed out that foreign governments looked to the United States Air Force for guidance in UFO matters but the Air Force had opened no official lines of inquiry or scientific exchange with any other government. Brown countered Hynek by saying the Air Force had no scientific information to exchange, and the thrust of the program had been to give the public a certain kind of evidence so that the UFO phenomenon did not "get more out of hand." Following the questioning there was a general discussion about public pressure and press publicity, especially the *Life* magazine article which had appeared the previous week. The hearings closed amidst much tongue-in-cheek humor, a few questions to Quintanilla, and an expression of satisfaction that the Air Force would implement the O'Brien recommendations.[25]

The committee had presented a *fait accompli* to Brown. Although he had only been considering the O'Brien recommendations, that afternoon—as soon as the hearing concluded—he directed the Air Force chief of staff to accept the O'Brien committee recommendations and to make arrangements for a scientific team to investigate selected UFO sightings. By deciding to contract out the UFO study to a university, the Air Force tacitly acknowledged that its nineteen years of investigation and analysis had been inadequate.

The UFO program had constantly embarrassed the Air Force: private groups continually attacked the Air Force, citizens who thought something must be up there distrusted the Air Force, congressmen threatened it with hearings, and, above all, the sighting reports continued. Since 1947 the Air Force had been in the unenviable position of having to pass judgment on every report of an unusual occurrence in the sky. And because these judgments were not always convincing, for years the Air Force tried to placate the public and Congress with fact sheets and special briefings. Even high-ranking government officials tried to help until the very end. In a session of the House Foreign Affairs Committee, just five days before the UFO hearings, Secretary of Defense Robert McNamara and Joint Chiefs of Staff Chairman General Earle Wheeler both stated for the record that UFOs did not represent a unique phenomenon and that the Air Force's investigation was adequate. But none of these efforts stopped the mounting discontent and, in April 1966, the Air Force finally moved to extricate itself from the UFO dilemma. The open congressional hearings did not directly force the Air Force to support a scientific investigation of UFOs but certainly did insure that it would take place.[26]

The Air Force formed a panel of six people to help carry out the O'Brien committee recommendations. The panel consisted of O'Brien and another member of the original ad hoc committee, two military personnel from the Air Force Scientific Advisory Board, a representative from the Air Force Office of Public Information, and Lieutenant Colonel Robert Hippler of the Office of Scientific Research, who was responsible for obtaining university participation in the project. General James Ferguson (deputy chief of staff for research and development) assumed the duty of administering all the panel's decisions.[27]

The panel first decided to find a "lead university" that could best coordinate a set of investigation teams, and with assistance from the National Academy of Sciences, the panel prepared a list of twenty-five prospective universities. Because the UFO problem was "an emotional phenomenon," Dr. O'Brien said, he thought his friend Dr. Horton G. Stever, president of the Carnegie Institute of Technology, should write letters to university presidents to get a feel for their attitudes toward the project. Recognizing that the UFO program was "99%" public relations, the panel recommended that the proposed investigating teams have the necessary skills "to give good Air Force public relations." The panel wanted both Hynek and Menzel to be on the investigating teams, but then reversed this decision because both men had made public their feelings on the subject. The results of the proposed investigation hopefully would allow the Air Force finally to know whether to continue the UFO program in its present capacity, to increase efforts, or, as the panel put it, to "discontinue the effort and get the Air Force out of the business." [28]

It was not until May 9, 1966, that the Air Force disclosed publicly its plan to contract with scientists for a UFO investigation. But by that time the prospects looked dim. According to Colorado psychologist and future project member David R. Saunders, none of the universities Colonel Hippler tried to interest in the UFO project would have it, presumably because of the public relations problem and the topic's "illegitimacy." Harvard, the Massachusetts Institute of Technology, the University of North Carolina, the University of California, and others had turned down the project. During the search the Air Force abandoned its plan to have several universities coordinate investigating teams and looked for only one university to conduct the entire study. When Colonel Hippler failed, Dr. William T. Price (Air Force Office of Scientific Research) tried; he too was unsuccessful. Finally, Dr. J. Thomas Ratchford (Office of Scientific Research) joined in the hunt for a "buyer." He first tried to interest the National Center for Atmospheric Research in Colorado—to no avail. The center's director, Dr. Walter Orr Roberts, suggested the University of Colorado. When Ratchford asked

Colorado in August 1966 to take the project, he assured the administration and faculty chairmen that the National Center for Atmospheric Research had been the Air Force's first choice and Colorado its second. The University of Colorado was interested.[29]

The decision to accept the Air Force's proposal rested in large part on the composition of the Department of Psychology faculty. Because the Air Force Office of Scientific Research required at least one clinical psychologist to be attached to the project and other psychologists in the fields of perception, cognition, and data gathering to help if possible, the Department of Psychology had to be sure it could recruit people with these qualifications. It did not see this as a problem and was receptive to the idea of taking the study. Furthermore, the Air Force offered an appealing incentive: it would forgo congressional cost-sharing regulations for federal grants so that the university would have to pay only one dollar to receive $300,000. David Saunders thought that as a result of legislative budget cuts for the university, the $300,000 government offer may have looked especially good to Colorado and may have been a factor in the decision. Also, in its zeal to induce the University of Colorado to take the project, the Air Force turned the grant into a contract; this meant that the government added $13,000 to the $300,000 to cover the university's cost of operating the program. (Eventually an extension brought the total sum to over $500,000.)[30]

Ratchford and Price tried to interest internationally known physicist and former head of the National Bureau of Standards, Dr. Edward U. Condon, in being the project director. But Condon was not anxious to accept the job. He was revising his book on atomic spectra and running for public election to the University of Colorado's Board of Regents. Ratchford told him that the job was "a dirty chore" but somebody had to do it. If Condon did, people would believe him more than "just some ordinary guy." Condon later said: "I fell for this. Flattery got him somewhere." [31]

Condon's credentials made him the ideal person for the Air Force, which wanted the project leader to be a prestigious scientist and to have the proper political outlook. Condon fit the job description in every way. He had coauthored the first textbook on quantum mechanics in this country, and he had written the standard work in the field of atomic spectra. He was a world renowned physicist. He was also politically acceptable. The Air Force did not want someone so far left or right of center that his credibility would be impaired. When Condon headed the National Bureau of Standards, he ran afoul of Richard Nixon and the House Committee on Un-American Activities. The committee, spearheaded by Nixon, thought Condon was a security risk because Secretary of Commerce Henry A. Wallace, whom the committee thought to be a Communist, had appointed Condon to his post. Also, Condon's wife was Czechoslovakian, and he had fraternized with various liberals and foreigners. Hauled before the committee, Condon refused to knuckle under, and after a long and hard fight between him and the committee and various loyalty review boards, Condon was completely exonerated. He came out of the fight with his scientific and political credentials intact, and he appeared to be a fighter against the establishment. Now as he took on the UFO project, he embarked on one of the most difficult and troublesome tasks of his career.[32]

On October 7, 1966, the Air Force publicly announced that the University of Colorado had accepted the UFO study project and that Edward U. Condon would be in charge. With the announcement Condon named three other men to work on the project: Assistant Dean of the Graduate School Robert Low as project coordinator, and psychologists Franklin Roach and Stuart Cook as principal investigators. The use of psychologists fulfilled the Air Force's requirement. The program, the *Denver Post* reported, was "designed to quiet public fears of the aerial objects." [33]

Reactions to the announcement varied. The *Denver Post* favored the decision, which it called "wise" because the Air Force had not been able to satisfy the American people. Although John Lear, of the *Saturday Review*, personally thought UFOs had something to do with "dying comets," he felt that the Condon committee would have a "fairer chance of clearing the air" of the bitterness that had developed over the UFO argument in recent years. Two Colorado congressmen were delighted over the Air

Force's selection of the university; they thought this proved that the University of Colorado "has the academic climate to satisfy and stimulate the scientific community" and that therefore the Atomic Energy Commission would be more prone to place the National Accelerator Laboratory in Colorado.[34]

Hynek and Keyhoe, of course, were positive. Writing in the *Saturday Evening Post*, Hynek said the establishment of the Condon committee gave him a feeling of "personal triumph and vindication." He was especially pleased that the committee would have enough time to review the phenomenon thoroughly, for he could not consider anyone an authority on the subject unless that person had read "at least a few thousand original (not summary) reports" and studied the phenomenon's global nature. Keyhoe called the establishment of the committee "the most significant development in the history of UFO investigation." The study of UFOs, he said, is now in the hands of civilian scientists "where it belongs." NICAP also felt vindicated in its policies of pushing for congressional hearings and trying to end Air Force secrecy. Keyhoe said NICAP would refrain from criticizing the Air Force unless it "releases counter-to-fact explanations" of sightings or "false information," and NICAP would help by giving the committee all "significant evidence." [35]

Not everyone was satisfied, however. Columnist Don Maclean charged, in a New Jersey newspaper, that the government was spending money to "check up" on another branch of the government—making the Condon committee "the most insulting thing that has happened to one of our armed services in some time." Hollywood columnist Austin Connor suggested that the government was cheating the taxpayers: the Air Force, for legitimate reasons, would not give the committee all its classified files, and therefore nothing would come of the UFO study. An editorial in the *Nation*, which publicly had backed Condon's unsuccessful campaign for regent, said if Condon did not come up with anything other than "little green men," the UFO enthusiasts would crucify him; yet it hoped the study could provide some useful results, such as insight about why people "must look to beings from beyond the earth as the only hope for escape from the tensions, dangers and boredom of modern life." [36]

Robert Low, the project coordinator, also had reservations. He was troubled because the study did not fulfill the three criteria for acceptable research projects: teaching, research, and public service. But, he added, the University of Colorado was the only institution that the Air Force asked to take the study, and "when you're asked to do something (as opposed to applying for it) you don't say no—not to the Air Force." Besides, he said, by examining people who reported UFOs, the study could uncover some new knowledge in the behavioral sciences.[37]

Soon after the committee's establishment, Condon started making statements that, at least to Keyhoe and others, seemed inconsistent with Condon's supposed impartiality and open-mindedness. The day after his appointment he informed a reporter for the *Denver Rocky Mountain News* that there was "just no evidence that there is advanced life on other planets," and he did not think flying saucers had visited the earth: "I haven't seen any convincing evidence. It is possible I suppose—but improbable. I would need a lot of convincing." Condon thought the Air Force had been doing a good job of handling UFO reports.[38]

The next day he explained that the committee would do more than conduct field interviews with UFO witnesses; it would experiment with swamp gas and similar phenomena as well, to give the public a "better understanding of ordinary phenomena, which, if recognized at once, would reduce the number of UFO reports." He suggested that this educational program could be accomplished through news media and school science classes. A few days later, Condon wrote to the *Denver Post* explaining that the UFO project could make "valuable contributions to knowledge of atmospheric effects and of people's behavior observing them under unusual conditions." Because "well-known natural phenomena" caused the great majority of UFO reports, this "clearly indicates an appalling lack of public understanding of such phenomena [and] this calls for improved teaching about these things." [39]

On October 30, R. Roger Harkins, reporter for the *Boulder Daily Camera*, quoted Condon as saying the committee would use social psychologists to study large groups of people and their reactions to "unusual stimuli," which included the field of "rumor phenomena, as exemplified by the hysterical popular reaction to H. G. Welles' [*sic*] radio program, 'War of the Worlds,' in the late 1930's." In a mid-November interview with a reporter from the *New York Times*, he admitted that he did not expect to find visitors from outer space, "but I'm not against it. . . . After all that would be the discovery of a century—the discovery of many centuries—of the millennia, I suppose." In a speech before the Corning Section of the American Chemical Society on January 25, 1967, Condon confessed: "It is my inclination right now to recommend that the government get out of this business. My attitude right now is that there's nothing to it." He added that "it would be a worthwhile study for those groups interested in meteorological phenomena." Condon seemed to be headed toward studying only two facets of the UFO problem: misinterpretations of natural phenomena, and the psychological bases for UFO reports.[40]

Having decided to place the study of UFOs in a university, the Air Force thought this was the right time to proceed with its 1959 plan to transfer the UFO program out of the intelligence community. In June 1966 General James Ferguson, now deputy chief of staff for research and development, assumed primary responsibility for the UFO program. This move put Blue Book in the Air Force's scientific community, under the Foreign Technology Division of the Air Force Systems Command. The Air Force changed AFR 200-2 to AFR 80-17 (the 200 series refers to intelligence and the 80 series to miscellaneous), thereby formalizing the new arrangement and also allowing Blue Book to send UFO cases directly to the Condon committee.[41]

At this same time, 1966 to 1967, the public debate on UFOs became more serious than it had been before, for it increasingly involved professional people. John Fuller was partially responsible for this. His articles in *Saturday Review* and *Look* contributed to widespread public interest in UFOs, and his book, *Incident at*

Exeter, was sober, well written, well researched, and nonsensational. Because of Fuller's national reputation and because he was not affiliated with any private UFO organizations, many people who previously had not been involved in the UFO debate expressed a favorable reaction to the book and its subject matter. For instance, Oscar Handlin, professor of history at Harvard, in a review in the *Atlantic Monthly*, summed up the growing serious attitude toward UFOs. The answer to the UFO enigma was "not now knowable," he said. Eyewitness testimony, the human eye being fallible, was inconclusive; yet because very little else existed to corroborate eyewitness testimony, "the confession of ignorance is the safest policy." Handlin attacked the Air Force for its "unwillingness . . . to concede that anything is unknown" and for its "bland public relations assurances," which had "heightened popular anxiety." Although scientists disliked admitting the limits of their knowledge, Handlin said, "there is . . . nothing inherently implausible about extraterrestrial visitors." Intelligent life probably existed elsewhere in the universe and it might "be much more advanced than that on earth." Therefore, "to dismiss out of hand the evidence for UFOs will not quiet the fears that we may be living through the first stages of exploration from elsewhere." [42]

John Fuller's work in the UFO field provoked enough interest at *Saturday Review* for science editor John Lear to write a series of articles about the Robertson panel and the CIA's involvement with it. The Air Force let Lear look through its UFO files, except for the classified and uncensored version of the 1953 Robertson panel report. It gave him an edited version instead, leaving out the participants' names and the key recommendation that national security agencies should embark on a public education program to explain the dangers of reporting UFOs. The fact that the CIA had edited the document disturbed Lear. He compared the edited version with Ruppelt's 1956 version, and since Lear had no way of knowing what the CIA had deleted, he stated that a doubt would always remain about what the CIA had found as long as the Robertson panel report remained censored.

Concern over the exact contents of the Robertson report became more intense when Dr. James E. McDonald, the senior atmospheric physicist at the University of Arizona's Department of Atmospheric Sciences, accidentally saw the classified version of the report at Wright-Patterson Air Force Base. McDonald had been interested in the UFO phenomenon privately for the last ten years, and the 1965 sighting wave strengthened his growing conviction that the phenomenon had scientific importance and that the extraterrestrial hypothesis might be the answer to the mystery. By 1966 he emerged as one of the nation's leading scientific authorities on UFOs and embarked on a national speaking tour to explain his views. After seeing the classified version of the Robertson report, McDonald placed the blame for the Air Force's secrecy policies on the CIA, and he resolved to make this information public. Speaking before members of the University of Arizona's Department of Meteorology, McDonald claimed that the CIA had ordered the Air Force to debunk UFOs, as seen in the unedited version of the Robertson report. The national news services picked up this story and publicized it widely on the same day that the Air Force announced the establishment of the Condon committee.[43]

Many professional people who became interested in the UFO phenomenon were scientists. Dr. Frank Salisbury, head of the Plant Science Department at Utah State University, Dr. Leo Sprinkle, psychologist at the University of Wyoming, Stanton Friedman, a nuclear physicist at Westinghouse Astronuclear Laboratories, Jacques Vallee, a mathematician at Northwestern University, and other scientists who had not been involved in the UFO controversy before now aligned themselves with the view that UFOs merited scientific study and that the extraterrestrial hypothesis might be valid. This new scientific interest probably was in part due to the establishment of the Condon committee. Condon's prestige was so great that he helped legitimize the subject and made it easier for scientists to discuss the matter without fearing as much ridicule as they had before 1966 (although ridicule still persisted). Condon's stature and Hynek's vigorous public statements about UFOs came together in October 1966, when *Science* magazine (the official organ of the American Association for the Advancement of Science) printed a letter

Hynek had written in August 1966. *Science* at first had refused to publish the letter but changed its policy and published it in abridged form after Condon agreed to take the UFO project.[44]

Since the Lonnie Zamora sighting in 1964, Hynek had become more determined in his request for a "respectable scholarly study of the UFO phenomenon." The swamp gas incident had placed him in a defensive position, and the result in 1966 was a more liberal view toward UFOs. Hynek's letter to *Science* was his most forthright statement to date. His main purpose was to refute several common misconceptions about the phenomenon. Truly puzzling reports came not from UFO buffs, he said, but from people who had given little or no thought to the subject before a sighting. Although unreliable, unstable, or uneducated people did generate some UFO reports, Hynek explained, "the most articulate reports come from obviously intelligent people." Moreover, the notion that scientifically trained people did not report UFOs was "unequivocably false," and, in fact, some of the *best* reports came from this group. Contrary to popular opinion, Hynek continued, people saw UFOs at close range and reported explicitly and in detail.[45]

As for the Air Force statement that it had no evidence that UFOs were extraterrestrial or represented advanced technology, Hynek said this was true but it "is widely interpreted to mean that there is evidence against the two hypotheses. As long as there are 'unidentifieds,' the question must obviously remain open." Hynek also countered the commonly held notion that publicity generated UFO reports: while it was true that widely publicized reports might stimulate other reports, "it is unwarranted to assert that this is the sole cause of high incidence of UFO reports." Finally, in answer to the charge that neither radar nor meteor and satellite tracking cameras had picked up UFOs, Hynek said these instruments had indeed tracked "oddities" that remained unidentified. For these reasons, Hynek said, he could not "dismiss the UFO phenomenon with a shrug." Twentieth-century scientists tended to forget "that there will be a 21st-century science, and indeed, a 30th-century science, from which vantage points our knowledge of the universe may appear quite different." He concluded that "we suffer, perhaps, from temporal provincialism, a form of arrogance that has always irritated posterity." [46]

Hynek's letter was just one example of scientists speaking out about the phenomenon. Condon reported receiving many letters from scientists volunteering to help the committee and none ridiculing him personally for accepting the project. Nevertheless, some scientists with an urge to explain persisted in ridiculing UFOs and the people who reported seeing them. Dr. Edward Teller, on a nationwide broadcast of CBS's "Face the Nation," said UFOs were "miracles," and "the human soul needs a miracle"; given a scientific age, "what is more proper than that the miracles should be scientific miracles?" The celebrated British astronomer Sir Bernard Lovell, on an American speaking tour, explained that people who reported UFOs were "tremendous emotionalists"; UFOs were nothing but natural phenomena and hoaxes, and the entire subject was "incredible nonsense." Science fiction writer and biochemist Isaac Asimov displayed his lack of knowledge about the subject by confusing what contactees reported and what reputable witnesses reported. He was convinced that "most flying saucer enthusiasts" believed "spaceship-crews are benevolent guardians of our welfare and anxious to keep us from destroying ourselves in nuclear warfare." According to Asimov, people who believed in the extraterrestrial origin of UFOs were "clinging to a fantasy." [47]

Other scientists skeptical about the subject at least offered arguments based on some knowledge of UFOs and related fields. Philip Klass, avionics editor of *Aviation Week and Space Technology*, added a new dimension to the scientific inquiry into the nature of the phenomenon when he proposed that ball lightning or plasmas caused UFOs. He expanded his theories into a book, *UFOs—Identified*. Basically Klass believed virtually all UFO sightings were due to coronal discharges—the result of free floating packets of charged air that a lightning bolt had ignited; this phenomenon occurs most often near high-voltage power lines. Klass formulated his theory after reading *Incident at Exeter*, in which many of the witnesses told of seeing UFOs near high-tension wires. Klass was convinced that he had found the solution to the UFO mystery: plasmas could cause automobile engine failure, appear luminous, hover, and create radar echoes.[48]

Many magazines and newspapers featured articles about the plasma idea. While admitting that plasmas might account for a few UFO reports, most UFO researchers, including Hynek, McDonald, Richard Hall of NICAP, and some electrical engineers, discounted the Klass theory as a solution because it did not explain the majority of UFO sightings. Because plasmas existed at most for a few seconds only near high-tension lines in a severe thunderstorm with lightning, the researchers said, the theory failed to account for sightings not in the area of high-power lines, that occurred in fair weather, and that lasted longer than a few seconds.[49]

Marquette University Professor of Physics William Markowitz found his own explanation of the mystery by studying how the objects moved. In a 1967 article in *Science*, "The Physics and Metaphysics of Unidentified Flying Objects," Markowitz discussed the idea that reported UFO maneuvers did not obey the "elemental laws of celestial mechanics and physics." He constructed a theoretical model, based on known laws, of the physics of interstellar space travel, giving special attention to takeoffs and landings. Reports of UFO takeoffs and landings did not conform with this model, he discovered, and therefore extraterrestrial space vehicles did not account for the phenomenon. Markowitz concluded by stating that he had now investigated UFOs, and because he had seen no valid reports of occupant sightings and no crashed UFOs had turned up, he doubted extraterrestrial visitation. Furthermore, because the data on extraterrestrial visitation was so meager, people should not waste time studying it and the Air Force should terminate its investigation activities. He had mentioned this prospect to Quintanilla, Markowitz said, and the major "raised no objections."[50]

This article provoked a lively response from the readers of *Science*. Richard J. Rosa, of the Avco Everett Research Laboratory, agreed with Markowitz's conclusion but found the argument "irrelevant"; although interstellar travel was impossible for our society now, Rosa wrote, Markowitz's arguments "in no way prove or imply that it is beyond someone else's—or . . . what we will have 100 years from now." William T. Powers, a friend of Hynek from Northwestern University's Dearborn Observatory, said Markowitz's argument "bears no relationship to the contents of UFO reports"; all his foolish model for space flight proved was that "his own design does not explain reports of takeoffs or landings." Furthermore, Powers stated, "the contrast between the notion of an advanced civilization's mode of transport (as one may legitimately attempt to imagine it) and Markowitz's sketchy design for a starship is ludicrous." Jacques Vallee, one of Hynek's colleagues at Northwestern and the author of two books on UFOs, charged that Markowitz deliberately selected "borderline cases in an effort to cast doubt on the validity of current official and private attempts at data-gathering." Furthermore, Vallee insisted, being concerned with only one idea (the extraterrestrial hypothesis), as Markowitz was, meant one had to "abandon entirely the rational process upon which science is based." The argument, Vallee concluded, was "grossly irrational." [51]

Although the scientific debate focused, in large part, on finding answers for or alternatives to the extraterrestrial hypothesis, some scientists took a middle-of-the-road position. Dr. Carl Sagan was representative of this view. Sagan was an astronomy professor at Cornell University and also had been a member of the Ad Hoc Committee to Review Project Blue Book (the O'Brien committee). He believed, on the one hand, in the possibility that extraterrestrial visitors had journeyed to earth in prehistoric times. Although highly unlikely and seemingly fantastic, this possibility definitely existed, he said, and scientists should examine closely ancient myths and legends for possible extraterrestrial contact. On the other hand, Sagan thought the prospect of extraterrestrial visitation to contemporary civilization was dim. Scientists had obtained no photographs of UFOs as they had of meteors, he argued, and the majority of sightings were actually common astronomical objects or atmospheric phenomena. Although "no unambiguous evidence" for even simple forms of extraterrestrial life existed, Sagan said, "the situation may change in the coming years." Therefore, Sagan warned scientists who had "a tendency to reject out of hand the possibility of extraterrestrial intelligence as baseless, improbable or unscientific" to avoid this danger.[52]

Hynek, too, publicly placed himself in this camp. He neither denied nor supported any theory; rather, he spent much of 1966 and 1967 calling for increased scientific scrutiny of the UFO problem because "no truly scientific investigation of the UFO phenomenon has ever been undertaken." Much of this Hynek did through the media: the letter in *Science* in October 1966, an article about the Air Force study and his involvement in it in the *Saturday Evening Post* in December 1966, a full-page interview with Hynek in the *Christian Science Monitor* in May 1967, and an article in *Playboy* in December 1967 discussing the inadequacies of the Air Force program. In the latter, Hynek outlined the dangers of the Soviets deciphering the UFO mystery before the Americans could and recommended increased study to avoid a "UFO gap." If the United States could do this, wrote Hynek, "Mankind may be in for the greatest adventure since dawning human intelligence turned outward to contemplate the universe." [53]

If Sagan and Hynek spoke for the middle position, Dr. James McDonald certainly was the advocate for the extraterrestrial position. Unafraid of ridicule, McDonald was an extremely intense and energetic individual whose research into UFOs had far outstripped all other researchers save Hynek. In March 1966 McDonald had succeeded in obtaining the National Academy of Science's approval for a discreet, one-man study of UFOs. But when the Academy heard of the Air Force plans to contract a UFO study to a university, it withdrew its offer of support. McDonald used his own money for UFO investigation, and he meticulously investigated scores of sightings and personally interviewed hundreds of witnesses. He concluded that "the extraterrestrial hypothesis [was] the only presently plausible explanation for the now-available facts."[54]

Armed with this idea and with the perhaps naive but unshaken faith that scientists, once alerted to the depth and enormity of the UFO data, would be swayed by logic and reason, McDonald launched a crusade to alert the scientific community to the seriousness of the problem. Over the next few years he wrote thousands of letters about the UFO problem to scientists, UFO researchers, military personnel, and private citizens. He stumped the country giving innumerable lectures, speeches, talks, and private discussions. His method of argumentation was to over-whelm listeners with a wealth of exhaustively documented and detailed UFO reports. He personally investigated all the reports he used, and he uncovered some of the best substantiated and strongest cases known. McDonald also did original research on many of the classic cases, such as the Mantell, Chiles and Whitted, Washington, D.C., and Zamora sightings. He printed his lectures and distributed them to anyone interested.

McDonald rushed into the fray with Menzel and Klass. Since his field was atmospheric physics, he was best equipped to counter Menzel's and Klass's arguments that most UFOs resulted from unusual atmospheric conditions. McDonald worked intensively on Menzel's books and painstakingly showed the implausibility of Menzel's theories. Phil Klass presented easier pickings. After demonstrating the weaknesses of Klass's ideas, McDonald re-marked: "Klass dismissed." McDonald's drive, tireless energy, keen intelligence, and remarkable productivity made him a major force in the UFO controversy.

McDonald also took on the Air Force. He vigorously attacked it for its lack of scientific investigation and its pro-nouncements designed to soothe the public. He attacked the CIA for its involvement in the Robertson panel report. While not subscribing to Keyhoe's conspiracy ideas, McDonald did believe the Air Force had been involved in a *"grand foulup"* because of the "limited scientific competence" of the personnel attached to the UFO project.[55]

The Air Force feared McDonald. It saw him as a major threat to its public relations efforts. When the American Society of Newspaper Editors asked the Air Force to allow Quintanilla to join McDonald and others in a symposium on UFOs, the Air Force Office of Information (SAFOI) thought long and hard about subjecting Quintanilla to McDonald's attacks. SAFOI decided to let Quintanilla appear, but he would have to be "brainwashed thoroughly" beforehand. "Two colonels with 30 years' experience in the information business will be holding his hands. They will work him over—ask him every leading dirty question he might get. He will be ready for them." Besides that, Klass would be on the panel, and since he was eager to promote his book and debate with McDonald, Quintanilla would be able to sit back and listen.[56]

McDonald's contacts with the scientific community also worried the Air Force. When McDonald wrote to the Air Force Office of Aerospace Research telling it that he would be in Washington and wanted to discuss the UFO situation with the staff, SAFOI knew that the Office of Aerospace Research would not be receptive but that "they dare not turn him down." The Air Force, as SAFOI put it, wanted to "fireproof" McDonald.[57]

McDonald's civilian adversaries, particularly Phil Klass, also wanted to fireproof him. Klass, who was rapidly becoming the new leader of the anti-UFO forces, engaged in a protracted battle of attrition with McDonald. He printed and distributed detailed critiques of McDonald's speeches and statements. McDonald charged that Klass had told columnist Jack Anderson that McDonald used navy funds on a trip to Australia to study UFOs. This caused a minor scandal and the navy sent an auditor to look at McDonald's contract. The navy found nothing irregular, but the resulting pressure from the university administration caused McDonald some embarrassment. The McDonald-Klass struggle continued until McDonald's death.[58]

In addition to his fight with Klass, McDonald also had a simmering feud with Hynek. It started in early June 1966 when McDonald visited Project Blue Book at Wright-Patterson Air Force Base. Quintanilla allowed him to examine some case reports. McDonald was astonished. The sighting reports he saw confirmed his suspicions. The Air Force was holding an enormous quantity of impressive reports, and Hynek had said nothing about them to the scientific community. He went directly from Wright-Patterson Air Force Base to Northwestern University and Hynek's office. He pounded on Hynek's desk and asked, "How could you sit on this information for so many years without alerting the scientific community?" Hynek later said this incident was "like a breath of fresh air," for here at last was a reputable scientist who was not afraid to say UFOs deserved scientific study.[59]

But McDonald was not through with Hynek yet. McDonald believed Hynek had committed an unpardonable scientific sin— he had been scientifically dishonest. Hynek had a key and unique role in being the only scientist working on UFOs. Hynek had known of the strong evidence of the possibility of extraterrestrial visitation but had remained quiet. He had known of the Air Force's inadequate investigatory methods but had gone along with them in the crucial early years. McDonald thought Hynek was as bad as, if not worse than, Menzel. In fact, McDonald characterized Hynek as "the original Menzel" and saw Hynek's later open-minded stand toward the UFO mystery as a self-serving way to assuage his guilt. Although in later years Hynek and McDonald were cordial to each other and appeared on forums together, McDonald never trusted Hynek and never forgave him.[60]

McDonald and Hynek did work together, to a certain extent, to interest the scientific community in UFOs. As a result of their urgings, the American Institute of Aeronautics and Astronautics (AIAA) decided to convene a panel of scientists for an unbiased discussion of the UFO problem. Joachim P. Kuettner of the Environmental Research Laboratories in Boulder, Colorado, chaired the eleven-member panel, which hoped to reach some conclusions before 1969.[61] Clearly, the events from 1965 to 1967 opened wider the door to scientific inquiry than ever before.

The events of 1965 to 1967 increased not only scientists' interest in UFOs but public interest in the various UFO organizations and clubs as well. The private UFO groups enjoyed increased memberships. Peter Bail in the *New York Times* reported that membership in UFO organizations was "soaring" and that "predictably the number of sightings of 'saucers' seemed to be growing apace." He reported that NICAP had doubled its membership to 11,000 and that the Amalgamated Flying Saucer Clubs of America (the California-based contactee group) claimed 3,700 members. George Van Tassel's contactee convention at

Giant Rock, California, drew crowds of at least 2,000—more than double what it had drawn in previous years. Hector Quintanilla's analysis of this new interest in UFOs was that it was due to an "upsurge in magazine stories and television shows devoted to the topic." [62]

Although Quintanilla's reason for the increase in UFO reports might be dubious, it was true that more people were writing more books on the subject. From 1966 to 1968 over two dozen books on UFOs were published. Frank Edwards, Keyhoe's old friend, led the way in 1966 with his best-selling *Flying Saucers—Serious Business*, an amalgam of sighting tales, history, and a large dose of speculation. Edwards's research was shoddy at best, but his book rivaled Keyhoe's books for sheer volume of sales. Edwards followed the next year with *Flying Saucers—Here and Now!*, which gave the reader more of the same.[63]

John Fuller's *The Interrupted Journey* told the story of the Barney and Betty Hill case, which involved an extremely credible and reliable interracial couple who claimed that extraterrestrials abducted them, took them aboard a UFO, gave them physical examinations, and then released them. Ordinarily UFO researchers would shy away from a case like this, but it bore no resemblance to contactee stories and the Hills had circumstantial evidence to bolster the credibility of their claim. Excerpted in *Look* magazine, the book was an instant success.[64]

Jim and Coral Lorenzen's 1962 *The Great Flying Saucer Hoax*, a comprehensive exposition of the worldwide UFO phenomenon coupled with their ideas on Air Force secrecy, came out in paperback in 1966 under the title *Flying Saucers: The Startling Evidence of the Invasion from Outer Space*. It too was popular and underwent numerous printings. They followed that with *UFOs Over the Americas*, which concentrated on recent sightings in the Western Hemisphere, *Flying Saucer Occupants*, the first book to treat reports of occupants seriously, and *UFOs: The Whole Story*, which outlined UFO sightings, the government's secrecy policies, and brought the history up to the Condon committee.[65]

Jacques Vallee, a mathematician and computer expert from Northwestern University, published two books on UFOs in 1965 and 1966, *Anatomy of a Phenomenon* and *Challenge to Science*. Both of these well-reasoned and scientifically based books attempted to give a scholarly basis for studying UFO reports. Vallee discussed the reports statistically, analytically, and categorically. His scientific training made these books the most solid scientific works on the UFO phenomenon during this period.[66]

Numerous other books that tried to capitalize on the current high level of interest also appeared in book stores. These works ranged from naked exploitation, like reprinted contactee books, to the standard potboiler. They all sold well as public interest seemed insatiable in light of the tremendous number of sightings during these years.

The Air Force received nearly three thousand sighting reports from 1965 through 1967. Public interest in them and massive publicity had finally forced a congressional hearing on UFOs which, in turn, compelled the Air Force to look for outside aid in dealing with the UFO problem. Finding the University of Colorado and especially Edward U. Condon to direct the civilian study allowed the Air Force to get rid of the UFO problem at least for a while. Condon's prestige also made UFOs a more legitimate area of study for some members of the scientific community. The spokesmen for the private UFO groups seemed less vocal; prominent professional people, such as Hynek and McDonald, more vocal; and many previously hostile sectors of the society began to treat the subject seriously.

Although hostility still prevailed, a growing number of scientists took a closer look at the UFO phenomenon during these years and independently concluded that the topic had scientific merit. As the UFO debate moved away from in-group and public relations haggling and toward the scientific community, the Condon committee's work became, necessarily, the focal point of attention. Many scientists as well as UFO proponents adopted a wait-and-see attitude before judging the work of this first university-based scientific investigation of the UFO phenomenon. The Condon committee assumed paramount importance, and, eventually, most concerned citizens and scientists looked to it to give them the answer to the problem.

THE CONDON COMMITTEE
AND ITS AFTERMATH

The establishment of the Condon committee was the culmi-
nation of years of pressure from Keyhoe, Hynek, private UFO
groups, Congress, and the news media. Because the committee
had a university rather than a military base, because its members
were trained in the physical and social sciences, and because its
purpose was a long-term and in-depth study of the UFO
phenomenon, it assumed extraordinary importance for people on
all sides of the UFO controversy. But the committee fell prey to
internal divisions, methodological disputes, and personality
clashes, and it did not resolve or clarify most of the issues
surrounding the UFO controversy. In fact, its final report raised
more questions than it answered. Although the Condon committee successfully helped the Air Force eliminate its UFO problem,
the committee failed to add substantially to knowledge about the
phenomenon.

The Condon committee began its work in October 1966 with
optimism on all sides. Even though no one connected with the
project had any prior experience in the field, the staff of
twelve—including psychologists David Saunders and Stuart Cook,
chemist Roy Craig, astronomer Franklin Roach, and project
coordinator Robert Low—formulated workable plans to attack
the UFO problem on many fronts. The staff planned to keep a
case book of the best available sightings, and Saunders was to

study them statistically. The staff compiled a library containing most of the important works on the subject. It planned to create investigation teams to study sightings as soon as they occurred. Psychologist William Scott began work on a standard questionnaire to gather information about sightings and their witnesses. Condon hired outside consultants to write reports about physical phenomena, such as ball lightning and plasmas, associated with UFO sightings. To orient project members about problems in UFO research, the staff brought in Hynek, Jacques Vallee, Quintanilla, Keyhoe, and NICAP assistant director Richard Hall.[1]

Trouble developed almost as soon as the first rush of optimism faded. David Saunders outlined the problems in a 1968 book about the Condon committee's early problems. According to Saunders, one of the first disagreements was over Scott's questionnaire: of its twenty-one pages, only one covered items about the sighting itself; the remaining twenty pages asked questions about the psychological reactions of the witnesses. Some staff members objected to this method, a dispute ensued, and Scott resigned. A second problem centered on project coordinator Robert Low who, Saunders said, seemed insensitive to the project members' work. He preoccupied himself with adding reports to his case book. Saunders later charged that Low improperly screened and analyzed these cases and they only increased the projected length of the final report. In August 1967 Low went to Europe for a month's stay to represent the committee at the International Astronomical Union in Prague. The staff thought this would be an excellent opportunity for Low to meet with two of Europe's leading UFO researchers, Charles Bowen of England and Aime Michel of France. Low, however, decided not to visit Bowen and Michel and went instead to Loch Ness because, he said, although neither UFOs nor the monster existed, it was important to compare the two phenomena.[2]

A third source of irritation was Condon's attitudes. Early in the project, on January 25, 1967, in his speech before the Corning Section of the American Chemical Society, he said that the government should get out of the UFO "business" and that the UFO phenomenon had nothing to it. Saunders explained that not only did the speech upset and puzzle some project staff members but it almost caused a break with NICAP. The Condon committee needed APRO's and NICAP's help, both of which had agreed to supply it with good sighting reports. The Air Force was inefficient; Blue Book personnel had misfiled and misplaced many reports, and air base officers sent reports slowly and contributed many of poor quality. Saunders, who joined NICAP to keep up with current sightings when the university accepted the UFO project, found that NICAP reports were of a higher quality than those of the Air Force. Many NICAP members thought Condon's speech at Corning proved both his bias and the Air Force's influence, and they put pressure on Keyhoe to withdraw support. Under Saunders's urging and with much reluctance, Condon wrote to Keyhoe explaining that the press had misquoted what he said and he managed to head off a serious problem with NICAP.[3]

But Condon still had problems concealing his negative attitude toward UFOs. He showed a distinct partiality to contactee-like claims—claims that serious UFO investigators viewed as hoaxes. Not only did these stories provide Condon with excellent after-dinner anecdotes, but they occupied an unusually large portion of his project efforts as well. Of the four of five cases he personally investigated, all were either hoaxes or had contactee overtones. In addition, he made a special trip to New York City in June 1967 to appear at a meeting of the contactee-oriented Congress of Scientific Ufologists where Howard Menger was the guest speaker. Condon took a bow in the audience. The project staff was not happy with this behavior.[4]

A major source of conflict, beginning as early as January 1967, surrounded the validity of the extraterrestrial hypothesis. Saunders rapidly emerged as the champion of the idea that the committee should consider the extraterrestrial hypothesis equally with other theories. Psychologist Michael Wertheimer and Low took the position that the extraterrestrial hypothesis was not only unprovable but probably absurd as well. A dispute over this point ensued between Saunders and Low and Wertheimer; as a result, Wertheimer lost interest in the project and participated only minimally. But Low and Saunders continued at odds over the issue, and in March 1967 Low wrote a position paper in which he called the extraterrestrial hypothesis nonsense.[5] He maintained this attitude until the end of the project.

The disagreement over the extraterrestrial hypothesis indicated deeper disputes within the committee. One concerned the committee's policy of releasing no information to the press before completing the final report. Condon and Low had instituted this policy, the one exception being any public remarks Condon might make, but Saunders disagreed with it. The policy seemed to bear directly on the committee's scientific intent. Saunders hoped and perhaps assumed that the staff would find at least several solid cases to support the recommendation for continued scientific study of UFOs; he had found some sightings he thought were solid, one being the 1950 Nicholas Mariana film.[6]

For Saunders, recommending continued study implied that UFOs were a unique phenomenon and that the extraterrestrial hypothesis might have merit. Therefore, he reasoned, the committee should release selected information to the public to soften the shock of this kind of recommendation. But Condon, also assuming that a "positive" report would mean that the extraterrestrial hypothesis had merit, refused to change the policy; if a positive final report seemed likely, he explained, he would not release the information to the press but would take it personally to the president of the United States. Saunders interpreted this statement to mean that no matter what the staff found the final report would be negative, that the report would not recommend continued study because the idea that UFOs represented an anomalous phenomenon of possible extraterrestrial origin had no validity.[7]

While this dispute simmered beneath the surface, a second issue emerged that unquestionably became the project's most dramatic by-product—the release of the so-called Low memorandum. In August 1966, as people at the University of Colorado tried to decide whether to accept the UFO project, Low wrote a memorandum to the university's administrators explaining his views. In it he dealt with the question of what could be the final result of the study.[8]

The memorandum, ambiguously and loosely worded, ex-

pressed the basic premise that UFOs were not a unique phenomenon, that they had no physical reality and were not extraterrestrial. But, Low stated, even though the staff would be composed of
"nonbelievers," it was practically impossible to prove these
negative propositions. Yet the staff could collect an impressive
body of evidence to bolster these commonsense negative assumptions. Such bolstering, Low cautioned, might involve a public
relations dilemma in which "the trick would be to describe the
project so that, to the public, it would appear a totally objective
study but, to the scientific community, would present the image of
a group of nonbelievers trying their best to be objective but having
an almost zero expectation of finding a saucer." Low decided that
the best way to accomplish this dual objective would be to stress
the investigation of "the psychology and sociology of persons and
groups who report seeing UFOs." By placing emphasis on the
witnesses, Low said, "rather than on examination of the old
question of the physical reality of the saucer, I think the scientific
community would quickly get the message." [9]

The Low memorandum found its way to a file marked "AF
Contract and Background," where it sat, as Saunders said,
"ticking away like a time bomb" until July 1967, when staff
member Roy Craig discovered it. Puzzled over its contents, Craig
showed it to coworker Norman Levine, who showed it to
Saunders. Saunders then showed the memorandum to Keyhoe because he wanted to be open with NICAP. He wanted Keyhoe to
know about Low's apparent bias, but he also wanted Keyhoe's
continued cooperation with the project so that Saunders would
have data to write a minority report. Keyhoe, in turn, told James
McDonald about the memorandum. Later McDonald received a
copy of it. All this went on without Low's knowledge. [10]

No one brought up the memorandum until February 1968,
when McDonald wrote a seven-page letter to Low criticizing the
project's methodology and expressing concern over the negative
conclusion to which the project seemed headed. In the letter
McDonald mentioned the memorandum, quoting the section
about "the trick would be. . . ." Low became exceptionally upset
and showed Condon McDonald's letter. Condon, who had not

known about the memorandum until this time, was outraged. He accused Saunders and Levine of stealing the letter from Low's personal files and releasing it to McDonald; Condon told Saunders he ought to be "professionally ruined" for leaking the memorandum. The next day Condon fired Saunders and Levine. Their dismissal brought other staff problems to the fore. Condon's administrative assistant, Mary Lou Armstrong, resigned, citing "an almost unanimous 'lack of confidence' " in Low's ability to direct the project. She also accused Low of misrepresenting the majority of the senior staff's opinion that the UFO phenomenon deserved further scientific study.[11]

The Low memorandum and Condon's handling of it reflected the philosophical divisions in the project and the conflicts between staff members. Condon was unable to maintain a continuous project staff; out of the original twelve, only Low and two other full-time staff members remained with the project for its duration.[12] Much of the personal conflict was based on the philosophical issue of what assumption to make in investigating cases. Neither of the two groups involved saw the primary focus as being to determine whether UFOs constituted an anomalous phenomenon. Instead, one group, with Saunders as spokesman, thought the committee should consider the extraterrestrial hypothesis and other theories about the origin of UFOs; this group wanted to look at as much of the data as possible. The other group, with Low as spokesman, thought the extraterrestrial theory was nonsense and believed the solution to the UFO mystery was to be found in the psychological makeup of the witnesses. The main conflict was over whether UFOs were an extraterrestrial phenomenon rather than whether they constituted a unique aerial phenomenon.

Perhaps the reason the two groups focused on the efficacy of the extraterrestrial hypothesis as a measure of the objects' reality was that none of the project staff had any experience in investigating UFO reports. Even though Condon asked Hynek, Keyhoe, and Jacques Vallee at the beginning to brief the project staff on problems in UFO research, he did not use these men as consultants for the project's methodology. Therefore, its methodological problems led the staff members to tangential concerns.

Disclosure of the Low memorandum became the central event in the Condon committee's stormy history. Journalist John Fuller found out about the firings soon after they occurred and in May 1968 wrote an article, "Flying Saucer Fiasco," for *Look* magazine. Fuller discussed the divisions in the project, Condon's seeming preoccupation with contactees, the Low memorandum, McDonald's letter to Low, the firing of Saunders and Levine, and Mary Lou Armstrong's subsequent resignation. To Fuller these events meant that "the hope that the establishment of the Colorado study brought with it has dimmed. All that seems to be left is the $500,000 trick." Condon sent a telegram to *Look* charging that the Fuller article contained "falsehoods, and misrepresentations" but not specifying what they were. The *Denver Post* quoted Mary Lou Armstrong as saying the article was accurate.[13]

In addition to the article, *Look* printed a short piece Keyhoe had written to say that NICAP had withdrawn its support from the Condon committee. NICAP had been wavering about continuing its support even before the Low disclosure. Although Saunders encouraged Keyhoe to withhold judgment, Keyhoe knew about the project's difficulties and became increasingly wary of its objectivity. The dismissals convinced him that his fears were justified; he could see the direction the project was taking and wanted no part of it. (He actually had withdrawn support before the *Look* article but made his decision public in the magazine.) APRO, claiming that NICAP had tried to influence the committee through Saunders, decided to continue to give sighting reports to the committee and not to prejudge the study.[14]

Fuller's article had far-reaching effects. Technical and professional journals carried the story and opened a forum for debate. In an interview with *Scientific Research*, Saunders and Levine said they planned a libel suit against Condon and attacked him for an " 'unscientific' approach" to the study. In reply, Condon said calling him unscientific was grounds for libel, and one factor in dismissing Saunders and Levine was that they gave "outsiders" material from "personal" files. Until the final report became available to the public in the fall of 1968, Condon said, "fair-minded people will reserve judgment." *Industrial Research* printed excerpts from the "stolen" Low memorandum, as Condon called it, and a statement from Thomas Ratchford of the Air Force Office of Scientific Research. He said it would be "inappropriate and premature" for the Air Force to comment on the matter until the Condon committee completed the final report. But, asserted Ratchford, he believed Condon to be "outstandingly open-minded" and unbiased. According to Air Force Public Information Officer David Shea, the Low memorandum caused a stir in the Air Force and Secretary Brown organized a task force "to keep a close eye on the project." [15]

Science magazine's news department was working on an article about the project's problems, and Condon, a past president of AAAS, agreed to cooperate with the author in hopes that this would be his counterattack to Fuller. But during the preparation of the article, the expected public interest in the committee's problems did not materialize, and Condon, according to *Science* editor Daniel S. Greenberg, decided it was "inappropriate for *Science* to touch the matter, withdrew his offer of cooperation, and proceeded to enunciate high-sounding principles in support of his new-found belief that *Science* should not touch the subject until after publication of his report." When Greenberg reminded Condon that he had wanted the article and had offered complete cooperation, "Condon flatly refused to discuss the matter further." *Science* printed the piece anyway. Condon became so angry that he resigned from AAAS.[16]

One of Condon's friends at the University of Colorado's Joint Institute for Laboratory Astrophysics criticized the magazine for writing about the controversy: because the public did not understand the workings of scientists, it tended to base its judgments on commentators' reactions to scientific controversies; the "tragedy" of the article was that "*Science* apparently fails to perceive that public acceptance of the rationality of science is at stake." Condon's colleague may have overstated his case. In spite of the debate the Fuller article created, the majority of people interested in the UFO controversy seemed to agree with the

Denver Post when it said that although it would have liked Condon to answer Fuller's charges, "everyone [should] wait for the project report before passing judgment." [17]

Fuller's article even prompted reaction in Congress. Indiana Congressman J. Edward Roush delivered a speech on the House floor saying the article raised "grave doubts as to the scientific profundity and objectivity of the project." In an interview with the *Denver Post*, Roush cited the Low memorandum as evidence of the Air Force's influence in the project from the start. Roush, who had a prior interest in UFOs and with McDonald's urgings, recommended a new congressional investigation, took steps immediately to initiate such an investigation, and scheduled it for July 29, 1968. [18]

Under the auspices of the House Science and Astronautics Committee, this hearing was more encompassing and ambitious than the one in 1966. Conceived of as a symposium, the participants were Hynek, McDonald, astronomer Carl Sagan, sociologist Robert L. Hall, engineer James A. Harder, and astronautics engineer Robert M. Baker. Menzel submitted a written statement, saying he was "amazed . . . that you [Roush] could plan so unbalanced a symposium, weighted by persons known to favor Government support of a continuing expensive and pointless investigation of UFOs without inviting me, the leading exponent of opposing views and author of two major books on the subject." Psychologists Leo Sprinkle and Roger N. Shepard, nuclear physicist Stanton Friedman, geophysicist Garry C. Henderson, and exobiologist Frank B. Salisbury also submitted prepared statements. The Science and Astronautics Committee set up symposium ground rules prohibiting any criticism of the Condon project or the Air Force, because the committee said, the House Armed Services Committee was the appropriate place to criticize the Air Force or an Air Force sponsored project. [19]

Hynek spoke first. He recounted his involvement in the UFO controversy and his change of mind over the years. At first he believed that the subject was "rank nonsense, the product of silly seasons, and a peculiarly American craze that would run its course as all popular crazes do." But as he examined more of the data over the years, he recounted, he realized that there might indeed be "scientific paydirt" in the phenomenon. He had not alerted the scientific community to the seriousness of the problem before, he said, because scientists had to be sure of their facts; he did not want to cry wolf unless he was reasonably sure there was a wolf. Now he was sure.[20]

Hynek offered two reasons for why scientists had not shown interest in UFOs previously. First, he said, was the lack of hard-core data and a method for obtaining this data; the Air Force failed to uncover such data because it only wanted to determine whether UFOs threatened national security. The second reason, Hynek explained, was the contactees and the sensational treatment of UFOs in pulp magazines. Hynek noted that the subject was so illegitimate for scientists that "there appears to be a scientific taboo on even the passive tabulation of UFO reports." It would be foolhardy for a scientist to present a paper on UFOs to the American Physical Society or to the American Astronomical Society—"the paper would be laughed down." [21]

In contrast, Hynek noted, the recent 1966–67 wave of sightings increased scientific interest, and all for the good. Scientists' misconceptions about the nature of UFO information have been "so powerful and all-encompassing," he said, "that an amazing lethargy and apathy to investigation has prevailed. This apathy is unbecoming to the ideals of science and undermines public confidence." The new scientific interest, Hynek explained, gave the impression that "we should either fish or cut bait." He wanted to fish and recommended establishing a "UFO Scientific Board of Inquiry properly funded, for the specific purpose of an investigation in depth of the UFO phenomenon." He also recommended using the United Nations for a free interchange of international sighting reports and data. Due to continued reports of close encounters with "unexplainable craft" from sane, reputable people, Hynek said, he had to believe that either the reports had scientific value or world society contained people "who are articulate, sane, and reputable in all matters save UFO reports." Either way, the phenomenon deserved study.[22]

The second speaker was McDonald. He began his testimony by saying that even though scientists had been lax to investigate UFOs because of the anecdotal evidence involved, the UFO matter was of "extraordinary scientific importance." He outlined his own change in attitude about UFOs: he, too, had placed little credence in UFO reports at first, but his research during the past few years convinced him that the extraterrestrial hypothesis was capable of explaining the majority of unexplained UFO reports whereas other hypotheses were not. For example, he had researched independently the 1952 Washington, D.C., sightings and found that the temperature inversion theory was untenable. UFOs were "entirely real," he said, and "we do not know what they are because we have laughed them out of court." He supported Hynek's suggestion for an ongoing UFO study on a global scale and urged further House hearings to enable scientists to debate the issue.[23]

Former O'Brien committee member and Cornell Professor of Astronomy Dr. Carl Sagan testified third. Taking a skeptical attitude toward UFOs being extraterrestrial, he confined his remarks to the possibilities of extraterrestrial life and the problems of space travel. He thought extraterrestrial life probably existed elsewhere in the universe, although intelligent life was most unlikely in our solar system; yet interstellar space travel, while encountering the difficulties of the time over great distances, Sagan said, was not physically impossible.[24]

The fourth person to speak was Dr. Robert L. Hall, chairman of the Department of Sociology at the University of Illinois and the brother of NICAP assistant director Richard Hall. He examined the theory that "hysterical contagion" caused UFO reports and found it "highly improbable," for "hard-core" cases and "the weight of evidence is strongly against it." Hall had discovered strong evidence that physical phenomena underlay a portion of the reports. To alleviate panic over UFOs, Hall said, the government should circulate freely all available information about the phenomenon and scientists should study carefully 100 to 200 cases per year for "recurring patterns, with emphasis on the way they react to their environment, the way they react to light sources, the way they react to presence of humans and so on." Hall "enthusiastically agreed with Hynek's suggestion of a Board of Inquiry." [25]

Dr. James A. Harder, associate professor of civil engineering at the University of California and an APRO consultant, did not mince words: "On the basis of the data and ordinary rules of evidence, as would be applied in civil or criminal courts, the physical reality of UFO's has been proved beyond a reasonable doubt." The objects were "interplanetary" and their propulsion was based on "an application of gravitational fields that we do not understand." As did the previous witness, Harder recommended a continued scientific investigation of UFOs. [26]

The last witness was Dr. Robert M. Baker, senior scientist with the Computer Sciences Corporation in southern California, editor of the *Journal of Astronomical Sciences*, and a former UCLA professor of astronomy and engineering. Baker had analyzed the Mariana and Newhouse films and had concluded that the Mariana film exhibited anomalistic objects and the Newhouse film "most probably anomalistic objects." Addressing himself to why American sky photography projects, radar surveillance systems, telescopes, and military detection equipment had not provided many photographs of unidentified flying objects, he explained that the majority of astronomical equipment was specialized and "would probably not detect the anomalous luminous phenomena reported by the casual observer." Only one American surveillance system had a "slight opportunity" to detect UFOs above the earth's atmosphere, Baker said. He had visited Air Defense Command headquarters and confirmed that since this equipment had been operative, "there have been a number of anomalistic alarms. Alarms that, as of this date, have not been explained on the basis of natural phenomena interference, equipment malfunction or inadequacy, or manmade space objects." [27]

Baker concluded: "We have not now, nor have we been in the past, able to achieve a complete—or even partially complete—surveillance of space in the vicinity of the earth, comprehensive enough to betray the presence of or provide quantitative information on anomalistic phenomena." He recommended instituting a long-term, properly funded, interdisciplinary, mobile scientific task force to study the surveillance problem and develop UFO sensing and tracking equipment. Baker also suggested a system of "listening posts" for possible extraterrestrial communication and studies to forecast technological and behavioral patterns of advanced extraterrestrial life.[28]

Finally, a House committee staff member placed into the record the papers prepared by Menzel, Stanton Friedman, Frank Salisbury, Leo Sprinkle, Garry Henderson, and Roger Shepard. Menzel's paper included his familiar theories that UFOs were mirages, reflections, temperature inversions, and the like. In his paper, Friedman criticized the positions of Menzel, Klass, and Markowitz and concluded that "the earth is being visited by intelligently controlled vehicles whose origin is extraterrestrial." Dr. Frank Salisbury's paper discussed the issue of noncontact and the danger of attributing human motivation to nonhuman intelligence: "To inductively extrapolate from our own current sociological approaches to those of other intelligent entities would be to commit the logical sin of extrapolation in a most flagrant manner." In their papers, Dr. Leo Sprinkle (psychologist at the University of Wyoming), Dr. Garry C. Henderson (senior research scientist for General Dynamics), and Dr. Roger N. Shepard (psychology professor at Stanford) took issue with Menzel's theories and criticized him for not giving enough credit to human observations, perceptions, and witnesses' ability to reconstruct accurately what they saw.[29]

Thus ended the second congressional hearing on UFOs. Although the House Science and Astronautics Committee prohibited all participants from criticizing the Colorado project openly, the criticism was apparent nonetheless. Each witness recommended an ongoing systematic investigation of UFO's; none suggested or implied that the Condon project would settle the debate over UFOs or would add significantly to knowledge about the subject. The hearing-symposium made the strongest case to date for continued study of UFOs. It also represented growing academic interest in the subject: a few years before the 1968 hearing Hynek was the only American scientist capable of discussing the UFO phenomenon knowledgeably and from a research basis, but at the time of the hearing at least twenty specialists in the physical and social sciences (apart from the Condon committee) were taking an active interest in the subject, and the number was growing. The 1965–67 sighting wave helped create this new scholarly interest and the Condon committee's work helped legitimatize the subject. In 1968 many academicians interested in UFOs joined APRO, which, with the help of Assistant Director Richard Greenwell, had launched an active recruitment program to gain these consultants for its work.[30]

The July 1968 House hearings came at the end of a peak period of sightings and of public interest in and press coverage of the phenomenon. Membership in the two national organizations had dropped as all interested groups waited for the Condon committee's final report, due in the fall of 1968.[31] After the firing of Saunders and Levine in February 1968, press coverage of the Condon committee became virtually nonexistent; Condon stopped making public speeches and very few people knew what was happening in the project. The only event to mar the quietude of this period was the publication of Saunders and Harkins's book, *UFOs? Yes!*, a blow-by-blow account of the early problems in the Colorado project. Saunders, sure that the Condon committee's final report would not recommend further systematic study, attempted in his book to prepare the public for this and to raise the issue of the committee's objectivity. Saunders and Levine hoped the book would appear just before the Condon report came out.

In November 1968, before Condon released the final report publicly, he turned it over to the National Academy of Sciences (NAS) for review and approval. NAS's review panel consisted of eleven scientists, who praised the report's scope, methodology, and concurred with all its conclusions and recommendations. The panel found the study to be a "creditable effort to apply objectively the relevant techniques of science to the solution of the UFO problem." It agreed that systematically studying UFO reports was not a fruitful way to expand knowledge of the phenomena and concluded that "the least likely explanation of

UFOs is the hypothesis of extraterrestrial visitations by intelligent beings." Frederick Sietz, president of the National Academy of Sciences and one of Condon's ex-students, wrote to Assistant Secretary of the Air Force Alexander Flax in January 1969 to say he hoped NAS's review would "be helpful to you and other responsible officials in determining the nature and scope of any continuing research effort in this area." Flax added that the National Academy of Sciences had made its report for the "sole purpose" of helping the Air Force make this decision.[32]

The Condon committee final report, 1,485 pages in hard cover and 965 pages in paperback, contained a collection of analyses from various individuals who were either project staff or consultants. It had six sections and extensive appendices. The *New York Times* science editor, Walter Sullivan, wrote the preface to the paperback edition. In it he basically answered Saunders's charges and hinted of what was to come in the body of the text. Sullivan called proponents of the extraterrestrial hypothesis "UFO enthusiasts" or "UFO believers." People who believed in the extraterrestrial theory did so, said Sullivan, because of "a hope that some sort of superior beings are watching over our world prepared to intervene if things get too bad"; although these UFO enthusiasts tried to discredit the report before it came out, the National Academy of Sciences gave it "straight As." [33]

Turning then to the project's critics and internal disputes, Sullivan claimed that Keyhoe, "as author of *Flying Saucers Are Real*, has a vested interest in the confirmation of his theories" and therefore tried to discredit the project. Sullivan explained that Condon's negative statements about UFOs and his apparent interest in contactee stories were the products of a "garrulous soul who loves to spin a yarn"; Condon found it hard to resist recounting some of the "sillier episodes" in UFO research. The project's biggest problem, according to Sullivan, was the release of the Low memorandum. Condon did not agree with its contents, Sullivan explained, and had not seen it before the release; the *Look* article resulted from leaking the memorandum to "disgruntled UFO believers." [34]

The final report included chapters from thirty-six people.

Condon had contracted with most to write sections on, for example, the history of the UFO phenomenon, and public opinion. The Stanford Research Institute had written sections on plasmas, in which it criticized Klass's theories, radar, meteorological optics, and so on. Condon's staff wrote the remaining sections. The result was a rather unorganized compilation of independent articles on disparate subjects, a minority of which dealt with UFOs.

The main UFO sections looked at ninety-one cases. Most were neither the cases Low had compiled nor those NICAP had donated. Of the ninety-one cases, the project staff identified sixty-one as misperceptions, hoaxes, and the like. The remaining thirty were either possible, probable, inconclusive, or unidentified. Because of the tentative nature of these unsolved cases, the committee listed all of them as unexplained. This finding was significant in view of the project's working definition of a UFO: "The stimulus for a report made by one or more individuals of something seen in the sky (or an object thought to be capable of flight but seen when landed on the earth) which the observer could not identify as having an ordinary natural origin" and which seemed sufficiently puzzling to report to the authorities.[35] By using this definition, the project concerned itself not with extensive evaluation of UFO reports that had defied previous analysis but with any UFO report *prior* to *any* analysis; this method greatly increased the project's chances of identifying the cases it studied. Still, the staff could not identify about one-third of the cases.

The final report divided the cases into five categories: astronaut sightings, optical and radar sightings, old cases, current cases, and photographic evidence. In the astronaut sighting section, author Franklin Roach said three observations from astronauts McDivitt and Borman were "a challenge to the analyst" and "puzzling." Of the ten cases Roach examined that predated the report, he listed only one as identified; two were possible, one probable, one inconclusive, one "part unidentified and part astronomical," and four unidentified.[36]

Gordon Thayer wrote the section on optical and radar sightings, dividing them into two groups: those with unidentified visual phenomena but identified radar phenomena, and those with both unidentified visual and radar phenomena. An example of the latter was the Lakenheath, England, case in August 1965, which featured two different ground radar-station, aircraft radar, and visual observations of an object that seemed to act in an intelligently controlled manner as it successfully evaded a jet intercept. Thayer concluded that "this is the most puzzling and unusual case in the radar-visual files. The apparently rational, intelligent behavior of the UFO suggests a mechanical device of unknown origin as the most probable explanation of this sighting." Later in the report, the staff discussed this case again and found "the probability that at least one genuine UFO was involved appeared to be fairly high." In another case Thayer said the "sighting defies explanation by conventional means." Describing a radar-visual report in Colorado Springs, Colorado, Thayer concluded: "This must remain as one of the most puzzling radar cases on record, and no conclusion is possible at this time." [37]

In the category of current, nonphotographic cases, the staff analyzed thirty-four reports, but some were multiple sightings and brought the total to fifty-one reports; thirteen of the sightings in these reports remained unidentified. Of the fourteen photographic cases (one of which occurred on two days and made a total of fifteen photos), photoanalyst William K. Hartmann listed three as positively identified, eleven as either possible, probable, or inconclusive, and one as unidentified. The latter involved two photographs that a farmer in McMinneville, Oregon, took in 1950; the project staff analyzed the original negatives and interviewed the farmer. Hartmann concluded: "This is one of the few UFO reports in which all factors investigated, geometric, psychological, and physical appear to be consistent with the assertion that an extraordinary flying object, silvery, metallic, disk-shaped, tens of meters in diameter, and evidently artificial, flew within sight of two witnesses." The number of reports the committee could not identify—thirty of the ninety-one analyzed—strongly suggested that some cases involved "genuine" UFOs. But the final report buried these findings: it devoted most space to the identified objects.[38]

Condon ignored these findings in his recommendations, which he placed at the beginning of the lengthy report. Condon's recommendations reflected more the speeches he gave during the course of the project than the evidence in the final report. His general conclusion was "that nothing has come from the study of UFOs in the past 21 years that has added to scientific knowledge. Careful consideration of the record as it is available to us leads us to conclude that further extensive study of UFOs probably cannot be justified in the expectation that science will be advanced thereby." Addressing himself to previous lack of scientific interest in the UFO phenomenon, Condon said scientists had ample opportunity to study the phenomenon and "have individually decided that UFO phenomena do not offer a fruitful field in which to look for major scientific discoveries." In light of this fact, Condon said, the federal government should not study UFO reports "in the expectation that they are going to contribute to the advance of science," and the Air Force's conclusions that UFOs did not threaten national security was valid. The Department of Defense, Condon suggested, should give UFOs attention "only so much as it deems necessary from a defense point of view" and could do this "within the framework established for intelligence and surveillance operations without the continuance of a special unit such as Project Blue Book." Condon found that, contrary to popular opinion, the subject of UFOs had not been "shrouded in official secrecy. . . . What had been miscalled secrecy has been no more than an intelligent policy of delay in releasing data so that the public does not become confused by premature publication of incomplete studies of reports." [39]

Condon argued that the staff had found "no direct evidence whatever of a convincing nature . . . for the claim that any UFOs represent spacecraft visiting Earth from another civilization." Although scientists said intelligent life elsewhere was "essentially certain," Condon argued, the great distances and time involved in interstellar travel made contact between societies on planets in different solar systems impossible. He concluded: "There is no relation between ILE [intelligent life elsewhere] at other solar systems and the UFO phenomenon as observed on Earth." By estimating the average life span of planets and civilizations, Condon could theorize that interplanetary travelers would not visit earth for at least 10,000 years. To illustrate that it was a "fantasy" to believe in the extraterrestrial hypothesis, Condon cited, among others, contactee Truman Bethurum's claim that the planet Clarion was located behind the sun and thus always out of Earth's view. Condon spent two pages proving that Clarion could not possibly exist and, therefore, that people who believed in the extraterrestrial hypothesis were misguided.[40]

Condon also offered his version of the project's conflict with NICAP. Although NICAP maintained friendly relations with the project at the beginning, he explained, "during this period NICAP made several efforts to influence the course of our study. When it became clear that these would fail, NICAP attacked the Colorado project as 'biased' and therefore without merit." [41]

Condon's final remarks in the opening section concerned the problem of "miseducation" in public schools. This arose because teachers allowed children to use their science study time to read books and magazine articles about UFOs. Because of errors in the material, children were "educationally harmed" or retarded in the "development of a critical faculty with regard to scientific evidence." To remedy this situation, Condon recommended that teachers withhold credit from students who study UFOs and instead "channel their interests in the direction of serious study of astronomy and meteorology, and in the direction of critical analysis of arguments for fantastic propositions that are being supported by appeals to fallacious reasoning or false data." [42]

Reactions to the Condon committee's final report followed expected lines. Keyhoe, McDonald, and Saunders held a news conference on January 11, 1969, a few days after the report appeared, and denounced it as a waste of money. McDonald and Saunders charged that Condon was biased against the extraterrestrial intelligence hypothesis, that the committee had failed to investigate the vast majority of significant UFO reports, and that Condon's conclusions did not represent the findings in the text. Furthermore, McDonald said, the National Academy of Sciences' review panel was not adequately prepared to assess the report.

Keyhoe claimed the Condon committee had examined only about one percent of the "reliable, unexplained" UFO sighting reports that NICAP had supplied.[43]

Keyhoe elaborated on his objections in a special January issue of NICAP's *UFO Investigator*. He accused Condon of not making field investigations himself, of trying to discredit some witnesses by calling them " 'inexpert, inept, or unduly excited'," and of concentrating on "kook cases." He pointed out those sections of the report that seemed to reaffirm that UFOs were a unique phenomenon and appealed to NICAP members for money to carry on a "full-scale campaign to bring the UFO subject out in the open in order to offset the Condon report." Keyhoe directed his main criticism at the inadequacy of the investigation: he accused Condon of ignoring numerous "top cases" involving highly credible witnesses who fit the project's requirements for witness reliability. Condon used only fifty cases from the 1947 to 1967 period, Keyhoe charged, whereas NICAP had 10,000 to 15,000 such cases in its files, and the fifty the project used did not represent the main body of solid UFO reports. In the next issue of the *UFO Investigator* Keyhoe emphatically denied Condon's charge that NICAP had withdrawn support after failing to influence the committee's direction. NICAP did indeed try to influence the project, Keyhoe said, but only "in the direction of objectivity, thoroughness, and concentration on the really significant reports." NICAP made every effort to cooperate with Condon and withdrew its support only "when it became evident that the project situation was beyond repair and foredoomed to be biased and superficial." [44]

APRO's reaction to the final report was as negative as NICAP's. Coral Lorenzen said that just as Condon dismissed many sighting reports because of internal inconsistencies, "we find that the report as a whole fails to pass the same test and should therefore be dismissed and/or discredited." The Lorenzens criticized the report for its "looseness and shallowness," citing as examples Condon's unsubstantiated conclusions that there was no evidence of Air Force secrecy and that school children should not be allowed to study the UFO phenomenon. Also, the project did not investigate enough cases adequately, the Lorenzens said, and the report tended to choose and emphasize cases with no particular significance. They attacked the report's methodology by offering case analyses that directly contradicted those in the report.[45]

As expected, other UFO groups and people connected with them also opposed the report. Nuclear physicist Stanton Friedman and electronics engineer Joseph Jenkins, members of a Pittsburgh UFO research group loosely affiliated with NICAP, criticized Condon for much the same things as Keyhoe and others had. Leonard Stringfield, an old-line UFO proponent, claimed that Condon's thinking was "Neanderthal" and "retrogressive" while Apollo flights showed that interplanetary flights were near. Earl J. Neff of the Cleveland Ufology Project said Condon was biased and the Air Force had for years "been on the hot seat." The Air Force would not admit UFOs were extraterrestrial "because there's no known defense against UFO's." [46]

McDonald, speaking before the DuPont Chapter of the Scientific Research Society of America (in Wilmington, Delaware), attacked the Condon committee on nine points. He criticized it for analyzing only a small fraction of scientifically puzzling UFO reports and for not discussing certain significant cases it did investigate, such as the 1957 Levelland sightings. Many of the reports were trivial and insignificant, McDonald said, and the committee should have ignored them. McDonald charged that scientifically weak and specious argumentation abounded in the case analyses. While Condon had said that scientists previously interested in the UFO phenomenon were biased, McDonald said the report itself was biased in the opposite direction. For example, the "disturbingly incomplete presentation of relevant evidence" in some cases was so severe that it was "little short of misrepresentation of case information." In addition, he asserted, the quantity of irrelevant padding was so great that scientists would find studying the report tedious. Moreover, Condon had casually ignored the significant number of cases that remained unidentified. In sum, McDonald said, the report "dismally" failed to support Condon's negative recommendations and the National

Academy of Sciences' endorsement would eventually be a painful embarrassment to it. He promised to devote all possible personal effort to air objectively the report's inadequacies because scientific clarification of the UFO problem would not come until the Condon report's negative influence was neutralized.[47]

Hynek's critique was perhaps the most cogent. Writing in the April 1969 issue of the *Bulletin of the Atomic Scientists*, he praised Condon for his previous contributions to physics but said his effort in the report was analogous to "Mozart producing an uninspired pot-boiler, unworthy of his talents." Hynek pointed out that the number of unexplained sightings in the report was higher than in Air Force files and that the Air Force's concern over unidentifieds was why Condon mounted the investigation in the first place. Hynek thought Condon had "grossly underestimated the scope and nature of the problem he was undertaking," as evidenced in his definition of UFOs. The definition, Hynek said, was so broad that the committee tried to study too much with its limited time and funds. Hynek proposed an alternate definition that limited the purpose: "A UFO is a report . . . the contents of which are puzzling *not only to the observer but to others who have the technical training the observer may lack.*" On the basis of his many years of experience, Hynek said, he would have deleted about two-thirds of the report's cases as scientifically profitless.[48]

Warming to his task, Hynek zeroed in on the report's underlying assumption. The project staff and the public, Hynek claimed, had confused the UFO problem with the extraterrestrial hypothesis. The issue was not the validity of the extraterrestrial hypothesis but the existence of a legitimate UFO phenomenon regardless of theories about its origin. Just as nineteenth-century scientists could not explain the aurora borealis with their physics, UFOs might be as inexplicable in terms of twentieth-century physics. Condon's conclusion that a phenomenon that thousands of people over a long period of time had reported was still unworthy of further scientific attention, Hynek said, did not serve science.[49]

Hynek hit hard at the project's selection of scientists. Asking an inexperienced group of scientists to take a fresh look at the UFO problem "was akin to asking a group of culinary novices to take a fresh look at cooking and then open a restaurant. Without seasoned advice, there would be many burned pots, many burned fingers, many dissatisfied customers." Concluding his critique, Hynek found a serious flaw in the report's methodology. "For any given reported UFO case, if taken by itself and without respect and regard to correlations with other truly puzzling reports in this and other countries," Hynek explained, "a possible natural, even though farfetched, explanation can always be adduced." The Condon committee found well-known causes for most UFOs because it operated solely on the hypothesis that these *were* the causes. As an example Hynek quoted a passage from the report: " 'This unusual sighting should therefore be assigned to the category of some almost certainly natural phenomenon which is so rare that it apparently has never been reported before or since.' " The final verdict on the Condon committee, Hynek said, "will be handed down by the UFO phenomenon itself. Past experience suggests that it cannot be readily waved away." [50]

Except for McDonald and Hynek, most other scientists did not react extensively to the Condon committee's report. Those who did speak out held opposing opinions. Dr. Robert M. L. Baker, who had testified at the 1968 House hearing, criticized the report in *Scientific Research*. He said it did contain evidence that scientists should continue to study the UFO phenomenon although the provocative and unexplained UFO sightings were hidden in the text among extensive discussions of explained cases and often superfluous technical background material. The report mixed the unexplained and explained UFO cases in "an almost contrived manner—and this tactic confuses or diverts all but the most dedicated reader." According to Baker, Condon should have highlighted the unexplained cases and juxtaposed them to the explained cases for comparison purposes. Baker thought the Condon committee should have determined the probability that UFOs were a new phenomenon, and if so, what patterns the sightings displayed. Then the committee should have formulated hypotheses to account for them. [51]

Frederick J. Hooven, who was a consultant to the committee and analyzed a case in which a low-flying UFO reportedly affected an automobile, also took issue with the final report. He did not think UFOs were extraterrestrial, but he held that the possibility of a visitor from space was reasonable enough to warrant continuing investigation of UFOs. Although man could not speculate about the state of science 50,000 years from now, Hooven explained, he could conceive of the idea that an extraterrestrial, technologically based civilization could be at least this far ahead of our own technological capabilities. Science was in its infancy, he said, and what we knew of physics was only a tiny fraction of what we would understand in the future.[52]

Yet most scientists seemed to support the Condon committee report. For example, Dr. Donald E. Ehlers, president of the Boothe Memorial Astronomical Society, wrote in a letter to the *New York Times* that the committee was courageous because it "discounted a growing religion." But as a taxpayer Ehlers was annoyed: the government spent "five hundred kilobucks" to investigate a phenomenon and came to the same conclusion which, "since the beginning of this hysterical witchhunt, has been that of all professional scientists worthy of the title." Dr. Hudson Hoagland, president emeritus of the Worcester Foundation for Experimental Biology and on the board of directors of the American Association for the Advancement of Science, claimed that the current concern with flying saucers resembled the old obsession with ghosts and seances. Even after investigators exposed seances as frauds, Hoagland said, the devout band of followers never relinquished their belief in them. For Hoagland the Condon study added "massive additional weight to the already overwhelming improbability of visits by UFOs guided by intelligent beings." But because science could not prove a negative, some UFOs would remain unexplained due to insufficient information; yet these unexplained cases did not justify continuing scientific investigation. Hong-Yee Chiu of NASA's Institute for Space Studies said now "ufology should be regarded as a pseudo-science." But the UFO enthusiasts would "find the truth a bitter pill" and would probably continue their "ufological career" with "greater vigor and bitterness toward scientists." He argued that it was "unthinkable" that extraterrestrial visitors would have visited our planet, which is indistinguishable "from the background noise of the Galaxy." [53]

A few politicians were annoyed enough to react to the Condon report. Congressman William F. Ryan (New York) attacked it on the House floor: the study did not explain conclusively the UFO phenomenon and its conclusions were not justified; accepting the conclusions might delay solving the UFO puzzle and make "a scientific breakthrough in an understanding of the problem" more difficult. Noting that in its July 1968 hearing the House Committee on Science and Astronautics had forbidden discussion of the Condon committee because it fell within the jurisdiction of the House Armed Services Committee, Ryan said Condon's conclusions were scientific judgments and therefore fell within the purview of the House Committee on Science and Astronautics. Therefore, Ryan said, the committee had a "duty and responsibility" to hold hearings on the Condon report and its implications. By trying to stop public discussion and governmental action on UFOs, Ryan charged, the report undermined confidence in its own conclusions and recommendations. "Public interest in UFOs cannot be wished away, and reported sightings will persist." Ryan recommended continued government involvement in UFOs, suggesting that NASA assume responsibility for the study. California Congressman Jerry Pettis, who had found the testimony at the July hearing impressive, announced that he too would seek a congressional investigation of the Condon report in the next session. Neither Ryan's recommendations nor Pettis's promise came to fruition.[54]

Newspaper reactions were divided. Most applauded the conclusions and recommendations of the Condon committee, saying the report was "reasonable," "thorough," "objective," and "sound" and the "eminent scientists" who served on the committee constituted an "impressive roster of experts." The *New York Times* ran full-page articles about the report, excerpted it, and gave it front-page coverage. Condon and his staff, the *New York Times* said, had made "a careful and extensive investigation" of the phenomenon, and the study would find "wide acceptance" from all except a few "true believers" who were "committed" to the extraterrestrial hypothesis. The rest of society could now worry about "more serious matters." *New York Times* science editor Walter Sullivan, who wrote the preface to the paperback edition of the report, suggested that the small number of unexplained cases could be identified if the committee had sufficient information. Similarly, the *Wall Street Journal* called Condon's suggestion that further UFO study would not serve science a "sound conclusion" and "common sense." [55]

The newspapers that praised the Condon committee's conclusions and recommendations almost always accompanied their remarks with the observation that "true believers," regardless of how convincing the report was, would not change their views. Frequently newspapers compared true believers to members of the British Flat Earth Society who, despite photographs and astronauts' eye-witness accounts, refused to believe the earth was round. One editorial said NICAP was akin to the "World is Flat Society" and accused it of trying to coerce one project investigator into making his findings "less positive." Moreover, many newspapers—in a turnabout of general press coverage in 1965 and 1966—resorted to ridiculing UFO proponents as "UFO enthusiasts," "diehard wishful thinkers," "die-hard flying saucer sighters," "nuts," "fanatics," and "dedicated disciples of the 'little green men from Mars' school." Syndicated science writer William Hines accused Keyhoe of being interested in UFOs for the money he received from "the sale of sensational paperbacks, hooh-hah magazine articles and the donations of excitable people." [56]

Not all newspapers and journalists supported the Condon report. Lucian Warren, writing in the *Buffalo Evening News*, called the report a "total bust" because it did not explain adequately the sightings in the Buffalo area. The *Knoxville Journal* expressed reservations because the report contained some unexplained photographs and sighting interpretations inconsistent with the facts. Chattanooga, Tennessee, columnist Sally Latham called the report a "$500,000 woolly eyeshade." Journalist Tom Tiede opposed the Condon report and defended NICAP. Once again

"America is laughing at Don Keyhoe," he said, but in the final analysis Keyhoe might have the last laugh. Mike Culbert, columnist for the *Berkeley Daily Gazette,* added a political twist by singularly attacking Condon for being a subversive (because of his past battles with the House Committee on Un-American Activities) and intimated that Condon was following Moscow's "new 'line' " in trying to discredit the existence of UFOs.[57]

Generally, magazine articles on the Condon committee's final report followed the same patterns as the newspaper reports. Magazines supporting the report thought it would not end the controversy. Philip Boffey, in *Science,* called the report the "most thorough and sophisticated investigation of the nebulous UFO phenomenon ever conducted" but doubted whether "flying saucer fans" or "UFO enthusiasts" would be satisfied: "scientific methods are not always able to resolve problems in fields where emotions run high and data are scarce." *Popular Science* writer Alden Armagnac thought the believers would not be quieted even though the "chances of ever finding a real saucer look a whole lot more remote, after you read the Condon report, than before." *U.S. News and World Report* and *Newsweek* agreed that the controversy would continue. *Newsweek* observed that saucer believers would continue to believe just as alchemy long resisted chemistry's discoveries and astrology survived in spite of modern psychology.[58]

Similarly, the *Nation* said that although we lived in an age of "ever-increasing rationality," science and the scientific method still inspired "stout resistance, especially when the subject is one of ancient myth and emotional connotation." The *Nation* theorized that we "yearn for neighbors among the stars" to help relieve our loneliness. For example, the article pointed out, "hardly any of these true believers have seen, or even thought they saw, anything" but insisted on believing witnesses who "on investigation almost invariably turn out to be unreliable or to have a naturalistic explanation." The *Nation* agreed with Condon's recommendation to keep school children from reading about UFOs and getting a warped view of science; this was a "public service of no small importance." *Time,* in "Saucers End," explained that the Condon report had destroyed saucer buffs' favorite theories with "rational, simple explanations." [59]

During the public debate over the report, Condon remained quiet. But he broke his silence in April 1969 in a speech before the American Philosophical Society in Philadelphia. The topic was "UFOs I Have Loved and Lost." Condon defended his conclusion that continued scientific study of UFOs was unwarranted, despite those who said otherwise. To reinforce this point, he related how "flying saucer buffs who have been making money from sensational writing and lecturing to gullible audiences, and collecting dues from the membership of their pseudo-science organizations" had bitterly denounced his conclusions. He told several humorous stories about contactees but allowed that some UFO proponents were "deeply sincere." He equated the study of UFOs with astrology, spiritualism, psychokinesis, and other pseudosciences, and he again said it was practically criminal for teachers to teach these subjects to young people: "In my view publishers who publish or teachers who teach any of the pseudo-sciences as established truth should, on being found guilty, be publicly horsewhipped, and forever banned from further activity in these usually honorable professions." [60]

Throughout the debate over the Condon committee's final report, the Air Force continued its public relations effort but with less sound and fury than before, for the Condon committee had taken some of the pressure off. Since 1966 the Air Force quietly had collected reports, submitted articles to magazines, and issued its usual press statements, fact sheets, and annual Project Blue Book reports. The Blue Book reports included statistical breakdowns of the number of reported sightings and the number of solved cases, a standard résumé on how the Air Force investigated and analyzed UFO reports, an explanation of the most common misidentifications of known objects, short histories of the Air Force's UFO project, discussions of the improbability of UFOs coming from other planets, and a bibliography that usually contained only one book treating the extraterrestrial hypothesis seriously. Using its standard definition of a UFO—"any aerial object or phenomenon which the observer is unable to identify"—

the Air Force claimed in 1969 that it had identified all but 701 of the 12,618 reports it had received since 1947. It reported a decline in reports, from the nearly 3,000 in 1965–67 to 375 in 1968 and 146 in 1969—the lowest number since 1947. Only one report in 1969 remained unidentified. Because of the Air Force's usual method of putting the probable and possible reports in with the identified category, the statistics overwhelmingly favored solved cases.[61]

The Air Force purposefully kept a low profile during the Condon committee's study. Fearful of being criticized for negatively influencing the committee, the Air Force was careful not to interfere with the committee's work and made no public statements about it. But the Air Force did not put aside work on its own UFO program. In 1966 and 1967, while the Condon committee was conducting its investigation, some people at the Foreign Technology Division (FTD) asked to strengthen Project Blue Book's scientific capabilities. This resulted from three factors: intense public interest in UFOs, the concomitant criticism of the Air Force, and the 1966 Gallup Poll finding that nearly half of the adult population believed flying saucers were real although not necessarily extraterrestrial. Noting this public interest, Colonel Raymond S. Sleeper, FTD's new commander, wanted to build a "new image for Project Blue Book" based on this "anchored public attitude." Sleeper thought Project Blue Book should begin a "positive program aimed at establishing contact with extraterrestrial life." But Air Force Director of Information General W. C. Garland had no interest in new images in 1967 and wanted no part of a program to search for extraterrestrial life. Besides, said Garland, "we would really open the flood gates on UFO problems if the public thought that the Condon group was about to involve in extensive research on extraterrestrial activities." Thus ended Sleeper's plan to energize Project Blue Book.[62]

Nonetheless, Sleeper was persistent. In September 1968 he wrote to Hynek asking for suggestions "towards defining those areas of scientific weakness" in Blue Book. Hynek remarked that this request marked the first time in the twenty years of his association with the Air Force that anyone had asked for his advice on Blue Book's scientific methodology. Hynek responded with a comprehensive critique of Blue Book's methods, attitudes, and conclusions. He attacked the Air Force in its most sensitive and potentially most responsive area: Blue Book had not fulfilled its twofold obligation, under AFR 80-17, to determine the potential danger of UFOs to the national security and to use the scientific and technical data garnered from the study of UFO reports. The Air Force claimed that UFO's were not dangerous, Hynek said, only because so far the objects had displayed no hostility, but this did not mean that UFOs were not hostile or that something could not happen in the future. Furthermore, Hynek charged, Blue Book had been inept, inefficient, and unscientific: it had emphasized explanations at any cost and failed to investigate significant cases adequately, spending too much time on obvious and routine cases; the staff was not trained to handle the most rudimentary scientific analyses, yet it routinely used explanations based on sophisticated scientific knowledge.[63]

Hynek also criticized the Air Force's policy of eliminating the possible, probable, and insufficient data categories from its year-end reports to make Blue Book seem efficient and most unidentifieds appear as misidentifications. Hynek complained that time and again his suggestions for improving the quality of Blue Book had gone unheeded, that even he did not have free access to the UFO case files, and that the Air Force did not tell him about significant UFO reports. Blue Book was a closed system where project officers only talked to one another and made no attempts to establish working relationships with Air Force scientists or with Air Force laboratories. Finally, as in his later critique of the Condon report, Hynek accused the Air Force of treating UFO reports as completely separate occurrences and not attempting to discern patterns of reported UFO behavior that could help solve the UFO mystery. By treating reports separately, Hynek argued, Project Blue Book personnel could always solve the case by explaining it as a misidentification of a natural phenomenon, an hallucination, or a hoax.[64]

Impassioned and critical as Hynek's letter was, it came too late for the Air Force to worry or do anything about, for the Condon report came out a few months later. Hynek's letter was the last major internal criticism of the Air Force. The Condon report recommended closing down Project Blue Book. In March 1969 a meeting took place at Air Force headquarters in Washington, D.C., with representatives of the Air Defense Command, Air Force Systems Command, Office of Aerospace Research, Office of Scientific Research, and Office of Information. "From the moment the meeting opened," Captain David Shea of SAFOI remembered, "there was no doubt that Project Blue Book was finished. Everyone agreed on that." The major question was where to place Blue Book's files to keep people "with a UFO axe to grind" from having easy access to them. For this reason SAFOI rejected Washington, D.C., as the site for the documents. It also thought the Air Force museum in Dayton, Ohio, was too accessible. Finally SAFOI decided on the less accessible Air Force Archives at Maxwell Air Force Base in Montgomery, Alabama.[65]

On December 17, 1969, Secretary of the Air Force Robert C. Seamans, Jr., officially announced the termination of the Air Force's twenty-two-year study of unidentified flying objects. An Air Force news release noted that Seamans, in a memorandum to Air Force Chief of Staff General John D. Ryan, said Blue Book's continuance " 'cannot be justified either on the ground of national security or in the interest of science.' " Seamans based his recommendation on the Condon study, the National Academy of Sciences' approval of the study, "past UFO studies," and previous UFO investigating experience.[66]

Most UFO investigators and researchers were not unhappy about the announcement. McDonald called it "no great loss," since Blue Book had been unsuccessful; he feared, though, that its closing might prompt people to believe no real problem existed. APRO's James Lorenzen thought terminating Blue Book eliminated a stumbling block that had hindered objective inquiry into the UFO problem. Stuart Nixon, assistant director at NICAP, said in a press conference that the Air Force's termination opened the way for a fresh look at the UFO problem free from military involvement, and he called for a federal or private agency to open new UFO investigations. The *New York Times* said nearly everyone in the country, except "saucer buffs," would applaud the

Air Force's decision, but "no doubt true believers will continue their quest more convinced than ever" of a conspiracy. The paper was puzzled that the Air Force had waited so long to act after Condon had "punctured the U.F.O. bubble." [67] Hynek, out of a job with Blue Book, remained in his position at Northwestern University and also began work on a book about the UFO phenomenon and the Air Force's and Condon's investigations of it.

The closing down of Blue Book, in addition to the dearth of sightings since 1968 and the Condon report, definitely affected public interest in the subject. NICAP, claiming 12,000 members in 1967, steadily lost members through 1968, 1969, and 1970; by 1971 the membership decreased to 4,000. APRO had the same problem, its membership declining from about 4,000 in 1967 to 2,000 in 1971. Newspaper and magazine publicity, with the exception of articles on the Condon committee and the closing of Blue Book, virtually ceased. Many of the popular UFO magazines stopped publication for lack of readership. The contactees, who had long since faded in popularity, although still somewhat in evidence, were no longer a factor in the UFO controversy.[68]

Furthermore, younger people were displacing some of the familiar figures. NICAP's chronic financial problems had become so severe by the end of 1969 that its board of governors, which had not held a meeting since 1960, decided to reassert its authority. In a stormy and angry meeting, the board determined that Keyhoe had to go. Keyhoe was furious about this "coup" but he stepped down, although he remained on the board. After twelve tumultuous years as director of NICAP, Keyhoe quietly retired to his home in Luray, Virginia, to begin work on his fifth book on UFOs. During his reign NICAP had become a force as a public pressure and education group that no other UFO organization could match. Its power and pressure were a major concern to the Air Force, and it had helped keep the UFO issue alive for the public and in Congress. But in the aftermath of the Condon report, Stuart Nixon, NICAP's new director, had all he could do to keep the organization alive. In 1968 Richard Greenwell, the young British assistant director of APRO, also tried to avert a financial crisis—the result of the Condon report and subsequent loss of membership. Interest on a popular level did not disappear completely, though. A new club, the Midwest UFO Network, appeared in 1969 and its membership rapidly climbed, although its numbers only amounted to several hundred by 1970.[69]

Even though the established private UFO organizations had serious problems at the end of 1969, scientific interest in UFOs still was at a peak. The American Institute of Aeronautics and Astronautics UFO Subcommittee continued its UFO study with a report promised for 1970, and the American Association for the Advancement of Science (AAAS) scheduled a symposium on UFOs for its December 1969 convention.

Thornton Page, who had been a member of the Robertson panel in 1953, and Carl Sagan had proposed a UFO symposium for the December 1968 meeting of AAAS in Dallas, but they decided to postpone it for a year when it became clear that the Condon report would not come out until after the symposium and when Condon and some influential AAAS members objected. McDonald said the symposium was "frowned upon by elder statesmen." [70]

The symposium was on again in 1969, but not without stiff opposition from Condon. He circulated three letters from Hudson Hoagland, National Academy of Sciences member C. D. Shane, and himself describing their objections. In his own letter he blasted AAAS in highly charged emotional terms: "The UFO buffs are a slippery lot, and do a great deal by 'insinuendo,' so that it is usually useless to try to find out what they are really contending. Some never had any critical faculty, some are suffering severely from progressive degeneration of whatever critical faculty they ever had." Since reputable scientists had not wasted time on such a worthless subject, Condon said, AAAS would not be able to get well-informed speakers "to criticize the fantasies of the UFO cult." The AAAS symposium would give the "UFO nonsense" a degree of legitimacy that would mislead the ignorant and "the intelligent will think AAAS is crazy." If AAAS gave a platform to the "UFO charlatans," it would aid them in their "deceptive and fradulent [sic] operations." Condon even appealed to Vice President Spiro Agnew to stop the symposium, but Agnew did not.[71]

The AAAS symposium went on as planned in December 1969 in Boston. The participants fell into three groups. McDonald, Hynek, Robert L. Hall, and Robert M. L. Baker presented the case for UFOs as anomalous phenomena. Thornton Page, psychologist Douglass Price-Williams, physicist Philip Morrison, and astronomer Frank D. Drake took a middle, "agnostic" position. Sagan, Menzel (who was sick but Walter Orr Roberts read his paper), journalist Walter Sullivan, Condon staff members William K. Hartmann and Franklin Roach, psychiatrists Lester Grinspoon and Alan D. Persky, and radar expert Kenneth Hardy presented the arguments for UFOs being explainable as known phenomena. Although heavily weighted with speakers against the idea that UFOs were anomalous phenomena, the symposium was the best scientific discussion of the subject to date.[72]

Even though the AAAS symposium featured only four scientists who thought UFOs were anomalous, many more scientists, less fearful of ridicule because of the legitimacy the Condon committee had given the topic, became increasingly active in the field. Through Richard Greenwell's and the Lorenzens' aggressive recruiting of consultants for APRO, over twenty-five physical and social scientists joined the APRO consultant roster.

By 1970 the UFO controversy was practically a forgotten episode in the press. NICAP's and APRO's losses of membership had depleted their finances and the heads of these organizations began to redirect their efforts. They no longer cried for a scientific investigation. Instead, Stuart Nixon of NICAP and the Lorenzens and Richard Greenwell of APRO began projects to computerize and microfilm all their sighting reports so that investigators would have easy access to the raw data. The new theory among UFO investigators was that individual scholars would have to study selected aspects of the phenomenon and come to independent conclusions. The shift was away from asking the "outside" community to consider the origins of UFOs and toward encouraging the growing number of individual scientists interested in the subject to conduct their own internal investigations free from the encumbrances of the "scientific establishment." Reflecting this new attitude, APRO held three symposiums on the UFO phenomenon, in Baltimore in January 1971, in Santa Ana (California) in June 1971, and in Tucson in November 1971. The Tucson symposium featured papers by thirteen APRO consultants in various scientific disciplines. The Midwest (later, Mutual) UFO Network also established an annual conference on the subject.[73]

The American Institute of Aeronautics and Astronautics released its promised UFO subcommittee report in November 1970. The subcommittee included Hynek, McDonald, Page, Phil Klass, Condon committee member Gordon Thayer, and chairman Joachim Keuttner. They found no basis for Condon's conclusion that nothing of scientific value would come from further study of UFOs. In fact, the subcommittee found it "difficult to ignore the small residue of well-documented but unexplainable cases which form the hard core of the UFO controversy." It recommended increased study with an emphasis on data collection and high-quality scientific analysis, and it expressed hope that scientists, engineers, and government agencies would consider "sound proposals in this field without bias or fear of ridicule and repercussion." Finally, the subcommittee announced it would publish examples of "hard-core" UFO cases so that AIAA members could form their own opinions. In July and September 1971 the AIAA journal *Astronautics and Aeronautics* carried two important UFO encounter cases. Also in 1971 *Industrial Research* polled its readers about the UFO phenomenon. Of the 2,700 respondents, 54 percent thought UFOs "probably" or "definitely" existed, 8 percent claimed to have seen a UFO, 32 percent thought the objects came from "outer space," 32 percent thought they were conventional phenomena, and 35 percent was undecided about their origin.[74]

The ridicule attached to the study of UFOs revived in 1970. *Science* magazine refused to publish electrical engineer William T. Powers's paper on UFOs, explaining to him that "at the present time the overwhelming majority of our readers are not interested in a further discussion" of the phenomenon. *Science* also refused to publish a critique of the Condon report by UCLA psychologist Douglass Price-Williams. Yet the magazine did print social worker Donald Warren's article espousing the theory that most people who reported UFOs suffered from "status inconsistency": UFO witnesses had a higher educational level than their employment indicated.[75]

To scientists, ridicule certainly loomed as the most fearful aspect of becoming involved on the positive side of the UFO controversy. Hynek, mindful of ridicule's destructive potential, had skillfully maneuvered around its pitfalls to prevent harming his academic and professional credibility. Loss of credibility would have destroyed any influence he may have had in urging other scientists to take the UFO problem seriously. His change of attitude toward UFOs had taken so long that he had not only succeeded in establishing his credentials as a scientist but had also learned methods of avoiding ridicule in the process. Other researchers were not so fortunate. McDonald's case is a good example.

During the years of his intense activity in UFO research, McDonald had managed to avoid the ridicule that plagued and hindered so many others. With the exception of Klass's vitriolic attacks on him, McDonald's bold stands on UFOs had not incurred censure from his colleagues, the press, or others. But in 1971 he found himself in a position of having ridicule used against him to discredit his professional credibility.

The House Committee on Appropriations called McDonald to testify about the supersonic transport (SST) plane because, as part of a National Academy of Sciences panel on weather and climate modification, he had worked arduously for three months on how the SST would affect the atmosphere. McDonald had discovered that the SST would reduce the protective layer of ozone in the atmosphere, and this might cause an additonal 10,000 cases of skin cancer each year in the United States. During McDonald's testimony, Congressman Silvio Conte of Massachusetts abruptly pointed out that McDonald was an expert on UFOs and believed power failures in New York "were caused by these flying saucers." Conte thought this point was "very, very important." McDonald calmly replied that he had not come to that conclusion but that he did think enough of a correlation existed between UFO sightings in the areas of power outages and the failures to warrant further investigation. During this exchange spectators and some congressmen openly laughed at McDonald. Conte kept after him, obviously trying to impugn his credibility. Congressman William Minshall of Ohio joined in and mentioned that Congress had held open and closed hearings on the subject and Department of Defense "experts" had "absolutely discounted any possibility of actual incursion into airspace by people from the outer planets." After a recess, Conte again brought up UFOs, trying to link McDonald's views on skin cancer with his views on UFOs—as if both of them were somewhat deranged. McDonald protested that no relationship existed between the two.[76]

The next day a general discussion ensued about McDonald's credentials, and Congressmen Yates of Illinois, McFall of California, and witness Will Kellogg, director of the National Center for Atmospheric Research, tried to recover some of the damage done to McDonald by stating that he was a "very distinguished atmospheric physicist." They said they deplored the snickering that some congressmen had indulged in the day before. Yet that afternoon Conte again hit hard at McDonald's credibility. First he read a section of McDonald's testimony before the Roush committee hearing in July 1968 when McDonald said he thought some reports of UFO occupants might be valid. Then Conte said, "A man who comes here and tells me that the SST flying in the stratosphere is going to cause thousands of skin cancers has to back up his theory that there are little men flying around the sky. I think this is very important." [77]

McDonald's work on the SST was his last project. In June 1971 he committed suicide at the age of fifty-one. He had not had the success with scientists in the area of UFOs that he had hoped for. He had not induced NASA to take on a study of UFOs, something he worked on for years. He had not convinced the scientific community to accept UFO research as a worthwhile endeavor. And he had not reduced the ridicule that so hindered systematic investigation of the phenomenon. Even after his death the ridicule of him that came out in the hearings did not stop. The eminent paleontologist George Gaylord Simpson called McDonald's advocacy of the extraterrestrial hypothesis a "monument to gullibility." Condon said bluntly that McDonald was a "kook." In 1972 Vice President Agnew derided Senator Edward Kennedy of Massachusetts for quoting McDonald's opposition to the SST without also mentioning that McDonald " 'had declared that the electric power failures in New York City were caused by aircraft from outer space, otherwise known as flying saucers.' " Agnew conceded that " 'there is always a remote possibility that flying saucer people can be right about some things,' " yet he placed McDonald and Kennedy, for their opposition to the SST, in the ranks of English doctors who had opposed smallpox vaccinations because they would make people look like cows.[78]

Nevertheless, McDonald's efforts did have an effect on the scientific community. His correspondence, speeches, and discussions had brought the UFO problem to the attention of many scientists who had not previously been aware of it. His research and investigation of case histories had uncovered a multitude of strong cases that other UFO researchers could point to as being virtually irrefutable and the crux of the UFO controversy. In the final analysis, perhaps McDonald's greatest contribution was to help legitimize the study of UFOs by lending his prestige to the field and joining Hynek in publicly advocating serious academic attention to the subject. Partially as a result of McDonald's and Hynek's efforts, a growing core of scientists became more interested in the UFO mystery. Many were younger men who had not gone through the wars with the Air Force, the contactees, and the scientific community. They formed the nucleus of a group of scientists who quietly studied the UFO phenomenon in the early 1970s.

The year 1972 was calm. The national UFO organizations tried to regroup the membership they had lost as a result of the Condon report and the lack of widespread sightings. UFO reports had increased somewhat, but not enough to gain publicity or renew public interest. Hynek's book, *The UFO Experience: A Scientific Inquiry*, came out in 1972. In it, he criticized the Air

Force's handling of UFO reports and the Condon committee's methods and conclusions, and he dispassionately described the UFO phenomenon and issues in UFO research. He set up new procedures whereby scientists could study the problem. His book brought the study of UFOs to a new level of sophistication. With an unemotional and undogmatic approach, Hynek helped bring the subject back to respectability and even obtained a favorable review in the pages of *Science*.[79] Condon, embittered from the criticism he had faced in the previous three years, had only harsh words for his adversaries, who he believed based their scientific judgments on unsound evidence. Saunders was a "kook," McDonald was a "kook," Hynek was "sort of nuts" and the Air Force should have fired him early on. Obviously disgusted with the entire controversy and wanting no more to do with it, Condon claimed to have burned the project's records.[80]

By the end of 1972 many people, including scientists and news reporters, thought flying saucer crazes were a quaint part of the popular culture of bygone years. The early 1970s' nostalgia fad curiously resurrected UFOs as a part of the tensions of the 1950s. For the public, UFOs were yesterday's news.

10

1973:

ECHOES OF THE PAST

Thousands of people in the United States in 1973 and 1974 said they saw unidentified flying objects in the skies over nearly every state in the Union, including Alabama, Arkansas, California, Illinois, Indiana, Kentucky, Louisiana, Mississippi, Missouri, North Carolina, Ohio, Oklahoma, Pennsylvania, South Carolina, Tennessee, Texas, Virginia, and West Virginia.

The sighting wave ranked with those of 1896–97, 1947, 1952, 1957, and 1965–67 in intensity, making it one of the largest in American history. Sighting reports had slowly increased since 1970, and a flurry of reports in 1972 preceded the massive wave of the following year.

January began the 1973 wave when private UFO organizations received reports from northern Alabama and Rhode Island. Sightings continued through March with reports from the Piedmont, Missouri, area and eastern Pennsylvania. From May through July the reports dwindled. The National Investigations Committee on Aerial Phenomena (NICAP), sure that the minor wave had ended, called 1973 the "Year of the 'Miniflap'." But in August people in Georgia started reporting UFOs again. By September the South seemed to be involved in a wave, and by October it was clear that the entire nation was in its grips. Mid-October was the peak period. Reports continued at a high rate in November, dipped in December, increased again in January 1974, and continued through April 1974. By June the wave had subsided. UFO researchers were unable to determine the exact number of sightings in the 1973–74 wave. One researcher catalogued over five hundred reports in Pennsylvania alone. If, as the Air Force estimated in the early 1950s, generally only about 10 percent of the people who had sightings reported them, then the 1973–74 wave must have produced thousands of sightings.[1]

The 1973–74 wave mirrored previous large waves, although by mid-1974 not enough time had passed for investigators to scrutinize the reports thoroughly for misidentifications, hoaxes, and the like. Reports fell into a wide range of UFO sighting categories. Among them were high-level and distant sightings, low-level sightings, car-chasing incidents, sightings causing electrical and/or mechanical effects or interference, sightings affecting animals, sightings affecting people physically, sightings causing psychological and mental effects on people, landings with traces left behind, and occupant cases.

High-level and long-distance night sightings constituted, as always, the largest category of reports. Although witnesses often could give only vague, general descriptions of the objects, they considered the objects strange enough to notify local police and newspapers.

Police officers in Manassas Park, Virginia, watched a glowing, circular object for over two hours late one night in December 1973. Through binoculars the officers could see a green light on one side of the object and a red light on the other side. A short distance away another police officer watched two lights hover in the sky. Suddenly one dropped to tree-top level and hovered silently while the other light remained stationary. After fifteen minutes the first light moved back up, and then both lights disappeared.[2] In Waverly, Illinois, the police chief and three other citizens saw an object with a white light in the middle and red and green flashing lights on each side early in the morning of October 17, 1973. As the astonished men watched, the object sent out glowing "embers" that burned in the sky as they fell to the ground. They watched the object with binoculars for an hour and forty-five minutes.[3]

Ohio governor John Gilligan and his wife were driving near Ann Arbor, Michigan, when they saw a "vertical amber colored" object for about half an hour. It ascended, penetrated the cloud cover, and then disappeared. Governor Gilligan told reporters that what he had seen was not a bird or plane.[4]

In October a young couple staying in a hotel near Dallas called two bellmen outside to view a strange, blindingly bright, red "ball" hovering over another hotel near the Texas Stadium. As the ball came closer to the witnesses, two smaller red balls came out of the larger object. The smaller balls grew large and flew off to the north and south.[5]

Witnesses in Magnolia, Mississippi, saw a round object, "colored like shiny new aluminum," hanging in the sky. As they watched, the object opened up and a rectangular, darkly colored "parachute-like thing" came out of it. The witnesses flagged down a passing motorist, and together they watched as the round object opened up again after a few minutes and the rectangular parachute-like device reentered it. The object then rose higher and disappeared into the clouds.[6]

Several high school students in Palmyra, Missouri, reported a strange spectacle similar to the 1896–97 sightings. An object with flashing lights appeared near the Mississippi River and shone a spotlight on a passing barge, lighting up the entire river bottom. The object then circled the river bottom several times and approached spectators on shore before leaving the area. Four days later Palmyra police and citizens observed an object with red, white, and amber lights on it and two extremely powerful "headlights" in front. It silently and slowly circled the town at a low level. When it flew over an elementary school police officers shone a spotlight on the object and it immediately moved away. The object made a humming sound similar to an electrical transformer.[7]

As in previous sighting waves, witnesses in 1973–74 claimed that beams of light came out of objects. Near Fayetteville, Arkansas, a woman saw a bright light the size of a "No. 3 washtub" with a beam of light radiating from it in a whirlwind motion. People in Felton, Pennsylvania, observed three oval-shaped UFOs revolving with orange coloring around the middle of them. One of the objects had a red beam radiating from it. In

Washington Township, New Jersey, witnesses described a spinning object that resembled an amusement park "whip" car with red and green lights and a red ray coming down from it.[8]

Many people observed strange objects at a low altitude, usually at night. For instance, an elementary school bus driver in London, Ohio, saw a yellow orange, football-shaped UFO the size of a barn hovering above some trees. The object's glow lighted up the trees and the ground around them. The object rose straight up and flew away. "People will think I've gone off the deep end," the witness declared, "but I know what I saw." [9]

Citizens summoned Los Angeles police officers to investigate a strange object on the east side of the city. Arriving at the scene, the police officers saw from their car an object "oblong shaped and very bright and bluish-white, like a mercury vapor lamp." The object then descended to the ground, and a sign obscured it from the officers' view. They continued toward it in their squad car, sighted it again, and estimated that it was the size of a half dollar at arm's length. The object rose at a 45 degree angle to a height of between 1,000 and 1,500 feet and sped off. After the sighting about a dozen other people called the police to report seeing a similar object at the same time the police had their sighting.[10]

A woman in St. Joseph, Missouri, glanced out the window before going to bed and noticed an object with a brilliant red and blue light coming down near the front lawn of the house across the street. The object hovered approximately six feet above the street for about six minutes. The witness said she was too "petrified," surprised, and curious to move. At first the object was still, but then it began to rotate slowly and the witness saw a "ribbed shield" that extended "about 10 inches from the side of the circular object up and slanting inward toward the translucent dome." The object had a round bottom, a high domed top, and blue and red lights glowing from inside it and flickering. It continued to rotate slowly, and after five or six minutes it gradually moved back in the direction from which it had come and drifted north. The witness looked through a pair of binoculars and found the object in the sky. Shortly another object joined it and "the two seemed to dart back and forth from north to south at very rapid speed for a time, then both shot upward out of sight at tremendous speed." [11]

A group of people in Goldsboro, North Carolina, observed a triangular object with lights at each apex of the triangle. The entire object changed colors, blinking red, then green, and then yellow. At first the object was high in the sky, but then it "shot downward at tremendous speed" and hovered. The witnesses could hear a whirring sound at this time. The object seemed as big as a house and had three long legs with a "chute" extending from one side of it. The observers watched it for thirty minutes. Then the object slowly turned and rapidly flew across the sky in four to five seconds. [12]

A Phoenixville, Pennsylvania, couple had what they described as a traumatic experience in December 1973 when they noticed a very bright light in the sky while driving on Route 252. As they approached the light they thought it might be a plane in distress or about to land. One of the witnesses described it as having "two blue lights on the wings, and it kind of looked like a plane, but it was moving very slowly, parallel to the road, like it was observing us. We weren't alone on the road. There were plenty of other cars around, going in both directions." The noiseless object came to within fifty feet of the couple's car, and they saw that underneath it seemed triangular with rounded edges and had a flashing red light in the center. The couple was too afraid to stop the car. [13]

This last case is similar to what UFO researchers have labeled car-chasing incidents. A good example occurred in Baton Rouge, Louisiana, where two sisters claimed that a cylindrical UFO, with red, yellow, and green lights, followed them for nearly eighty miles while what appeared to be its identical companion remained stationary in the sky. The next day they summoned the sheriff's office as they once again saw a UFO following them home. The sheriff also observed the object. "I know some people will think I'm crazy," the sister who was driving said, "but I know what I saw." [14]

The next night, on October 11, 1973, at 8:00 P.M., a woman, her daughter, and her thirteen-year-old grandson were driving west of their home in Madisonville, Kentucky, when they spotted an egg-shaped object, which they estimated to be five or six feet long, giving off white, then red, pink, and blue lights that illuminated the road. The object was twenty to twenty-five feet in the air and began to follow them. The daughter, who was driving, was too scared to stop the car and continued to travel at speeds over seventy miles per hour. The silent object paced the car, turned when it did, and always stayed on the left. "I know it's hard to believe, but it's God's fact," said the mother. At the same time on the same night 100 miles west in Cairo, Illinois, four members of a family and a friend also reported a car-chasing incident. They claimed that a twenty-five-foot circular object, with red and white lights blinking in a circle, followed their car, slowing down when it did, for five miles before the driver stopped. They all got out of the car and watched as the object performed loops in the air, turned somersaults, stopped, backed up, and generally behaved erratically. The object stayed about one-half mile off the ground, and the witnesses heard no sound from it.[15]

A month later two Cameron County deputy sheriffs were driving prisoners from Brownsville, Texas, to the state penitentiary in Huntsville when a strange object appeared over their station wagon early in the morning. The deputies found it difficult to discern the object's shape but said it had a red light on top and a yellow light on the bottom. The object stayed at from fifty to sixty feet above the station wagon at all times and followed the car for twenty miles. When the driver speeded up, slowed down, or stopped, the object did the same. The sheriffs called police units in Harlingen and San Benito, Texas. These officers converged with the sheriffs near San Benito, and they all watched the object hover in the sky for thirty minutes before it zoomed straight up and disappeared."[16]

Another frequent feature of UFO sightings was electrical or mechanical effects on or interference with automobiles, radios, televisions, and the like. These incidents date back to 1947, the beginning of the modern era of sightings, and 1973–74 had its share of them. A woman in Osyka, Mississippi, went outside to burn some trash and noticed an oblong, shiny, aluminum-colored object in the sky. Her radio inside the house stopped working when the object passed overhead and came on again when the object moved out of sight. "It scared me so I'm still shaking," she told reporters. The police chief of Pierce, Nebraska, and other citizens observed a brilliant blue flashing light early one morning. The light was so bright that it turned off several street lights in the area, which supposedly shut off automatically only when sufficient daylight triggered a photosensitive device. Two deputy sheriffs investigating a ringing burglar alarm near Santa Cruz, California, were surprised to hear the alarm ringing in synchronization with the blinking lights of an object hovering over the coast. The deputies said the alarm stopped ringing when the object disappeared.[17]

At times UFO appearances seemed to have a noticeable effect on animals, just as they did in the 1896–97 wave. The majority of animal effect cases involved dogs barking at strange objects or else cowering and behaving uncharacteristically. However, witnesses reported that the appearance of a UFO affected other animals as well. For example, a dairyman spotted a strange object at 4:30 A.M. about forty miles northeast of Tulsa, Oklahoma. It appeared to be taking off from his pasture and made a high-pitched, shrill, whistling sound. The object was silvery and had red or orange flashing lights. The witness saw it take off and land two more times before it shot straight up into the sky and vanished. The object so frightened the dairyman's herd dog that he ran into the house and refused to come out. It also scared the herd of forty-two cows, which scattered around the pasture. Their milk production was 100 pounds below normal for the next week.[18]

Some people reported that strange objects affected them physically during a sighting. Often witnesses said they experienced a tingling feeling or the sensation of heat or cold. Sometimes witnesses reported that alleged UFOs caused injuries. In Zeigler, Illinois, near Carbondale, a bright light awoke a woman early in the morning. She thought she had forgotten to turn her hallway light off. When she got out of bed she noticed that the light was coming from outside her house. She then saw an object about 60

feet off the ground and 400 feet away giving off an extremely
intense light. She repeatedly tried to look at the light, but it
burned her eyes and she had to turn away each time. After fifteen
minutes the object disappeared. The woman's eyes hurt after the
sighting and that day she claimed that her vision was reduced.
Four days later her eyes still bothered her.[19]

One of the strangest vision-affecting cases of the 1973–74
wave occurred near Cape Girardeau, Missouri, in early October
1973. The witness, a truck driver, and his wife were driving a
tractor-trailer about dawn when he noticed, in his rearview mirror,
an unusual lighted object about a mile behind them. Its lights
glittered red and yellow, and the object traveled at about four to
five feet above the ground. The object rapidly moved up on the
witness as he drove at sixty miles per hour. He told his wife about
the lights, but she saw nothing out of the rearview mirror on her
side of the cab. He looked again, and this time he observed that
the object was turnip shaped, about thirty feet in diameter, and
very close behind the truck. It had three sections: the top and
bottom sections were spinning and appeared to be made of
aluminum or chrome; the middle section did not move and had
red and yellow lights on it that glittered and seemed to mix
together. The driver faced the windshield as the truck entered a
patch of fog. Then he put his head out the window, looked back
again, and saw a spotlight come out of the object at the same time
that it began to rise. He also heard for the first time a humming
sound coming from the object. The humming rose in pitch as the
object rose in altitude. He thrust his head out a little farther and
suddenly a bright white flash like a ball of fire struck him in the
face. The instant this happened the noise stopped and the object
disappeared. The driver pulled his head back in, put his hands
over his eyes, and screamed that he could not see. He stopped the
truck in the middle of the highway. His wife, who had neither seen
nor heard anything, turned the light on in the cab and saw that
her husband's forehead was red and hot, the frames of his glasses
were melted and twisted, and one lens had fallen out. An
ambulance took the driver to the hospital where he received
emergency treatment. His sight returned gradually, but five days

later a St. Louis ophthalmologist found that the driver still had only 20 percent vision. Also, he complained of pain deep inside his forehead. Later a physicist examined the glasses and said the frames appeared to have been internally heated.[20]

Perhaps some of the most puzzling and elusive cases, occurring in previous sighting waves as well as in 1973–74, were those that seemed to have mental effects on witnesses. Although subjective and difficult to pinpoint as the results of an object, these effects happened so often that serious UFO researchers considered them a legitimate part of the UFO phenomenon. For instance, a man and his family were fishing late at night near Madison, Wisconsin, when they saw three lights in the sky darting about and moving erratically. The man ran to another campsite to get other people's confirmation of the sighting. As he returned to his camp, he looked up again and saw another light. This one was bright orange, at a lower level than the other three, and hovered. When he looked at it he immediately received the sensation that beings were inside the object and "they" saw and knew everything. The witness was terrified and said he felt he would not be able to make it back to his campsite. The feeling went away when the object disappeared.[21]

In a similar case near Tulsa, Oklahoma, a husband, wife, and their ten-year-old daughter were in their pickup truck at 12:20 A.M. on October 17 when they saw a gigantic object with an intricate set of lights on it. The object seemed big enough to dwarf a 747 jet. It came within 250 feet of the truck at one time, and the witnesses noticed four "prongs" with red lights on them coming out of the tail end and a white light in the object's center. The witnesses heard low-pitched and high-pitched humming sounds. The driver stopped the truck and the family watched the object. During the sighting they experienced what they called an all-around-you feeling, and they said they felt "powerless." The same night in Ohio two Adams County deputy sheriffs on routine patrol in the town of West Union saw an unusual object hanging about 200 feet in the sky. The arrangement of pulsating, brilliant, red, green, blue, and white lights apparently made the object's shape difficult to discern. The amazed men watched as the object zigzagged and made tight circles in the sky. During this time they both felt mesmerized or transfixed as they watched the object.[22]

The 1973–74 wave had its share of landing cases. Reported since 1896, they have represented some of the most unusual and sensational cases. Yet UFO researchers believed these cases were among the best to study because often a UFO would leave "proof" of its existence in the form of markings on the ground. UFO researchers called these *trace cases.*

In mid-October in Clay County, Mississippi, two witnesses reported independently that they had to swerve their vehicles into a ditch to avoid an elliptical object, with blue and orange lights, sitting in the middle of the road on legs about four to six feet in height. The next day one of the witnesses and other people searched the area where the sighting occurred and discovered that the grass on either side of the road was "burned and smelled like oil." They also found two padlike marks in the ditch.[23]

An Ohio National Guardsman reported seeing pulsating, bright lights in the night sky near his home in Columbus. The lights swooped down in a zigzag pattern and disappeared behind some trees. Later the man checked the area of the supposed landing, a field of waist-high weeds, and found a semioval area about twenty feet wide and thirty feet long of weeds crushed to the ground.[24]

One of the most interesting trace cases of the 1973–74 wave occurred in Lawrenceburg, Tennessee. In the afternoon of September 30, 1973, a hunter quietly perched in a tree saw a white, fluorescent, perfectly round ball about ten feet in diameter silently glide across a nearby soybean field and pass directly in front of him. The object stopped about four feet above an old roadbed. Three legs unfolded from under the object and formed a tripod. Two legs came down on the roadbed and the third leg rested on the field next to it. A few seconds later the hunter heard two loud squawks which sounded like high-pitched crow calls. Although the witness could see no seams, windows, or openings in the object, suddenly a door, about three feet wide and four feet high, appeared. It swung down to form a ramp. The hunter had had a cold and unconsciously sniffed. The object apparently detected the sound because the door immediately snapped shut, the tripodal legs disappeared into the object, and it shot away at a tremendous speed. The witness then saw a whitish vapor or fog where the object had landed. He climbed down from the tree and went to the landing site. Breathing the fog gave him the sensation that his lungs were about to burst. He ran out of the foggy area and was able to breathe normally in the fresh air. He returned to the spot (presumably after the fog had dissipated) and found three spots of depressed grass where the tripodal legs had rested. The depressions were about eight inches long.[25]

As fascinating as this case was, some of the 1973–74 occupant reports overshadowed it. These reports of alleged occupants did not follow the contactee tradition. Instead of having continual communication with space beings who imparted knowledge and a mission to the selected earth people, the witnesses of alleged occupants usually only caught a fleeting glimpse of the "beings." The 1964 Lonnie Zamora sighting, in which the police officer briefly saw two occupants beside an object on the ground, is a classic example of this type of report. Yet on rare occasions reputable witnesses claimed to have interacted with an occupant. So-called legitimate occupant cases illustrate the more bizarre aspects of the UFO phenomenon. They required the most extensive and meticulous investigation to eliminate hoaxes. For years occupant cases caused conflict within UFO organizations. Some investigators wanted to avoid these cases because they smacked of contacteeism. Others wanted to accept and study them as a valid part of the phenomenon. By 1973 most groups, including the conservative NICAP, regarded well-documented occupant sighting cases as a legitimate part of the UFO mystery.

The following is an example of the most typical type of occupant sighting. The witness saw the object and the occupant only briefly and had no interaction with the being. The sighting began when the witness was driving home from work on a freeway in southern California and noticed a blimp-like object hovering over a crest of hills. The object sank below the hills and he lost sight of it. As he approached the top of a rise in the freeway, he looked down into the area where the object had descended. At first he saw nothing unusual, but as he continued driving he noticed what he described as dust rising from the canyon below the freeway. Curiosity made him stop his car, back up fifty feet, and get out to look into the canyon. He then observed, at a distance of from eighty to a hundred feet, a grayish pink object that resembled a giant Jaguar XKE car about fifty feet long and thirty feet wide. It hovered about ten feet above the ground. On one side it had what the witness thought was either a series of vents or an insignia in the shape of a large V with progressively smaller Vs inside it. A hose about eight feet long and one foot in diameter protruded from the bottom of the object but did not touch the ground. The witness saw no doors or windows, but he noticed a glasslike "bubble" three feet in diameter and swiveling like a ball on top of the object. He also discerned a colored mass inside the bubble.

Suddenly the witness spotted an occupant crawling from the opposite side of the object toward the front. The occupant appeared to be of normal size and dimensions and was wearing apparel that resembled a silvery or light-colored wet suit. The man did not get a good look at the occupant's face. The occupant looked at the witness and quickly scrambled to the other side of the object and disappeared. At the same time the witness heard a few clicking sounds coming from the UFO which reminded him of distant automatic weapons fire. With the occupant out of sight, the bubble rotated and disappeared inside the body of the object. The object made a whirring or humming sound and a fog-like substance, which exuded a sweet incense-like odor, began to envelop it. Then suddenly the object just disappeared and the fog and scent dissipated quickly. The witness did not see it fly away or leave the area. After the sighting he told the police what he had seen. A week later a woman called the witness to tell him that she had seen a similar object in the same general area a week before.[26]

The case of a twenty-five-year-old woman in New Hampshire was atypical and more bizarre because it contained physical and mental effects on the witness and because she claimed to have interacted with the alleged occupant. Driving home from work on Route 114A near Manchester, New Hampshire, at 4:00 A.M. in early November 1973, the witness noticed a bright orange light in the sky that seemed to vanish and then reappear. She watched the object for about seven miles. She veered left on Route 114 and was amazed to see the object now larger, lower, and closer than before—about 1,600 feet in front of her. It looked like a large ball, honeycombed with a design of hexagons. In its upper left sector she saw what appeared to be an oval window of a paler color. The object had a "peculiar translucent quality about it." Red, green, and blue rays emanated from the center of the object. The woman heard a steady, high-pitched whine that she felt throughout her body as a tingling sensation.

The witness panicked when she felt unable to remove her hands from the steering wheel. She felt that the object was drawing her toward it and she was unable to take her eyes off it. As she drove toward it, she claimed to have experienced memory loss during a half mile stretch, and she remembered nothing about it. Then she suddenly became aware of her surroundings and found herself and the car hurtling toward the UFO. She acknowledged after the sighting that she could have unconsciously been pressing on the accelerator because of fright. She approached to within 500 feet of the object when the whining noise grew louder. She now saw that the object was about 30 feet above the ground and noticed a figure in the window.

The occupant was looking at her. She could see the being only from the waist up because a dark area obscured the lower part of its body. Its head was grayish, round, and dark on top. Its face had large egg-shaped eyes. Underneath the eyes the occupant's skin seemed loose or wrinkled like "elephant's hide." The occupant's mouth turned down at the corners. The witness did not notice a nose or ears. As the witness looked, her attention riveted on the occupant's eyes, she claimed that she received an impression that the occupant was in some way telling her not to be afraid. Overcome by panic, she thought the UFO was about to capture her.

The woman spied a house on the left side of the street at the same time that the object became so bright she covered her face with her arms. She turned the car half blindly into the driveway of the house and stopped across the front lawn. The witness was only three-fourths of a mile from her own home. She jumped out of the car, leaving the headlights and motor on, and a German shepherd dog charged up to her. Although usually afraid of strange dogs, the woman smacked the dog across the mouth, ran to the front door, and pounded on it, yelling "Help me! Help me!" She looked over her shoulder and saw that the UFO, still making a whining noise, had moved across from the house. The witness found the whine unbearable. She pounded and yelled for about two minutes until the owner, who had been upstairs asleep with his wife, came to the door. The witness, panic-stricken, hysterical, and crying, grabbed the man, sank to her knees almost in a faint, and sobbed "Help me! I'm not drunk! I'm not on drugs! A UFO just tried to pick me up!" The witness covered her ears with her hands, but the man heard nothing.

By this time the man's wife had awakened and come downstairs. It was 4:30 A.M. After a few minutes in the couple's kitchen, the witness said the sound and tingling sensation had stopped but she noticed a spot in her vision similar to staring too long at a bright light. The woman of the house called the police and an officer arrived about ten minutes later. He turned the headlights and motor off in the witness's car. After he arrived the four people went outside and saw a light some distance off moving slightly and changing colors. The light appeared to go off when the officer shined his spotlight on it. When the local newspapers heard about the sighting, the witness, fearful of ridicule, only mentioned the occupant phase of the sighting briefly and in vague terms.[27]

Probably much to the witness's relief, this case received little publicity except in UFO organization literature and related journals. This was not so for the Pascagoula, Mississippi, incident, which ranks with the 1947 Kenneth Arnold sighting and the 1952 Washington, D.C., sightings as one of the most publicized and publicly discussed cases on record.

The incident occurred on October 11, 1973, at the peak of the 1973–74 wave. Calvin Parker (nineteen years old) and Charles Hickson (forty-two years old), both from Gautier, Mississippi, were fishing at the mouth of the Pascagoula River in Pascagoula when they became aware of a buzzing sound. The men looked behind them and instantly froze with fright as they saw a large, egg-shaped, glowing object hovering a few feet above the ground and about forty feet from the river bank. The object, about ten feet wide and eight feet high, had blue lights on the front of it and seemed to transmit a buzzing sound, like air escaping from a pressure hose. Paralyzed with fear, the men watched as a door seemed to appear out of nothing and three occupants came toward them. The occupants floated instead of walked and their legs did not move. The occupants were human-like, about five feet tall, with bullet-shaped heads but no necks, pointed conical appendages jutting straight out where noses and ears would be, and a slit for a mouth. The witnesses saw no eyes. They described the occupants' skin as light gray and resembling elephant's skin with many wrinkles. The occupants had round feet and hands that looked like crab claws.

Two of the occupants took hold of Hickson and the third grabbed Parker, who, overcome by fear, fainted. Hickson claimed that the occupants lifted him by putting their hands underneath his arms, at which time he felt a numbness in his body, and then "floated" him into the UFO. Inside he found himself in a round and brightly lighted room, but he said he could not see the source of the light. As the two occupants held Hickson, an object resembling an eye and apparently not attached to anything appeared in front of him. The two occupants moved Hickson in different positions in front of the object, as if it were an examining device, and the apparatus also moved over his body during the "examination." The occupants at one time seemed to communicate by making humming sounds. When the examination ended, the occupants left Hickson suspended in the middle of the air. He could not move except to blink and shift his eyes. Hickson thought the occupants had Parker in another room but was unable to tell for sure.

After about twenty minutes from the time Hickson first saw the UFO, the occupants "floated" him outside and put him down. He was so weak-kneed that he fell over. He saw Parker crying and praying near him. Hickson then watched the hissing object fly straight up into the sky and disappear almost instantly. Hickson calmed down his hysterical friend and the two ran from the area.

At first they decided not to tell anyone about their experience, assuming that no one would believe them and that they would encounter a lot of ridicule. But then they thought the government might want to know what happened. They called Keesler Air Force Base in Biloxi and a sergeant there referred them to the sheriff. But afraid that the sheriff would not believe them, they drove to the local newspaper office to see a reporter. A janitor there told them the office was closed and suggested that they go see the sheriff, which they did at 10:30 that night. The next day the local press heard about the story and publicized it. The wire services picked it up, and within a few days it became sensational news across the country.

The Aerial Phenomena Research Organization (APRO) sent one of its consultants, University of California engineering professor James Harder, to investigate. J. Allen Hynek also went to Pascagoula, and he and Harder interviewed the witnesses. Harder hyponotized Hickson but had to break off the hypnosis when Hickson found it too painful and frightening to go on. The hypnosis, Harder said, was too soon after the traumatic event. On the night of the sighting the local sheriff had put Hickson and Parker in a room equipped with hidden sound-monitoring equipment and thought they would reveal the hoax when left alone, but the two men passed this "test" to the satisfaction of the authorities. Eventually Hickson and Parker took lie detector tests and passed them. Hynek and Harder believed the events had happened as the witnesses had described them. After interviewing the two men, Hynek said he was certain that they had had "a very real, frightening experience." He said this "fantastic" experience "should be taken in context with experiences that others have had elsewhere in this country and in the world." Later, newspapers and television, which gave Hynek as much publicity for this sighting as for the 1966 swamp gas episode, quoted him as saying "there was definitely something here that was not terrestrial."[28]

The 1973–74 wave echoed previous sighting waves, including

the airships of 1896–97, in many respects. The large variety of reports, ranging from high-level, nocturnal meandering lights to occupant encounter cases, and the disparate people who made them, ranging from children to policemen, were common elements in all sighting waves. The 1973–74 wave also had its share of radar reports and photographs of UFOs as well as a few motion pictures of objects. As in the past, people in rural areas made most of the reports, but many citizens in urban areas also reported seeing strange objects. Perhaps the most unifying element was fear. Witnesses throughout the UFO controversy, from 1896 on, reported, first, that their sightings frightened them and, second, that as a result of relating their experiences they feared public ridicule. Thus some witnesses preferred anonymity while others took great care to explain that they were not lunatics, drunk, or on drugs, and that they saw what they said they saw. In the 1973–74 wave, as in previous sighting waves, hoaxes and the media's treatment of them compounded the witness ridicule problem. Hoaxes seemed more widespread than they actually were because of publicity and thus cast doubt on what reputable people reported and on the legitimacy of the UFO phenomenon.

Yet in many ways the 1973–74 wave was different from previous waves. For the first time since 1947 the Air Force stayed on the sidelines. In all previous sighting waves, especially since the large one in 1952, the Air Force had acted as the official body that made pronouncements and judgments about the reports. It had served as a restraining influence, especially on scientists and members of the press interested in the subject. Through its press releases, its system of classifying reports, and its assumed authority and expertise on the subject, the Air Force had pushed public opinion toward disbelieving and ridiculing UFO witnesses and denying that UFOs were an anomalous phenomenon. In 1969 the Air Force gave up its role as overseer of the phenomenon. From then on it refused to investigate any UFO sightings and usually told people who reported them to call their local police departments. It made one exception and cursorily investigated the Pascagoula case, but it did not release conclusions to the press. Thus in 1973–74, without the Air Force's influence, and without an official government body assuring the public that it had found no evidence to suggest that UFOs were extraterrestrial, or even anomalous or extraordinary, the American people for the first time in twenty-five years could indulge in unrestrained interest in the phenomenon.

Not only could the public speculate more freely about UFOs, but it could also take a fresh look. The 1973–74 wave came at a time when many people thought "flying saucer scares" were a quaint, and somewhat ludicrous, part of the 1950s and, to a lesser extent, the 1960s. The Air Force and the Condon committee had solved the UFO mystery, the public thought, and lack of widespread publicity about UFO sightings seemed to prove this. Therefore the sighting wave in the early 1970s generated a certain amount of surprise and shock in the country. It stimulated people to confront the UFO mystery anew and to take a fresh look at a phenomenon that refused to take its place with outmoded fads and crazes. The very persistence of the phenomenon may have contributed to the change in public attitudes toward UFOs.

Also, the 1973–74 wave was the first since the historic 1969 manned moon landing. Although the impact of the moon landing is unclear, it may have made extraterrestrial hypotheses more acceptable: if people on earth could visit other heavenly bodies, then possibly others from the skies could visit earth. Moreover, in the early 1970s scientists increasingly began to say that the probability for life existing elsewhere in the universe seemed fairly high, and the media widely publicized the efforts of astronomers like Carl Sagan and Frank Drake, both of Cornell University, who were actively searching for extraterrestrial life.

Furthermore, the 1973–74 wave came at a time when many scientists had publicly expressed interest in the UFO phenomenon. In the middle and late sixties, as a result of dissatisfaction with the Air Force's and the Condon committee's "solutions," many scientists privately began studying the phenomenon. The Air Force's exit from the UFO battles and its release of its accumulated sighting reports removed a barrier that had long hindered scientific interest and research in the subject. Thus by 1973 many scientists had already researched the phenomenon extensively and began to present new methods of studying UFOs, especially through the use of computers.

The incipient scientific interest in UFOs that had started in 1965 progressed quietly in the early 1970s without fanfare or major publicity. In March 1974 the American Institute of Aeronautics and Astronautics revitalized its UFO subcommittee, which had laid dormant for several years because its chairman, Joachim Keuttner, was working in England. The subcommittee decided to petition for full committee status so that it could remain permanently active. In addition, many scientists teaching at small colleges around the country independently organized a variety of courses on the UFO phenomenon.[29]

One of the most ambitious of the scientific research projects on UFOs took place in mid-1973 under the direction of Harley D. Rutledge, who was chairman of the physics department at Southeast Missouri State College, a former president of the Missouri Academy of Sciences, and skeptical about UFOs. Rutledge, James E. Sage (an electronics professor at Southeast Missouri State College), and several graduate students achieved a unique feat: they succeeded in photographing and taking scientific measurements of high-level unidentified flying objects over a seven-month period in 1973. Rutledge and his colleagues had at least seventy sightings, and they measured speed, distance, and altitude for many of them. Rutledge classified twenty-three sightings as strange objects that he thought might be aircraft although they did not exhibit aircraft characteristics. Another twenty-seven he catalogued as sightings of lights that turned on and off in the sky or had "extraordinary" flight characteristics. And he listed twenty-one sightings as lights that behaved so puzzlingly that he called them "incredible or bizarre—miracles of physical science." Rutledge said that at his first sighting of lights he knew he was investigating "very mysterious phenomena."[30]

At the front of the growing corps of scientists actively researching the UFO phenomenon stood Hynek. After twenty-six years of nearly continual involvement with UFOs, he had become the premiere authority on the subject. His unique position as the only man in the country to have studied firsthand the entire history of the phenomenon since 1948 made him the one unifying link with the UFO controversy in previous years. Remarkably, he had successfully steered through the treacherous waters of emotionalism, anger, and ridicule during the early years and had emerged practically unscathed. He had gone from initial hostility toward the subject to skepticism and misgivings, to cautious calls for more study, to muted criticism of the Air Force, and eventually to open hostility toward the Air Force and complete acceptance of the idea that UFOs represented potentially one of the most serious problems he had confronted. His change was gradual and often agonizing. Although others had roundly, and at times deservedly, attacked him for his actions or inactions during the first ten years of the controversy, he had survived this criticism and emerged as an activist in the fight to gain scientific legitimacy for the UFO phenomenon.

In 1973, at the age of sixty-four, Hynek became more involved with intensive UFO research than ever before in his career. He established the first UFO study group under the complete direction of scientists, the Center for UFO Studies in Northfield, Illinois. The Center consisted of scientists, engineers, and other professionals who donated their time to study specific problems arising from UFO reports. The research involved five main areas: analysis of soil and plants that a UFO may have affected, medical examination of people and animals affected, theoretical studies of UFO movements and luminescent properties, psychological studies of witness credibility, and photographic and spectrographic analyses of UFOs. The Center also had a computer data bank for information retrieval and analysis of reports. Hynek arranged with the Mutual UFO Network (MUFON) to have its investigators send reports to the Center. In addition, Hynek sent a toll-free number to every major police department in the country so that they could phone in reports. The Center for UFO Studies functioned in much the same way as the Air Force had claimed to function, and Hynek hoped that, with the cooperation of NICAP and APRO as well as MUFON, it would become a national clearinghouse for sighting reports.[31]

The three established UFO organizations, somewhat lethargic because of the Condon report's effect, began to revive in the early 1970s and especially as a result of the 1973–74 wave. NICAP underwent personnel and policy changes during this time. John Acuff, a photography analyst engineer, became chairman of the NICAP Board of Governors in 1970. He clashed with Stuart Nixon, director of NICAP, over organization and financial policy, and Nixon left the organization at the end of 1973. Acuff was determined to pull NICAP out of its long-standing financial difficulties and did not hire a replacement for Nixon. Instead he decided to direct the organization himself more along the lines of a small business, and he hired a person to manage the daily affairs and help edit the *UFO Investigator*. NICAP's financial and organizational problems since Keyhoe's retirement had forced it to concentrate on keeping alive. It received a boost in 1974 when Senator Barry Goldwater agreed to join the board of governors. Goldwater had been interested in UFOs since the early years of the controversy and had no qualms about expressing his belief in the extraterrestrial hypothesis to the press. Many NICAP members hoped that Acuff's new policies and Goldwater's activities would help pull the organization out of its seemingly unending financial and organizational difficulties.[32]

APRO also went through a realignment in its staff in 1973. Richard Greenwell, the assistant director, resigned early in the year and the Lorenzens reassumed more direct control over the organization. They continued APRO's increasingly successful program of scientific symposiums and added to its scientific consulting staff, which consisted of forty members by mid-1974. As a result of the 1973–74 wave, APRO's membership increased to levels approaching the high point in 1967, before the Condon report. *The A.P.R.O. Bulletin* carried some of the most thoroughly investigated foreign and domestic sighting reports available in the United States.[33]

MUFON thrived during 1973 as scientists, engineers, and other professional people volunteered their time for analysis and investigation of UFO reports. MUFON's annual UFO symposiums enjoyed continuing success, and its magazine, *Skylook*, took on a new professional look reflecting the organization's growing influence in UFO research, under Walt Andrus's direction.

Scientific support for Hynek's center and public interest in the three national organizations indicated the subtle change in society's attitudes toward the UFO phenomenon in general and the 1973–74 wave in particular. Scientists, the news media, the general public, and even the Air Force seemed less opinionated about UFOs, less enmeshed in the traditional line of reasoning, and more willing to suspend judgment on the phenomenon. The 1973–74 sighting wave lacked the emotionalism and rancor that had characterized the opposing viewpoints in the waves of the 1950s and 1960s. In general, society seemed more open than ever to the theory that the UFO phenomenon might be legitimate regardless of the objects' origins. The bitter battles of previous years had ended, and only the phenomenon remained. Yet not all the battle scars had healed, and the spectrum of opinion on UFOs was as wide as ever.

The 1973–74 wave brought out a resurgence of an aspect long a part of the UFO controversy: the urge to explain. This mechanism was mainly at work in the scientific and academic communities, where many people refused to acknowledge that witnesses had observed extraordinary or potentially anomalous objects or that the subject deserved systematic attention. The academics voiced the familiar refrains that had become a staple in all the sighting waves. Psychologists and psychiatrists most frequently used the hoary societal-stress-and-anxiety explanation. "Mass hysteria," "collective hallucinations," "UFO hysteria," public "suggestibility"—these, the psychologists said, explained why people reported UFOs. Social scientists related UFO reports to societal and political anxieties in 1973, which presumably were higher than in previous years.[34]

Astronomers usually found that people were actually seeing stars, planets, other astronomical bodies, and disintegrating satellites. Several astronomers asserted that people could not possibly be seeing anomalous craft because of the great distances between the stars, too great for humans to traverse. Some astronomers used simple reason to deny the legitimacy of the problem. Why would UFOs visit the insignificant planet Earth, they asked rhetorically, and why would they visit remote places on earth? Some limited their remarks on the subject to paraphrasing the National Academy of Sciences's review of the Condon report: the extraterrestrial hypothesis was the least likely explanation for UFO reports. Other scientists in other fields had their own pet theories. A chemist explained a rash of sightings in Piedmont, Missouri, as being "a combination of stars, airplanes, reflecting sunlight, excess moisture, and hot plasma gas." A physician theorized that UFOs were "specks of antimatter."[35]

The urge to explain did not confine itself to those new to the UFO controversy. Thornton Page, a member of the 1953 Robertson panel, who also had helped organize the 1969 American Association for the Advancement of Science Symposium on UFOs, asserted that the great distances between stars ruled out the possibility that UFOs were extraterrestrial. Besides, he asked, why would extraterrestrials want to visit earth? Astronomer Carl Sagan also relied on the distance-between-stars theory. Isaac Asimov explained that one sighting set off others like a "mania." He said the first sighting in the 1973–74 wave was the Pascagoula incident and the rest multiplied from it. "There is no such thing as a single UFO sighting," he declared.[36]

Phil Klass, busy at work on a new book that would "solve" the UFO mystery, got in his licks as well. He told United Press International that "there simply is not a shred of physical evidence [for UFOs] after more than 25 years of sightings. Quite literally. Not a shred, in any of the tens of thousands of UFO sightings that have been reported, that you could take before the National Academy of Sciences and ask: 'Have you ever seen its like on Earth?'" Curiously, Donald Menzel remained quiet on this UFO wave, but Edward U. Condon, apparently unable to detach himself from the controversy, gave his views to a Florida newsman. He said that UFO reports were "pretty much fantasy stuff." Ninety percent of the sightings could be explained, he claimed, and "the other 10% only had vague details." This was one of the embattled physicist's last statements on the subject.

Condon died in March 1974, after a prolonged bout with heart disease.[37]

Although the great majority of scientists who made statements to the press came out against the idea that UFOs represented an anomalous phenomenon, a small number of scientists advocated impartiality. Most of these stressed the need for an open mind about UFOs because of the probability of extraterrestrial life. They admitted the possibility that people saw extraordinary things and did not just misidentify known phenomena. Some cautioned about the "unscientific" stance of dismissing reports automatically because they seemed ridiculous. Others suggested that scientists pay serious attention to the subject.[38]

Just as the wave elicited scientists' explanations and opinions, as in the past it also brought out widespread newspaper coverage. Editorial writers adopted a slightly different tone than they had used previously. The frustration evident in so many editorials advocating a thorough study of UFOs during the 1965–67 wave was absent in 1973. Few newspapers called for a governmental study and virtually no newspapers called for the Air Force to "do something."

Like the scientists, newspaper editorial writers exhibited a wide range of opinion on UFOs. Of the newspapers that considered the sighting wave nonsense, most gave the standard reasons that the press had used since 1947. Some editorials likened UFOs to the Loch Ness monster, and some called the wave a product of the "silly season." "Benign hysteria" or the "power of suggestion" supplied easy answers for others.[39]

These views were in the minority, however, and the majority of the press adopted a neutral attitude toward the phenomenon. Some newspapers considered the wave simply a pleasant and harmless diversion from the world's ills, and a few reflected that the UFO wave had a nostalgic quality to it. For instance, the *Washington, D.C. Star-News* said the reappearance of UFOs was a "nice reprise from the 1960s, in retrospect a simpler age." Many journalists advocated keeping an open mind because intelligent life probably existed elsewhere in the universe. Most of the newspapers that recognized the legitimacy of the UFO problem claimed, as did some scientists, that given the probabilities of life in space, one had to assume that some of the sightings were valid and some of the UFOs extraterrestrial.[40]

Many newspaper columnists also seemed more disposed in 1973–74 to accept the validity of the phenomenon than they had been in the past. Syndicated columnist and popular radio commentator Paul Harvey wrote seriously about UFOs, discussing Harley Rutledge's study and Hynek's views. Lydel Sims, in the *Memphis Commercial Appeal,* equated people's ready acceptance of politicians' statements on world affairs with people's ready rejection of UFO reports. He called it "gullicism," made up of "equal parts of abject gullibility and uninformed skepticism," and thought the country needed a lot less of both. Roscoe Drummond continued his efforts to give the subject legitimacy by writing two columns in successive weeks saying "UFOs are real" and advocating attempts at communication with the extraterrestrials. Other columnists claimed that the evidence suggested "there does seem to be something out there" or urged the public to believe people who reported UFOs. Even Walter Sullivan, science editor of the *New York Times,* who, in the introduction to the paperback edition of the Condon report, had severely criticized those who accepted the legitimacy of the UFO problem, had changed his view somewhat in the early 1970s. He wrote that although hoaxes, misidentifications, and the like accounted for most sightings, a small residue of perplexing cases remained, and some of these "involved seemingly reliable observers and could not be dismissed out of hand."[41]

Yet several columnists still took hostile and uninformed stands. Nationally syndicated columnist Clayton Fritchey called UFOs a figment of the imagination and people who accepted reports of UFOs true believers and gullible. Lawrence Maddry labeled people who reported UFOs "Utterly foolish odd-balls," "mentally infirm," "drunks, deadbeats, hot-gospel goodfellows, goatherders, pool hall perverts, and other glaucoma cases with eyeglasses thicker than bulletproof windows." They were "all seeking and getting headlines," he claimed.[42]

Many people could not help but treat the phenomenon humorously. Since 1896–97, political cartoonists had found UFOs an effective vehicle for their statements. The 1973–74 wave, coming at a time of domestic political problems, presented rich material. Some political cartoonists linked the circular UFO to the disputed circular White House tapes in the Watergate scandal. Cartoonist Herblock drew a man looking at an occupant talking to him from a UFO after the man had finished reading a newspaper with articles on Watergate, Nixon's finances, Agnew's resignation, inflation, and fuel shortages. The caption read: "On The Other Hand, Can You Rule Out Anything Anymore?" [43] All the humor did not take a political form. A short poem, reminiscent of the 1896–97 wave, made the point:

> I never saw a flying saucer,
> I never hope to see one.
> But I can tell you anyhow,
> I'd rather see than be **in** one.[44]

The 1973–74 wave did not receive the magazine coverage other waves had. *Life* and *Look* had folded in the early 1970s before the wave and most other magazines and journals virtually ignored the sightings. Only four major articles on UFOs and the 1973–74 wave appeared in popular magazines. *Rolling Stone*, the rock music and counterculture magazine which expanded its scope to articles on politics and current news, featured a long article on the Pascagoula incident. Writing in the breezy "new journalism" style of the Tom Wolfe school, the author described the town and its leading citizens in an often biting and uncomplimentary manner. He was fair and accurate in his details of the actual sighting but concentrated on the incident's impact on the townspeople rather than on the scientific implications of the sighting.[45]

Newsweek gave the sighting wave a tongue-in-cheek and skeptical treatment. It hinted that the Pascagoula sighting was a hoax, having "as much moonshine as stardust in the story." *U.S. News and World Report*'s article took the UFO reports seriously. It posited an explanation for the sightings: they were a "freakish—but very real and natural—electronic phenomenon" that resembled ball lightning. In experiments conducted in a private laboratory, the magazine explained, scientists ignited ammonia with a high-voltage spark and produced a one-inch round mass of glowing gas that darted about. This experiment, reminiscent of Phil Klass's ball lightning theories and Donald Menzel's bell jar demonstrations in the early 1950s, accounted for "perhaps all" UFO sightings—according to an unnamed scientist and *U.S. News and World Report*.[46]

Perhaps the best article of the four, in terms of the treatment of the phenomenon, appeared in *Cosmopolitan*. This was *Cosmopolitan's* first article on UFOs since Bob Considine, with Air Force sponsorship, attacked the subject and UFO witnesses in 1951. In a total reversal from the 1951 piece, journalist Ralph Blum wrote an impartial review of the scope of the UFO phenomenon, including some of the more bizarre sightings and incidents, and seriously considered the extraterrestrial hypothesis.[47]

Donald Keyhoe, now seventy-five years old, released his fifth book on UFOs in 1973. Called *Aliens From Space,* the book traced Keyhoe's trials and tribulations in his battle with the Air Force and the government when he attempted to end official secrecy about UFOs and initiate congressional hearings on the matter. Keyhoe had at last discovered the identity of his old nemesis, the silence group: it was the Central Intelligence Agency. He told how the CIA had directed the Robertson panel and then had orchestrated the Air Force's program to thwart NICAP's efforts to reveal the truth about UFOs. Keyhoe also described his dispute with the Condon committee and roundly criticized its report. For Keyhoe the most important part of the book was Operation Lure, a plan to induce UFOs down to a prescribed meeting place so that the United States could make official contact with their occupants. Keyhoe wanted to set aside a large parcel of vacant land, allow no planes to fly over it, and build a large model of a UFO to attract the attention of the aliens. The area would also contain "education buildings" stacked with "a variety of exhibits intended to interest the UFO crews." Hidden television cameras and microphones would record the aliens' reactions. Eventually live contact would take place.[48]

Keyhoe's book indicated a change in his attitude toward occupant reports. Although Keyhoe had in the past refused to accept these reports because of their similarity to the infamous contactee stories, he now admitted the reality of the Lonnie Zamora sighting and other fleeting sightings of occupants yet balked at occupant-witness interaction cases.[49]

Publishers quickly capitalized on renewed interest in the phenomenon in 1973 by reprinting a barrage of books on UFOs. Frank Edwards's and John Fuller's books appeared in bookstores once again as did French UFO investigator Aime Michel's 1956 book, *The Truth About Flying Saucers.* The contactees enjoyed a minor resurrection as well. George Adamski's *Flying Saucers Farewell* (1961), wherein he recounted for the last time philosophical conversations with the space brothers, and Howard Menger's "fact/fiction" *From Outer Space* resurfaced with new covers and assumed their old role of confusing the public about which UFO reports were reputable and which were not.[50]

By far the biggest economic bonanza for publishers came not in reprinting old books but in publishing new ones on extraterrestrial visitation in ancient times. Although UFO researchers had published books with similar themes for over twenty years, Erich von Däniken, the Swiss writer, hit the publishing jackpot with his wildly successful *Chariots of the Gods?* A big seller in Europe before it appeared in American markets, its success in this country was unparalleled. Von Däniken theorized that the "gods" of many ancient cults and religions may have been extraterrestrial visitors. He went further than this, though. He posited the theory that the extraterrestrials might have landed, lived with the people, and offered basic technological help and skills. Von Däniken's evidence consisted of myth, legend, ancient drawings and paintings, and artifacts from ancient societies around the world, particularly those in Latin America.[51]

Although von Däniken had a certain amount of evidence to back up his ideas, he failed to discuss a wide range of anthropological theories that may have accounted for the data or to grant to ancient people the intelligence and creativity they deserved. Nevertheless, the book was stimulating enough to provoke widespread discussion, and eventually von Däniken published two more books espousing the same theories.[52] He also contributed to a television show and movie based on his ideas. Other authors, seeing gold in the "gods," rushed to partake in von Däniken's success. In little more than a year, over a dozen books came out with the same general theme of extraterrestrial intervention in ancient times. Moreover, they either had the word *god* in their titles or had the same block lettering style as von Däniken's book covers.

As a spin-off of the von Däniken craze, the public became interested in the so-called Bermuda Triangle, an enormously large area of the Atlantic Ocean and Caribbean Sea. Mysterious disappearances of planes and ships since 1945 had caused speculation about their fate. In 1973 John Wallace Spencer wrote a book claiming that in some way UFOs had either kidnapped the ships and planes and their crews or caused them to disappear. Spencer went on a national tour promoting his book, and sales and profits swelled.[53]

Although the contactees themselves did not make a comeback in the 1970s, the wave of sighting reports thrust a few of them into the press again. Daniel Fry's "Understanding units," still in existence, continued to hold meetings with speakers who claimed to be on intimate terms with space brothers. Contactee Hal Wilcox, who had visited other planets, spoke on "Chariots and Other Vehicles" at one meeting. Dr. Frank Stranges, an evangelist turned contactee supporter who once wrote a book revealing the hitherto unknown facts that space brothers had infiltrated the Pentagon and even conversed with President Kennedy, made the news as the sponsor of a contactee-oriented space and science national convention.[54]

The early 1970s bred a new type of contactee. The new contactees evolved from the popular fascination in the late 1960s and and early 1970s with the occult and the psychic. They claimed to possess psychic powers and abilities and either alleged, as did the popular Israeli psychic Uri Geller, that their psychic powers derived from a close encounter with a UFO or that they, through their special talents, communicated with space brothers. Psychic Ray Stanford belonged to this latter group. He claimed in 1974 that he had had many meetings with space people and had taken motion pictures of UFOs on several occasions. One of the motion pictures, he said, was a spectacular film of a UFO that the Air Force had analyzed and classified as unidenfified—the only unidentified film in Air Force files. But Air Force records show that it classified the object in Stanford's film as Venus—positively identified. Like the contactees of the 1950s, the new contactees in the early 1970s added yet another confusing element to the UFO controversy. By linking psychic and occult phenomena to UFOs, the new contactees threatened to complicate the subject even more for the public.[55]

Television, however, somewhat prevented this confusion from escalating. Whereas in previous years television had aided the contactees' cause, in 1973–74 in the main it did not couple either the old or new contactees with UFOs. During the earlier sighting waves, television news had concentrated on giving vent to contactee claims or ridiculing legitimate UFO reports as part of a national "silly season." But in 1973–74, for the first time television news squarely confronted the UFO problem. CBS, NBC, and ABC gave the UFO sightings the fairest and most impartial coverage the networks had ever given the subject. CBS and ABC nightly news shows carried two-minute and three-minute news features on the UFO sightings and noticeably refrained from tongue-in-cheek humor, "silly season" editorializing, or ridiculing witnesses. NBC's John Chancellor took the boldest stand of the network commentators. In his October 18, 1973, newscast, Chancellor summed up what seemed to be the prevailing opinion among broadcasters: "Many people would like the UFOs to go away. But the UFOs won't go away, and many scientists are taking them very seriously. It's likely that we will hear more and more about the UFOs." In fact, the only major exception to the new television news stance was CBS newsman Hughes Rudd, who continually resorted to sarcasm and ridicule when he read news accounts of UFO sightings.

The only prime time dramatic show to have a plot capitalizing on the interest in UFOs was CBS's March 31, 1974, episode of "Apple's Way." The leading character spotted a UFO, underwent severe ridicule as he bravely told his story to the public and the press, and then encountered several contactee types and lunatics who confided their experiences with the space brothers to him. No one on the show spoke of reputable UFO witnesses. In the end the hero discovered that he actually saw a secret weather device. The show left the viewer with the inference that UFOs were misidentifications of known phenomena and that most UFO witnesses were crazy.

Generally the many syndicated and network talk shows so popular in the late 1960s and early 1970s gave UFOs the most attention. Of talk show hosts, David Susskind reacted most antagonistically toward the subject. When he featured a show with author John Fuller, UFO researcher Stanton Friedman, Betty Hill (of the 1961 Barney and Betty Hill abduction case), and militant UFO debunker Phil Klass, Susskind indulged in heavy ridicule, taunting comments, and general derision of his guests and the subject during the entire show.

Susskind's attitude, however, was not typical. The hosts of the NBC "Today" show discussed the subject seriously with Friedman, Hynek, and Ralph Blum who, with his wife Judy, wrote a book about his investigation of UFOs during 1973. The program with the Blums also included Congressman Roush of Indiana, who had chaired the 1968 House hearings on UFOs and was a member of the NICAP board of governors, and Air Force general and astronaut James A. McDivitt, who had sighted a UFO while aboard the Gemini IV mission and who believed the subject deserved serious attention.

NBC's late-night "Tomorrow" show devoted one full program to UFOs. Host Tom Snyder, a Los Angeles newsman, talked with Hynek, James A. Harder, the University of California engineering professor who had hypnotized one of the Pascagoula witnesses, and Phil Klass. Most of the discussion consisted of a dispute between the two scientists and Klass. As the 1973–74 wave continued, the "Tomorrow" show displayed some confusion about the reputable UFO phenomenon by having some minor contactees on. The "Tonight Show" with Johnny Carson had very little on UFOs per se, but Carson did interview Erich von Däniken and Bermuda Triangle authority John Wallace Spencer.

Without doubt, "The Dick Cavett Show" (ABC) presented the best discussion of the UFO phenomenon on television. Cavett opened his October 25th ninety-minute show with a half hour interview with Charles Hickson, who calmly and articulately described the events of the Pascagoula incident. Then Hynek, astronomer Carl Sagan, John Wallace Spencer, astronaut James McDivitt, and army helicopter pilot Laurence Coyne talked about the UFO wave. (Several months before the show Coyne and his crew of four had had a close encounter with a UFO in their helicopter.) Cavett did not engage in ridicule, and the participants discussed the subject calmly and seriously.

The 1973–74 wave prompted several ambitious television projects. In May 1974 NBC, after an abortive start in October 1973, began production on a news documentary concentrating on the changing societal reactions to the UFO phenomenon over the years. Hynek and producer Craig Leake were working on the program, and it promised to be the best news presentation on UFOs to date.[56]

Independent film maker and producer Allan Sandler began to produce a highly popularized television and motion picture semi-documentary on UFOs in 1973. Surprisingly, Sandler obtained complete Air Force support for the production. The Air Force appeared to be engaging in a dramatic but low-keyed reversal of policy. Instead of telling Sandler to obtain his information from the Air Force Archives at Maxwell Air Force Base in Montgomery, Alabama, it decided to cooperate with him in every way possible. Even though the Air Force knew that the script mildly criticized it and suggested increased study of UFOs, it assigned a public information officer to look after Sandler's needs and to give him virtually everything he wanted for the show. The Air Force approved the appearances on the show of former Project Blue Book directors Hector Quintanilla and Robert Friend as well as other Air Force personnel. Furthermore, rumor had it that the CIA also supported the project. Whatever the reasons the Air Force may have had for cooperating with Sandler, through this open policy the Air Force circumvented potential charges of secrecy, collusion, and dishonesty and thereby removed itself as an easy target for criticism.[57]

The 1973–74 sighting wave, as all other sighting waves, had an impact on American public opinion. A November 1973 Gallup Poll indicated that 51 percent of adult Americans believed UFOs were "real" and not products of imagination or hallucination. Furthermore, 11 percent, a projected fifteen million people, said they had seen a UFO, which was more than double the 5 percent figure in 1966. The poll showed that UFO sightings were not confined to any particular population group. College-educated people reported seeing UFOs as often as those with less education. But people living in the eastern part of the United States saw fewer UFOs than people living in the north, west, or south. The poll also revealed the remarkable statistic that 95 percent of the adult population in the United States had read or heard about UFOs. This awareness was one of the highest in the history of the Gallup Polls.[58]

Here was a phenomenon that virtually the entire adult population of the United States had heard about, and that millions of people claimed to have seen, yet after twenty-seven years no one knew for sure what it was. The controversy over unidentified flying objects, from 1896 on, centered around two issues: identification and credibility. Identification lay at the heart of the opposing positions. Credibility formed the basis for a continuing controversy.

In the 1896–97 mystery airship sightings these two issues had not yet jelled. The public at first had a simple explanation for the existence of the airships: an unknown individual had secretly invented a flying machine and had put man into the skies. But when no authentic inventor appeared on the scene, the focal point of the controversy shifted from identification of the strange objects to the credibility of the witnesses, and ridicule entered the debate. Scientists compounded the ridicule problem when they asserted that witnesses had seen stars and planets or had contrived hoaxes. But ridicule of witnesses in 1896–97 did not become as severe as it did after 1947. The American public in the late 1890s could more easily believe witnesses because it sensed that the invention of flight was near. Also, the 1896–97 sightings lasted only a few months. The public did not have to confront the phenomenon on a continuing basis and could view the airship mystery as a minor episode.

Fifty years later when the modern era of sightings began, the United States could not afford to treat reports of strange objects in the sky as a minor matter. Identifying the unidentified flying objects was for the Air Force, the scientific community, and the civilian UFO organizations the most important issue. The problem of identification involved asking the most appropriate question. The history of the controversy demonstrated that these three groups usually failed to pose the basic question: Did UFOs constitute an anomalous phenomenon? Given the anecdotal and ephemeral nature of the data, the sighting reports, this question was the only remotely answerable one. All other questions about the origin of UFOs were at best highly theoretical and speculative. The available data provided no way to determine the objects' origins. Yet all three groups focused in vain on the unanswerable question of origin. Because neither the Air Force, most scientists involved in the controversy, nor the civilian UFO organizations concentrated on the limited and less sensational issue of anomalousness, each group seriously weakened its position and prolonged the debate.

The task of identifying the unknown flying objects fell first and appropriately to the Air Force—the official group responsible for defending the nation against attack from the air. Public pressure and Air Force concern that UFOs might be secret foreign weapons prompted the study. When Project Sign concluded in 1948 that the objects were not foreign weapons and did not threaten the national security, some staff members speculated that UFOs therefore had to be extraterrestrial. Without first proving that the objects represented an anomalous phenomenon, however, this conclusion remained untenable. Since the Air Force found no proof for the extraterrestrial hypothesis, it rejected this theory completely after 1948 and operated under the unproven assumption that UFOs did not constitute an anomalous phenomenon.

By concluding that UFOs were not anomalous, the Air Force put itself in the position of denying the credibility of witnesses. People who reported UFOs, the Air Force said, either misidentified natural phenomena, lied, or suffered from delusions. But the public, and especially people who claimed to have seen a UFO, found it difficult to believe many of the Air Force explanations for the strange observations.

In 1953 the Robertson panel intensified the Air Force's need to explain all sightings as ordinary occurrences. By recommending that the Air Force reduce UFO reports to a minimum for the sake of national defense, the Robertson panel encased the Air Force in a difficult public relations problem and gave it a rationale for making misleading and deceptive statements to the public and to Congress. The Air Force had to protect the country not against the objects but against the reports. It had to allay public fears by assuring the people that nothing unusual was in the sky. It had to avert congressional hearings because they might create popular interest in UFOs, which would result in "flying saucer hysteria," which, in turn, would generate more UFO reports and thus threaten the national security.

To do all these things, as well as to safeguard the intelligence community that presided over the UFO project, the Air Force gave out only limited information and kept its files classified, thus preventing civilians from examining the data. More importantly, it tried to eliminate sighting reports. If hoaxes, delusions, and misidentification of known phenomena accounted for the sightings, as the Air Force believed, then the Air Force needed to educate the public and especially Congress about this fact to prevent a recurrence of UFO reporting. Hence the problem of unidentified flying objects for the Air Force lay primarily in public relations.

These public relations policies created a credibility problem for the Air Force. UFO organizations vociferously criticized Air Force methods of investigating and analyzing sightings and the public doubted its explanations for UFOs. To counteract these attacks and maintain its credibility, the Air Force engaged in a protracted struggle with the UFO groups. But the Air Force's position was weak. After the Robertson panel's recommendations, the Air Force had abandoned systematic study of UFOs and confined its activities to collecting reports and performing statistical breakdowns of the broad identified category. Systematically studying UFOs wasted time and effort because people did not see uniquely unusual objects.

The Air Force's conviction that scientific investigation would prove worthless deepened even more its public relations bind because the public looked to the Air Force for scientific answers to the problem. To placate the public, the Air Force insisted, on the basis of the incomplete and inconclusive Battelle Memorial Institute study and the Robertson panel, that it had thoroughly investigated the phenomenon and had found no evidence for unusual craft in the sky. The Air Force also effectively used this argument to prevent congressional scrutiny of its UFO program. Consequently, from the early 1950s to the late 1960s, the Air Force was in the unenviable position of playing a conflictiing role: it supplied "scientific" answers to a question it had not studied by releasing incomplete and misrepresentative statistics based on poorly analyzed sighting reports, and it attempted to quiet public criticism of it for not treating the UFO issue scientifically by making misleading and often deceptive public relations statements.

Almost all scientists involved in the UFO controversy also assumed that UFOs were misidentifications, hoaxes, delusions, and not anomalous. The ephemeral, nonreproducible, anecdotal, and unpredictable nature of the data made study within established disciplines and the methodologies difficult. And most raw reports, in fact, did fall in the category of misidentification of known phenomena. But the crux of the controversy rested on the reports that analysts could not identify. Few scientists confronted the basic question for these unidentified reports: Did the objects constitute a uniquely unusual phenomenon? If scientists answered this question affirmatively, they then could have asked whether the objects were natural or artificial. Only after this could they have dealt with the objects' origins. Instead, they made the same logical leap as the Air Force and tried to explain the origins before asking the other questions. Many scientists used logical fallacies to attack the extraterrestrial hypothesis. They argued that since human technology could not overcome the problems of time and distance in space, then neither could extraterrestrial technology. Even if "aliens" controlled the objects, the argument went, the occupants would surely have made "official" contact with earth people. Because they had not, it followed that the objects were not under intelligent control, not extraterrestrial, and not anomalous.

A central problem in the scientific community's treatment of the subject was that the UFO phenomenon did not fit into the purview of any one scientific discipline. Each scientist assumed that UFOs fell within an established scientific field—usually his own. Most scientists failed to recognize that UFOs might constitute a complex and interdisciplinary field of study with its own precepts and methodology. This was why scientists never could account for those reports that remained unidentified after extensive analysis. In fact, most scientists refused to see the phenomenon as a legitimate field of study.

Ridicule played a critical role in perpetuating the idea that the UFO phenomenon was nonsense and undeserving of study. Ridicule touched everyone in the private sector involved in investigating the phenomenon, especially active members of UFO research organizations. The threat of ridicule inhibited scientists from studying the phenomenon and reinforced the idea that UFOs were not anomalous. Fear of ridicule deterred people from reporting UFO sightings. Although the ridicule problem began to lessen slightly by 1973, it remained one of the most important barriers to research on UFOs.

The contactees' unsubstantiated claims of trips in flying saucers and ongoing personal communication with aliens in the mid-1950s increased the ridicule problem, added more confusion to the subject, and strengthened the scientific community's position that UFOs did not merit study. The media and entertainment industry compounded the confusion between contactees and reputable UFO witnesses by giving the contactees widespread publicity and by producing movies with contactee-like themes. As a result, the national UFO organizations had to expend much energy not only disassociating themselves from the contactees but also trying to correct the public confusion they engendered.

The contactees represented only one obstacle for the UFO organizations. Two greater impediments were the Air Force, with its public relations policies, and the scientists, with their attitudes toward the UFO phenomenon. Yet like these two adversaries, the UFO groups became ensnarled in asking inappropriate questions. The leaders, especially Keyhoe, presumed that UFOs were anomalous and therefore extraterrestrial. For Keyhoe this "fact" lay buried in the inner reaches of Air Force and CIA classified files. With this conviction, Keyhoe evolved a complex belief system that assumed the Air Force was lying to the public and conspiring to keep information from it to prevent panic. In view of the Air Force's classification policies, investigatory techniques, and public statements, Keyhoe's suspicions seemed well founded. But through Keyhoe's influence the focus of the controversy shifted away from the UFO problem and onto the Air Force. This outlook weakened the potential effect of NICAP and, to a lesser extent, other UFO organizations.

The Air Force effectively combated Keyhoe's calls for congressional investigations and denied charges of cover-up by referring to its scientific studies which found no evidence for the extraterrestrial hypothesis. Furthermore, the Air Force impeached Keyhoe's credibility by using the Robertson panel report to show that his activities might threaten the national security. With Keyhoe's credibility undermined, and with his assumption that UFOs were extraterrestrial, he never could convince the scientific community to study the phenomenon.

The charges and countercharges of the Air Force, some scientists, and the national UFO organizations in the 1960s planted a seed of doubt in many people's minds about the Air Force's capability to handle the UFO problem. The 1965–66 sighting wave led to widespread press criticism of the Air Force as well. Hynek's 1966 swamp gas pronouncement stretched credibility to the limit as many people simply refused to believe him.

Furthermore, the sightings themselves, always present, had a renewing effect on the controversy and on public interest. The UFOs seemed immune to public discussion about them, came at quasi-predictable times regardless of societal events, and cut across geographic boundaries. Also, people who reported sightings represented all strata of American life. The Air Force, after trying to disengage itself from investigating UFOs, became frustrated over its helplessness to reduce reports after years of effort. Under tremendous public pressure and criticism, it tacitly admitted defeat in 1966 and established the Condon committee. Still confident that UFOs were a nonsense problem, the Air Force took a calculated risk in creating the committee and won.

The Condon committee fell into the same trap as the others: it primarily concerned itself with the validity of the extraterrestrial hypothesis and not with the possible anomalous nature of the phenomenon. Finding no evidence for the extraterrestrial origin of UFOs, the committee, and especially Condon, fell prey to the common mistake of concluding that UFOs did not constitute an anomalous phenomenon and therefore did not merit further study. The Air Force seized upon these conclusions and used the Condon committee's recommendations to close Project Blue Book and end its involvement with the UFO phenomenon in 1969.

The failure of the Air Force, the scientific community, and the UFO organizations to ask the one question that offered some possibility of empirical resolution perpetuated the UFO mystery and the confusion surrounding it. Thus in 1969, although no official UFO project existed, many people still sought a solution to the mystery. Among them was a growing corps of scientists under the leadership of James McDonald and J. Allen Hynek.

By the time of the 1973–74 wave, the tone of the controversy, while for the most part following established lines, began to change. The Air Force had removed itself from the controversy, Keyhoe had retired, the fight for congressional hearings had ended, and the Condon committee was history. Between 1969 and 1974 scientists interested in UFOs quietly and slowly chipped away at the granite wall of disreputability and illegitimacy so long associated with the subject of UFOs. The moon landing and scientists' acceptance of the probability of life elsewhere in the universe helped ease ridicule of UFO witnesses and the phenomenon itself. The focus began to shift from credibility back to identification, the heart of the issue.

By mid-1974 many scientists had answered affirmatively the question of UFO anomalousness and were clarifying some of the basic issues that had muddied the controversy. New perspectives emerged based on the increased awareness of the global nature of the phenomenon. The excellent British journal, *Flying Saucer Review,* provided a forum for international exchanges of data and ideas. Hynek's Center for UFO Studies served as a focal point for scientific analysis of the phenomenon. Free from the debates of previous years, researchers for the first time focused on identification and confronted head-on the mystery of unidentified flying objects.

Changes in Air Force Annual UFO Report Statistics, 1960–69

Year in Which Public Reported UFO Sightings	Yearly Totals as Reported by the Air Force								Total No. Uniden- tified*
	1960– 61	1962– 63	1964	1965	1966	1967	1968	1969	
1947	79	79	79	79	122	122	122	122	12
1948	143	143	143	143	156	156	156	156	7
1949	186	186	186	186	186	186	186	186	22
1950	169	169	169	210	210	210	210	210	27
1951	121	121	121	156	169	169	169	169	22
1952	1,501	1,501	1,501	1,501	1,501	1,501	1,501	1,501	303
1953	425	425	425	425	509	509	509	509	42
1954	429	429	429	487	487	487	487	487	46
1955	404	404	404	543	545	545	545	545	24
1956	778	778	667	670	670	670	670	670	14
1957	1,178	1,178	1,004	1,005	1,006	1,006	1,006	1,006	14
1958	573	590	623	623	627	627	627	627	10
1959	364	364	386	387	390	390	390	390	12
1960	462	514	556	556	557	557	557	557	14
1961	—	488	584	585	591	591	591	591	13
1962	—	—	469	469	474	474	474	474	15
1963	—	—	382	393	399	399	399	399	14
1964	—	—	—	532	562	562	562	562	19
1965	—	—	—	—	886	887	887	887	16
1966	—	—	—	—	—	1,060	1,112	1,112	32
1967	—	—	—	—	—	—	937	937	19
1968	—	—	—	—	—	—	—	375	3
1969	—	—	—	—	—	—	—	146	1
TOTAL								12,618	701

NOTE: The Air Force failed to explain adequately why changes existed in its annual statistics. It stated in 1968 that some press releases had not included all the sightings and that this was later corrected, but the Air Force never explained why some yearly totals decreased over time.

* The unidentified list does not include sightings in the *possible* and *probable* categories.

Notes

1 The Mystery Airship: Preliminaries to the Controversy

1. See Savante Stubilius, *Airship, Aeroplane, Aircraft* (Goteborg, Sewden: Almqvist Wiksell, 1966), for a complete analysis of nineteenth-century usage of words dealing with aircraft.

2. *Omaha Morning World-Herald*, 6 April 1897, p.5; *Chicago Tribune*, 10 April 1897, p.2; *Dallas Morning News*, 17 April 1897, p.8, and 16 April 1897, p.5.

3. *Milwaukee Sentinel*, 11 April 1897, p.11; *Detroit Free Press*, 14 April 1897, pp.3, 2; *Chicago Tribune*, 12 April 1897, p.5; *Dallas Morning News*, 8 April 1897, p.3; *Galveston Daily News*, 24 April 1897, p.3.

4. *Dallas Morning News*, 8 April 1897, p.3; *Chicago Times-Herald*, 6 April 1897, p.1.

5. *Dallas Morning News*, 16 April 1897, p.5.

6. *Detroit Free Press*, 10 April 1897, p.2; *Chicago Tribune*, 2 April 1897, p.14; *Dallas Morning News*, 19 April 1897, p.5.

7. *Chicago Times-Herald*, 10 April 1897, p.1, and 13 April 1897, p.2; *Detroit Free Press*, 16 April 1897, p.3.

8. *Sacramento Daily Record-Union*, 18 November 1896, p.4, and 19 November 1896, p.8; *Dallas Morning News*, 18 April 1897, p.4; *Chicago Tribune*, 2 April 1897, p.14; *Des Moines Leader*, 13 April 1897, p.3; *Houston Post*, 22 April 1897, p.9.

9. *Milwaukee Sentinel*, 15 April 1897, p.10; *Cincinnati Commercial-Tribune*, 25 April 1897, p.10.

10. *Galveston Daily News*, 22 April 1897, p.4; *St. Louis Post-Dispatch*, 14 April 1897, p.7; *Chicago Times-Herald*, 16 April 1897, p.1; *Houston Post*, 22 April 1897, p.9; *Sacramento Daily Record-Union*, 19 November 1896, p.8; *Dallas Morning News*, 18 April 1897, p.4.

11. *Chicago Times-Herald*, 17 April 1897, p.6; *Harrisburg (Arkansas) Modern News*, 23 April 1897, p.2; *San Francisco Call*, cited in *Sacramento Daily Record-Union*, 24 November 1896, p.8.

12. *St. Louis Post-Dispatch*, 25 April 1897, p.9.

13. *Houston Post*, 25 April 1897, p.13.

14. *Dallas Morning News*, 19 April 1897, p.5.

15. Ibid.

16. Ibid.

17. *Houston Post*, 21 April 1897, p.2.

18. *Galveston Daily News*, 24 April 1897, p.3, and 28 April 1897, p.6; *Houston Post*, 25 April 1897, p.5.

19. *Houston Post*, 26 April 1897, p.2.

20. *Houston Post*, 30 April 1897, p.7.

21. *Yates Center* (Kansas) *Farmer's Advocate*, 23 April 1897, cited in Jerome Clark, "The Strange Case of the 1897 Airship," *Flying Saucer Review* 12 (July–August 1966): 10–17, especially 13.

22. Ibid.

23. *St. Louis Post-Dispatch*, 11 April 1897, p.2; *Des Moines Leader*, 11 April 1897, p.3; *Chicago Record*, 17 April 1897, cited in Donald Hanlon, "The Airship in Fact and Fiction," *Flying Saucer Review* 16 (July–August 1970): 20–21; *Milwaukee Sentinel*, 15 April 1897, p.1; *Cincinnati Commercial-Tribune*, 19 April 1897, p.1; *Des Moines Daily News*, 12 April 1897, p.3.

24. *Dallas Morning News*, 19 April 1897, p.5.

25. Frank Masquellette, "Physical Evidence of Great Airships of 1897," *Houston Post*, 13 June 1966, p.8.

26. *Sacramento Daily Record-Union*, 23 November 1896, p.4, and 24 November 1896, p.8.

27. *Chicago Tribune*, 12 April 1897, p.6, and 26 April 1897, p.3.

28. *Louisville Courier-Journal*, 19 April 1897, p.1.

29. *Detroit Free Press*, 1 April 1897, p.9.

30. *Chicago Times-Herald*, 12 April 1897, p.1; *Chicago Tribune*, 12 April 1897, p.5; *Des Moines Daily News*, 12 April 1897, p.3.

31. *Cincinnati Commercial-Tribune*, 16 April 1897, p.1.

32. *Detroit Free Press*, 10 April 1897, p.2; *Dallas Morning News*, 18 April 1897, p.4; *St. Louis Globe-Democrat*, 2 April 1897, p.2; *Milwaukee Sentinel*, 10 April 1897, p.1; *St. Louis Post-Dispatch*, 10 April 1897, pp.1, 2; *Chicago Times-Herald*, 10 April 1897, p.4.

33. *Galveston Daily News*, 20 April 1897, p.2; *Louisville Courier-Journal*, 15 April 1897, p.5; *Dallas Morning News*, 17 April 1897, p.8.

34. *Dallas Morning News*, 19 April 1897, p.5.

35. *Chicago Times-Herald*, 11 April 1897, p.2; *Chicago Tribune*, 12 April 1897, p.5.

36. *Chicago Times-Herald*, 8 April 1897, p.1; *Milwaukee Sentinel*, 11 April 1897, p.11; *Chicago Tribune*, 10 April 1897, p.2; *Galveston Daily News*, 15 April 1897, p.1; *Chicago Times-Herald*, 4 April 1897, p.1; *Chicago Tribune*, 5 April 1897, p.4; *Omaha Morning World-Herald*, 6 April 1897, p.5; *Galveston Daily News*, 23 April 1897, p.3.

37. *Sacramento Daily Record-Union*, 24 November 1896, p.1; *Chicago Tribune*, 10 April 1897, p.1, and 11 April 1897, p.1.

38. *Omaha Morning World-Herald*, 8 April 1897, p.5; *Chicago Tribune*, 10 April 1897, p.2, and 11 April 1897, pp.32, 1.

39. *Milwaukee Sentinel*, 13 April 1897, p.1.

40. *St. Louis Post-Dispatch*, 10 April 1897, pp.1, 2, and 13 April 1897, pp.1, 2.

41. *St. Louis Post-Dispatch,* 13 April 1897, pp.1, 2; *Chicago Tribune,* 20 April 1897, p.4.

42. *Sacramento Daily Record-Union,* 20 November 1896, p.2, and 21 November 1896, p.4; *Birmingham* (Alabama) *News,* cited in *Cincinnati Commercial-Tribune,* 22 April 1897, p.4; *Chicago Tribune,* 19 April 1897, p.6; *Kansas City* (Missouri) *Star,* 28 March 1897, p.2, and 29 March 1897, p.8.

43. *Chicago Tribune,* 4 April 1897, p.32.

44. *Des Moines Leader,* 11 April 1897, p.3; *Wisconsin State Journal* (Madison), 12 April 1897, p.2; *Cincinnati Commercial-Tribune,* 16 April 1897, p.1; *Baltimore News,* cited in *Cincinnati Commercial-Tribune,* 22 April 1897, p.4.

45. *Memphis Commercial Appeal,* cited in *Cincinnati Commercial-Tribune,* 22 April 1897, p.4; *Dallas Morning News,* 21 April 1897, p.6; *Galveston Daily News,* 2 May 1897, p.20; *St. Louis Post-Dispatch,* 18 April 1897, p.20.

46. *Sacramento Daily Record-Union,* 24 November 1896, p.8; *St. Louis Post-Dispatch,* 17 April 1897, p.1; *Dallas Morning News,* 18 April 1897, p.4.

47. *Chicago Times-Herald,* 12 April 1897, p.1; *St. Louis Post-Dispatch,* 12 April 1897, pp.1, 2, and 18 April 1897, p.1.

48. James O. Bailey, *Pilgrims Through Space and Time* (New York: Argus, 1947), p.96.

49. *St. Louis Post-Dispatch,* 11 April 1897, p.4, and 14 April 1897, p.7; *Houston Post,* 22 April 1897, p.9; *Washington Times* and *Memphis Commercial Appeal,* cited in *Cincinnati Commercial-Tribune,* 22 April 1897, p.4.

50. *St. Louis Globe-Democrat,* 13 April 1897, p.11; *Milwaukee Sentinel,* 13 April 1897, p.1; *St. Louis Post-Dispatch,* 14 April 1897, p.5.

51. *Omaha Morning World-Herald,* 8 April 1897, p.5.

52. *Galveston Daily News,* 16 April 1897, p.2; *Sacramento Daily Record-Union,* 30 November 1896, p.3; *Houston Post,* 22 April 1897, p.9.

53. Basil Clarke, *The History of Airships* (London: Herbert Jenkins, 1960), pp.31–44. See also Joseph H. Hood, *The Story of Airships* (London: Arthur Barker Ltd., 1968); John Toland, *Ships in the Sky* (New York: Henry Holt Co., 1957); Charles H. Gibbs-Smith, *The Invention of the Aeroplane, 1799–1901* (New York: Taplinger, 1966); C. Gibbs-Smith, *A History of Flying* (London: B. T. Batsford, 1953); C. Gibbs-Smith, *Aviation: An Historical Survey* (London: Her Majesty's Stationery Office, 1970).

54. Ibid.

55. Ibid.

56. "Pennington's Airship," *Scientific American*, 7 March 1891, p.150; Howard Scamehorn, *Balloons to Jets* (Chicago: Henry Regnery, 1957), pp.14–15.

57. For a photograph of Professor Barnard's pedal-powered airship, see Herman Justi, ed., *Official History of the Tennessee Centennial Exposition* (Nashville: Brandon Printing Co., 1898), p.404.

58. Scamehorn, p.15.

59. Charles H. Gibbs-Smith, "Historical Note," *Flying Saucer Review* 12 (July–August 1966): 17.

2 The Modern Era Begins: Attempts to Reduce the Mystery

1. Gordon I. Lore and Richard Deneault, *Mysteries of the Skies* (Englewood Cliffs, N.J.: Prentice-Hall, 1968), pp.116, 123–25; David R. Saunders and R. Roger Harkins, *UFOs? Yes!* (New York: Signet, 1968), p.53; *Washington Star*, 6 July 1947, reprinted in Donald E. Keyhoe, *The Flying Saucers Are Real* (New York: Fawcett, 1950), pp.34–35; *New York Times*, 2 January 1945, pp.1, 4; Jo Chamberlain, "The Foo Fighter Mystery," *American Legion Magazine*, December 1945, pp.9, 43–47; Frederic O. Sargent, *Night Fighters: An Unofficial History of the 415th Night Fighter Squadron* (Madison, Wis.: By the Author, 1946).

2. United States Air Force, "Unidentified Flying Objects: Project 'Grudge'," 1 August 1949, No. 102-AC 49/15-100, Appendix A (in the Air Force Archives at Maxwell Air Force Base in Montgomery, Alabama, hereafter referred to as MAFB); *New York Times*, 12 August 1946, p.1, 13 August 1946, p.4, 14 August 1946, p.11, 11 October 1946, p.3; Saunders and Harkins, p.54.

3. Kenneth Arnold's testimony and sighting information are in the sighting files at MAFB.

4. Herbert Strentz, "An Analysis of Press Coverage of Unidentified Flying Objects, 1947–1966" (Ph.D. dissertation, Northwestern University, 1970), p.2.

5. Ted Bloecher, *Report on the UFO Wave of 1947* (By the Author, 1967), pp.I-1, I-2.

6. Bloecher, p.I-11; Frank M. Brown, Memorandum for the Officer in Charge, 16 July 1947 (MAFB).

7. DeWayne B. Johnson, "Flying Saucers—Fact or Fiction?" (Master's thesis, University of California at Los Angeles, 1950), pp.105–15. This thesis contains some little known information about this famous incident.

8. Bloecher, p.I-14; *New York Times*, 9 July 1947, pp.1 and 10, 12 July 1947, p.11.

9. Bloecher, p. I-11, and p.I-5.

10. *New York Times*, 27 December 1947, p.28, 6 July 1947, p.36.

11. *New York Times*, 10 July 1947, p.23.

12. "A Rash of Flying Discs Breaks Out Over the U.S.," *Life*, 21 July 1947, pp.14–16.

13. George H. Gallup, *The Gallup Poll: Public Opinion 1935–1948* (New York: Random House, 1972), p.666.

14. *New York Times*, 4 July 1947, p.26.

15. Edward J. Ruppelt, *The Report on Unidentified Flying Objects* (Garden City, N.Y.: Doubleday, 1956), p.23; "Project 'Grudge'," pp.2–3.

16. Ruppelt, *Report on UFOs*, p.22.

17. *New York Times*, 7 July 1947, p.5.

18. General Nathan F. Twining to Commander, Air Material Command, 23 September 1947, contained in Edward U. Condon, project director, *Scientific Study of Unidentified Flying Objects* (New York: Bantam ed., 1969), pp.894–95, hereafter referred to as *Condon Report*.

19. Major General L. C. Craigie to Commanding General Wright Field, "Flying Discs," 30 December 1947, contained in *Condon Report*, pp.896–97. See also Edward J. Ruppelt, "What The Air Force Has Found Out About Flying Saucers," *True* (May 1954), reprinted in *The TRUE Report on Flying Saucers* (reprints of articles in *True Magazine*; New York: Fawcett, 1967), pp.36–39, 57–74.

20. Captain Mantell sighting information on file at MAFB. Reports that Mantell noticed heat in his cockpit are untrue.

21. Ruppelt, *Report on UFOs*, pp.33, 37–38.

22. Ruppelt, *Report on UFOs*, pp.27–28.

23. Ruppelt, *Report on UFOs*, p.28.

24. Chiles and Whitted sighting information is on file at MAFB. The information contained in Ruppelt, *Report on UFOs*, p.40, relating to a "tight left turn" by Chiles and "turbulent air" by the object is incorrect. Chiles and Whitted told James E. McDonald that the object vanished into thin air (letter from James McDonald to Richard H. Hall, 13 January 1968).

25. Ruppelt, *Report on UFOs*, pp.41, 45. J. Allen Hynek, the Air Force's scientific consultant on UFOs, confirmed the existence of the "Estimate of the Situation" in an interview with the author, February 1971.

26. Ruppelt, *Report on UFOs*, pp.58–59. Albert M. Chop, Air Force public information officer, confirmed the factionalism at AMC in an interview with the author, 7 January 1974.

27. United States Air Force, "Unidentified Aerial Objects: Project 'Sign'," February 1949, No. F-TR-2274-IA, pp.vi–vii (MAFB).

28. Ibid.

29. Project 'Sign'," pp.32–35.

30. Ruppelt, *Report on UFOs*, pp.57, 59–60. Interview with J. Allen Hynek, February 1971.

31. "Project 'Grudge'," p.2. Ruppelt, *Report on UFOs*, pp.60–61.

32. Sidney Shallett, "What You Can Believe About Flying Saucers (Part II)," *Saturday Evening Post*, 7 May 1949, pp.36, 184–86.

33. Sidney Shallett, "What You can Believe About Flying Saucers (Part I)," *Saturday Evening Post*, 30 April 1949, p.20; Shallett, Part II, p.186.

34. "Project 'Grudge'," p.1; Ruppelt, *Report on UFOs*, p.63.

35. "Project 'Grudge'," incident No. 207, Appendices B, n.p., I, n.p., C-2, p.4. This incident is discussed in Ruppelt, *Report on UFOs*, pp.67–68.

36. "Project 'Grudge'," incident No. 33 a–g, Appendix B, n.p.; see also Ruppelt, *Report on UFOs*, pp.34–35.

37. "Project 'Grudge'," Part V, Appendix G, n.p.; A. M. Wood to Lieutenant Colonel A. J. Hemstreet, 29 March 1949, contained in "Project 'Grudge'," Appendix D–I, n.p.; "Project 'Grudge'," p.10.

38. "Project 'Grudge'," p.10.

39. Department of Defense, News Release No. 629–49, "Air Force Discontinues Flying Saucer Project," 27 December 1949, contained in Leon Davidson, ed., *Flying Saucers: An Analysis of the Air Force Project Blue Book Special Report No. 14*, 4th ed. (Clarksburg, W. Va.: Saucerian Publications, 1970), p.7; Major Boggs, Memorandum for the Record, 31 August 1949 (MAFB).

40. Project Twinkle final report, 27 November 1951 (MAFB). Includes letters and memoranda.

41. Ruppelt, *Report on UFOs*, p.67; George H. Gallup, 2 (1949–1958), p.911.

42. Keyhoe cited in Ruppelt, *Report on UFOs*, pp.64–65.

43. Donald E. Keyhoe, "The Flying Saucers Are Real," *True* (January 1950), reprinted in *The TRUE Report on Flying Saucers*, p.93. Keyhoe, *True*, p.7. Ruppelt, *Report on UFOs*, pp.64–65.

44. Robert B. McLaughlin, "How Scientists Tracked a Flying Saucer," *True* (March 1950), p.28.

45. Frank Scully, *Behind The Flying Saucers* (New York: Henry Holt, 1950), p.137.

46. Roland Gelatt, "Flying Saucer Hoax," *Saturday Review of Literature*, 6 December 1952, p.31.

47. Roland Gelatt, "In a Saucer From Venus," *Saturday Review of Literature*, 23 September 1950, pp.20–21, 36; "More About Flying Saucers," *Science News Letter*, 16 September 1950, p.181; "Visitors From Venus; Flying Saucer Yarn," *Time*, 9 January 1950, p.49.

48. Keyhoe, *The Flying Saucers Are Real*, p.73.

49. Keyhoe, *The Flying Saucers Are Real*, p.173.

50. "Flying Saucers—The Real Story: U.S. Built First One in 1943," *U.S. News and World Report*, 7 April 1950, pp.13–15; "Flying Saucers Again," *Newsweek*, 17 April 1950, p.29; Ruppelt, *Report on UFOs*, p.82; *Condon Report*, p.515.

51. *New York Times*, 5 April 1950, p.24.

52. Bob Considine, "The Disgraceful Flying Saucer Hoax," *Cosmopolitan* (January 1951), pp.33, 100–102.

53. Saunders and Harkins, pp.98–99.

54. "Belated Explanation on Flying Saucers," *Time*, 26 February 1951, p.22; *New York Times*, 14 February 1951, p.28, 26 February 1951, p.25.

55. *Condon Report*, p.514.

3 The 1952 Wave: Efforts to Meet the Crisis

1. "Project Grudge Special Report No. 1," 28 December 1951, contained in United States Air Force, *Projects Grudge and Bluebook Reports 1–12* (Washington, D.C.: National Investigations Committee on Aerial Phenomena, 1968), pp.23–28. All subsequent references to Project Grudge and Blue Book reports in this chapter are from this volume and are cited by report number and date only. For Edward Ruppelt's discussion of this sighting, see his *The Report on Unidentified Flying Objects* (Garden City, N.Y.: Doubleday, 1956), pp.91–92.

2. Ruppelt, p.93.

3. Letter from Ruppelt to Max Miller, 13 February 1956 (files of the National Investigations Committee on Aerial Phenomena, Kensington, Maryland, which I hereafter refer to as NICAP); Ruppelt, p.94; "Status Report No. 2," 31 December 1951, p.33; "Status Report No. 3," 31 January 1952, p.58; "Status Report No. 4," 29 February 1952, p.67.

4. Ruppelt, p.114; "Status Report No. 1," 30 November 1951, p.2; Ruppelt, p.14.

5. "Status Report No. 2," 31 December 1952, p.33; "Status Report No. 3," 31 January 1952, p.59.

6. "Status Report No. 1," 30 November 1951, pp.3–4; "Status Report No. 2," 31 December 1951, pp.33–34; "Status Report No. 3," 31 January 1952, p.59; "Status Report No. 4," 29 February 1952, p.67; "Status Report No. 5," 31 March 1952, p.84; "Status Report No. 6," 30 April 1952, p.99; Ruppelt, pp.136–37.

7. Letter from Ruppelt to Max Miller, 13 February 1956 (NICAP); Ruppelt, p.94; "Status Report No. 2," 31 December 1951, p.34; "Status Report No. 3," 31 January 1952, p.59.

8. "Status Report No. 1," 30 November 1951, p.4. See also David R.

Saunders and R. Roger Harkins, *UFOs? Yes!* (New York: Signet, 1968), p.59.

9. Ruppelt, pp.131, 143.

10. "Status Report No. 5," 31 March 1952, pp.85–86; "Status Report No. 6," 30 April 1952, pp.98–99.

11. Ruppelt, pp.137, 140, 143.

12. Department of the Air Force, Air Force Letter No. 200–5, 29 April 1952 (from the Air Force Archives at Maxwell Air Force Base in Montgomery, Alabama, which I hereafter refer to as MAFB); Ruppelt, pp.133–34.

13. Department of Defense, Office of Public Information, "Press Release," 3 April 1952, reproduced in Leon Davidson, ed., *Flying Saucers: An Analysis of the Air Force Special Report No. 14*, 4th ed. (Clarksburg, W.Va.: Saucerian Publications, 1971), p.A4.

14. "Status Report No. 5," 31 March 1952, pp.84–85.

15. H. Bradford Darrach and Robert Ginna, "Have We Visitors from Space?," *Life*, 7 April 1952, p.80.

16. Darrach and Ginna, p.86.

17. Ibid.

18. "Status Report No. 6," 30 April 1952, p.99.

19. *New York Times*, 12 April 1952, p.10, and 13 April 1952, Sec. IV, p.9.

20. Ruppelt, p.132. Two months later *Life* published a follow-up: Robert Ginna, "Saucer Reactions," 9 June 1952, pp.20–26. Ginna noted that there had been a "tremendous barrage" of letters and that more were coming in every day (p.20).

21. Ruppelt, pp.131, 138. Accurate statistics on the number of reports sent to ATIC are difficult to obtain; the Condon committee final report, Project Blue Book reports, and Ruppelt all give slightly different figures on monthly sighting report totals but are substantially in agreement about the yearly totals.

22. Ruppelt, p.149; "Status Report No. 7," 31 May 1952, p.115.

23. "Status Report No. 8," 31 December 1952, pp.134, 136, passim.

24. Ruppelt, pp.147–49.

25. Donald H. Menzel, "The Truth About Flying Saucers," *Look*, 17 June 1952, pp.35–39; "Those Flying Saucers" (an interview with Donald Menzel), *Time*, 9 June 1952, pp.54–56. These articles are essentially similar in expounding Menzel's views.

26. "Status Report No. 6," 30 April 1952, p.99.

27. J. Robert Moskin, "Hunt for the Flying Saucers," *Look*, 1 July 1952, pp.37, 40.

28. Moskin, p.41.

29. "Status Report No. 8," 31 December 1952, pp.134, 136, 143; Ruppelt, p.132.

30. Ruppelt, p.157.

31. For a more complete description of the Washington, D.C., sightings, see: file on Washington, D.C., sightings at MAFB; Ruppelt, pp. 156–72; Donald E. Keyhoe, *Flying Saucers From Outer Space* (New York: Holt, 1953), pp. 63, 68–69; Richard Hall, ed., *The UFO Evidence* (Washington, D.C.: NICAP, 1964), pp.35, 77, 132, 149, 159; *Washington Post*, 22, 25, 27, 28, 29, 30 July 1952.

32. Interview with Albert M. Chop, 4 January 1974. See also Washington, D.C., file at MAFB.

33. Ruppelt, pp.160, 162.

34. Hall, p.159; Ruppelt, pp.161, 165.

35. Hall, p.159; Ruppelt, p.166; interview with Albert M. Chop, 4 January 1974.

36. Ruppelt, p.167; Memorandum for the Record, "Trip to Washington, D.C.," 26 July 1952 (Personal files).

37. *Washington Post*, 29 July 1952, p.1.

38. Interview with Albert M. Chop, 4 January 1974.

39. Department of Defense, "Minutes of Press Conference held by General John A. Samford," 29 April 1952 (MAFB); Keyhoe, p.76. Keyhoe's transcription of the Samford new conference is a fairly accurate and complete account. See also *Christian Science Monitor*, 31 July 1952, p.1; *Washington Post*, 30 July 1952, p.1; Ruppelt, p.168.

40. *New York Times*, 31 July 1952, p.22, 30 July 1952, p.10; *Christian Science Monitor*, 31 July 1952, p.12, 30 July 1952, p.1.

41. *Baltimore Sun*, 1 August 1952, p.10; *Milwaukee Journal*, 30 July 1952, p.24; Lawrence Elliot, "Flying Saucers: Myth or Menace?," *Coronet*, 19 November 1952, p.50.

42. *Washington Post*, 25 July 1952, p.18; *Denver Rocky Mountain News*, 28 July 1952, cited in Keyhoe, pp.69–70.

43. Allen cited in *San Francisco Chronicle*, 4 August 1952, p.3 (Allen was part of the *New York Tribune* news service); "Washington's Blips," *Life*, 4 August 1952, p.40.

44. Edgar Mauer, "Of Spots Before Their Eyes," *Science*, 19 December 1952, p.693; *New York Times*, 29 July 1952, p.20, 28 July 1952, p.5; *Milwaukee Journal*, 30 July 1952, p.2.

45. *Milwaukee Journal*, 4 August 1952, p.2; *Baltimore Sun*, 3 August 1952, p.1; "No Visitors From Space," *Science News Letter*, 30 August 1952, p.143; *San Francisco Chronicle*, 30 July 1952, p.2; *Washington Post*, 30 July 1952, p.1; *Milwaukee Journal*, 30 July 1952, p.2.

46. J. Allen Hynek, "Special Report on Conferences with Astronomers on Unidentified Flying Objects," 6 August 1952, p.18 (MAFB). See also "Status Report No. 8," 31 December 1952, pp.137–38.

47. *New York Times*, 1 August 1952, p.19; *Christian Science Monitor*,

30 July 1952, p.10; *New York Times*, 4 August 1952, p.3; *Baltimore Sun*, 4 August 1952, p.1.

48. *Baltimore Sun*, 31 July 1952, p.1.

49. Chester Morrison, "Mirage or Not, Radar Sees Those Saucers Too," *Look*, 9 September 1952, p.99.

50. Ruppelt, p.13; *Milwaukee Journal*, 1 August 1952, p.1; "Wind is Up in Kansas," *Time*, 8 September 1952, p.86; Ohio Northern University, "Project A: Investigation of Phenomena," 18 March 1953, p.1 (from the files of the Aerial Phenomena Research Organization, Tucson, Arizona).

51. Darrach and Ginna, p.86; interview with Coral Lorenzen, head of the Aerial Phenomena Research Organization, June 1972.

52. Donald H. Menzel, "Abstract," *Journal of the Optical Society of America* 42 (November 1952): 879. Menzel did not submit his paper for publication but the journal published his abstract.

53. Urner Liddel, "Phantasmagoria or Unusual Observations in the Atmosphere," *Journal of the Optical Society of America* 43 (April 1953): 314, 315, 317.

54. J. Allen Hynek, "Unusual Aerial Phenomena," *Journal of the Optical Society of America* 43 (April 1953): 312.

55. Hynek, "Unusual Aerial Phenomena," p.313; "Status Report No. 9," 31 January 1953, p. 158.

56. "Special Report No. 1," 28 December 1951, pp.23–28. See also the complete report on the Fort Monmouth sightings at MAFB.

57. "Status Report No. 8," 31 December 1952, p.138.

58. Ruppelt, pp.190–91.

59. Ruppelt, p.149.

60. "Status Report No. 8," 31 December 1952, pp.139, 141.

61. "Status Report No. 8," 31 December 1952, p.139.

4 The Robertson Panel and Its Effects on Air Force UFO Policy

1. Transcript of UFO briefing to Subcommittee on Atmospheric Phenomena, House Select Committee on Astronautics and Space Exploration, 8 August 1953, p.3 (from the Air Force Archives at Maxwell Air Force Base in Montgomery, Alabama, which I hereafter refer to as MAFB).

2. Memorandum, Air Technical Intelligence Command to Air Defense Command, 23 December 1952 (MAFB); letter from S. A. Goudsmit to author, 9 February 1972: "communication channels had been nearly saturated during an outbreak of UFO hysteria shortly before our meeting. We considered this a real danger. . . ."

3. The duration of the meetings is a subject of controversy. Ruppelt said the meeting started on 12 January and went for five days. The

Robertson panel minutes puts the date at 14–18 January. According to a copy of the minutes, the date of 14–17 January is correct.

4. *Who Was Who in America*, no. 4 (New York: Marquis Co., 1968), p.800; *Who's Who in America*, no. 36 (New York: Marquis Co., 1971), p.865, and also Edward U. Condon, project director, *Scientific Study of Unidentified Flying Objects* (New York: Bantam ed., 1969), pp.516–17; *Who's Who*, p.37; *Who's Who*, p.1733; *Who Was Who*, p.1051.

5. Edward J. Ruppelt, *The Report on Unidentified Flying Objects* (Garden City, N.Y.: Doubleday, 1956), p.241.

6. Frederick C. Durant, "Report of Meetings of Scientific Advisory Panel on Unidentified Flying Objects," 14–18 January 1953, p.3 (MAFB), which I hereafter refer to as Robertson report; also contained in Condon, pp.896–99. Ruppelt, p.219.

7. Robertson report, pp.3–5, 17.

8. Robertson report, pp.4–6, 17.

9. Robertson report, pp.12–13; letter from S. A. Goudsmit to author, 9 February 1972.

10. Robertson report, pp.9, 11–12.

11. Robertson report, Tab A.

12. Robertson report, pp.18–24, Tab A.

13. Robertson report, pp.21–22.

14. Letter from Thornton Page to Author, 7 February 1972; letter from S. A. Goudsmit to J. A. Hennessey, 25 February 1965 (in the files of the National Investigations Committee on Aerial Phenomena, Kensington, Maryland, which I hereafter refer to as NICAP); letter from S. A. Goudsmit to J. A. Hennessey, 10 March 1965 (NICAP); J. Allen Hynek, "Are Flying Saucers Real?" *Saturday Evening Post*, 17 December 1966, p.19.

15. Interview with J. Allen Hynek, February 1972.

16. See chapter 2, pp.61–62, 66–69.

17. Letter from Edward J. Ruppelt to Leon Davidson, 7 May 1958, contained in Leon Davidson, ed., *Flying Saucers: An Analysis of the Air Force Special Report No. 14*, 4th ed. (Clarksburg, W.Va.: Saucerian Publications, 1970), p.B3. Exactly when the CIA released the summary to Blue Book is not known.

18. Ruppelt, p.228; Donald E. Keyhoe, *The Flying Saucer Conspiracy* (New York: Holt, 1955), pp.39–40.

19. United States Air Force, "Status Report No. 10," 27 February 1953, *Projects Grudge and Bluebook Reports 1–12* (Washington, D.C.: NICAP, 1968), p.180 (hereafter I will refer to all status reports by number and date only); "Status Report No. 11," 31 May 1953, p.204. Also see Ruppelt, p.229.

20. Ruppelt, p.231; letter from Major Robert C. Brown to Command-

ing General, Air Defense Command, 5 March 1953 (MAFB); Memorandum, "Division of Responsibility ATIC-ADC," December 1953 (MAFB); "Status Report No. 10," 27 February 1953, p.179; Memorandum, "Briefing of ADC Forces and Divisions of Project Blue Book," 12 November 1952 (MAFB); Memorandum, "Project Blue Book Special Briefing for Air Defense Command," March 1953 (MAFB).

21. Ruppelt, pp.231–32.

22. Interview with J. Allen Hynek, February 1972.

23. Keyhoe, *Conspiracy*, p.44.

24. Donald E. Keyhoe, "Flying Saucers From Outer Space," *Look*, 20 October 1953, pp.114–20.

25. Keyhoe, *Look*, p.114; Keyhoe, *Conspiracy*, p.55; telegrams from Albert M. Chop to Keyhoe, n.d., December and October 1953? (NICAP); interview with Keyhoe, April 1972.

26. Donald E. Keyhoe, *Flying Saucers From Outer Space* (New York: Holt, 1953), pp.124, 249.

27. Donald H. Menzel, *Flying Saucers* (Cambridge, Mass.: Harvard University Press, 1953), passim.

28. Menzel, pp.22, 15, 149–66.

29. Menzel, p.80.

30. Menzel, pp.57, 171, 143–44, 148.

31. Norman J. Crum, "Flying Saucers and Book Selection," *Library Journal* 79 (October 1954): 1719–25; David Flick, "Tripe for the Public," *Library Journal* 80 (February 1955): 202.

32. Department of the Air Force, "Air Force Regulation 200-2," 26 August 1953, 2 November 1953, 12 August 1954 (MAFB), and also contained in Davidson, pp.135–38; Department of the Air Force, "Air Force Letter 200-5," 29 April 1952 (MAFB). See also "Status Report No. 12," 30 September 1953, p.219.

33. *Joint-Army-Navy-Air Force-Publication 146*, December 1953, contained in Lawrence J. Tacker, *Flying Saucers and the U.S. Air Force* (Princeton, N.J.: Van Nostrand, 1960), pp.127–35.

34. "Status Report No. 11," 31 May 1953, p.200; "Status Report No. 12," 30 September 1953, p.216.

35. *Special Report No. 14*, 5 May 1955, contained in Davidson. See section in chapter 6 on *Special Report No. 14*.

36. Ohio Northern University, "Project A: Investigation of Phenomena," 18 March 1953 (from the files of the Aerial Phenomena Research Organization, Tucson, Arizona).

5 Contactees, Clubs, and Confusion

1. For a discussion of occupant reports, see Coral and Jim Lorenzen, *Flying Saucer Occupants* (New York: Signet, 1967); J. Allen Hynek, *The*

UFO Experience: A Scientific Inquiry (Chicago: Henry Regnery, 1972); and Charles Bowen, ed., *The Humanoids* (London: Neville Spearman, 1969).

2. Jung's psychoanalytic description of a flying saucer sighting pertains to these individuals. See Carl G. Jung, *Flying Saucers: A Modern Myth of Things Seen in the Sky,* trans. R. F. C. Hull (New York: Harcourt, Brace, 1959; Signet, 1969).

3. Paris Flammonde, *The Age of Flying Saucers* (New York: Hawthorn, 1971), p.53. See also Bryant and Helen Reeve, *Flying Saucer Pilgrimage* (Amherst, Wis.: Amherst Press, 1957), for a discussion of the contactees' personalities.

4. Flammonde, p.54. The title of Adamski's novel is *Pioneers of Space.*

5. Desmond Leslie and George Adamski, *Flying Saucers Have Landed* (London: Werner Laurie, 1953), pp.172–73.

6. Leslie and Adamski, p.205.

7. George Adamski, *Inside the Spaceships* (New York: Abelard-Schuman, 1955); the paperback edition is *Inside the Flying Saucers* (New York: Paperback Library, 1967), pp.78, 95, 104–5, 123, 157, 179. All subsequent references are to the paperback edition.

8. Truman Bethurum, *Aboard A Flying Saucer* (Los Angeles: De Vorss, 1954), pp.143, 123, 145.

9. Bethurum, pp.25–26.

10. Daniel Fry, *The White Sands Incident* (Los Angeles: New Age Publishing Co., 1954), p.19. One year later Fry wrote *Alan's Message to Men of Earth* (Los Angeles: New Age Publishing Co., 1955). Both books were combined in *The White Sands Incident* (Louisville, Ky.: Best Books, 1966), to which the notes in this chapter refer.

11. Fry, pp.20–21.

12. Fry, pp.67, 70, 90–92.

13. Orfeo M. Angelucci, *The Secret of the Saucers* (Amherst, Wis.: Amherst Press, 1955), pp.113, 33–36. For an extensive psychoanalytic study of this book, see Jung, pp. 119–27.

14. Angelucci, pp.76–78, 121, 138–40.

15. Howard Menger, *From Outer Space to You* (Clarksburg, W. Va.: Saucerian Books, 1959). The paperback is *From Outer Space* (New York: Pyramid, 1967), pp. 34–38, 149, 119–24, 127. All notes refer to the paperback edition.

16. Bethurum, p.141; Angelucci, pp.106, 31.

17. Adamski, p.78; Angelucci, p.130.

18. Leslie and Adamski, p.202; Fry, p.71; Menger, p.155.

19. Adamski, p.75; Bethurum, p.103; Fry, pp.26, 46; Angelucci, p.9; Menger, p.158.

20. Adamski, p.73; Bethurum, p.75; Fry, p.67; Angelucci, pp.46, 30, 110; Menger, pp.23, 41, 63.

21. Edward J. Ruppelt, *The Report on Unidentified Flying Objects* (Garden City, N.Y.: Doubleday, 1956). In 1959 Doubleday published a revision of this book which included three additional chapters, one of which discussed contactees (p. 263); however, the revision does not have the word *revision* on it and carries the 1956 date. Also Bethurum, pp. 120–25; Menger, pp.113, 132, 172–75. See also Flammonde, pp.94–100.

22. Leslie and Adamski, pp.177, 183; Bethurum, p. 10; Angelucci, pp.74, 26.

23. Flammonde, pp.87–88, 211; Civilian Saucer Investigations of New York, *CSI Newsletter*, 15 July 1959, p.11. George Van Tassel, *I Rode A Flying Saucer* (by the Author, 1952); George Van Tassel, *The Council of Seven Lights* (Los Angeles: De Vorss, 1958). George Hunt Williamson and Alfred C. Bailey, *The Saucers Speak* (Los Angeles: New Age Publishing Co., 1954). Flammonde, pp.179–80. *Nexus* 2 (May 1955): 9. For additional descriptions of some of these minor figures, see: Flammonde, passim; John Nebel, *The Way Out World* (Englewood Cliffs, N.J.: Prentice-Hall, 1961; New York: Lancer, 1962); John Nebel, *The Psychic World Around Us* (New York: Hawthorn, 1969; New York: Signet, 1970).

24. *CSI Newsletter*, 15 December 1956, p.8. *CSI Newsletter*, 15 July 1959, pp.5–8; see also Flammonde, pp.128–31. *Thy Kingdom Come* became *AFSCA World Report* (1959–61), then *UFO International* (1962–65), and then *Flying Saucers International* (1966–72). John Godwin, *Occult America* (Garden City, N.Y.: Doubleday, 1972), p. 147.

25. James Moseley's reports on the Giant Rock conventions are in: *Nexus* 2 (May 1955): 9; *Saucer News* 7 (September 1960): 3–9; *Saucer News* 8 (December 1961): 12–13; *Saucers, Space and Science* 60 (1971): 7–8. James Moseley, "Non-Scheduled Newsletter No. 11," *Saucer News* (10 September 1960): 1; see also *Saucer News* 7 (September 1960): 3–9.

26. "AMFSCA Souvenir Program," *Thy Kingdom Come* (May–June 1959): 2–3. James Moseley, "Recent News Stories," *Saucer News* 6 (December–January 1958): 13–14. *CSI Newsletter*, 15 July 1959, p.11.

27. Flammonde, passim; Nebel, *The Way Out World*, passim. Letter from Keyhoe to Lorenzen, 30 March 1954 (in the files of the Aerial Phenomena Research Organization, Tucson, Arizona, to which I hereafter refer as APRO).

28. For an index of some of these clubs and their locations, see *Thy Kingdom Come* (April–May 1957): 13–15 (published by the Los Angeles Interplanetary Study Groups, later called the Amalgamated Flying Saucer Clubs of America).

29. Flammonde, p.67; *The Flying Saucer Review* (official publication of the Space Observers League, Seattle, Washington), see particularly 1 (October 1955), 2 (February 1956), 2 (April 1956), 2 (June 1956), 2 (August 1956); *The Spacecrafter* 3 (January–March 1960): 3.

30. Gray Barker, *They Knew Too Much About Flying Saucers* (New York: University Books, 1956); Albert K. Bender, *Flying Saucers and the Three Men* (New York: Paperback Library, 1968).

31. *UFORUM* 1 (February–March 1957): 4–5; *CSI Newsletter*, 1 May 1957, pp.1–2; *Nexus* (January 1955, March 1955, May 1955); *Saucer News* 2 (June–July 1955), 4 (February–March 1957), "Confidential Newsletter No. 4." (October 1957), "Confidential Newsletter No. 8" (August 1958), 6 (December–January 1958–59), 6 (February–March 1959), 7 (September 1960), "Non-Scheduled Newsletter No. 11" (10 September 1960), 8 (December 1961), 11 (March 1964), 13 (March 1966).

32. Letters from Keyhoe to Lorenzen, 22 September 1954, and 2 July 1954 (APRO).

33. See "Special Adamski Exposé Issue," *Saucer News* (October 1957); James Moseley, "Strange New Ideas from Howard Menger," *Saucer News* (Non-Scheduled Newsletter No. 26 [25 January 1966]): 1; an account of the Van Tassel-St. Germain episode can be found in *CSI Newsletter*, 1 May 1957, pp. 9–10; Ruppelt (1959 revision), p.268; *Saucer News* (December 1961): 15.

34. *CSI Newsletter*, 1 November 1957, p.16.

35. Ruppelt (1959 revision), pp.270–71; letter from Keyhoe to Lorenzen, 17 July 1958 (APRO); interview with Mrs. Ruppelt, 4 January 1974; interview with Robert Friend, 4 January 1974.

36. Godwin, p.144.

37. Robert Ellwood, *Religious and Spiritual Groups in Modern America* (Englewood Cliffs, N.J.: Prentice-Hall, 1973), pp. 132–33, 11–19.

38. H. Taylor Buckner, "Flying Saucers are For People," *Trans-Action* 3 (May–June 1966): 10–13; Buckner, "The Flying Saucerians: An Open Door Cult," in Marcello Truzzi, ed., *Sociology and Everyday Life* (Englewood Cliffs, N.J.: Prentice-Hall, 1968), pp.223–30; Leon Festinger, *When Prophecy Fails* (Minneapolis, Minn.: University of Minnesota Press, 1956), passim.

39. No good analysis of science fiction movies exists. However, three fair attempts are: John Baxter, *Science Fiction in the Cinema* (New York: A. S. Barnes, 1970); Dennis Gifford, *Science Fiction Film* (London: Dutton, 1969); Susan Sontag, "The Imagination of Disaster," *Against Interpretation* (New York: Dell, Laurel edition, 1969), pp.212–28.

40. *The Day the Earth Stood Still, It Came From Outer Space*, and *This Island Earth* are at the Library of Congress. *The Thing* is at the State Historical Society, Madison, Wisconsin.

41. Letter from Keyhoe to Lorenzen, 3 October 1956 (APRO).

6 1954 to 1958: Continued Skirmishes and the Rise of NICAP

1. James Moseley, *Saucer News* 3 (June–July 1956): 3. Leon David-

son, "The Air Force and The Saucers, Part I," *Saucer News* 3 (February–March 1956): 13–16, and "The Air Force and The Saucers, Part II," *Saucer News* 4 (June–July 1957): 9–16. Leon Davidson, ed., *Flying Saucers: An Analysis of the Air Force Special Report No. 14*, 4th ed. (Clarksburg, W.Va.: Saucerian Publications, 1970), pp.145–54 (all subsequent references to *Special Report 14* are to this volume and are listed by report title only).

2. Letter from Donald Keyhoe to Coral Lorenzen, 30 March 1954 (in the files of the Aerial Phenomena Research Organization, Tucson, Arizona, to which I hereafter refer as APRO); letters from Keyhoe to Lorenzen, 15 August 1954 and 22 September 1954 (APRO).

3. Department of the Air Force, "Air Force Regulation 200-2," 13 August 1954, contained in Davidson, ed., pp.135–38, and at the Air Force Archives at Maxwell Air Force Base in Montgomery, Alabama, to which I hereafter refer as MAFB. Edward J. Ruppelt, *The Report on Unidentified Flying Objects* (Garden City, N.Y.: Doubleday, 1956), pp.231–32; Major Robert C. Brown to Commanding General Air Defense Command, "Utilization of 4602nd Personnel in Project Blue Book Field Investigations," 5 March 1953 (MAFB).

4. Colonel John M. White, Jr., to Commander, Air Technical Intelligence Center, "Report of Visit of ATIC Representatives," 23 November 1954 (MAFB); United States Air Force, "Status Report No. 11," 31 May 1953, *Projects Grudge and Bluebook Reports 1–12* (Washington, D.C.: National Investigations Committee on Aerial Phenomena, 1968), p.203; Lt. Mary L. Storm to Commander 4602nd (ADC), "Unidentified Flying Object Guide," 14 January 1955 (MAFB).

5. Interview with J. Allen Hynek, March 1974.

6. Project Blue Book press releases, which are on file at MAFB and at National Investigations Committee on Aerial Phenomena (NICAP) in Kensington, Maryland.

7. Interview with J. Allen Hynek, March 1974.

8. For complete statistics listed in ATIC and 4602nd reports during these years, see addition to *Special Report Number 14*, which is a typed insert (MAFB); Department of Defense, News Release No. 1108–57, 15 November 1957 (APRO & NICAP).

9. Interview with J. Allen Hynek, March 1974.

10. Department of Defense, "Fact Sheet," n.d. late 1953 and early 1954? (NICAP & APRO); Department of Defense, News Release No. 1053–55, 25 October 1955, attachment (NICAP & APRO). See also *New York Times*, 2 January 1954, p.5; J. Allen Hynek, "Are Flying Saucers Real?" *Saturday Evening Post*, 17 December 1966, pp. 17–21.

11. Department of Defense, "Fact Sheet," n.d. late 1953 and early 1954? (NICAP & APRO).

12. Charlotte Knight, "Report on Our Flying Saucer Balloons," *Collier's*, 11 June 1954, pp.50–57; Siegfried Mandel, "The Great Saucer Hunt," *Saturday Review*, 6 August 1955, pp. 28–29; "Waiting for the Little Green Men," *Newsweek*, 28 March 1955, p.64.

13. *New York Times*, 2 September 1955, p.3, 16 December 1954, pp.24, 1, 26, and 19 December 1954, Sec. IV, p.8.

14. "The Saucers Again," *American Aviation* 17 (March 1954): 3.

15. Donald E. Keyhoe, *The Flying Saucer Conspiracy* (New York: Holt, 1955), p.7 and passim.

16. Letters from Keyhoe to Lorenzen, 6 November 1955 and 28 October 1955 (APRO).

17. *Special Report 14*, pp.57, 68.

18. *Special Report 14*, p.24.

19. Department of Defense, Office of Public Information, News Release No. 1053–55, 25 October 1955, contained in Davidson, ed., pp.D5–D6. Letters from Keyhoe to Lorenzen, 1 December 1955 and 29 February 1956 (APRO). See also Donald E. Keyhoe, *Flying Saucers: Top Secret* (New York: Putnam, 1960), pp.157–60.

20. Letters from Keyhoe to Lorenzen, 1 December 1955 and 29 February 1956 (APRO). See also Keyhoe, *Top Secret*, pp.157–60.

21. Letter from Ruppelt to Max Miller, 13 February 1956 (NICAP).

22. Information supplied by Stanton T. Friedman, nuclear physicist and private UFO researcher.

23. *New York Times*, 22 January 1956, Sec. 7, p.25; letter from Charles A. Hardin to General Watson, 7 February 1956 (MAFB).

24. Colonel John G. Eriksen, Memorandum for Director of Intelligence, "Proposed Reply by the Secretary of the Air Force to the letter from the Honorable John E. Moss, Chairman, Government Information Subcommittee of the Committee on Government Operations," 25 June 1956 (MAFB); letter from Donald A. Quarles to Representative John E. Moss, 5 July 1956 (MAFB); A. Francis Arcier to George T. Gregory, "Request—Progress on Status of 'Blue Book' Printing and Dissemination," 8 April 1958 (MAFB); letter from John E. Moss to Donald A. Quarles, 17 June 1956 (MAFB).

25. Captain George T. Gregory, "Lecture on UFO Program for the ATI School," n.d., pp.1–11 (MAFB).

26. J. Allen Hynek, *The UFO Experience: A Scientific Inquiry* (Chicago: Henry Regnery, 1972), p.181.

27. The information in this section was derived from case files at MAFB.

28. This film is in the Library of Congress Film Archives.

29. *Christian Science Monitor*, 1 May 1956. Captain Gregory's marginal comments are contained in a special file at MAFB. George T.

Gregory, "Memorandum for AFOIN—4X1," 17 May 1956 (at MAFB; AFOIN, and later AFCIN, is the Air Force Office of Assistant Chief of Staff for Intelligence); Gregory, "Memorandom for The Scientific Advisor," 21 May 1956 (MAFB); Gregory, "Memorandum for Office of the Scientific Advisor," 5 June 1956 (MAFB); Colonel John Eriksen, "Memorandum for Director of Intelligence," 1 June 1956 (MAFB); Brigadier General Harold E. Watson to A. M. Rochlen, n.d. (MAFB). See also file on motion picture at MAFB.

30. For a convenient compilation of most years of sighting reports, see Edward U. Condon, project director, *Scientific Study of Unidentified Flying Objects* (New York: Bantam ed., 1969), p.514. Many of the statistics are not consistent with Blue Book statistics. For Blue Book's version, see "Project Blue Book, 1964–1968" (MAFB, APRO, NICAP).

31. *UFO Investigator*, October 1971, pp.1–4; letters from Keyhoe to Lorenzen, 3 October 1956 and 21 October 1956 (APRO).

32. Letters from Keyhoe to Lorenzen, 22 January 1957 and 1 February 1957 (APRO); Keyhoe, *Top Secret*, p.44. See also Morris K. Jessup, "A Report on Washington, D.C.'s NICAP," *Saucer News* 4 (February–March 1957): 5.

33. Letter from Keyhoe to Lorenzen, 30 March 1954 (APRO). See also letter from Keyhoe to Lorenzen, 6 November 1955 (APRO).

34. Keyhoe, *Top Secret*, p.20. See also *UFO Investigator*, July 1957, for short biographies of members of the board of governors. *UFO Investigator*, July 1957, pp.28, 30.

35. *UFO Investigator*, October 1971, p.1; letters from Keyhoe to Lorenzen, 1 February 1957 (APRO).

36. Letter from Keyhoe to Lorenzen, 10 June 1957 (APRO); Donald Keyhoe, "Statement by Major Donald E. Keyhoe, Director of NICAP," 7 March 1957 (NICAP & APRO).

37. *UFO Investigator*, July 1957, p.1.

38. Colonel Leonard T. Glaser, Memorandum to Commander, Air Technical Intelligence Center, "UFO Program," 17 December 1958 (MAFB); letter from Major Robert F. Spence to Max Miller, 11 June 1957 (NICAP); letter from Major General Joe W. Kelly to Donald Keyhoe, 15 November 1957 (NICAP).

39. Colonel Frank B. Chappell to Chief, AFOIN-X, "New AFOIN-4 Plan on UFOBs," 15 May 1957 (MAFB); Colonel Frank B. Chappell to AFOIN-XI Colonel Hurley, "New AFOIN-4 Plan on UFOBs," n.d. (MAFB); Memorandum (unsigned) to Chief, AFCIN-XI, "New AFCIN-4 Plan on UFOBs," 13 February 1958 (MAFB); A. Francis Arcier, Memorandum for Director of Intelligence, "Publication of UFO Special Report No. 14," 4 January 1957 (MAFB).

40. Air Force Regulation 200-2, 5 February 1958 (MAFB); Memoran-

dum to Director AFOIN-4, "Publication of UFO Special Report No.
14," 10 May 1957 (MAFB); Keyhoe, *Conspiracy*, pp.24–25.

41. Colonel John W. Meador, AISS, to the Assistant Chief of
Staff/Intelligence, Headquarters, USAF, "Processing of Reports of UFO
Sightings," 8 October 1953 (MAFB); Deputy Assistant Chief of Staff
Harold E. Watson to General Charles B. Dougher, Commander ATIC,
"The UFO Program," 21 July 1959 (MAFB); Air Force Regulation
200-2, 14 September 1959, contained in Lawrence J. Tacker, *Flying
Saucers and the U.S. Air Force* (Princeton, N.J.: Van Nostrand, 1960),
pp.91–98.

42. Condon, *Scientific Study of UFOs*, p.514.

43. These sightings are more fully discussed in Hynek, *The UFO
Experience*, pp.123–28; his analysis is based on a NICAP study. The
information for the Levelland sightings is contained in "Air Intelligence
Information Report," No. 141957, 2–8 November 1957 (MAFB). See
also *New York Times*, 4 November 1957, p.4.

44. Hynek, *The UFO Experience*, p.124.

45. "Air Intelligence Information Report," No. 141957, 2–8 November 1957, p.5 (MAFB); Hynek, *The UFO Experience*, p.125.

46. Hynek, *The UFO Experience*, pp.125–26.

47. Hynek, *The UFO Experience*, pp.126, 10, 126.

48. "Air Intelligence Information Report," No. 141957, 2–8 November 1957, p.16 (MAFB).

49. *New York Times*, 5 November 1957, p.22; Hynek, *The UFO
Experience*, p.128.

50. George T. Gregory, Disposition Form, "Request for Air Science
Division Review of Levelland Case," 4 December 1957 (MAFB);
Department of Defense, News Release No. 1108–57, 15 November 1957
(NICAP & APRO).

51. George T. Gregory, Disposition Form, "Request for Air Science
Division Review of Levelland Case," 4 December 1957 (MAFB).

52. Department of Defense, News Release No. 1083–58, 5 November
1957 (NICAP & APRO); *New York Times*, 7 November 1957, p.24.

53. *New York Times*, 6 November 1957, p.12; Condon, *Scientific Study
of UFOs*, p.514.

54. Memorandum (unsigned) to Chief, AFCIN-XI, "New AFCIN-4
Plan on UFOBs," 13 February 1958 (MAFB).

55. Keyhoe, *Top Secret*, pp.155–65.

56. Letter from Lawrence J. Tacker to unspecified person, 12 March
1958 (MAFB); Memorandum (unsigned) to Chief, AFCIN-XI, "New
AFCIN-4 Plan on UFOBs," 13 February 1958 (MAFB).

7 The Battle for Congressional Hearings

1. Letter (unsigned) from Air Force Office of Legislative Liaison to
Frelinghuysen, 12 September 1957 (in the files of the National Investiga-

tions Committee on Aerial Phenomena, Kensington, Maryland, to which I hereafter refer as NICAP); letter from Major General Joe W. Kelly, Director of Legislative Liaison to Lee Metcalf, 11 January 1957 (NICAP).

2. Colonel Glen W. Clark, Chief Public Information Division, OIS, Memorandum for Deputy Director of Information Services, SAFS, "Congressional Public Hearings—Unidentified Flying Objects," 3 February 1958 (in the files of the Air Force Archives, Maxwell Air Force Base, Montgomery, Alabama, to which I hereafter refer as MAFB). See also Donald E. Keyhoe, *Flying Saucers: Top Secret* (New York: Putnam, 1960), pp.81–96. Memorandum for Chief AFCIN-XI, "New AFCIN-4 Plan on UFOBs," 13 February 1958 (MAFB; AFCIN stands for Air Force Office of Assistant Chief of Staff for Intelligence).

3. Memorandum for Chief AFCIN-XI, "New AFCIN-4 Plan on UFOBs," 13 February 1958 (MAFB); Major General Arno H. Luehman, Memorandum for Director of Legislative Liaison, "McClellan Subcommittee Statement Concerning Air Force Handling of UFO Reports," 28 February 1958 (MAFB); Major General Joe W. Kelly, Memorandum for Director of Information Services, "McClellan Subcommittee Statement Concerning Air Force Handling of UFO Reports," 3 March 1958 (MAFB).

4. Letter from John E. Henderson to Secretary of Defense Neil H. McElroy, 8 May 1958 (MAFB); Major Byrne, Memorandum for the Record, "Briefing of Representative Henderson and Colleagues on the Air Force Unidentified Flying Object (UFO) Program," 23 June 1958 (MAFB).

5. Major General W. P. Fisher, Director of Legislative Liaison, Memorandum for the Under Secretary of the Air Force, "Hearings on Unidentified Flying Objects," n.d. (MAFB); Colonel Bourne Adekson, Deputy Director of Legislative Liaison, Memorandum for the Assistant Chief of Staff/Intelligence, "Hearings on Unidentified Flying Objects," 6 August 1958 (MAFB); Major Byrne, Memorandum for the Record, "Hearings on Unidentified Flying Objects (UFO)," 12 August 1958 (MAFB).

6. Major General W. P. Fisher, Memorandum for the Under Secretary of the Air Force, "Air Force Briefing for the Subcommittee on Atmospheric Phenomena, House Select Committee on Astronautics and Space Exploration, on Unidentified Flying Objects," 11 August 1958 (MAFB); George T. Gregory, Transcript of UFO Briefing, "UFO Program," 8 August 1958, pp.1–11 (MAFB).

7. George T. Gregory, Transcript of UFO Briefing, "UFO Program," 8 August 1958, pp.1–11 (MAFB).

8. Ibid.

9. For examples, see: letters from Major General Fisher to Senator Harry F. Byrd, 20 January 1959; Fisher to Senator Mike Monroney, 4 June 1959; Fisher to Senator Barry Goldwater, 29 July 1959 (NICAP).

10. Letter from Richard Horner, Assistant Secretary of the Air Force for Research and Development, to Senator Barry Goldwater, January 1958 (NICAP); letter from Major General Fisher to Senator Byrd, 20 January 1959 (NICAP).

11. Department of Defense, Air Force Fact Sheet No. 986–58, 6 October 1958 (NICAP).

12. Ibid.

13. Colonel Leonard T. Glaser, Memorandum for Commander of Air Technical Intelligence Center, "UFO Program," 17 December 1958 (MAFB); Major General Charles B. Dougher to Assistant Chief of Staff/Intelligence, Draft, 16 December 1958 (MAFB); Draft of proposed message to all Major Commands, n.d. (MAFB).

14. Colonel Glaser, "UFO Program," 17 December 1958 (MAFB); Major General Dougher, Draft, 16 December 1958 (MAFB); Draft of proposed message to all Major Commands, n.d. (MAFB).

15. Colonel William E. Boyd, Disposition Form, "Support of the UFO Program," n.d. (MAFB); William E. Boyd, Disposition Form, to AFCIN-4X4, "UFO Program," n.d. (MAFB); Boyd, Disposition Form, to AFCIN-4X5, "Support of UFO Program," n.d. (MAFB); Boyd, Disposition Form, to AFCIN-4X6, "UFO Program," n.d. (MAFB); Charles B. Dougher to Brigadier General Howe, "UFO Program," 17 December 1958 (MAFB); Leonard T. Glaser, Memorandum for the Record, 16 December 1958 (MAFB).

16. J. Allen Hynek, *The UFO Experience: A Scientific Inquiry* (Chicago: Henry Regnery, 1972), p.187.

17. Interview with Robert Friend, 7 January 1974.

18. Robert J. Friend, Memorandum for the Record, "Unidentified Flying Object Conference," n.d. (20 February 1959?), pp.2–3 (MAFB).

19. Ibid.

20. Ibid.

21. Colonel H. K. Gilbert to Lt. Colonel Parris, Disposition Form, "Unidentified Flying Objects Advisory Panel," 16 March 1959 (MAFB); Colonel Vincent C. Rethman to Theodore Hieatt, 29 April 1959 (MAFB); Rethman to Chaplain Graham, 8 May 1959 (MAFB); R. J. Friend, "AFCIN-4E4g Weekly Activity Report," 8 May 1959 (MAFB).

22. Memorandum for the Record, "Meeting of UFO Panel," 7 April 1960, 12 April 1960 (MAFB); interview with J. Allen Hynek, 27 September 1972.

23. "USAF UFO Program," unsigned, 28 September 1959, pp.1–3 (MAFB). See also Dougher to AFCIN (General Walsh), "UFO Program," n.d. (MAFB).

24. Colonel Richard R. Shoop, "Study by AFCIN-4E4, Unidentified Flying Objects—Project #5771 (Blue Book)," 28 September 1959, pp.1–2 (MAFB).

25. Colonel Shoop, "Study by AFCIN-4E4 on UFOs," 28 September 1959, pp.1, 2, 3 (MAFB).

26. Ibid.

27. "Study by AFCIN-4E4, Unidentified Flying Objects Program Project #5771 (Blue Book)," unsigned, n.d., p.2 (MAFB); this document differs somewhat from the Shoop memorandum above. Colonel Shoop, "Study by AFCIN-4E4 on UFOs," 28 September 1959, pp.2, 3 (MAFB). See also Charles B. Dougher to AFCIN (General Walsh), "UFO Program," 28 September 1959 (MAFB).

28. Shoop to Lt. General Bernard A. Schriever, "Transfer of USAF Aerial Phenomena Program," 1 December 1959 (MAFB); Major General James Ferguson to Headquarters, USAF (AFCIN), "Transfer of USAF Aerial Phenomena Program," 5 February 1960 (MAFB); Colonel Aaron J. Boggs, Referral Notice, "Transfer of USAF Aerial Phenomena Program," 7 March 1960 (MAFB); letter from J. Allen Hynek to General Holzman, 17 February 1960 (MAFB); letter from General Holzman to J. Allen Hynek, 8 March 1960 (MAFB).

29. Colonel Philip G. Evans to AFCIN-4 (M/Gen. Dougher), "Transfer of USAF Aerial Phenomena Program," 31 March 1960 (MAFB); A. Francis Arcier, Memorandum for Major General Dougher, "Transfer of UFO," 1 April 1960 (MAFB); letter (unsigned) to AFCIN (Major General Walsh), "Transfer of USAF Aerial Phenomena Program," n.d. (MAFB); Major General Walsh to SAFOI (Major General A. H. Luehman), "Transfer of USAF Aerial Phenomena Program," n.d. (MAFB).

30. Keyhoe, *Top Secret*, p.274, passim.

31. Robert J. Friend, "Memorandum for the Record," n.d. (MAFB); interview with Robert Friend, 7 January 1974.

32. *UFO Investigator* 1 (December–January 1960–61): 3.

33. Lawrence J. Tacker, *Flying Saucers and the U.S. Air Force* (Princeton, N.J.: Van Nostrand, 1960), pp.12, 16, 17, 18.

34. Tacker, p.83.

35. Tacker, p.84.

36. Tacker, pp.85, 47, 87. See also letter from Colonel Carl M. Nelson to Senator Philip A. Hart, 4 April 1960 (NICAP).

37. Transcript, "Washington Viewpoint," 20 December 1960 (MAFB).

38. Robert J. Friend to AFCIN-4E (Colonel Evans), "Possible Congressional Hearing," 7 June 1960 (MAFB); Richard R. Shoop, "UFO Briefing," 11 July 1960 (MAFB); Robert J. Friend, Task Activity

Report, 18 July 1960 (MAFB); Colonel Philip G. Evans, "UFO Case Summaries," 28 July 1960 (MAFB).

39. Friend, Task Activity Report, 18 July 1960 (MAFB); Hynek, *The UFO Experience*, pp.267–69.

40. Major General Arno H. Luehman, Director of Information, Memorandum for Assistant Chief of Staff/Intelligence, "Unidentified Flying Objects," 2 August 1960 (MAFB).

41. Task Activity Report, 20 July 1960 (MAFB); Richard R. Shoop to AFCIN-4X6, "ATIC Capability for Investigating Sightings of Uniden-tified Aerial Phenomena," 20 July 1960 (MAFB); Philip G. Evans to Lt. Colonel Sullivan, "ATIC Capability for Investigating Sightings of Unidentified Aerial Phenomena," 29 July 1960 (MAFB); Luehman to Assistant Chief of Staff/Intelligence, 2 August 1960 (MAFB); Colonel Barton S. Pulling, Chief of Staff, ATIC, to AFCIN-P, 17 August 1960 (MAFB).

42. Shoop to AFCIN-4X6, "ATIC Capability," 20 July 1960 (MAFB); Friend to AFCIN-R, Joint Messageform, 26 January 1961 (MAFB).

43. Philip G. Evans to Lt. Colonel Tacker, "ATIC UFO Investigation Capability," 17 March 1961 (MAFB).

44. Department of Defense, News Release, "Fact Sheet Air Force UFO Report," No. 812-60, 21 July 1960 (NICAP and the files of the Aerial Phenomena Research Organization, Tucson, Arizona, to which I hereafter refer as APRO); Philip G. Evans to Headquarters USAF, "Unidentified Aerial Phenomena," 27 December 1960 (MAFB).

45. Letter from Carl M. Nelson to Senator Oren E. Long, 27 April 1960 (NICAP); letter from Joseph Kingsley to John Carstarphen, 26 May 1960 (NICAP); letter from Gordon B. Knight to Estes Kefauver, 6 April 1960 (NICAP).

46. *Springfield* (Massachusetts) *Union*, contained in *UFO Investigator* 11 (January–February 1962): 3; *UFO Investigator* 11 (July–August 1961): 1; *UFO Investigator* 11 (October 1961): 1.

47. *UFO Investigator* 11 (July–August 1961): 1–4.

48. Colonel Edward H. Wynn to Brigadier General Arthur A. Pierce, Commander, Air Force Systems Command, "Congressional Investiga-tion of the UFO Program," 14 July 1961 (MAFB); Robert Friend to AFSC (SCGP), "Congressional Committee Staff Member Visit," 25 August 1961 (MAFB).

49. Letter from Richard P. Hines to Robert J. Friend, 21 August 1961 (MAFB).

50. Letter from Joseph E. Karth to Donald E. Keyhoe, 28 August 1961 (NICAP & MAFB); Robert J. Friend to Colonel Wynn, "Uniden-tified Flying Objects," 4 December 1961 (MAFB).

51. *UFO Investigator* 11 (October 1961): 2; letter from Joseph E. Karth to Donald Keyhoe, 19 September 1961, contained in *UFO Investigator* 11 (October 1961): 1.

52. Interview with Coral Lorenzen, June 1971.

53. *The A.P.R.O. Bulletin*, July 1962; letter from Richard Hall to Coral Lorenzen, 7 September 1962 (APRO); letter from Coral Lorenzen to Richard Hall, 20 September 1962 (APRO).

54. *Saucer News* 5 (August–September 1958): 11–13. See also Winston F. Gardlebacher, "Does NICAP Really Exist?," *Saucer News* 15 (Summer 1968): 9–11; Frank Strange, "NICAP Has Gone Too Far!," *Saucer News* 15 (Summer 1968): 2–3. Letter from Donald Keyhoe to Zan Overall, 19 September 1958 (NICAP). See also telegram from Donald Keyhoe to Gabriel Green, 6 July 1959 (APRO): "This is to warn you against repeating any claim that the National Investigations Committee on Aerial Phenomena is part of your flying saucer clubs organization." Letter from Donald Keyhoe to NICAP membership, 30 June 1961 (APRO).

55. See also *UFO Investigator*, special issue (October 1962), for basic outline of this compendium.

56. Edward U. Condon, project director, *Scientific Study of Unidentified Flying Objects* (New York: Bantam ed., 1969), p. 514.

57. Robert J. Friend to Colonel Wynn, "Trip Report (UFO)," 9 April 1962 (MAFB); Edward H. Wynn to Headquarters USAF, "Project Blue Book (Unidentified Flying Objects)," 20 April 1962 (MAFB).

58. Friend to Wynn, "Trip Report (UFO)," 9 April 1962 (MAFB); Wynn to Colonel Carlisle, "Unidentified Aerial Phenomena," n.d. (MAFB).

59. Friend to Wynn, "Trip Report (UFO)," 9 April 1962 (MAFB); Wynn to Headquarters USAF, "Project Blue Book (Unidentified Flying Objects)," 20 April 1962 (MAFB); Wynn to Carlisle, "Unidentified Aerial Phenomena," n.d. (MAFB).

60. Hynek, *The UFO Experience*, p.198. See also James E. McDonald, *Unidentified Flying Objects: Greatest Scientific Problem of Our Times*, address to the American Society of Newspaper Editors (Washington, D.C.: Pittsburgh Subcommittee of NICAP, 1967; published at author's request).

61. Interview with Quintanilla, in Herbert Strentz, "A Survey of Press Attitudes Toward UFOs, 1947–1966" (Ph.D. dissertation, Northwestern University, 1970), pp.216–17.

62. Draft (unsigned) of letter to Carl Vinson, n.d. (MAFB). See also Commander Arthur J. Pierce to Lt. Colonel Desert, 18 July 1963 (MAFB); Colonel Eric de Jonckheere, Staff Summary Sheet, "Congressional Correspondence on the U.S. Air Force UFO Program, Congress-

man Carl Vinson," 18 July 1963 (MAFB); Colonel de Jonckheere, Memorandum to Headquarters, USAF, "Unidentified Flying Objects," 22 July 1963 (MAFB).

63. Richard Hall, ed., *The UFO Evidence* (Washington, D.C.: NICAP, 1964); see United States Air Force, "Project Blue Book, 1964–1967" (MAFB, NICAP, APRO).

64. Donald Menzel and Lyle G. Boyd, *The World of Flying Saucers* (Garden City, N.Y.: Doubleday, 1963), pp.15, 133, 134.

65. Menzel and Boyd, pp.142, 143; "Project Blue Book, 1964–67" (MAFB, NICAP, APRO).

66. Socorro, New Mexico, sighting information on file at MAFB. See also Hynek, *The UFO Experience*, pp.144–45.

67. Ibid.

68. Ibid.

69. Socorro, New Mexico, sighting information on file at MAFB. See also Hynek, *The UFO Experience*, pp.144–45; *Christian Science Monitor*, 1 May 1964, p.3.

70. Socorro, New Mexico, sighting information on file at MAFB.

8 1965: The Turning Point in the Controversy

1. Herbert Strentz, "A Survey of Press Coverage of Unidentified Flying Objects, 1947–1966" (Ph.D. dissertation, Northwestern University, 1970), p.47.

2. *Charleston* (South Carolina) *Evening Post*, 16 July 1965; *Orlando* (Florida) *Sentinel*, 21 September 1965, p.13-b.

3. *Fort Worth Star Telegram*, *Richmond* (Virginia) *News Leader*, and *Alameda* (California) *Times-Star*, cited in *Orlando Sentinel*, 21 September 1965, p. 13-b.

4. *Christian Science Monitor*, 16 August 1965, p.1, 21 August 1965, p.E-1, 3 September 1965, p.5.

5. Edward U. Condon, project director, *Scientific Study of Unidentified Flying Objects* (New York: Bantam ed., 1969), p.514; *San Fernando* (California) *Valley Times*, 4 August 1965.

6. *Wall Street Journal*, 13 December 1965, pp.1, 20.

7. John Fuller, "Tradewinds: Report of an Unidentified Flying Object in Exeter, N.H.," *Satruday Review*, 2 October 1965, p.10; John Fuller, *Incident at Exeter* (New York: G. P. Putnam, 1966), passim; Fuller, "Incident at Exeter," *Look*, 22 February 1966.

8. Fuller, "Tradewinds: Exeter People Give Accounts of Observations," *Saturday Review*, 22 January 1966, p.14; Fuller, "Tradewinds: U.S. Air Force's Reactions to Recent Sightings," *Saturday Review*, 16 April 1966, p.10; *UFO Investigator* 3 (January–February 1966): 5.

9. *UFO Investigator* 3 (January–February 1966): 5–6.

10. J. Allen Hynek, *The UFO Experience: A Scientific Inquiry* (Chicago: Henry Regnery, 1972), p.198; General E. B. LeBailly, Memorandum for Military Director, Scientific Advisory Board, "Unidentified Flying Objects (UFOs)," 28 September 1965 (in the files at the Air Force Archives at Maxwell Air Force Base in Montgomery, Alabama, to which I hereafter refer as MAFB), and also contained in Condon, pp.816–17.

11. LeBailly, Memorandum for Military Director, Scientific Advisory Board, "Unidentified Flying Objects (UFOs)," 28 September 1965 (MAFB), and also contained in Condon, pp.816–17.

12. "Special Report of the USAF Scientific Advisory Board Ad Hoc Committee to Review Project 'Blue Book'," March 1966, pp.1–9 (MAFB and in Condon, pp.811–15).

13. Ibid.

14. Ibid.

15. *Gallup Political Index*, Report No. 11, April 1966 (American Institute of Public Opinion), p. 13. See also George H. Gallup, *The Gallup Poll: Public Opinion 1935–1971*, vol. 2 (New York: Random House, 1972), p.2004.

16. *New York Times*, 23 March 1966, p.22. For a good summary of the Dexter sighting, see "Well-Witnessed Invasion by Something: Australia to Michigan," *Life*, 1 April 1966, pp.24–31.

17. J. Allen Hynek, "Are Flying Saucers Real?," *Saturday Evening Post*, 17 December 1966, p.20; David R. Saunders and R. Roger Harkins, *UFOs? Yes!* (New York: Signet, 1968), p.61.

18. Hynek, "Are Flying Saucers Real?," p.20; Strentz, "A Survey of Press Coverage of UFOs," p.52. See also *Raleigh* (North Carolina) *News and Observer*, 27 March 1966, pp.1, 3.

19. *Life*, 1 April 1966, pp.24–31; "Notes and Comment: Saucer Flap," *The New Yorker*, 9 April 1966, p.33; "Fatuus Season: Ann Arbor and Hillsdale Sightings," *Time*, 1 April 1966, p.25B; *Wisconsin State Journal* (Madison), 26 March 1966, p.1, and 29 March 1966 (private clipping).

20. *New York Times*, 27 March 1966, Pt. 4, p.2 and p.61, 23 March 1966, p.43; *Christian Science Monitor*, 30 March 1966, p.24, 11 April 1966, p.16.

21. *New York Times*, 26 March 1966, p.31; Gerald Ford to L. Mendel Rivers, 28 March 1966, in U.S. House, Committee on Armed Services, *Hearings, Unidentified Flying Objects*, 89th Cong., 2d sess., 5 April 1966, pp.6046–47 (I hereafter refer to this as *Hearings*); *Detroit News*, 30 March 1966, p.10.

22. *Hearings*, pp.6011–42.

23. *Hearings*, pp.5991–6005.

24. *Hearings*, pp.6007–8.

25. *Hearings*, pp.6045, 6069–74.

26. Lieutenant Colonel Thomas J. Hester, "History of the Directorate of Science and Technology Deputy Chief of Staff, Research and Development, 1 January 1966 through 30 June 1966," n.d., pp.27–28 (typescript at MAFB); Lt. Colonel Harold A. Steiner, Memorandum for the Record, "Implementing SAB Ad Hoc Committee on Project Blue Book Recommendations," 20 April 1966 (MAFB); U.S. House, Committee on Foreign Affairs, *Hearings, Foreign Assistance Act of 1966*, 89th Cong. 2d sess., 30 March 1966, pp.330, 332.

27. Steiner, Memorandum for the Record, "Implementing SAB Ad Hoc Committee on Project Blue Book Recommendations," 20 April 1966, pp.1, 2 (MAFB).

28. Steiner, Memorandum for the Record, "Implementing SAB Ad Hoc Committee on Project Blue Book Recommendations," 20 April 1966, pp.1, 2 (MAFB); Lt. Colonel Robert R. Hippler, Memorandum for the Record, "Scientific Panel to Investigate Reported Sightings of Unidentified Flying Objects (UFOs)," 22 April 1966 (MAFB).

29. Office of the Assistant Secretary of Defense (Public Affairs), "Air Force to Contract with Scientists for UFO Investigations," 9 May 1966 (MAFB). Most of the information for the section on placing the Colorado project was obtained from Saunders and Harkins, pp.25–29.

30. Saunders and Harkins, pp.29, 28, 29.

31. *Nation*, 26 September 1966, p.269; Major David J. Shea, "The UFO Phenomenon: A Study in Public Relations" (Master's thesis, University of Denver, 1972), Appendix C, pp.150–51, 157.

32. Letter from James E. McDonald to T. F. Malone, 20 July 1966 (personal files); Saunders and Harkins, pp.39–41.

33. *Denver Post*, 7 October 1966, p.3, and 6 October 1966, pp.1, 19; see also *New York Times*, 14 August 1966, pp.1, 70.

34. *Denver Post*, 7 October 1966, p.22; John Lear, "Research in America: Dr. Condon's Study Outlined," *Saturday Review*, 3 December 1966, p.87; *Denver Post*, 7 October 1966, p.3.

35. Hynek, *Saturday Evening Post*, pp.17–21; *UFO Investigator* 3 (October–November 1966): 2.

36. *Union City* (New Jersey) *Hudson Dispatch*, 21 October 1966 (from the files of the National Investigations Committee on Aerial Phenomena, Kensington, Maryland, to which I hereafter refer as NICAP); *Hollywood* (California) *Citizen-News*, 27 October 1966, p.A-2; "Can Dr. Condon See It Through?," *Nation*, 31 October 1966, p.436; see also "Condon for Regent," *Nation*, 26 September 1966, p. 269.

37. Quoted in *Denver Post*, 9 October 1966, p.29.

38. *Denver Rocky Mountain News*, 8 October 1966; see also *Denver Post*, 8 October 1966, p.26.

39. *Denver Post*, 9 October 1966, p.47, and 11 October 1966, p.21.

40. *Boulder Daily Camera*, 30 October 1966, pp.1, 6; *New York Times*, 16 November 1966, p.28; *Elmira* (New York) *Star-Gazette*, 26 January 1967 (NICAP).

41. Lt. Colonel Robert R. Hippler, Memorandum for the Record, "Scientific Panel to Investigate Reported Sightings of Unidentified Flying Objects," 22 April 1966 (MAFB); Colonel Raymond S. Sleeper, Deputy Chief of Staff for Foreign Technology, to Foreign Technology Division, "Scientific Panel Investigation of Unidentified Flying Objects," 2 June 1966 (MAFB); U.S. Air Force, "Air Force Regulation 80-17," 19 September 1966, contained in Condon, pp.819–28.

42. See Walter Sullivan's review in the *New York Times*, 27 August 1966, p.27; Daniel Cohen, "Review of *Incident at Exeter*," *Science Digest*, October 1966, pp.42–44; "Heavenly Bogeys," *Time*, 2 September 1966, pp.81–82; Oscar Handlin, "Readers Choice," *Atlantic Monthly* 218 (August 1966): 117.

43. John Lear, "The Disputed CIA Document on UFOs," *Saturday Review*, 3 September 1966, pp.45–50; *New York Times*, 21 October 1966, p.9; *Denver Post*, 9 October 1966, p.29.

44. "UFO's For Real?," *Newsweek*, 10 October 1966, p.70.

45. J. Allen Hynek, "UFOs Merit Scientific Study," *Science*, 21 October 1966, p.329.

46. Ibid.

47. *New York Times*, 16 November 1966, p.28, 4 April 1966, p.33; *Christian Science Monitor*, 21 April 1966, p.18; Isaac Asimov, "UFOs— What I Think," *Science Digest*, June 1966, p.47.

48. Philip J. Klass, "Plasma Theory May Explain Many UFOs," *Aviation Week*, 22 August 1966, pp.48–50+; Klass, "Many UFOs Are Identified as Plasmas," *Aviation Week*, 3 October 1966, pp.54–55+; Klass, *UFOs—Identified* (New York: Random House, 1968); *New York Times*, 23 August 1966, p.36; John Lear, "Scientific Explanation for the UFOs?," *Saturday Review*, 1 October 1966, pp.67–69; "Great Balls of Fire," *Newsweek*, 5 September 1966, p.78; "Management Newsletter," *Electrical World*, 15 April 1968, pp.57–60; *Chicago Tribune*, 9 October 1966, pp.1B, 2B; "UFOs or Kugelblitz?," *Popular Electronics*, September 1966, p.84.

49. For critiques of Klass's theory, see: James McDonald, *Unidentified Flying Objects: Greatest Scientific Problem of Our Times*, address to the American Society of Newspaper Editors, April 1966 (Washington, D.C.: Pittsburgh Subcommittee of NICAP, 1967; published at the Author's request); *Chicago Tribune*, 9 October 1966, pp.1B, 2B. For electrical engineers' critique, see: "Management Newsletter," *Electrical World*, 15 April 1968, pp.57–60. Also see Richard Hall's letter to the editor, *Aviation Week*, 10 October 1966, p.130.

50. William Markowitz, "The Physics and Metaphysics of Unidentified Flying Objects," *Science*, 15 September 1967, pp.1274–79.

51. Richard J. Rosa, "Letters," *Science*, 8 December 1967, p.1265; William T. Powers, "Letters," *Science*, 8 December 1967, p.1265; Jacques Vallee, "Letters," *Science, 8 December 1967, p.1266.*

52. Carl Sagan and I. S. Shklovskii, Intelligent Life in the Universe (San Francisco: Holden-Day, 1966); see also John Lear, "What Are the Unidentified Aerial Objects?," *Saturday Review*, 6 August 1966, pp.41–49. Carl Sagan, "The Saucerian Cult," *Saturday Review*, 6 August 1966, pp.50–52.

53. Hynek, *Science*, 21 October 1966, p.329; Hynek, "White Paper on UFOs," *Christian Science Monitor*, 23 May 1967, p.9; Hynek, "The UFO Gap," *Playboy*, December 1967, pp.143–46, 267, 269–71.

54. McDonald, *UFOs: Greatest Scientific Problem*, pp.6, 17.

55. McDonald, *UFOs: Greatest Scientific Problem*, p.11.

56. "Resume of telephone conversation between Colonel Stanley (in Col. Jack's office, SAFOI) and Colonel Holum 4 April 1967," n.a. (typescript at MAFB).

57. Ibid.

58. Letter from James E. McDonald to Richard Hall, 8 March 1969 (personal files).

59. Interview with J. Allen Hynek, February 1972.

60. Letter from James McDonald to Richard Hall, 10 February 1971 (personal files).

61. See "AIAA Committee Looks at UFO Problem," *Astronautics and Aeronautics*, December 1968, p.12; "Background," *Astronautics and Aeronautics*, November 1970, p.51. I will discuss the AIAA's conclusions and recommendations in chapter 9.

62. *New York Times*, 16 November 1966, p.28; "Out of This World: Convention of the Amalgamated Flying Saucer Clubs of America," *Newsweek*, 7 November 1966, p.38; *New York Times*, 16 November 1966, p.28.

63. Frank Edwards, *Flying Saucers—Serious Business* (New York: Bantam Books, 1966); Frank Edwards, *Flying Saucers—Here and Now!* (New York: Bantam Books, 1967).

64. John Fuller, *The Interrupted Journey* (New York: Dial Press, 1966).

65. Jim and Coral Lorenzen, *Flying Saucers: The Startling Evidence of the Invasion from Outer Space* (New York: Signet Books, 1966); Jim and Coral Lorenzen, *UFOs Over the Americas* (New York: Signet Books, 1968); Lorenzen, *Flying Saucer Occupants* (New York: Signet, 1968); Lorenzen, *UFOs the Whole Story* (New York: Signet Books, 1969).

66. Jacques Vallee, *Anatomy of a Phenomenon* (Chicago: Henry

Regnery, 1965); Jacques and Janine Vallee, *Challenge to Science: The UFO Enigma* (Chicago: Henry Regnery, 1966).

9 The Condon Committee and Its Aftermath

1. David Saunders and R. Roger Harkins, *UFOs? Yes!* (New York: Signet, 1968), pp.67–74; I obtained much of the information on the internal methodology and disputes from this book. Edward U. Condon, project director, *Scientific Study of Unidentified Flying Objects* (New York: Bantam edition, 1969), p.15, to which I will hereafter refer as *Condon Report*; see also Saunders and Harkins, p.50.

2. Saunders and Harkins, pp.67–69, 135. See also Mary Lou Armstrong's letter of resignation in J. Allen Hynek, *The UFO Experience: A Scientific Inquiry* (Chicago: Henry Regnery, 1972), p.245.

3. Saunders and Harkins, pp.115–17, 119; letter from Edward U. Condon to Donald E. Keyhoe, 2 February 1967 (in the files of the National Investigations Committee on Aerial Phenomena, Kensington, Maryland, to which I will hereafter refer as NICAP).

4. *1967 Congress of Scientific Ufologists* (New York: privately printed, 1967), p.14.

5. Saunders and Harkins, pp.78–80, 132–33.

6. Saunders and Harkins, p. 141.

7. Ibid.

8. Saunders and Harkins, pp.81–108, 136–37.

9. Memorandum from Robert J. Low to E. James Archer and Thurston E. Manning, "Some Thoughts on the UFO Project," 9 August 1966, typed copy (NICAP, and in the files of the Aerial Phenomena Research Organization, Tucson, Arizona, to which I hereafter refer as APRO); also contained in Saunders and Harkins, pp.242–44.

10. Saunders and Harkins, p.130.

11. Letter from James E. McDonald to Robert J. Low, 31 January 1968, contained in Saunders and Harkins, pp.244–52. Saunders and Harkins, pp.188–95; see also *Denver Rocky Mountain News*, 10 February 1968, p.31. Letter from Mary Lou Armstrong to Edward U. Condon, 24 February 1968, contained in Hynek, *The UFO Experience*, pp.243–45; see also *Denver Post*, 29 February 1968, p.61.

12. Saunders and Harkins, passim and p.21.

13. John Fuller, "Flying Saucer Fiasco," *Look*, 14 May 1968, p.63; *Denver Post*, 30 April 1968, p.15.

14. Fuller, "Flying Saucer Fiasco," *Look*, 14 May 1968, p.63.

15. "Libel Suit May Develop from UFO Hassle," *Scientific Research*, 13 May 1968, p.11; Edward U. Condon, letter to *Scientific Research*, 27 May 1968, p.5; "UFO Study Credibility Cloud?," *Industrial Research*, June 1968, p.27; David J. Shea, "The UFO Phenomenon: A Study in

Public Relations" (Master's thesis, University of Denver, 1972), p. 39.

16. Daniel S. Greenberg, letter to *Science*, 25 October 1968, pp.410–11.

17. Lewis M. Branscomb, letter to *Science*, 27 September 1968, p.1297. See also Philip M. Boffey, "UFO Project: Trouble on the Ground," *Science*, 26 July 1968, pp.339–42. *Denver Post*, 2 May 1968, p.18.

18. U.S., *Congressional Record*, 90th Cong., 2d sess., 30 April 1968, vol. 114, part 9, p.11043; *Wall Street Journal*, 3 May 1968, p.10; *Denver Post*, 2 May 1968, p.4.

19. U.S. Congress, House, Committee on Science and Astronautics, *Hearings, Symposium on Unidentified Flying Objects*, 90th Cong., 2d sess., 29 July 1968, p.205; I hereafter refer to this as *Hearings*. The transcript of the hearings is included without material submitted for the record in John Fuller, *Aliens In The Skies* (New York: Berkeley Medallion, 1969). *Hearings*, p.2.

20. *Hearings*, pp.4, 14.

21. *Hearings*, p.5.

22. *Hearings*, pp.14–15.

23. *Hearings*, pp.18–19, 21, 26, 30.

24. *Hearings*, pp.86–98.

25. *Hearings*, pp.106, 107.

26. *Hearings*, pp.113–21.

27. *Hearings*, p.131.

28. *Hearings*, pp.135, 137.

29. *Hearings*, pp.199–205, 214–24, 238, 208–9.

30. See *The A.P.R.O. Bulletin* from 1968 to present for list of scientists connected with the organization.

31. *New York Times*, 17 January 1968, p.14.

32. "Review of the University of Colorado Report on Unidentified Flying Objects by a Panel of the National Academy of Sciences" (National Academy of Sciences, 1969), pp.1–6. (Mimeographed; NICAP and in the Air Force Archives at Maxwell Air Force Base in Montgomery, Alabama, to which I hereafter refer as MAFB). Letter from Frederick Sietz to Alexander H. Flax, 8 January 1969 (MAFB & NICAP).

33. *Condon Report*, p.viii.

34. *Condon Report*, pp.x, xi.

35. *Condon Report*, p.9.

36. *Condon Report*, pp.245–80.

37. *Condon Report*, pp.164, 256, 143, 171.

38. *Condon Report*, pp.280–369, 396–480, 407.

39. *Condon Report*, pp.1, 5.

40. *Condon Report*, pp.25, 28, 29, 30–31.

41. *Condon Report*, p. 14.

42. *Condon Report*, pp.6–7.

43. Philip Boffey, "UFO Study: Condon Group Finds No Evidence of Visits from Outer Space," *Science*, 17 January 1969, pp.260–62; *New York Times*, 11 January 1969, p.30.

44. "The Truth About the Condon Report," *UFO Investigator* (Special Edition), January 1969, pp.1–2; *UFO Investigator*, February–March 1969, p.2.

45. *The A.P.R.O. Bulletin*, January–February 1969, pp.1, 5.

46. *Cincinnati Enquirer*, 13 January 1969, p.13; *Cleveland Press*, 10 January 1969, p.B3.

47. *UFO Investigator*, February–March 1969, p.5. See also *Wilmington (Delaware) Morning News*, 13 February 1969, p.19; *Daily Wildcat* (University of Arizona), 3 February 1969, p.6A.

48. J. Allen Hynek, "The Condon Report and UFOs," *Bulletin of the Atomic Scientists*, April 1969, pp.39–42.

49. Hynek, *Bulletin of the Atomic Scientists*, pp.39–42.

50. Hynek, *Bulletin of the Atomic Scientists*, pp.39–42. See also *Condon Report*, p.140.

51. Robert M. L. Baker, "The UFO Report: Condon Study Falls Short," *Scientific Research*, 14 April 1969, p.41.

52. Frederick J. Hooven, "UFOs and the Evidence," *Saturday Review*, 29 March 1969, pp.16–17, 62.

53. *New York Times*, 27 January 1969, p.32; Hudson Hoagland, "Beings From Outer Space—Corporeal and Spiritual," *Science*, 14 February 1969, p.7; Hong-Yee Chiu, Review of Condon committee report, *Icarus*, November 1969, pp.447–50.

54. U.S., *Congressional Record*, 91st Cong., 1st sess., 1969, vol. 115, part 1, pp.373–74; *Tucson Daily Citizen*, 13 January 1969 (NICAP).

55. *New York Times*, 8 January 1969, pp.1 and 2, 9 January 1969, p.36, 10 January 1969, pp.32 and 46, 11 January 1969, p.30, 12 January 1969, Sec. IV, p.6; *New York Times*, 10 January 1969, p.46, and 12 January 1969, Sec. IV, p.6; *Wall Street Journal*, 16 January 1969, p.18.

56. *Ogden (Utah) Standard-Examiner*, 10 January 1969, p.6A; *Los Angeles Herald-Examiner*, 19 January 1969, p.C–2.

57. *Buffalo Evening News*, 11 January 1969 (NICAP); *Knoxville Journal*, 11 January 1969 (NICAP); *Chattanooga Post*, 14 January 1969 (NICAP); *Fort Smith* (Arkansas) *Times Record*, 30 January 1969, p.2–B; *Berkeley Daily Gazette*, 13 January 1969 and 14 January 1969 (NICAP).

58. Boffey, *Science*, 17 January 1969, pp.260–62; Alden Armagnac, "Condon Report on UFOs: Should You Believe It?," *Popular Science*, April 1969, pp.72–76; "Flying Saucers, Not Real But—," *U.S. News and World Report*, 20 January 1969, p.6; "Shooting Down the UFOs: Condon Report," *Newsweek*, 20 January 1969, p.54.

59. "Lost Cause: Condon Report," *Nation*, 27 January 1969, p.100; "Saucers End," *Time*, 17 January 1969, pp.44–45.

60. Edward U. Condon, "UFOs I Have Loved and Lost," address to the American Philosophical Society, Philadelphia, Pennsylvania, 26 April 1969 (typed transcript at NICAP). This address was slightly revised and printed under the same title in the *Bulletin of Atomic Scientists*, December 1969, pp.6–8.

61. U.S. Air Force, "Project Blue Book," 1967, p.1 (MAFB, NICAP, APRO); "Project Blue Book," 1968 (MAFB, NICAP, APRO). See also "Project Blue Book," 1966 (MAFB, NICAP, APRO); and U.S. Air Force, Press Release, "Total UFO Sightings 1947–1969," n.d. (MAFB, NICAP, APRO).

62. William F. Marley, Transcript of Briefing to General William C. Garland, 7 July 1967, pp.18–19 (MAFB); see also Raymond Sleeper to William Garland, 28 July 1967 (MAFB). William C. Garland to Raymond Sleeper, 2 August 1967 (MAFB).

63. Letter from Raymond Sleeper to J. Allen Hynek, 4 September 1968, contained in Hynek, *The UFO Experience*, p.167.

64. Hynek, *The UFO Experience*, pp.251–70.

65. Shea, p.48.

66. U.S. Air Force, News Release, "Air Force to Terminate Project 'Blue Book'," No. 1077–69, 17 December 1969 (NICAP & APRO).

67. *Tucson Daily Star*, 19 December 1969, p.12 (NICAP); *New York Times*, 18 December 1969, p.41, and 19 December 1969, p.54.

68. Interviews with Stuart Nixon, April 1972 and May 1974.

69. Letter from Stuart Nixon to author, 29 May 1974; interview with Richard Greenwell, April 1972.

70. Letter from Carl Sagan to James E. McDonald, 18 September 1968 (personal files); letter from McDonald to Richard Hall, 16 October 1968 (personal files).

71. Letter from Edward U. Condon to Walter Orr Roberts, 5 September 1969 (personal files); letter from Thornton Page to J. Allen Hynek, 23 September 1969 (from Hynek's files); *Birmingham Post-Herald*, 29 September 1969.

72. See Carl Sagan and Thornton Page, *UFOs: A Scientific Debate* (Ithaca, N.Y.: Cornell University Press, 1973).

73. See *The A.P.R.O. Bulletin*, November–December 1971, for information on the Tucson symposium. Also see Coral Lorenzen, ed., *Proceedings of the Eastern UFO Symposium*, 23 January 1971, Baltimore, Maryland (Tucson, Ariz.: APRO, 1971).

74. "UFO, An Appraisal of the Problem," *Astronautics and Aeronautics*, November 1970, pp.49–51; "UFO Encounter I," *Astronautics and Aeronautics* 9 (July 1971): 66–70; "UFO Encounter II," *Astronautics and*

Aeronautics 9 (September 1971): 60–64; "UFOs Probably Exist," *Industrial Research*, April 1971, p.75.

75. J. Allen Hynek, "Commentary on the AAAS Symposium," *Flying Saucer Review* 16 (March–April 1970): 5; Donald I. Warren, "Status Inconsistency Theory and Flying Saucer Sightings," *Science*, 6 November 1970, pp.599–604.

76. U.S. Congress, House, Committee on Appropriations, *Hearings, Civil Supersonic Aircraft Development (SST), 92d Cong., 1st sess.*, 1–4 March 1971, pp.334, 336, 340–41. See also *New York Times*, 3 March 1971, p.87.

77. *SST Hearings*, pp.587, 592.

78. George Gaylord Simpson's remarks in Carl Sagan, ed., *Communication with Extraterrestrial Intelligence* (Cambridge, Mass.: The M.I.T. Press, 1973), pp.363–64; Shea, Appendix C, p.157; *Washington Post*, 13 July 1972, p.A35.

79. Bruce C. Murray, "Reopening the Question," *Science*, 28 August 1972, pp.688–89.

80. Shea, Appendix C, pp.150–51, 157.

10 1973: Echoes of the Past

1. For more analyses of the 1973–74 wave, see: Eileen Buckle, "Major 'Flap' in the United States," *Flying Saucer Review* (London) 19 (November–December 1973): 2–5; George D. Fawcett, "1973—Big for UFOs," *Skylook*, February 1974, pp.10–11; Ted Phillips, "14 Ring Reports in 1973 Landings," *Skylook*, March 1974, pp.16–17; Jacques Vallee, "The UFO Wave of 1973," *Flying Saucer Review* (London) 19 (November–December 1973): 15; *UFO Investigator*, September 1973; and *The A.P.R.O. Bulletin*, November–December 1973.

2. *Culpeper* (Virginia) *Star-Exponent*, 29 December 1973. Newspaper citations without page numbers are from clipping services and personal files.

3. *Springfield* (Illinois) *Register*, 17 October 1973.

4. *Lima* (Ohio) *News*, 17 October 1973.

5. *Irving* (Texas) *News*, 28 October 1973.

6. *Jackson* (Mississippi) *Clarion-Ledger*, 18 October 1973.

7. *Palmyra* (Missouri) *Spectator*, 10 October 1973.

8. *Fayetteville* (Arkansas) *Northwest Arkansas Times*, 18 March 1974; *York* (Pennsylvania) *Recorder*, 16 October 1973; *Hackensack* (New Jersey) *Record*, 10 October 1973.

9. *The Madison Press* (London, Ohio), 17 October 1973.

10. *Los Angeles Times*, 14 November 1973.

11. *St. Joseph* (Missouri) *Gazette*, 9 October 1973.

12. *Goldsboro* (North Carolina) *News Argus*, 28 October 1973.

13. *Today's Post* (King of Prussia, Pennsylvania), 3 December 1973.
14. *Baton Rouge State Times*, 12 October 1973.
15. *Madisonville* (Kentucky) *Messenger*, 17 October 1973; *Cairo* (Illinois) *Evening Citizen*, 17 October 1973.
16. *Wisconsin State Journal* (Madison), 16 November 1973, sec. 2, p.8.
17. *McComb* (Mississippi) *Enterprise Journal*, 16 October 1973; *Pierce Co.* (Nebraska) *Leader*, 22 November 1973; *Wisconsin State Journal* (Madison), 8 December 1973, p.6.
18. *Oklahoma City Times*, 18 February 1974.
19. *So. Illinoisian* (Carbondale), 9 October 1973.
20. *Cape Girardeau Southeast Missourian*, 4 October 1973. For follow-up reports, see: *Cape Girardeau Southeast Missourian*, 9 October 1973; and *Wisconsin State Journal* (Madison), 6 October 1973, p.3.
21. Personal files.
22. *Tulsa World*, 19 October 1973; *West Union* (Ohio) *People's Defender*, 18 October 1973.
23. *West Point* (Mississippi) *Times-Leader*, 17 October 1973.
24. *Columbus* (Ohio) *Evening Dispatch*, 14 October 1973.
25. *Lawrenceburg* (Tennessee) *Democrat-Union*, 18 October 1973.
26. *Simi Valley* (California) *Enterprise Sun and News*, 12 October 1973. For the complete police report on this sighting, see *Skylook*, December 1973, p.4.
27. *The A.P.R.O. Bulletin*, January–February 1974, pp.5–7.
28. The press has covered this sighting innumerable times. Two of the best accounts are: Ralph Blum with Judy Blum, *Beyond Earth: Man's Contact with UFOs* (New York: Bantam Books, 1974); and Joe Eszterhas, "Claw Men From The Outer Space," *Rolling Stone*, 17 January 1974, pp. 27+.
29. Interview with J. Allen Hynek, June 1974.
30. *Milwaukee Journal*, 28 December 1973, pp.1, 3 of green sheet.
31. *Skylook*, March 1974, pp.6–7, and April 1974, pp.6–7.
32. Interview with Stuart Nixon, May 1974; *UFO Investigator*, May 1974, p.1.
33. Interview with Jim and Coral Lorenzen, January 1974.
34. For examples of psychologists', psychiatrists', and social scientists' explanations, see: *San Francisco Examiner*, 19 October 1973; *Louisville Times*, 19 October 1973; *Buffalo* (New York) *Courier-Express*, 19 October 1973; and *Milwaukee Journal*, 21 October 1973.
35. For examples of astronomers' and other scientists' explanations, see: *Wisconsin State Journal* (Madison), 18 October 1973, p.9, and 26 April 1973, sec. 5, p.4; *Glendale* (California) *News, 18 October 1973; Austin* (Texas) *Statesman*, 18 October 1973; *Pottstown* (Pennsylvania) *Mercury*, 19 October 1973; and *Pittsburgh Post-Gazette*, 23 March 1974.

36. *Cape Girardeau Southeast Missourian*, 8 February 1974; *Valley News & Green Sheet* (Van Nuys, California), 24 March 1974; and *Trentonian* (Trenton, New Jersey), 19 October 1973.

37. *Wisconsin State Journal* (Madison), 23 October 1973, p.12; *Pensacola* (Florida) *News*, 19 October 1973.

38. For examples of scientists impartial to the UFO phenomenon, see: *Wisconsin State Journal* (Madison), 23 October 1973, p.12; *Bellefontaine* (Ohio) *Examiner*, 19 October 1973; *New Orleans States-Item*, 17 October 1973; *Philadelphia Daily News*, 18 October 1973; *Newport Beach* (California) *Daily Pilot*, 18 October 1973.

39. For examples of editorials criticizing the validity of the UFO phenomenon, see: *Springfield* (Massachusetts) *Union*, 19 October 1973; *Pensacola* (Florida) *Journal*, 18 October 1973; *Charlotte* (North Carolina) *Observer*, 11 October 1973; *Trentonian* (Trenton, New Jersey), 19 October 1973; and *Lyons* (Kansas) *Daily News*, 18 October 1973.

40. *Washington, D.C., Star-News*, 19 October 1973. See also *New Orleans States-Item*, 18 October 1973; and *Oregon State Barometer* (Corvallis), 18 October 1973.

41. *Santa Monica* (California) *Evening Outlook*, 25 March 1974; *Memphis Commercial Appeal*, 16 October 1973; *San Francisco Examiner*, 28 December 1973, and 4 January 1974; *New York Times*, 21 October 1973, p. 65.

42. *Chicago Tribune*, 30 October 1973, p.12; *Norfolk* (Virginia) *Pilot*, 18 October 1973.

43. *Madison* (Wisconsin) *Capital Times*, 27 October 1973.

44. *Trentonian* (Trenton, New Jersey), 19 October 1973.

45. Joe Eszterhas, "Claw Men From The Outer Space," *Rolling Stone*, 17 January 1974, pp.27+.

46. "UFO: Stardust and Moonshine," *Newsweek*, 29 October 1973, p.31; "Are Flying Saucers Real? Latest on an Old Mystery," *U.S. News and World Report*, 5 November 1973, pp.75–76.

47. Ralph Blum, "UFOs: Those Heavenly Bodies are Alive and Well," *Cosmopolitan*, 1 February 1974, pp.176+.

48. Donald E. Keyhoe, *Aliens From Space* (Garden City, N.Y.: Doubleday, 1973), passim.

49. Keyhoe, pp.107, 123, 239.

50. Aime Michel, *The Truth About Flying Saucers* (New York: Pyramid Books, 1974); George Adamski, *Behind the Flying Saucer Mystery* (New York: Warner Paperback Library, 1974); Howard Menger, *From Outer Space* (New York: Pyramid Books, 1974).

51. Erich von Däniken, *Chariots of the Gods?* (New York: Bantam Books, 1971).

52. Erich von Däniken, *Gods From Outer Space* (New York: Bantam

Books, 1972); Erich von Däniken, *The Gold of the Gods* (New York: Bantam Books, 1973).

53. John Wallace Spencer, *Limbo of the Lost* (New York: Bantam Books, 1973).

54. *Culver City* (California) *Evening Star News*, 22 March 1974; *Glendale* (California) *News-Press*, 25 June 1974, p.8–A.

55. "Interview: Ray Stanford," *Psychic*, April 1974, pp.6–10, 36–38.

56. Interview with J. Allen Hynek, June 1974.

57. Interviews with Allan Sandler, February, March, April 1974.

58. *New York Times*, 29 November 1973, p.41.

A Note on Sources

There is no central depository for documents and other material relating either to the UFO controversy or to UFO sightings. Researchers must cull what they can from several public and private agencies. Some individuals, aware of the problem of sources, have begun collecting whatever documents they can find for their own files. I consulted three of the best private collections—those of J. Allen Hynek, Richard Greenwell, and the late James McDonald. McDonald's collection is without a doubt the best, containing reports of his own excellent investigations of sightings, copies of hundreds of Air Force reports, and an enormous amount of correspondence between him and other scientists and UFO researchers. J. Allen Hynek's collection includes cases, correspondence, and documents, as well as a large volume of newspaper sighting reports and articles. Richard Greenwell's collection of books, pamphlets, and privately printed material is one of the most complete in the country. For the researcher interested in the controversy, though, the Air Force, the National Investigations Committee on Aerial Phenomena, and the Aerial Phenomena Research Organization are the best places to obtain material.

The Air Force Archives at Maxwell Air Force Base in Montgomery, Alabama, contain the bulk of Projects Sign, Grudge, and Blue Book documents. The voluminous collection of sighting reports includes a wealth of information about UFO report investigation and identification procedures. I found most of the major documents, reports, and studies in the unsystematically arranged project files. In addition, the project files contain many unpublished letters, memoranda, and other documents about the Air Force's struggle with NICAP, its attempts to avert congressional hearings, and its efforts to transfer the UFO program. While providing much information about the Air Force's UFO program and policies, the project files are still disappointingly incomplete. Strongest on the 1953–61 period, the files have few documents for the years before or after. Moreover, these potentially significant missing documents are not available from any other known source.

In the files of NICAP, which moved from Washington, D.C., to Kensington, Maryland, in 1973, I found essential supplemental information about NICAP's fight for congressional investigations and its struggle with the Air Force. NICAP files contain letters from the Air Force to congressmen and private citizens in addition to the organization's own correspondence. NICAP's collection also includes some of Donald E. Keyhoe's private correspondence with Al Chop, Edward Ruppelt, and other figures prominent in the early years of the controversy. Although not all of Keyhoe's correspondence is at NICAP, enough is there to provide invaluable supplementary material. The organization also has many Air Force documents, reports, press releases, and some office files, most of which are duplicates of the material at the Air Force Archives. NICAP's newspaper file includes many articles that it has collected from clipping services since 1957. The organization's book collection contains its own holdings as well as that of the defunct Civilian Saucer Intelligence of New York, which makes the book collection one of the most complete on UFOs in the country, with many rare and out-of-print contactee books. Finally, NICAP's large sighting files do not significantly overlap those of the Air Force and the organization's investigations are usually more complete than the Air Force's.

APRO, located in Tucson, Arizona, offered me access to the largest collection of UFO club and contactee periodicals in the country. The Coral Lorenzen–Donald Keyhoe correspondence at APRO is invaluable for an understanding of their early theories and the beginnings of NICAP. APRO also has a collection of Air Force press releases and reports and some Air Force correspondence with APRO members and private citizens. Most of the Air Force documents are duplicates of material in the Air Force Archives. APRO's sighting files supplement those at NICAP and the Air Force Archives and its investigation work is generally very good.

The Library of Congress has a limited but valuable collection of books and periodicals. It has some important contactee and UFO club literature unavailable elsewhere. The library's unspecialized motion picture collection includes a few movies with flying saucer themes and several interesting television films about UFOs, some dating back to the mid-1950s.

I found the facilities of the Wisconsin State Historical Society in Madison useful for researching newspaper accounts of the 1896–97 and recent sightings. The most helpful newspapers for the 1896–97 sightings were the *Chicago Tribune, Chicago Times–Herald, St. Louis Post–Dispatch, Dallas Morning News, Houston Post, Detroit Free Press, Sacramento Daily Record–Union,* and *Cincinnati Commercial–Tribune.* For recent sightings and the controversy over them, I found the *New York*

Times, *Christian Science Monitor*, and other major city newspapers indispensable. Also, local newspapers in or near a sighting area contained important UFO reports. In addition, I found that newspaper clipping services often obtained sighting reports that large city newspapers or the wire services did not carry.

Selected Bibliography

Personal Interviews and Correspondence

Alvarez, Luis. Lawrence Radiation Laboratory, University of California, Berkeley, California. Letter, 9 February 1972.

Chop, Albert M. Downey, California. Interview, January 1974.

Friend, Lieutenant Colonel (ret.) Robert. Irvine, California. Interview, January 1974.

Goudsmit, Samuel. Brookhaven National Laboratory, Upton, Long Island, New York. Letter, 9 February 1972.

Greenwell, Richard. Aerial Phenomena Research Organization, Tucson, Arizona. Continuous correspondence from August 1971 to June 1973.

Hynek, J. Allen. Northwestern University, Evanston, Illinois. Interviews, February 1971, February 1972, September 1972, April 1973, and continuous through July 1974.

Keyhoe, Donald E. Luray, Virginia. Interview, April 1972.

Lorenzen, James and Coral. Aerial Phenomena Research Organization, Tucson, Arizona. Interviews, June 1971, January 1974.

Nixon, Stuart. National Investigations Committee on Aerial Phenomena, Kensington, Maryland (formerly in Washington, D.C.). Interview and correspondence, April 1973, May 1974.

Page, Thornton. Wesleyan University, Middletown, Connecticut. Letter, 7 February 1972.

Ruppelt, Mrs. Edward J. Long Beach, California. Interview, January 1974.

Shea, Major David J. Dayton, Ohio. Interview, May 1974.

Reports and Public Documents

National Academy of Sciences. Panel. "Review of the University of Colorado Report on Unidentified Flying Objects." Washington, D.C., 1969. (In the Air Force Archives, Maxwell Air Force Base, Montgomery, Alabama.)

U.S. Air Force. *Projects Grudge and Bluebook Reports 1–12.* Washington, D.C.: National Investigations Committee on Aerial Phenomena, 1968.

U.S. Air Force. Air Materiél Command. "Unidentified Aerial Objects: Project 'Sign'." No. F-TR-2274-IA. February 1949. Montgomery, Alabama, Maxwell Air Force Base, Air Force Archives. (Mimeographed.)

————. "Unidentified Flying Objects: Project 'Grudge'." No. 102-AC 49/15-100. August 1949. Montgomery, Alabama, Maxwell Air Force Base, Air Force Archives. (Mimeographed.)

————. "Project Twinkle Final Report." 27 November 1951. Montgomery, Alabama, Maxwell Air Force Base, Air Force Archives. (Mimeographed.)

————. Air Technical Intelligence Center. "Special Report No. 14." 1955. Montgomery, Alabama, Maxwell Air Force Base, Air Force Archives. (Mimeographed.)

————. Scientific Advisory Board. Ad Hoc [O'Brien] Committee to Review Project Blue Book. "Special Report." Washington, D.C., 1966. (Mimeographed.)

U.S. Congress. House. Representative Roush speaking against the Condon Committee's methods. 90th Cong., 2d sess., 30 April 1968. *Congressional Record*, vol. 114, p. 11043.

————. House. Representative Ryan speaking against the Condon Committee's findings. 91st Cong., 1st sess., 9 January 1969. *Congressional Record*, vol. 115, pp. 373–74.

————. House. Committee on Appropriations. *Civil Supersonic Aircraft Development (SST). Hearings before The Committee on Appropriations, House of Representatives.* 92d Cong., 1st sess., 1–4 March 1971.

————. House. Committee on Armed Services. *Unidentified Flying Objects. Hearings before the House Committee on Armed Services, House of Representatives.* 89th Cong., 2d sess., 5 April 1966.

————. House. Committee on Foreign Affairs. *Foreign Assistance Act of 1966. Hearings before the Committee on Foreign Affairs, House of Representatives.* 89th Cong., 2d sess., 30 March 1966.

————. House. Committee on Science and Astronautics. *Symposium on Unidentified Flying Objects. Hearings before the Committee on Science and Astronautics, House of Representatives.* 90th Cong., 2d sess., 29 July 1968.

Books

Adamski, George. *Behind the Flying Saucer Mystery.* New York: Paperback Library, 1967. (Original title: *Flying Saucers Farewell.* New York: Abelard-Schuman, 1961.)

————. *Inside the Flying Saucers.* New York: Paperback Library, 1967. (Original title: *Inside the Spaceships.* New York: Abelard-Schuman, 1955.)

Angelucci, Orfeo M. *The Secret of the Saucers.* Amherst, Wis.: Amherst Press, 1955.

Bailey, James O. *Pilgrims Through Space and Time.* New York: Argus, 1947.

Baxter, John. *Science Fiction in the Cinema.* New York: A.S. Barnes, 1970.

Bethurum, Truman. *Aboard a Flying Saucer.* Los Angeles: De Vorss, 1954.

Bloecher, Ted. *Report on the UFO Wave of 1947.* Washington, D.C.: By the Author, 1967. (Available from California UFO Research Institute, P. O. Box 941, Lawndale, Calif. 90260).

Blum, Ralph with Blum, Judy. *Beyond Earth*: *Man's Contact with UFOs.* New York: Bantam Books, 1974.

Buckner, H. Taylor. "The Flying Saucerians: An Open Door Cult." *Sociology and Everyday Life.* Edited by Marcell Truzzi. Englewood Cliffs, N.J.: Prentice-Hall, 1968.

Clarke, Basil. *The History of Airships.* London: Herbert Jenkins, 1960.

Condon, Edward U., project director. *Scientific Study of Unidentified Flying Objects.* New York: Bantam Books, 1969.

Daniels, George H. *Science in American Society.* New York: Knopf, 1971.

Davidson, Leon, ed. *Flying Saucers*: *An Analysis of the Air Force Project Blue Book Special Report No. 14.* Clarksburg, W.Va.: Saucerian Publications, 1971.

Edwards, Frank. *Flying Saucers—Here and Now!* New York: Bantam Books, 1967.

———. *Flying Saucers—Serious Business.* New York: Bantam Books, 1966.

Ellwood, Robert S. *Religious and Spiritual Groups in Modern America.* Englewood Cliffs, N.J.: Prentice-Hall, 1973.

Festinger, Leon. *When Prophecy Fails.* Minneapolis: University of Minnesota Press, 1956.

Flammonde, Paris. *The Age of Flying Saucers*: *Notes on a Projected History of Unidentified Flying Objects.* New York: Hawthorn, 1971.

Fry, Daniel. *The White Sands Incident.* Louisville, Ky.: Best Books, 1966.

Fuller, John. *Aliens in the Skies.* New York: Berkeley Medallion, 1969.

———. *Incident at Exeter.* New York: G. P. Putnam, 1966.

———. *The Interrupted Journey.* New York: Dial Press, 1966.

Gallup, George H. *The Gallup Poll*: *Public Opinion 1935–1972.* 3 vols. New York: Random House, 1972.

Gibbs-Smith, Charles H. *Aviation*: *An Historical Survey.* London: Her Majesty's Stationery Office, 1970.

———. *A History of Flying.* London: B. T. Batesford, 1953.

———. *The Invention of the Aeroplane.* New York: Taplinger, 1966.

Gifford, Dennis. *Science Fiction Film.* London: Dutton, 1969.

Godwin, John. *Occult America.* Garden City, N.Y.: Doubleday, 1972.

Hall, Richard, ed. *The UFO Evidence*. Washington, D.C.: National Investigations Committee on Aerial Phenomena, 1964.

Hood, Joseph. *The Story of Airships*. London: Arthur Barker, Ltd., 1968.

Hynek, J. Allen. *The UFO Experience: A Scientific Inquiry*. Chicago: Henry Regnery, 1972.

Johnson, DeWayne B. "Flying Saucers—Fact or Fiction?" Master's thesis, University of California at Los Angeles, 1950.

Jung, Carl G. *Flying Saucers: A Modern Myth of Things Seen in the Sky*. Translated by R. F. C. Hull. New York: Harcourt, Brace, 1959; Signet, 1969.

Justi, Herman, ed. *Official History of the Tennessee Centennial Exposition*. Nashville: Brandon Printing Co., 1898.

Keyhoe, Donald. *Aliens From Space*. Garden City, N.Y.: Doubleday, 1973.

————. *The Flying Saucers Are Real*. New York: Fawcett Publications, 1950.

————. *The Flying Saucer Conspiracy*. New York: Holt, 1955.

————. *Flying Saucers From Outer Space*. New York: Holt, 1953.

————. *Flying Saucers: Top Secret*. New York: G. P. Putnam, 1960.

Klass, Philip J. *UFOs—Identified*. New York: Random House, 1968.

Leslie, Desmond, and Adamski, George. *Flying Saucers Have Landed*. London: Werner Laurie, 1953.

Lore, Gordon, and Deneault, Harold H. *Mysteries of the Skies: UFOs in Perspective*. Englewood Cliffs, N.J.: Prentice-Hall, 1968.

Lorenzen, Coral, ed. *Proceedings of the Eastern UFO Symposium*, 23 January 1971, Baltimore, Maryland. Tucson, Ariz.: Aerial Phenomena Research Organization, 1971.

Lorenzen, Coral and Jim. *Flying Saucer Occupants*. New York: Signet, 1967.

————. *Flying Saucers: The Startling Evidence of the Invasion from Outer Space*. New York: Signet, 1966.

————. *UFOs Over the Americas*. New York: Signet, 1968.

————. *UFOs: The Whole Story*. New York: Signet, 1969.

McDonald, James E. *Unidentified Flying Objects: Greatest Scientific Problem of Our Times* (address to the American Society of Newspaper Editors, April 1966). Washington, D.C.: Pittsburgh Subcommittee of NICAP [National Investigations Committee on Aerial Phenomena], 1967.

Menger, Howard. *From Outer Space to You*. Clarksburg, W.Va.: Saucerian Publications, 1959. (Paperback edition title: *From Outer Space*. New York: Pyramid, 1967.)

Menzel, Donald. *Flying Saucers*. Cambridge, Mass.: Harvard University Press, 1953.

Menzel, Donald, and Boyd, Lyle G. *The World of Flying Saucers.* Garden City, N.Y.: Doubleday, 1963.

Nebel, John. *The Psychic World Around Us.* New York: Hawthorn, 1969; Signet, 1970.

———. *The Way Out World.* Englewood Cliffs, N.J.: Prentice-Hall, 1961; Lancer, 1962.

1967 Congress of Scientific Ufologists. New York: Privately Printed, 1967. (Available at the Library of Congress.)

Reeve, Bryant and Helen. *Flying Saucer Pilgrimage.* Amherst, Wis.: Amherst Press, 1957.

✓Ruppelt, Edward J. *The Report on Unidentified Flying Objects.* Garden City, N.Y.: Doubleday, 1956. (In 1959 Doubleday published a revision of this book which included three additional chapters; however, the revision does not have the word *revision* on it and carries the 1956 date.)

Sagan, Carl, and Page, Thornton, eds. *UFOs: A Scientific Debate.* Ithaca, N.Y.: Cornell University Press, 1973.

Sagan, Carl, and Shklovskii, I. S. *Intelligent Life in the Universe.* San Francisco: Holden-Day, 1966.

✓ Saunders, David R., and Harkins, R. Roger. *UFOs? Yes!: Where the Condon Committee Went Wrong.* New York: Signet, 1968.

Scamehorn, Howard. *Balloons to Jets.* Chicago: Henry Regnery, 1957.

Scully, Frank. *Behind The Flying Saucers.* New York: Henry Holt, 1950.

Shea, David J. "The UFO Phenomenon: A Study in Public Relations." Master's thesis, University of Denver, 1972.

Strentz, Herbert. "A Survey of Press Coverage of Unidentified Flying Objects, 1947–1966." Ph.D. dissertation, Northwestern University, 1970.

Tacker, Lawrence S. *Flying Saucers and the U.S. Air Force.* Princeton, N.J.: Van Nostrand, 1960.

Toland, John. *Ships in the Sky.* New York: Henry Holt Co., 1957.

✓Vallee, Jacques. *Anatomy of a Phenomenon.* Chicago: Henry Regnery, 1965.

✓———. *Challenge to Science: The UFO Enigma.* Chicago: Henry Regnery, 1966.

Van Tassel, George. *The Council of Seven Lights.* Los Angeles: De Vorss, 1958.

———. *I Rode A Flying Saucer.* By the Author, 1952. (Not available.)

Williamson, George Hunt, and Bailey, Alfred C. *The Saucers Speak.* Los Angeles: New Age Publishing Co., 1954.

Articles and Periodicals

AFSCA World Report. Edited by Gabriel Green. Los Angeles: Amalga-

mated Flying Saucer Clubs of America, 1959–60. (In the files of the
Aerial Phenomena Research Organization, Tucson, Arizona.)

"AIAA Committee Looks at the UFO Problem." *Astronautics and Aeronautics*, December 1968, p.2.

The A.P.R.O. Bulletin. Edited by Coral Lorenzen. Tucson, Ariz.: Aerial Phenomena Research Organization, 1953–74.

"Are 'Flying Saucers' Real? Latest on an Old Mystery." *U.S. News and World Report*, 5 November 1973, pp.75–76.

Armagnac, Alden. "Condon Report on UFOs: Should You Believe It?" *Popular Science*, April 1969, pp.72–76.

Asimov, Isaac. "UFO's, What I Think." *Science Digest*, June 1966, pp.44–47.

"Background." *Astronautics and Aeronautics*, November 1970, p.51.

Baker, Robert M. L. "The UFO Report: Condon Study Falls Short." *Scientific Research*, 14 April 1969, p.41.

"Belated Explanation on Flying Saucers (Balloons)." *Time*, 26 February 1951, p.22.

Black, Victor. "Flying Saucer Hoax." *American Mercury*, October 1952, pp.61–66.

Blum, Ralph. "UFOs: Those Heavenly Bodies are Alive and Well." *Cosmopolitan*, February 1974, pp.176–78, 200–201, 221.

Boffey, Philip M. "UFO Project: Trouble on the Ground." *Science*, 26 July 1968, pp.339–42.

———. "UFO Study: Condon Group Finds No Evidence of Visits from Outer Space." *Science*, 17 January 1969, pp.260–62.

Branscomb, Lewis M. "Letter." *Science*, 27 September 1968, p.1297.

Buckner, H. Taylor. "Flying Saucers Are for People." *Trans-Action* 3 (May–June 1966): 10–13.

"Can Dr. Condon See It Through?" *Nation*, 31 October 1966, p.436.

Carson, Charles. "Those Little Men From Venus: A Reply to R. Gelatt." *Saturday Review of Literature*, 21 October 1960, p. 25.

Catton, William R. "What Kind of People Does a Religious Cult Attract?" *Sociology and Everyday Life*. Edited by Marcell Truzzi. Englewood Cliffs, N.J.: Prentice-Hall, 1968.

Chiu, Hong-Yee. Review of Condon Committee Report. *Icarus*, November 1969, pp.442–47.

Clark, Jerome. "The Strange Case of the 1897 Airship." *Flying Saucer Review* (London) 12 (July–August 1966): 10–17.

Clark, Jerome, and Farish, Lucius. "The 1897 Story—I." *Flying Saucer Review* (London) 14 (September–October 1968): 13–16.

———. "The 1897 Story—II." *Flying Saucer Review* (London) 14 (November–December 1968): 6–8.

———. "The 1897 Story—III." *Flying Saucer Review* (London) 15 (January–February 1969): 26–28.

Cohen, Daniel. "Review of *Incident at Exeter.*" *Science Digest,* October 1966, pp.41–42.

Condon, Edward U. "Letter." *Scientific Research,* 27 May 1968, p. 5.

———. "UFOs I Have Loved and Lost: Adaptation of an Address— April 1969." *Bulletin of the Atomic Scientists* 25 (December 1969): 6–8.

"Condon For Regent." *Nation,* 26 September 1966, p. 269.

Considine, Bob. "The Disgraceful Flying Saucer Hoax." *Cosmopolitan,* January 1951, pp.33, 100–102.

Crum, Norman J. "Flying Saucers and Book Selection." *Library Journal* 79 (October 1954): 1719–25.

CSI Newsletter. Edited by Lex Mebane. New York: Civilian Saucer Intelligence of New York, 1955–59. (In the files of the Aerial Phenomena Research Organization, Tucson, Arizona.)

Darrach, H. Bradford, and Ginna, Robert. "Have We Visitors From Space?" *Life,* 7 April 1952, pp.80–82 + .

Draper, Hal. "Afternoon With the Space People." *Harper's Magazine,* September 1960, pp.37–40.

Elliott, Lawrence. "Flying Saucers: Myth or Menace?" *Coronet,* 19 November 1952, pp.47–54.

Eszterhas, Joe. "Claw Men From The Outer Space." *Rolling Stone,* 17 January 1974, pp.27 + .

"Fatuus Season: Ann Arbor and Hillsdale Sightings." *Time,* 1 April 1966, p.25B.

Flick, David. "Tripe for the Public." *Library Journal* 80 (February 1955): 202.

The Flying Saucer Review. Edited by Roger Gribble. Seattle, Washington: Space Observers League, 1955–56. (At the Library of Congress.)

"Flying Saucers Again." *Newsweek,* 17 April 1950, p.29.

"Flying Saucers, Not Real But—." *U.S. News and World Report,* 20 January 1969, p.6.

"Flying Saucers—The Real Story: U.S. Built First One in 1942." *U.S. News and World Report,* 7 April 1950, pp.13–15.

"Flying Saucers: The Somethings." *Time,* 14 July 1947, p.18.

Fuller, John. "A Communication Concerning UFOs." *Saturday Review,* 4 February 1967, pp.70–73.

———. "Flying Saucer Fiasco." *Look,* 14 May 1968, pp.58–63.

———. "Incident at Exeter." *Look,* 22 February 1966, pp.36 + .

———. "Tradewinds: Exeter People Give Accounts of Observations." *Saturday Review,* 22 January 1966, p.14.

———. "Tradewinds: Report of an Unidentified Flying Object in Exeter, N.H." *Saturday Review,* 2 October 1965, p.10.

———. "Tradewinds: U.S. Air Force's Reactions to Recent Sightings." *Saturday Review,* 16 April 1966, pp.10, 12, 77.

Gelatt, Roland. "Flying Saucer Hoax." *Saturday Review of Literature*, 6 December 1952, p.31.

―――. "In A Saucer From Venus." Review of *Behind the Flying Saucers*, by Frank Scully. *Saturday Review of Literature*, 23 September 1950, pp.20–21, 36.

Gibbs-Smith, Charles H. "Historical Note." *Flying Saucer Review* (London) 12 (July–August 1966): 17.

Ginna, Robert E. "Saucer Reactions." *Life*, 9 June 1952, pp.20, 23–24, 26.

"Great Balls of Fire! Philip Klass Theory." *Newsweek*, 5 September 1966, p.78.

Greenberg, Daniel S. "Letter." *Science*, 25 October 1968, pp.410–11.

Hall, Richard. "Letter." *Aviation Week*, 10 October 1966, p.130.

Handlin, Oscar. "Reader's Choice." Review of *Incident at Exeter*, by John G. Fuller. *Atlantic Monthly*, August 1966, pp.116–17.

Hanlon, Donald. "The Airship in Fact and Fiction." *Flying Saucer Review* (London) 16 (July–August 1970): 20–21.

"Heavenly Bogeys." *Time*, September 1966, pp.81–82.

Hoaglund, Hudson. "Beings From Outer Space—Corporeal and Spiritual." *Science*, 14 February 1969, p.7.

Hooven, Frederick J. "UFOs and the Evidence: Condon Report." *Saturday Review*, 29 March 1969, pp.16–17, 62.

Hynek, J. Allen. "Are Flying Saucers Real?" *Saturday Evening Post*, 17 December 1966, pp.17–21.

―――. "Commentary on the AAAS Symposium." *Flying Saucer Review* (London) 16 (March–April 1970): 5.

―――. "The Condon Report and UFOs." *Bulletin of the Atomic Scientists* 25 (April 1969): 39–42.

―――. "The UFO Gap." *Playboy*, December 1967, pp.143–46+.

―――. "UFOs Merit Scientific Study." *Science*, 21 October 1966, p.329.

―――. "Unusual Aerial Phenomena." *Journal of the Optical Society of America* 43 (April 1953): 311–14.

―――. "White Paper on UFOs." *Christian Science Monitor*, 23 May 1967, p.9.

Keyhoe, Donald E. "Flying Saucers Are Real." *True Magazine*, January 1950. Reprinted in *The TRUE Report on Flying Saucers*. New York: Fawcett, 1967, pp.6–7, 92–94.

―――. "Flying Saucers From Outer Space." *Look*, 20 October 1953, pp.114–20.

Klass, Philip J. "Many UFOs Are Identified as Plasmas." *Aviation Week*, 3 October 1966, pp.54–55+.

―――. "Plasma Theory May Explain Many UFOs." *Aviation Week*, 22 August 1966, pp.48–50+.

Knight, Charlotte. "Report on Our Flying Saucer Balloons." *Collier's*, 11 June 1954, pp.50, 52–53, 56–57.

Lear, John. "The Disputed CIA Document on UFOs." *Saturday Review*, 3 September 1966, pp. 45–50.

———. "Research in America: Dr. Condon's Study Outlined." *Saturday Review*, 3 December 1966, pp.87–89.

———. "Scientific Explanation for the UFOs?" *Saturday Review*, 1 October 1966, pp.67–69.

———. "What Are the Unidentified Aerial Objects?" *Saturday Review*, 6 August 1966, pp.41–42.

———. "UFOs and the Laws of Physics: Concerning Views of J. Allen Hynek and William Markowitz." *Saturday Review*, 6 October 1967, p.59.

Ley, Willy. "More About Out There." Review of *Is Another World Watching?*, by Gerald Heard. *Saturday Review of Literature*, 28 April 1951, pp.20–21, 30.

"Libel Suit May Develop From UFO Hassle." *Scientific Research*, 13 May 1968, p.11.

Liddel, Urner. "Phantasmagoria or Unusual Observations in the Atmosphere." *Journal of the Optical Society of America* 43 (April 1963): 314–17.

"Lost Cause: Condon Report." *Nation*, 27 January 1969, p.100.

McDonald, James E. Review of Condon Committee Report. *Icarus*, November 1969, pp.447–50.

McLaughlin, Commander R. B. "How Scientists Tracked Flying Saucers." *True Magazine*, March 1950, pp.25–27, 96–99.

"Management Newsletter." *Electrical World*, 15 April 1968, pp.57–60.

Mandel, Siegfried. "The Great Saucer Hunt." *Saturday Review*, 6 August 1955, pp.28–29.

Margolis, Howard. "UFO Phenomenon." *Bulletin of the Atomic Scientists* 23 (June 1967): 40–42.

Markowitz, William. "The Physics and Metaphysics of Unidentified Flying Objects." *Science*, 15 September 1967, pp.1274–79.

Masquellette, Frank. "Physical Evidence of Great Airships of 1897." *Houston Post*, 13 June 1966, p.8.

Mauer, Edgar F. "Of Spots Before Their Eyes." *Science*, 19 December 1952, p.693.

Menzel, Donald H. "Abstract." *Journal of the Optical Society of America* 42 (November 1952): 879.

———. "The Truth About Flying Saucers." *Look*, 17 June 1952, pp.35–39.

"More About Flying Saucers." Review of *Behind the Flying Saucers*, by Frank Scully. *Science News Letter*, 16 September 1950, p.181.

Morrison, Chester. "Mirage or Not, Radar Sees Those Saucers Too." *Look*, 9 September 1952, pp.98–99.

Moseley, James. "Giant Rock." *Saucers, Space and Science* 60 (1971): 7–9. (In the files of the Aerial Phenomena Research Organization, Tucson, Arizona.)

Moskin, J. Robert. "Hunt for the Flying Saucers." *Look*, 1 July 1952, pp.37–41.

Murray, Bruce L. "Reopening the Question." Review of *The UFO Experience: A Scientific Inquiry*, by J. Allen Hynek. *Science*, 28 August 1972, pp.688–89.

Nelson, Buck. "I Visited Mars, Venus and the Moon!" *Search*, no. 18 (December 1956): 6–20. (In the files of the Aerial Phenomena Research Organization, Tucson, Arizona.)

Nexus. Edited by James Moseley. Fort Lee, N.J.: James Moseley, 1955. (In the files of the Aerial Phenomena Research Organization, Tucson, Arizona.)

"No Visitors From Space." *Science News Letter*, 30 August 1952, p.143.

"Notes and Comment: Saucer Flap." *The New Yorker*, 9 April 1966, pp.32–34.

"Out of the Blue Believers: Civilian Saucer Intelligence of New York." *The New Yorker*, 18 April 1959, pp.36–37.

"Out of This World: Convention of The Amalgamated Flying Saucer Clubs of America." *Newsweek*, 7 November 1966, pp.38, 40.

"Pennington Airship." *Scientific American*, 7 March 1891, p.150.

Powers, William T. "Letter." *Science*, 8 December 1967, p.1265.

Proceedings. Edited by George Van Tassel. Yucca Valley, Ca.: College of Universal Wisdom, 1958–59. (In the files of the Aerial Phenomena Research Organization, Tucson, Arizona.)

"A Rash of Flying Disks Break Out Over the U.S." *Life*, 21 July 1947, pp.14–16.

Rogers, Warren. "Flying Saucers: Sightings and Study of UFOs." *Look*, 21 March 1967, pp.76–80.

Rosa, Richard J. "Letter." *Science*, 8 December 1967, p.1265.

Ruppelt, Edward J. "What the Air Force Has Found Out About Flying Saucers." *True Magazine*, May 1954. Reprinted in *The TRUE Report on Flying Saucers*. New York: Fawcett, 1967, pp.36–39, 57–71.

Sagan, Carl. "The Saucerian Cult." *Saturday Review*, 6 August 1966, pp.50–52.

Saucer News. Edited by James Moseley. Fort Lee, N.J.: Saucer and Unexplained Celestial Events Research Society, 1955–68. (In the files of the Aerial Phenomena Research Organization, Tucson, Arizona.)

Saucers. Edited by Max B. Miller. Los Angeles: Flying Saucers International, 1953–60. (In the files of the Aerial Phenomena Research Organization, Tucson, Arizona.)

"The Saucers Again." *American Aviation* 17 (March 1954): 3.
"Saucers End: Condon Report." *Time*, 17 January 1969, pp.44–45.
Shallett, Sidney. "What You Can Believe About Flying Saucers (Part I)." *Saturday Evening Post*, 30 April 1949, pp.20–21, 136–39.
———. "What You Can Believe About Flying Saucers (Part II)." *Saturday Evening Post*, 7 May 1949, pp.36, 184–86.
"Shooting Down the UFOs: Condon Report." *Newsweek*, 20 January 1969, p. 54.
Skylook. Edited by Dwight Connelly. Quincy, Ill.: Mutual UFO Network, 1969–1974.
Sontag, Susan. "The Imagination of Disaster." *Against Interpretation.* New York: Dell, Laurel ed., 1969.
The Spacecrafter. Phoenix, Ariz.: Spacecraft Research Association, 1960. (At the Library of Congress.)
Telonic Research Bulletin. Edited by George Hunt Williamson. Prescott, Ariz.: Telonic Research Center, 1955. (In the files of the Aerial Phenomena Research Organization, Tucson, Arizona.)
"Things That Go Whiz: Flying Saucers." *Time*, 9 May 1949, pp.98–99.
"Those Flying Saucers: An Astronomer's Explanation." *Time*, 9 June 1952, pp. 54–56.
Thy Kingdom Come. Edited by Gabriel Green. Los Angeles: Amalgamated Flying Saucer Clubs of America, 1957–59. (In the files of the Aerial Phenomena Research Organization, Tucson, Arizona.)
"UFO, An Appraisal of the Problem." *Astronautics and Aeronautics* 8 (November 1970): 49–51.
"UFO Encounter I." *Astronautics and Aeronautics* 9 (July 1971): 66–70.
"UFO Encounter II." *Astronautics and Aeronautics* 9 (September 1971): 60–64.
U.F.O. Investigator. Washington, D.C./Kensington, Md.: National Investigations Committee on Aerial Phenomena, 1957–74. (NICAP moved to Kensington in 1973.)
UFO Newsletter. Morristown, N.J.: New Jersey UFO Group, 1957. (In the files of the Aerial Phenomena Research Organization, Tucson, Arizona.)
UFORUM. Edited by Art Gibson, Bob Hillary, and Don Plank. Grand Rapids, Mich.: Flying Saucer Federation, 1956–57. (In the files of the Aerial Phenomena Research Organization, Tucson, Arizona.)
"UFO's for Real? J. Allen Hynek Calls for Serious Investigation." *Newsweek*, 10 October 1966, p.70.
"UFOs Not From Mars." *Science News*, 3 September 1966, p.165.
"U.F.O.'s or Kugelblitz?" *Popular Electronics*, September 1966, p.84.
"UFOs Probably Exist." *Industrial Research*, April 1971, p.75.
"UFO: Stardust and Moonshine." *Newsweek*, 29 October 1973, p.31.

"UFO Study Credibility Cloud." *Industrial Research*, June 1968, p.27.

Vallee, Jacques. "Letter." *Science*, 8 December 1967, p.1266.

———. "UFOs: The Psychic Component." *Psychic*, January–February 1974, pp.13–17.

"Visitors From Venus: Flying Saucer Yarn." *Time*, 9 January 1950, p.49.

"Waiting For the Little Green Men." *Newsweek*, 28 March 1955, p.64.

Warren, Donald I. "Status Inconsistency Theory and Flying Saucer Sightings." *Science*, 6 November 1970, pp. 599–604.

"Washington's Blips." *Life*, 4 August 1952, pp.39–40.

"Well-Witnessed Invasion by Something: Australia to Michigan." *Life*, 1 April 1966, pp. 24–31.

"Wind Is Up in Kansas." *Time*, 8 September 1952, p.86.

INDEX

Acuff, John, 284
Adamski, George, 110–25 passim, 137, 184, 202, 203, 291; books by, 110, 111, 117, 291
Ad Hoc Committee to Review Project Blue Book, 198, 203–7 passim; recommendations and conclusions of, 198–99; as part of Air Force policy, 199–200
Aerial Phenomena Research Organization (APRO), 84, 95, 124, 133, 149, 191, 192, 227, 236, 238, 258, 259, 279, 283, 284; conflict with NICAP, 183–84; and Condon committee, 231; and Condon report, 244, 256–57
Agnew, Spiro, 258, 262
Air Defense Command: UFO detection plans, 68, 87, 88, 163, 236, 255. *See* 4602d and 1006th AISS
Air Force, 35, 38, 41–44, 45–106 passim, 108, 109, 119, 129, 131–58 passim, 166–92 passim, 199, 206, 207, 217, 219, 224, 252, 280–81, 298–301; and public relations, 98, 136, 137, 138, 150, 155, 158, 166–78 passim, 185, 187, 191, 192, 199, 207, 252, 298, 299, 301; and congressional inquiries/briefings, 160–61, 176, 182, 191, 206; unofficial UFO panel, 167–68; staff studies, 163, 164–65, 168–70; and UFO program disbandment, 169, 170, 172, 186, 187, 225, 242, 255; and university contract, 199, 205–8, 211; and conflict with McDonald, 220, 221; and transfer of UFO program, 212; fact sheets, 155, 163–64, 179, 204, 206, 252
Air Force Letter *200–5*, 68–69, 104
Air Force Office of Aerospace Research, 186, 221, 255
Air Force Office of Scientific Research, 206, 207, 208, 232, 255
Air Force Regulation *80–17*, 212, 254

Air Force Regulation *200–2*, 104, 134, 138, 150, 151, 165, 212
Air Force Systems Command, 186, 212, 255
Air Materiel Command, 41–63 passim, 176
Air Research and Development Command (ARDC), 170–71, 176
Airships, history of, 30–32
Airships, mystery, *1896–97*, 33, 38, 39, 41, 102–3, 174, 264, 266, 270, 273, 280, 288, 296, 297; characteristics of, 5–16; "Wilson" reports of, 12–14; hoaxes, 16–19; photographs of, 19–20; reactions to, 21–29, 33–34; explanations of, 22–25, 28–30, 32
Air Technical Intelligence Center (ATIC), 63–74 passim, 78, 82, 87–92 passim, 104, 105, 106, 133–68 passim, 174, 177, 186–95 passim; and transfer of Blue Book, 169–71, 185–87; and congressional hearings, 178–79
Alvarez, Luis, 91, 92
American Association for the Advancement of Science (AAAS), 214, 232, 248, 257; symposium on UFOs, 258, 286
American Institute of Aeronautics and Astronautics (AIAA): UFO subcommittee, 222, 257, 259, 282
American Society of Newspaper Editors: UFO symposium, 220
Andrus, Walt, 285
Angelucci, Orfeo, 113–20 passim, 125; book by, 113
A.P.R.O. Bulletin, The, 84, 284
Arcier, A. Francis, 145, 171
Armstrong, Mary Lou, 230, 231
Armstrong Circle Theater, 156, 171, 175
Arnold, Kenneth: UFO sighting by, 36–38, 188, 277
Asimov, Isaac, 216, 286